Gender Studies

Terms and Debates

Anne Cranny-Francis
Wendy Waring
Pam Stavropoulos
Joan Kirkby

First published 2003 by
PALGRAVE MACMILLAN
Houndmills, Basingstoke, Hampshire RG21 6XS and
175 Fifth Avenue, New York, N.Y. 10010
Companies and representatives throughout the world

PALGRAVE MACMILLAN is the global academic imprint of the Palgrave Macmillan division of St. Martin's Press, LLC and of Palgrave Macmillan Ltd. Macmillan® is a registered trademark in the United States, United Kingdom and other countries. Palgrave is a registered trademark in the European Union and other countries.

ISBN 0–333–77611–9 hardback
ISBN 0–333–77612–7 paperback

This book is printed on paper suitable for recycling and made from fully managed and sustained forest sources.

A catalogue record for this book is available from the British Library.

Library of Congress Cataloging-in-Publication Data

Cranny-Francis, Anne.
    Gender studies : terms and debates / Anne Cranny-Francis, Wendy Waring ... [et al.].
        p. cm.
    Includes bibliographical references and index.
    ISBN 0–333–77611–9 (cloth) — ISBN 0–333–77612–7 (paper)
        1. Women's studies. 2. Feminist theory. 3. Women's studies—Terminology. I. Waring, Wendy Elizabeth, 1960– II. Title.

    HQ1180 C73 2002
    305.4'07—dc21   2002035792

Editing and origination by Aardvark Editorial, Mendham, Suffolk

10 9 8 7 6 5 4 3 2 1
12 11 10 09 08 07 06 05 04 03

Printed and bound in Great Britain by
Creative Print & Design (Wales), Ebbw Vale

Contents

Preface

This book is an attempt to approach the study of gender both as an academic practice and as a feature of our everyday lives. We encounter issues relating to gender even before we leave the womb – as parents plan for the birth of a girl or a boy by preparing clothes in appropriate colours or decorating a nursery with appropriate cultural motifs. As the protagonist of Ursula Le Guin's science fiction novel, *The Left Hand of Darkness* (1981), explains:

> I suppose the most important thing, the heaviest single factor in one's life, is whether one's born male or female. In most societies it determines one's expectations, activities, outlook, ethics, manners – almost everything. Vocabulary. Semiotic usages. Clothing. Even food. (p. 200)

In the same novel an interplanetary anthropologist reports from the planet Gethen, known to off-worlders as Winter because of its intense cold. She notes that indigenous Gethenians spend most of their time in no specific sexual identity: 'One is respected and judged only as a human being. It is an appalling experience' (Le Guin 1981, p. 86). Le Guin's fiction of the planet Gethen/Winter is an exploration of the significance of sex and gender in the lives of members of contemporary Western societies. As these quotes indicate, through her protagonists Le Guin argues that sex plays a critical role in the life of the individual, influencing everything from the way we dress to what we eat, the kinds of things we do, how we behave, what we are likely to achieve in our lives.

Gender Studies is an attempt to explore some of the practices and sites specified by Le Guin's protagonists. Gender theorists explore the ways in which we think about gender – how binaristic understandings of femininity and masculinity shape the ways we perceive gender, and how the assumption of heterosexuality determines the ways we constitute that femininity and masculinity. Chapter 1 deals with many of the commonsense terms we use to speak about gender and sexuality and how the history of these terms reveals something of the complexity of sexing and gendering practices in our society. For example, we look at the history of a term such as 'heterosexuality', which many people assume to be an ancient term coined to describe what is assumed to be the norm for human sexuality, only to find that it is a very recent term, coined as the reverse side of a relatively new term 'homosexuality'. This raises many fundamental questions about why we now think about sexuality and about sexed and gendered individuals in the way that we do.

In Chapter 1 we also introduce work on subjectivity; that is, how we come to know and understand ourselves as individuals living in a particular society. We introduce terms such as 'subjectivity' and 'the subject', which have specific, technical meanings in this context, and we trace the theoretical frameworks used in their formation and development. We also discuss the ways in which individual subjects, such as ourselves, are formed in relation to and delimited by the institutions of our society which include gendering practices such as patriarchy. Furthermore we consider the ways in which our own individual experiences (of sexing and gendering) are a crucial part of what makes us who we are, and introduce some of the ways we now use to evaluate those experiences critically.

This leads in Chapter 2 into a study of the ways in which we think about gender, which draws on the work of theorists from a wide range of disciplines including psychoanalysis, philosophy, history and critical theory. Not surprisingly, the work of Freud is a major source for gender theory, although this does not mean that contemporary theorists simply accept Freud's work. A lot of contemporary psychoanalytic theory is intensely critical of Freud's work, using it as a touch-stone or starting point from which to develop alternative accounts of sex and gender. Jacques Lacan, Luce Irigaray and Julia Kristeva are among the many recent commentators on Freud, whose own work subsequently provides wholly new ways of rethinking the feminine and the masculine, gendered subjectivity, and the relationship between the individual and her/his society.

Other ways of thinking about gender are derived from historians and philosophers such as Louis Althusser and Michel Foucault, who trace the ways in which we think about the role of the individual in society, and specifically the ways in which power and subjectivity are experienced. Feminist theorists such as Teresa de Lauretis utilise some of this work but correct its gender-blindness, to provide new perspectives on both gendering practices in society and the theories used to explain those gendering practices.

Feminist theory and the more recent men's movement and men's studies, which are also discussed in Chapter 2, have some very specific ways of thinking about identity and the role of sex and gender in formulating contemporary notions of identity. In particular, they look at the concept of difference and how it both rejects the self/other binary of Western thought and enables strategic alliances among those with shared purpose but diverse experience and being. We address the notion of identity and how it has been challenged by women of colour, who use this concept to critique the feminist movement from within. And we also consider the deconstruction of identity politics by poststructuralist theory and queer theory.

In Chapters 3 and 4 we consider how these ways of thinking about gender have guided the ways we now have of reading and seeing gender in the texts of our society, which include novels, films and television programmes as well as newspapers, street fashions and everyday conversation. In each case we are concerned with how gendered representations – or representations of gender – circulate in our society, and how those representations are consumed by individual subjects. Chapter 3 focuses on reading (although within that term we include viewing and listening), our ways of engaging with cultural products and practices and generating meaning from them.

We begin by introducing what we mean by text – a much broader category than book or novel – and why analysing texts is of particular interest to gender theorists. We then move to some of the concepts which have proved particularly useful in examining the kinds of meaning circulating in our society (discourse) and the ways texts operate (genre, disjunction, reading). This provides the critical reader with the analytical tools needed to specify the kinds of meaning she/he is reading from texts and with a way of talking about the text which is generating those meanings. We also consider the different readings that can be made from texts – readings which seem to be in line with a general cultural perception of that text (mainstream or compliant), readings which conflict with what a text seems to be saying (resistant), and readings which don't seem to have much to do with the text at all (tactical). In each case the reading practice is a crucial part of how we generate meanings, including gendered meanings, from texts which ultimately become a part of how we engender ourselves as individuals.

Chapter 4 focuses on issues related to seeing, including the critical notions of representation and stereotyping. We look at the ways we see, and the ways we see others and others see us, from within the frameworks of gender. Some of the major issues we deal with are: the processes of stereotyping; the formation of identification and desire through seeing; the processes of looking at cultural texts such as fashion magazines, photography and films; and the question of gender as a performance or masquerade.

We begin with a quote by John Berger who wrote in the early 1970s about the different ways men and women look or are looked at and move from there to the concept of the stereotype – its social function and purpose. Specific gendered stereotypes are then considered for the kinds of meanings they generate about women and men, with case studies such as the Clarence Thomas/Anita Hill case and the Ormond College Case used as illustrations. We also consider ways of resisting these gendered stereotypes and representations, including a description of the critical notion of 'the gaze' and the psychoanalytic theory which has generated these resistant stances. We end with a discussion of some overtly resistant representations or embodiments of gender such as transvestism – practices which are based on a fundamental challenge to the ways in which femininity and masculinity are signified through/by the bodies of individuals in our society.

Chapter 5 engages with the issue of embodiment, which has been such an important focus of recent critical writing. In Chapter 1 we talked about the split between mind and body which has been fundamental to Western thought. In this chapter we discuss recent critical work which has established the consequences for our gendering practices of that split. We also visit a number of sites at which notions of embodiment are now being explored, including the institutions of medicine, the law and fashion.

Finally, in Chapter 6, we consider ways in which the social fabric is woven into the gendered ways we live our lives by looking closely at the intersection between the social, the public and the private – a crucial nexus for gender studies. We discuss how we live and 'do' gender in light of these connections by focusing on the context of everyday lives. Reference is made to the specific sites of the workplace and home life, and activities such as using space, and the negotiaton of gender duality particularly by young children.

Some issues recur in a number of chapters and this enables us to present them from several different perspectives, and to show how different theories can engage at the one site. We hope that reading this book will engage you in the discussions and debates we set out.

Overall, *Gender Studies: Terms and Debates* is an attempt to introduce the theories used in the discussion of gender as a concept as well as of the media and modes by which gender is part of our lives and of ourselves as subjects. We relate these theories to the everyday situations in which we encounter gendering practices, focusing quite specifically on the ways in which we read and see gender in the world around – and within – us. Our aim is to provide you with some tools with which to think about gender, to understand some of the complex theoretical materials written about gender, and to locate the practices of gendering in your everyday lives.

All the contributors work at Macquarie University, Sydney, Australia: Anne Cranny-Francis is Associate Professor in the Department of Critical and Cultural Studies; Wendy Waring is Director, Institute for Women's Studies; Pam Stavropoulos is Senior Lecturer in the Department of Politics; Joan Kirkby is Associate Professor in the Department of Critical and Cultural Studies.

1

Ways of Talking

There are a number of terms that people use when they talk about gender. Many of these, such as 'heterosexual' and 'homosexual', seem self-evident and we tend to think that such terms have always existed. It's often surprising to discover that many of the terms we take for granted are relatively new, coined only in the nineteenth century. Somehow their Greek etymology (heterosexual using the Greek *heteros* meaning 'other, different'; homosexual using the Greek *homos* meaning 'same as') makes them seem much older. In this chapter, we explore many of the terms which recur in our discussions of gender and sexuality, to discover what their actual history is and how this history reflects and shapes attitudes and values. We also begin to look at how subjectivity is formed, and provide some of the initial terms that you will need to navigate through the complex terrain of the various hypotheses on what processes govern the formation of the self. To think about gender is to think about the self, or the subject, in formation. Let us start with the most obvious term: gender.

Gender

Gender divides humans into two categories: male and female. It is a system which organises virtually every realm of our lives; whether we are sleeping, eating, watching TV, shopping or reading, gender is at work. Yet because it is everywhere, it is sometimes difficult to see it in operation. Imagine trying to escape the division of gender in our daily lives – without the birth certificate which records our gender, we could not get a passport, or driver's licence (which also record our gender). But say we had managed to get by without paperwork. Every trip to a public toilet would demand that we declare our gender by which door we choose. Every human body in modern societies is assigned a place in a binary structure of gender.

Not only does the system of gender divide the human race into two categories, it privileges the male over the female. Gender operates as a set of hierarchically arranged roles in modern society which makes the masculine half of the equation positive and the feminine negative. We can trace this way of dividing up the world as far back as the ancient Greek philosopher Aristotle in Western European history (see Synnott 1993). In his *Metaphysics* Aristotle summarises what he calls the Pythagorean table of opposites and it shows clearly how these divisions work. On the one side are terms such as Limit, Odd, One, Right, Male, Resting, Straight, Light, Good, Square; on the other side, Unlimited, Even, Plurality, Left, Female, Moving, Curved, Darkness, Bad, Oblong (Aristotle 1968–69). Aristotle sets one series of nouns against another, sorting them into opposites, where the obviously opposite pairs reinforce the oppositionality of the merely different pairs (male is to female as an oblong is opposite to a square?). Aristotle took his curious set of binary oppositions even further in his *Economics* where he states that men were stronger, women weaker; men courageous, women cautious; men the outdoors type, women domestic; men educate children, women nurture them (Aristotle 1968–69). An examination of TV ads shows that ancient Greek philosophy continues to have its influence centuries later. Beer commercials show men shooting dangerous rapids, while women are pictured elsewhere decorating the home. Even our language is gendered: nouns which are feminine in English (as in many other languages) more often than not have negative connotations. A buddy (a word derived from brother) is a good thing to have, but no one wants to be a sissy (derived from sister).

This binary division of gender can take several forms. The two halves can be seen to be equal but opposite, in a complementary relationship, as in the Ying/Yang symbol of Chinese philosophy. However, often the two halves will be typified as opposite and with the female in the inferior position. An example of this can be found in the nineteenth-century work of Paul Broca, who weighed male brains against female ones, and came up with some rather dubious conclusions about male superiority based on his findings. Another formulation of the binary division has it that the two halves are opposite and the female is naturally superior. The pioneer of education, Maria Montessori, held opinions which would exemplify this view: she saw women's superiority in their guardianship of human morality, affectivity and honour (for a longer discussion of the binary division and more examples, see Synnott 1993). We have here several ways of configuring the relationship between the two sides of gender (equal but opposite; opposite but female-negative; opposite but female-positive; and so on), but while these formulations might reflect different political agendas, and different ways of understanding the world, they all share the view that human gender is binary, is made up of two halves, which each define the other. The male side of the equation is generally coded as the positive one, and so becomes the standard by which all others are judged; in effect it becomes the norm. This privileging of the masculine is generally the case in Western societies.

When gender is used in feminist analysis, it is traditionally defined in relation to sex: gender as the cultural or social construction of sex. As a sociological or anthropological category, gender is not simply the gender one is, that is, a man or a woman, but rather a set of meanings that sexes assume in particular societies. The operation of gender in our society takes up these sets of meanings, organises them as masculinity or femininity, and matches or lines them up with male and female bodies. Received opinion about gender would have it that a female body produces feminine behaviours, a feminine identity. Cross-cultural research from anthropologists such as Margaret Mead (1949) has often been used by feminists to show that if sex is a biological given, gender is a social construct (see also section on 'Sex'). This research has also made clear that a particular behaviour which is coded as masculine in one society may be coded feminine in another. A man holding hands with another man in public is interpreted as feminine behaviour in many Western nations. In countries in the Middle East, however, this activity would be coded as acceptable masculine behaviour. Moreover, in the nineteenth century in England, a man would often stroll arm in arm with another male friend without this being coded as effeminate. This allows us to consider the historical and cross-cultural constructedness of femininity and masculinity, of gender itself.

Many socialist feminists and theorists such as Christine Delphy (1984) maintain that sex roles became part of our bodies, not because they expressed masculinity or femininity, but because of a hierarchical division of labour which initiated the elaboration of hierarchies. For Delphy, gender came into being to reinforce an already existing dichotomy between workers and owners. For some theorists, gender and sex are overlapping constructs that differ in emphasis, where our understanding of biological sex is likely to be shaped by our culture's notion of gender. Other theorists argue that there is no body, no biological sex, outside gender; that in becoming human, one is always already gendered.

Feminist psychoanalysis in particular has looked very closely at this question of where gender begins. How, they ask, does one become a boy or a girl? Looking at two different answers to this question gives us a sense of the debates about the cultural construction of gender, and the two different notions of the 'subject', or the self, and its relation with gender. Is gender acquired in the course of socialisation and the internalisation of norms, *or* is gender part of a linguistic network that precedes and structures the formation of the ego and the linguistic subject? For the most part, Object relations theory (a school of thought associated with the work of Melanie Klein (1963), and taken up by US feminist psychologists such as Nancy Chodorow (1978a, 1978b)) would say that the first possibility is the case; these theorists tend to argue that gender is a set of roles and cultural meanings acquired in the course of ego formation within family structures, and that significant changes in child-rearing practices and kinship organisation can alter the meaning of gender and close the hierarchical gap between the genders of man and woman (Chodorow 1978b).

For Freudian-derived French Lacanian psychoanalysis, the second answer is the attractive one. Theorists reworking this Lacanian tradition tend to refer to sexual difference not gender; using this term sexual difference reflects their conviction that in order to become speaking subjects, we must be sexed. Sexual difference is a process, rather than something which is acquired. Whereas other theorists of gender presume a subject who takes on a gender in the course of its development, the Lacanian view insists that the subject itself is formed through a subjection to sexual difference. So these two schools show us two possibilities: in one, gender appears to be a cultural determination that a pre-existing subject acquires; in the other, sexual difference appears to constitute the very matrix which gives rise to the subject itself.

A further explanation for how gender comes to work in society is posited by Judith Butler (1990, 1993). She argues that gender is the process of embodiment which results from the repeated performance of acts of gendering, and that this debate over which comes first, gender or sex, nature or culture, is a red herring.

Gender is one of feminism's most central categories of inquiry, and it intersects with many other social systems (race, sexuality) which are also governed by binary opposition. Gender studies pays particular attention to how these markers of difference work to constitute and reinforce individual and social subjectivities.

Gender is the culturally variable elaboration of sex, as a hierarchical pair (where male is coded superior and female inferior).

Sex

While the debate over which comes first, gender or sex, may be a red herring, a discussion of how people have understood what sex is would seem to be crucial to a discussion of gender. We all know what sex is, don't we? It's easy to demonstrate. You point to someone's body to prove they're a man or woman, a boy or a girl. The idea of sex is so naturalised that it is hard to see it at work. Of course sex is natural. Men and women fit together, don't they? As only one chromosome out of 46 determines sex, human beings are biologically, or genetically, more similar than we are different. Yet this idea of sex, of a natural biological coupling and equivalence, is part and parcel of the establishment in certain Western cultures of a battle of the sexes, of a binary opposition, which makes this distinction and mutual exclusiveness between men and women appear natural.

To start thinking about what sex is, we must first concentrate on its naturalness. We believe that proof of the existence of two sexes is on the body, in the
body; it *is* the body. Yet biologists are not necessarily uninfluenced by their
own cultural beliefs about what is natural. The anatomist Herophilus of
Alexandria, who assumed that women were imperfect men, dissected
cadavers and found the proof for his theory; he thought he saw testes and
seminal ducts connected to the neck of the bladder, using the male body as a
template (see Synnott 1993). Of course, what he saw were ovaries and
Fallopian tubes, which do not connect to the bladder.

We began with the naturalness of sex, and now move to its binary quality.
Common knowledge has it that there are two sexes. How do we know?
Administrative forms ask us to tick male or female, doors to public toilets
make us choose one or the other, the birth of a new baby is invariably greeted
with the question, 'Boy or girl?' Many psychologists, biologists and medical
practitioners in particular rely on definitions of sex which refer to a person's
biological maleness or femaleness. When, in modern societies, a child is born
with ambiguous genitalia, parents are asked to make a difficult decision:
which of the two sexes will they choose for the sex of rearing? This decision
is framed by medical expertise, made largely on the basis of the reproductive
possibilities of the infant or its real genetic sex. In our highly medicalised
modern societies, the resolution of ambiguous sex reveals how our bodies are
rigorously policed into two sexes – male or female.

Sigmund Freud (1925, 1931, 1933), the 'father of psychoanalysis' who
developed his theories quite early in the twentieth century, didn't think that
the little boys and girls growing up into proper mothers and fathers was the
only possibility (although he did think it was the only sane one). He imagined
that this sexual distinction could be upset, and reviewed the possibilities of
other developmental trajectories, such as various forms of homosexuality
('inversion') and modes of anatomical hermaphroditism. But in our society it
is increasingly difficult to think outside the frame of male and masculine,
female and feminine.

What then is the relationship between gender and sex? There have been
quite important and consequential formulations of the distinction between
sex and gender, for example, in Simone de Beauvoir's *The Second Sex* (1972),
'One is not born, but rather becomes, a woman', and in cultural anthropology
where gender does not reflect or express sex as a primary given, but is the
effect of social and cultural processes. The 'sex/gender system' is a term feminist anthropologist Gayle Rubin (1974) coined to explain the variable ways
that kinship organisations produce gendered beings out of sexed bodies. In
1974, she argued that all societies had a sex/gender system, and that this
system produced social conventions on gender from the biological and
anatomical raw material of human sex and procreation.

Rubin's essay argues with the work of anthropologist Claude Levi-Strauss and psychoanalyst Jacques Lacan. Rubin questions Levi-Strauss's analysis of the universality of kinship relations. Levi-Strauss believed that universal structures required every human to submit to the incest taboo in order to enter into kinship and the cultural status of the human subject. Only through subjecting incestuous impulses to this taboo do subjects emerge. In other words, to have the status of a person, to be able to say 'I', everyone must first be positioned within kinship, that is, become a daughter, sister, brother, son. The individual is prohibited from desiring or becoming members of their own kinship group (family or clan) – the incest taboo. So human subjects emerge on the condition that they are first gendered through kinship relations.

Rubin goes on to explain that the law of kinship produces human subjects, by prohibiting not only incest, but also homosexuality; gendered subjects are thus produced through a series of prohibitions which regulate not only sexual behaviour, but sexual desire itself. One is a man to the extent that one does not desire other men, but desires only those women who are substitutes for the mother; one is a woman to the extent that one does not desire other women (the spectre of that desire has been transformed into an identification, into wanting to be like that woman rather than wanting that woman) and desires only those men who are substitutes for the father.

For both Levi-Strauss and Lacan, it is only through being subjected to this process of heterosexualised gendering that viable or coherent human subjects are produced. So, 'one' is not a one, that is, a speaking, human subject, except through subjection to this heterosexual imperative.

For Lacanian-based feminist psychoanalysis, this doesn't quite measure up. If feminists take Lacan seriously, then gender cannot be said to be the cultural construction of sex, for sex is established through the linguistic effect of sexual difference, and this effect is coextensive with language, and hence, culture as such. The initiation into language is the primary process by which sexual difference is required and constituted. If this scheme is right, gender cannot be overthrown, and the very wish to do so is a fantasy which is inevitably thwarted by the constraints of language itself. Such a view has critical implications for any effort to consider gender as that into which one is socialised, for the 'one' is always already marked by sexual difference; constituted in culture as a sexed being *before* the process called socialisation.

Understanding how the sex/gender system establishes not only the sex of bodies, but also the kinds of desire they can have is very important. The way that some kinship systems make all homosexual practices taboo, and others do not, is important for thinking about the ways in which heterosexuality is made natural by culture. Feminism has argued that these gendered, heterosexual positions are not as stable as some might have us believe. Some feminists think that our unconscious fantasies threaten the stability of the structure, or that these are historically specific ideas about becoming human, and so may be different in other cultures, and subject to change in the future. Informed by feminist and gay cultural movements, the future of kinship relations could lead to the destabilisation and overthrow of gender itself.

Imagine a world with five sexes, say, lesbian, man, hermaphrodite, woman and cyborg. This would be a project which would involve reinventing everything which surrounds us, language, architecture, painting, advertising and, most of all, ourselves.

Sex is a theory about human beings which divides them into two biologically based categories – male or female.

Sexuality

What is clear about the definitions and discussions of gender and sex is that ideas about sexuality are so intimately tied up with gender, that it is sometimes difficult to see where one ends and the other begins. To begin with, the hierarchy that privileges the male in dualist systems of gender, also gives the structure for how sexuality works in Western society. Female sexuality is marked as naturally masochistic, narcissistic and passive; male sexuality is inscribed as naturally aggressive, sadistic and active. Traditional notions of women's sexuality make it virtually synonymous with her reproductive function. Motherhood is seen as the natural expression of female sexuality. The myth of the vaginal orgasm (that is, the belief that an orgasm triggered by vaginal rather than clitoral stimulation is superior and normal for women), for example, is caught up in this notion that pleasure and desire in women will be tied to child-bearing. (This myth is one of Freud's less laudable contributions to thinking on gender and sexuality, and is one reason why his theories have been viewed with some suspicion by feminist theorists.) According to this way of seeing the world, the clitoris, because it has no reproductive function, has no sexual function. And so sex (doing it) is conflated with sex (which public toilet door is chosen).

To give an example of how this affects the working of society we might look at legal cases of personal injury, where injuries to the penis are often amply compensated. Courts in Australia have even considered awarding men who are seriously injured the services of a 'masseuse' to provide for their sexual gratification. For women, if penetration has become difficult due to an accident, some compensation might be awarded. But generally, damage to functions which affect women's sexual pleasure – loss of feeling, touch or difficulty in other associated sexual functions (painful menstruation, for example) – has gone uncompensated. As for lesbians, one wonders how a conservative legal court would deal with pleasure without penile penetration ... 'Well, if they don't really do it, then how can compensation be awarded?' In this way, legal decisions reveal how deeply entrenched is the idea that normal sexuality be organised around intercourse, around a penis penetrating a vagina.

Feminists have contested the naturalness of this version of (hetero)sexuality just as they have questioned the naturalness of gender roles. They have pried apart the automatic link between dominance and the male, and submission and the female. They have also argued that the personal is political, that our most personal experiences are shaped by their location within social divisions and histories. This distinction between what can be discussed openly and what should be hidden takes us back to Aristotle's Pythagorean table in the section on gender: men are on the side of the public; women hidden. Now we can identify a real paradox. On the one hand, as we saw with the court cases regarding compensation, a certain kind of male heterosexual desire defines what counts as real sex; on the other hand, women, paradoxically, are 'the sex', they stand in for, they come to represent, sex.

Thus heterosexuality is not just a choice of partners. Its construction through the binary oppositions of gender helps it to produce the hierarchies which systematically organise the oppression of women. For some, this system of 'compulsory heterosexuality' (a term Adrienne Rich (1993a) developed in 1979 which we will soon discuss) is so deeply implicated in women's oppression that real social change will involve challenging this norm. Other feminists have argued that to overturn patriarchal oppression, the link of female sexuality to motherhood must be severed. The demands for women's right to control their own sexuality, to determine whether and when to have children, targeted this system of compulsory heterosexuality. For Shulamith Firestone (1970), the elaboration of new contraceptive devices and the promise of reproductive technologies was that they would uncouple mothering from the female body, and so lead to new sexualities and new configurations of gender roles. For other theorists, lesbian separatism provided an escape route from the patriarchally dominated institutions of sexuality (for example Daly, 1978).

But to change something, we must understand it. How is sexuality constructed? In trying to understand where desire comes from, how sexuality works, a variety of theories have been advanced to explain these (relatively recent and Western) rigid categories of human sexuality. Until the gay liberation movement of the 1970s encouraged gays and lesbians to theorise their own existence, scientists and psychologists generally explained homosexuality and bisexuality as either exceptions to or aberrations from the norm of heterosexuality. Currently, theories on sexuality range from sexual identity to sexual activity, from pathology to preference. At one end of the spectrum, our sexuality could be seen to be a part of an essential us, with a biological basis – genetic and prenatal hormonal factors have determined our sexual orientation. Here it assumed that sexual orientation is 'set' early in life. We may have tried to repress the 'real (gay/lesbian/male heterosexual/female bisexual) us', but eventually we will no longer be able to deny our true self. This is one way of telling the story, that there is an essential core which is the identity with which we are born and which we will take to the grave. At the other end of the spectrum of sexual orientation is social constructivism: that events or the environment made us who we are (and formed what and who we want). Here the particular development of our sexual orientation is based on social and cultural factors. Under this theory, the overwhelming predominance of heterosexuality in society would be attributed to the compelling social pressures which are exerted on men and women, to the ways in which real men and real women only properly exist within the strictures and structures of heterosexuality, and as part of the natural fit between male and female bodies.

> Sexuality is a set of social processes which produce and organise the structure and expression of desire.

The Modern Subject

Several times in the first three sections of this chapter we have used the word 'subject' rather than the word 'individual' or even 'self'. Writers in this field often refer not only to the self, or the individual, but at times to the subject, and subjectivity. Much of the work in this book will consist of suggesting ways to think about how we come to be who we are. We will be analysing what it means to be human. In focusing on gender, sex and sexuality, we are focusing on the subject. For some analysts of what being human involves, gender is a supplemental category – for example the optional extra of air conditioning in an expensive car. For those who think it is a bit more crucial (the wheels? the chassis?), it then becomes important to choose appropriate theories of being human. When we think of our self, our ideas are formulated not only by our original insights into what it means to be, but also in part by what prominent philosophers have speculated about the self over the last few centuries. We will be gradually introducing this concept of the subject and subjectivity and its importance throughout the book, but we start here by discussing what is understood by the word 'individual' and what some of the major differences are between it and the modern subject.

When we speak about the self, we often imagine the individual, someone who knows their own mind, acts on their rational assessments of situations. For example, a friend decides to move cities to take a new job. When we ask them why, it is likely that they will present a series of reasons – that the money is better, that the work is more challenging. We, in turn, will probably accept that this is an appropriate way to talk about the situation. We will assume that someone acting in the world can take it upon themselves to make such a decision, to act autonomously. We are unlikely to hear from them an explanation that as their childhood was troubled, they neurotically move from place to place; that they have seen a vision from God which initiated their departure; that their boss has commanded that they do so; or that their parents have insisted. Of course, these are possibilities, but when people represent their actions to others, they generally like to show themselves as reasonable, and the source of their own decisions, that is, autonomous. 'Yes, my boss was very insistent, but finally, I am the one who made the decision.'

The model of the self, or subject, which is being used in this scenario, is one of the individual – an autonomous being who acts and thinks rationally, for whom flights of fancy, madness or spirit are aberrant, not part of a properly functioning self. Like many of the concepts we review in this book, this one is also not as natural as it seems at first glance. It comes to us from early modern European philosophers, and can be most clearly seen in René Descartes' treatise on scientific method (1979). Descartes, a seventeenth-century French philosopher and scientist, is generally acknowledged in Western thought to be the founder of modern scientific method. His famous dictum *cogito ergo sum* – 'I think therefore I am' – establishes the rational individual as the centrepiece of a variety of interlocking practices of knowing. This thinker is self-defining and self-sufficient. Coded as male, he is fully conscious to himself, in control of his actions, thoughts and meanings.

The Cartesian method also sees knowledge or science itself as universal, available to all who follow the appropriate rules of investigation. This implies that the idea of mind is a disembodied universal. Knowledge, particularly rationality, is imagined as the universal property of human beings. Not only does the thinking subject transcend its own corporeality in this model of knowledge, but it also sees itself as a neutral observer. This transcendent subject – the one which establishes itself by announcing, 'I think therefore I am' – is also capable of neutral observation.

This is the self upon which much of liberal politics is based. The self which acts as a citizen is, in this humanist political philosophy, a liberal self, one for whom individual rights are secured. This kind of humanism assumes that the individual, man, has individual free will and is autonomous; that is, that individuals can define themselves independently of the social structures and physical relations of which they are a part. Autonomy, free will and rationality – these capacities are defined as natural to humans.

One could ask: what's wrong with being rational, self-controlled and neutral? If certain qualities such as rationality are seen as coming naturally to certain kinds of humans (white European heterosexual men), it doesn't leave much space for women and other people who don't fall into those categories to see themselves as human. Two thinkers in the late nineteenth and early twentieth century began to challenge these ideas of the individual, and their challenges had a lasting impact on the ways we imagine that our selves function.

In the nineteenth century, Karl Marx articulated a powerful vision of the way that humans in capitalist society are shaped and determined by their work, by whether, how, to whom they sell their labour, by the kinds of work they do, and their relations to what he called the mode of production. For Marx, whether one worked in a factory or owned the factory made a big difference to what kind of self one might have. Marx argued that consciousness is determined by social and economic systems rather than the other way around. This puts paid to the idea of the sovereign individual who's running the show. For Marx, the economic system of capitalism makes the worker in our scenario a mobile one, and not his/her individual decisions. Certainly, such decisions are important for that person, but as a model for understanding the motivations and functioning of selves, Marx needed a theory of the subject that would take into account people acting collectively, and being acted upon collectively. The collective subject, the idea that based on the subjective shared experience of material circumstances we develop a collective identity, is one that we can trace to Marxism.

A second prominent thinker also upended these common notions about how people might develop. Psychoanalyst and philosopher Sigmund Freud undertook a detailed elaboration of the functioning of the human mind and the mental mechanisms by which it becomes adapted to the world. Two important innovative ideas are central to Freud's new perspective. First, that sexuality can be a source for somatic (physical) illness for both sexes at all ages, including children; second, that sexuality is linked to unconscious processes. Freud posited that all subjects have areas and activities of the mind not accessible to consciousness, repressed material including infantile aggressions, resentments, traumas and fixations too painful or conflicted for consciousness to bear but which nevertheless inform human actions, language and thought. He called this the unconscious.

This had enormous implications for concepts of subjectivity. Whereas since Descartes the individual had been conceived as autonomous, rational and masterful, Freud emphasised the structuring role played by the unconscious. The psychoanalytic concept of the 'subject', in opposition to the humanist term 'individual', implies that subjectivity is more than and goes beyond, even eludes, the conscious self. For Freud, subjectivity is a laborious and endless process, in which the subject is torn back and forth between desires and drives on the one hand and cultural and social demands on the other. Freud developed a model of the psyche which breaks it into three parts, and which reflects the fragmentation of the subject into dynamic components: the unconscious (the id), the conscious personality (the ego) and the cultural and symbolic image of the self (the superego). We can imagine the ego as a kind of maître d' in a restaurant, keeping control of the tables; the id, which is linked to the unconscious, is what goes in the kitchen and under the tables – it is a reservoir of psychical energy, drives and desires; and finally, the superego would be the restaurant critic, a censor who sits in judgement.

Although there are many critiques that can be made about Freud, and we will survey some of them, his work is interesting for feminists in that he is one of the few renowned theorists of the modern age who tries to understand why men end up as men, and women as women. Psychoanalysis is specifically interested in the formation of masculine and feminine identity at the level of the unconscious. Feminists interested in philosophy, literary criticism, history, fine art, theatre, film and so on have all taken up Freud and his ideas.

These new formulations of the subject also inform what we think of nowadays when we think of the self. Our society is imbued with psycho-analytic practices; we might say that we speak Freud without even being aware of it (Turkle 1992). Using Freudian psychoanalysis to think about the ways in which selves come into being has in some ways become as natural to us as the Cartesian individual acting rationally. Marx's elaboration of the self in relation to production is with us too, in the ways in which we think about class division and the collective struggle of embattled groups. We readily talk of Freudian slips, repressed desires, or wonder whether the actions of a friend are spurred on by some peculiar neurosis which is the product of a childhood trauma. We also use Marxist notions of collective struggle quite readily: we read the impact of social and economic forces into the narratives of the lives around us. Heroic films of groups of people battling against the wheels of industry are not that uncommon. Of course, it is unlikely that Marx would have imagined Sissy Spacek as the embodiment of the collective subject of the proletariat struggle. For him, the collective subject was more like the idea of a group identity – think perhaps of the Black Panthers in the 1960s. In a film such as *Coal Miner's Daughter* (1980), we can see two ideas of the subject – the individual and the collective – merged together in a rather strange marriage. But incoherent or not, they're both there.

These kinds of reading practice are specific to modernity (see Chapter 3 for more on reading practices). We believe that we can read deep meanings from surface manifestations, like dreams and banal actions, the trace of the uncon-scious on our conscious lives, or the manifestation of the underlying base of material production in the superstructure of our daily lives. What's on top hides what lies beneath – the nervous tic and the faceless bureaucracy are linked to deep structures: a neurosis developed in childhood and the capi-talist system of production. In fact, the very idea that we can 'read' humans, that we can analyse ourselves, is typically modern. We will take up this question of the self, the subject and the individual again. Now we look at a series of terms around sexuality, as a way of thinking about the subject in formation.

Institution

In the discussion of the term 'sexuality', we mentioned the 'patriarchally dominated institutions of sexuality'. Let us examine what we mean by these terms. By 'institution' we mean a set of relationships and/or practices which are expressions of mainstream social values and beliefs: for example, relationships such as the family, practices such as parliamentary democracy, the legal system and general education. In each case a specific form of the institution is given broad social approval and support – rhetorical and/or material. So in the case of the family, contemporary Western societies tend (in most cases) to favour the bourgeois nuclear family, and so family comes to mean that specific formulation: heterosexual, discrete, isolated and constituted on the basis of patrilinearity. Now this is not the only family structure to be found in contemporary Western societies; however, it is the structure which is assumed in government policy, and so receives the benefit – rhetorical and material – of government and its ministries.

When a particular set of relationships and practices attains the status of an institution, therefore, a number of consequences can be seen:

1. A specific formulation of this set of relationships and/or practices is not only identified with the institution, but *as* the institution – with the consequent exclusion of different formulations.

2. The institution effectively positions all individuals within the society as either part of it, or potentially part of it – with the consequent disapprobation of those who cannot or will not participate.

3. That formulation of the institution, which *is* the institution, is supported not only by general (although not unanimous) approval, but also by economic and other institutional advantage.

Taking the family as our example again, we might trace these consequences in its operation. For example, because the family assumed in government policy and in many of the cultural productions of Western societies is the bourgeois nuclear family, it is very difficult for other family formations to be granted legitimacy and the material and other support which make it possible to operate. For example, a family comprising a same-sex couple frequently encounters difficulties with regard to issues such as bank loans, workplace acceptance of the same-sex partner, sick leave to attend a same-sex partner and spousal allowances of many kinds (government and workplace). A family comprising same-sex partners with children encounter many of these issues as well as issues specifically concerning the children: who to contact in the case of illness, availability of sick leave to attend children and custody issues in the case of separation. Because this family arrangement is not socially legitimated (via policy arrangements and general social attitudes), its members encounter difficulties, and they are excluded from both the material benefits and social reinforcement offered to the institutional (bourgeois nuclear) family.

The coercive power of the institution in relation to individuals can be seen in the pressure on women and men to settle down and have a family. For those whose inclinations – sexual or otherwise – do not necessarily dispose them to this lifestyle (and note again that family here implicitly means a bourgeois, nuclear, patrilineal family), then social disapprobation is expressed in many ways; at its least virulent in slighting references to the individual's sexuality, fertility and/or social responsibility. While this may have a minimal effect on some people, for others it may be a constant reproach, a source of insecurity and even self-loathing.

As stated above, the family which is *not* the bourgeois, nuclear, patrilineal family may find it impossible to access the kinds of material benefits which society offers the correct family; for example in taxation allowances, sick leave entitlements and insurance payments. Alternative family structures also do not receive the social approval expressed in cultural productions such as advertisements, television programmes and films, and, in fact, are often defined negatively by contrast with the institutionalised family.

> An institution is a set of relationships and/or practices which are expressions of mainstream social values and beliefs, and have the support – explicit and implicit – of other social and cultural institutions.

Patriarchy

The institution which is probably the most talked about in feminist theory is patriarchy. The concept and widespread use of the term 'patriarchy' grew out of feminist debates about gender in the 1960s and 70s. Patriarchy replaced the earlier term 'sexism', emphasising the importance of institutions in gender oppression, rather than individual prejudice (Edley and Wetherell 1995). It is still used as a shorthand to indicate a social system in which maleness and masculinity confer a privileged position of power and authority; where man is the Self to which woman is Other. It was taken from anthropology where it referred to a kinship system in which the eldest male, sometimes literally the father or patriarch, was invested with authority over other men and over women. In this model of patriarchy, which continued in apprentice crafts in the early modern period, old men held authority, younger males were subservient, and women were excluded. Early feminist theorists used the term strategically to highlight men's dominance of women in the private (the family) and the public (work, politics, culture) spheres. Now, however, it is generally used to refer to the systematic structural differences in the cultural, economic and social position of men in relation to women.

> Patriarchy is a social system in which structural differences in privilege, power and authority are invested in masculinity and the cultural, economic and/or social positions of men.

Under a patriarchal regime, women are, by definition, excluded from positions of power and authority – except where that power and authority works to support individual men or the social system as a whole. So a woman might be authoritative towards her children in the home, in order to provide a calm and supportive environment for her husband. She might be authoritative as a teacher, in order to reinforce the values and attitudes constitutive of the social system. When writers refer to the patriarchy or patriarchal values, they indicate a set of values and beliefs which positions the male and masculine as the site of authority and power in society. Women are excluded from this power and authority unless it ultimately serves the ends of that social system, and then its actual status as power and authority may be challenged.

However, patriarchy has become a controversial term; it has been critiqued for its monolithic construction of men and masculinity as the enemy and the oppressor; for its lack of precision and its inability to account for complex social processes and cultural dynamics. For example, a working-class man may be subservient to a wealthy woman in social interactions, illustrating that the factor of class is one of the processes involved in the dynamics which some uses of the term patriarchy overlook. When 1970s' feminism spoke of patriarchy as the master pattern in human history, the argument was over-generalised. But the idea well captured the power and intractability of a massive structure of social relations: a structure that involved the state, the economy, culture and communications as well as kinship, child-rearing and sexuality (Connell 1996).

While many feminists are now wary of using the term, scholars of masculinity have retained the term but use it in conjunction with more detailed considerations of the relation between patriarchy and capitalism, and patriarchy and male hegemony, in an attempt to understand the multidimensional and historically and culturally specific forms of male dominance. Importantly, it is one of the few contexts in which 'the man question' or 'the man problem' can be raised. In almost all other social theories, the issue of gender is raised in terms of 'the woman question' or 'the woman problem'.

Recent studies in a wide range of disciplines (sociology, social psychology, psychoanalysis, anthropology, history and cultural studies) have focused on the importance of thinking structurally rather than personally about the issue of gender oppression. Contemporary studies of masculinity have turned their attention to several sites – capitalist work practices, the division of labour, the family, the state, colonialism, empire, rationality, sexuality and culture – as important patriarchal structures. In *Understanding Masculinities*, Martin Mac An Ghaill (1996) is concerned to build up a more complex model for understanding masculinity and male domination as cultural and social practices that are part of large-scale social structures and processes. Yet while Connell (1996) points out that 'the main axis of power in the contemporary European/American gender relations' remains 'the overall subordination of women and dominance of men – the structure Women's Liberation named "patriarchy"' (p. 74), the phrases 'male hegemony' or 'hegemonic masculinity' are used by some instead of the term 'patriarchy' in reference to the widespread domination of men in the social, economic and cultural spheres.

Male hegemony or hegemonic masculinity refers to the widespread domination of men in the social, economic and cultural spheres.

The concept of 'hegemony' refers to 'the cultural dynamic by which a group claims and sustains a leading position in social life' and is borrowed from Antonio Gramsci's analysis of class relations (Connell 1996, p. 77). Hegemonic masculinity consists of the current practices and ways of thinking which authorise, make valid and legitimise the dominant position of men and the subordination of women. This hegemony exists through institutions such as the family, corporate business, government and the military.

Connell uses the phrase 'patriarchal dividend' to refer to the ways in which all men benefit from patriarchal privilege without personally being engaged in direct acts of aggression or oppression of women. There is, he suggests, a widespread 'complicity with the hegemonic project' even among men who are never violent towards women, who do their share of the housework and make extensive compromises with women rather than exercising naked domination or uncontested displays of authority. (This does not mean that violence is not used in the maintenance of hegemonic masculinity; male on female domestic violence is still significantly present.)

David Buchbinder (1994, 1998) suggests that patriarchal social structures are not positive for men either. In addition to the subordination of women, he points out that in modern Western patriarchal societies there is also 'a differential power relationship among men', with access to power depending on 'physical build, and strength, age, (official) sexual orientation and prowess (even if only rumoured), social class and advantage, economic power, race of the individual, and so on' (1994, p. 34). Throughout their lives, boys and men find themselves under the supervision and surveillance of other males. Under these conditions many men come to feel that they may be publicly humiliated and deprived of their status as men. As a consequence of this, they may strive for 'an excessive masculinity, whether signified by a huge, muscular body, an impressive sexual scorecard', 'a powerful car or a high-flying job', or 'acts of violence toward women and children, and other men, especially gays, as an attempt to assert their masculinity in the eyes of their fellows' (p. 36). This rivalry towards other men, which is also a feature of hegemonic masculinity, leads to men's demands for unequivocal emotional support from women, which in turn leads to domestic violence if the woman is unable or unwilling to give it.

Patriarchy remains a contested term. But whether one speaks of patriarchy or hegemonic masculinity, conceiving of gendered differences in power and authority as structural allows scope to both men and women to work for changes in social policy, for childcare provisions, for flexible working conditions and working hours, and for policies that monitor the abuse of power and violence.

Heterosexuality

Perhaps another of the most prominent institutions in the study of gender is heterosexuality. Heterosexuality is defined in the *Shorter Oxford English Dictionary (SOED)* as 'pertaining to or characterized by the normal relations between the sexes'; although the *SOED* does not specify what normal means. The implication of such a definition is that the meaning of 'normal relations' is so apparent that it needs no definition, and any doubt on the part of the reader is a reflection on the reader her- or himself. Reading the dictionary in the context of contemporary Western society, which privileges heterosexuality in its institutional practices (more on this below), we can deduce that normal relations means men having procreative sex with women and vice versa. The other implication we might make from this definition is that heterosexuality is a universal and transhistorical concept, again because of the use of the term 'normal relations'. The concept of 'normal' closes down any suggestion that understandings might once have been different, or might not even have existed, by its evocation of its opposite abnormal or pathological. If we try to think differently about gender and sexuality, about a time perhaps when the term 'heterosexuality' did not exist, the definition implies that we are outside the realm of normal relations between the sexes.

Heterosexuality, the dictionary tells us, was devised after (that is, following, or in the style of) the term, 'homosexual', which had itself been coined some four years earlier in 1897. So heterosexuality, a term which many might assume to have a long history, which was used to describe relations between the sexes, is in fact quite a new term. The obvious question we might ask after this revelation is 'why?' Why did the English develop a term to describe normal relations between the sexes only in 1901?

The most obvious answer is that the term was developed, as the dictionary indicates, as the obverse of homosexuality. Yet even that explanation begs the question: why did it take so long for these terms to be generated? Was there no flexibility in human sexual relations before this time, so that terms such as 'heterosexual' and 'homosexual' were unnecessary? Or, is it the other way around, that there was so much flexibility that such defining and delimiting terms were irrelevant? The unspoken assumption here might be that before this time all human relations were heterosexual. Yet historians and archaeologists among others will tell us that the behaviour defined by the *SOED* as homosexual clearly existed before this time. Perhaps it had taken until the early twentieth century for the normal to be defined?

Another approach might be to ask why the terms 'homosexual' and 'heterosexual' were defined at this time. And here there is an answer: both homosexual and heterosexual were used by Charles Gilbert Chaddock in his 1892 translation of Richard von Krafft-Ebbing's *Psychopathia Sexualis: A Medico-Forensic Study* (*SOED*). This is the representative quote from Krafft-Ebbing given in the *SOED*: 'The object of post-hypnotic suggestion is to remove the impulse to masturbation and homosexual feelings and impulses, and to encourage heterosexual feelings with a sense of virility.' In other words, sexuality (whether heter- or homo-) was perceived not as a way of describing particular acts or behaviours, but as an element of the individual's emotional life and, subsequently, of her or his sense of identity. Furthermore, heterosexual, it appears, is both desirable and manly, in apparent contrast to homosexual. So heterosexual was part of a regime – a medicalised or psychoanalytic regime – whereby sexuality was not only located within the identity of the individual subject (rather than, for example, being located in the sexual act itself), but was also assigned a disciplinary or regulatory function, with one sexuality (hetero-) identified as positive and another (homo-) as negative.

In the early twentieth century, as Gayle Rubin claims, sexuality became 'a vector of oppression' (1992); that is, it became a way of classifying human beings – normal or abnormal, inside society or outside it, acceptable or unacceptable. The theorist whose work has most influenced the contemporary revaluations of sexuality and gender is Michel Foucault. His four-volume work *The History of Sexuality* argues convincingly that sexuality is socially and historically, rather than biologically, derived. From this perspective, hetero-sexuality is not a biological state or orientation, but is a socially and histori-cally constructed category which positions some people as good and others as bad. Furthermore, since sexuality is positioned as the critical point of contact between the genders, it is also used to regulate them. The genders male and female are themselves constructed by reference to socially and historically constituted definitions of heterosexuality – the positively coded sexuality. Male behaviour equates with heterosexual, masculine behaviour; female with heterosexual, feminine behaviour.

Gender and heterosexuality can, therefore, be seen as categories which regulate (and create) individual subjects, according to how they are prepared to perform their sexuality. At the same time, their performativity is clearly revealed; these are not categories to *be*, but to perform, as Judith Butler (1990) argues in her influential book, *Gender Trouble*. This recognition that neither gender nor sex are inherent, biological features but are socially and culturally constructed is fundamental to our current revaluation of 'heterosexuality' as a term which constructs, rather than simply classifies, human sexuality and the gendering of individual subjects.

When Adrienne Rich first used the phrase 'compulsory heterosexuality', it is this coercive power of heterosexuality to which she refers: 'I am suggesting that heterosexuality, like motherhood, needs to be recognized and studied as a *political institution*' (1993a, p. 232). Heterosexuality, she argues, is not just an innate biological function or practice, as had been previously assumed. Gayle Rubin refers specifically to this assumption as 'sexual essentialism' which she notes is 'embedded in the folk wisdoms of Western societies, which consider sex to be eternally unchanging, asocial, and transhistorical' (1992, p. 9). When a sexual practice is perceived or constructed as essential, in turn, it then has the power to construct those who do not practice it as aberrant, as non-essential in all senses of the word; that is, not possessing the innate or essen-tial capacity to be viable human beings, and so non-essential to human society. For Rich, then, heterosexuality is rendered compulsory for all who would participate in human society.

The power of compulsory heterosexuality is that for those whose lives conform to its demands, it acts as a constant reinforcement and regulatory mechanism, producing its compliant readers as viable social subjects and regu-lating any thoughts they might have about alternative gender roles or sexual choices. For those who do not conform to its demands, on the other hand, compulsory heterosexuality acts as a mechanism of exclusion and oppression, because it consistently constructs them as outsiders, aberrant and bad.

The term 'heterosexist' is used to describe a society in which heterosexual operates as a defining and regulating principle. The negative connotations of the term refer to the proscriptive function of (compulsory) heterosexuality.

> Heterosexism describes social or personal structures which are defined
> and regulated by exclusive and compulsory heterosexuality.

To be heterosexist is to assume that every person and every practice is heterosexual and, by implication, to suppress or silence all who are not heterosexual,
and devalue every practice which is not heterosexual. Another term used to
describe this assumption of heterosexuality is 'heteronormative'. The value of
this alternative term is that it captures the coercive power of this assumption –
its normative or regulatory power.

So heterosexuality is a powerful conceptual tool or category which has
been mobilised in the twentieth century to define and regulate not just sexual
behaviours, but the ways in which we define gender. As a result it plays a critical role in determining who is regarded as an acceptable social subject. For
this reason Judith Butler uses the phrase 'heterosexual matrix' to refer to
heterosexuality: 'to designate that grid of cultural intelligibility through
which bodies, genders, and desires are naturalized' (1990, p. 151).

> Judith Butler's phrase 'heterosexual matrix' refers to a grid or frame through
> which cultures make sense of the ways that our bodies, genders and
> desires seem to appear naturally heterosexual.

Butler's term captures the power of heterosexuality to make particular practices and behaviours seem natural and others unnatural, and it also identifies
this term as cultural or social, not biological. Butler also acknowledges the
work of Monique Wittig (1992), who uses a similar term, 'heterosexual
contract', to capture the regulatory function of the term 'heterosexuality'.

So heterosexuality is a concept, used to delineate, and so regulate, the nature
of contemporary sexual relations. It is not simply a biological category, as often
assumed; indeed biology developed for many years as a scientific study
without the use of this term. Instead it is a social construct which has the
power to regulate and (re)inforce not only particular kinds of sexual practice,
but also the gender categories based on them. Heterosexuality is the concept
which determines whether a man is recognised as a viable male subject and a
woman as a viable female subject.

Homosexual

As noted above, homosexual, meaning 'having a sexual propensity for
person's of one's own sex' (*SOED*), came into general usage following the

1892 translation of Krafft-Ebbing's *Psychopathia Sexualis*. Some earlier usages have been recorded: Swiss doctor Karoly Maria Benkert used the term 'homosexual' in a response to German anti-homosexual legislation in 1869 to describe an 'inborn, and therefore irrepressible, drive' (Plummer 1981, p. 142). Foucault also records the use of the term in an 1870 paper, *Archiv für Neurologie*, by Carl Westphal to describe 'less ... a type of sexual relations than ... a certain quality of sexual sensibility, a certain way of inverting the masculine and the feminine in oneself' (1981, p. 43). However, the 1890s marks the general adoption of the term by writers such as essayist J.A. Symonds and theorist Havelock Ellis. Like Benkert, all these theorists were involved in a debate about whether desires and behaviours described by the term 'homosexual' were innate or culturally acquired.

Writing about this debate, Foucault notes:

> The nineteenth-century homosexual became a personage, a past, a case history, and a childhood, in addition to being a type of life, a life form, and a morphology, with an indiscreet anatomy and possibly a mysterious physiology. (1981, p. 43)

Listing these attributes Foucault alludes to the various kinds of study of the homosexual undertaken in the nineteenth century: biographical (a personage), historical and archaeological (a past), medical (a case history), psychological (a childhood), anthropological (a type of life), biological (a life form), psycho-analytic/medical (a morphology), moral (an indiscreet anatomy) and forensic (a mysterious physiology). Foucault's point is not that homosexuality was first discovered or observed in the nineteenth century, but rather that, in the nineteenth century, sexuality and, particularly, aberrant sexuality, 'was implanted in bodies, slipped in beneath modes of conduct, made into a principle of classification and intelligibility, established as a *raison d'être* and a natural order of disorder' (1981, p. 44). In other words, Foucault sees the classification of homosexuality as part of the development of a regime of power which operates by means of its sexual classification of individuals. To accomplish that classification, this regime must first create those individuals, those identities – the homosexual, the heterosexual, the perverse of various kinds – and the structures of pleasure, histories, biologies, moralities, personalities and psychologies which characterise them.

Before the nineteenth century, we might argue, various kinds of sexual act were performed; they were not necessarily used to classify the individual who performed them. During and after the nineteenth century, however, sexuality was inscribed in the individual as a function of her or his sexual practice. Further, all sexualities were not considered equal. The *SOED* definition of homosexuality (above) seems relatively non-judgmental, but the textual examples it provides of the use of the term suggest otherwise: 'he had been free from homo-sexual inclinations' *Psychopathia Sexualis*. If we substitute heterosexual for homo-sexual, it is clear, by contrast, that this statement is a negative reference to homosexuality.

The debate around the use of the term 'homosexual' in the nineteenth century was stimulated by the proposal and passing of laws against acts associated with homosexual men. As historians of sexuality such as Jeffrey Weeks (1977) have argued, before this time there were laws against acts such as sodomy, but little distinction was made between sodomy between man and man, man and woman, man and beast. However, in 1885 in England the Laboucherie Amendment to the Criminal Law Act effectively outlawed all forms of homosexual male sexual activity. Following the passing of this Amendment, a number of scandals and trials followed, most famous of which was the prosecution of Oscar Wilde.

It must be noted that there is a causal relation between the scandal and the legal definition; that is, the legal act itself can be seen as having created the scandal by creating the conditions for it to happen.

The Wilde trial and associated debate revealed a great deal of indeterminacy about the meaning of homosexual, stemming in part from the basic issue of whether homosexuality was regarded as innate or learned behaviour. Yet in posing the question in that format, the debaters assumed that sexuality was somehow already innate. It was not that heterosexuality and homosexuality were both seen as possibly learned or culturally produced, but rather that homosexuality might be some sort of culturally produced perversion or inversion of 'normal' heterosexuality. The terms 'inversion' and 'invert' also became popular in the nineteenth century, to describe same-sex behaviours and individuals who engage in same-sex sexual activities. The negative construction of homosexuality at this time is evident in the use of these terms; further, its legal realisation was primarily masculine.

'Inversion' and 'invert' are popular nineteenth-century terms to describe same-sex behaviours and individuals who engage in same-sex sexual activities.

The acts outlawed by the Laboucherie Amendment are specifically masculine (for example sodomy, oral sex between men). Weeks (1977) records that the major sanction on sexuality before the nineteenth century was directed against 'non-purposive' or non-procreative sex; the inspiration being Judaeo-Christian ethics which claimed that sex was meant for procreation. Following from the same ethical base, male sexuality was targeted by these sanctions, with lesbianism virtually escaping any legal sanction whatsoever. The reason for this seems to be that women's role in procreation was not recognised in Judaeo-Christian ethics as active; women were merely receptacles for the male sperm which were the source of procreation. Lesbians, according to this view, could not be charged with interfering sexually with procreation. The focus on masculinity in the new laws seems to derive not only from the Judaeo-Christian ethic of the past but from a model of male sexuality as undifferentiated and uncontrollable. From Foucault's perspective, we might here recognise a legal construction or production of male sexuality, which can then be used to regulate and discipline male behaviours.

The reasons for the development of this model have been related to concerns about the stability of the family, required for the maintenance of bourgeois society, although a single explanation for such a complex phenomenon is unlikely to be completely sufficient. The Wilde trial, for example, has been seen as a rejection of Wilde's anti-bourgeois behaviour – his flamboyance and overt rejection of bourgeois society – rather than simply (or only) of his sexuality (Marshall 1993), although his homosexuality became emblematic of what was seen as his corrupting influence. The question remains whether that corruption was primarily sexual or social; was Wilde's crime to be homosexual or was it to be an intelligent, socially critical, anti-bourgeois Irishman?

For the history of homosexual as a term and an identity, this question is important because it signifies its social and cultural derivation and use. It was not clear at the end of the nineteenth century whether homosexuality was to be considered natural or cultural; after all, how did one classify homosexual acts performed by otherwise apparently heterosexual people? As Foucault noted (1986, 1988), the various domains of knowledge which characterised nineteenth-century society – for example law, medicine, psychology, anthropology, biology and ethics – were all involved in the production of rules of viable sexual conduct. 'Homosexual' had a role in the production of sexual identities and behaviours which might be used to regulate and discipline members of society. Paradoxically perhaps, while that identity was negative, it nevertheless enabled self-recognition among those who felt excluded by or outside the evolving definitions of 'normal' (hetero-)sexuality; in other words, it was also the genesis of homosexual liberation movements (see below).

Homosexuality

While it may seem redundant at this point to deal separately with homosexuality, it is important to note the genesis of homosexuality as a concept and the great variety of sexual behaviours and identities to which it originally referred. As the discussion above indicates, debates about homosexuality focused on the status of identities which could not be defined by a normative concept of heterosexuality. Terms such as 'invert' and 'pervert' evolved to differentiate between those who might be seen as innately non-heterosexual (invert) and those who choose to engage in behaviours which are outside the parameters of normal (normative) heterosexuality (pervert). Both terms were negative, however, and their functionality eventually called into question even by those who would police sexual behaviours (after all, how was it possible to tell one from the other?). The point here is that homosexuality as a concept was so broad that it was not only of dubious value in a variety of fields (medical, psychological, judicial), but it also lumped together a range of behaviours which have no necessary relationship, for example homosexuality, transvestism, transsexualism, bisexuality and paedophilia.

The most disturbing correlation of sexual behaviours in our contemporary society is homosexuality and paedophilia. It is striking that in a society in which child sexual abuse is overwhelmingly heterosexual (predominantly committed by men on girls), the focus of so much moral panic is abuse by men on boys, which is then sometimes identified as homosexual. On the same grounds, heterosexuality would have to be identified as fundamentally paedophilic, with homosexuality a pale copy. This conflation of homosexuality and paedophilia has also been related to the nature/nurture argument surrounding homosexuality. If homosexuality is constructed as a learned behaviour *unlike heterosexuality*, then perhaps it can be taught to young people by older people. As the discussion of compulsory heterosexuality above indicates, having learned homosexuality, those young people will then be unable to take their place as acceptably gendered social subjects. This kind of argument has been associated with the reviling of homosexuality as corruption, which can be found in many discussions, and played a major role in the Wilde trial. The metaphorical production of homosexuality as an infectious virus (still evoked around the material reality of the AIDS virus) followed. This is not to devalue the concern with paedophilia, but rather to identify what has been, and continues to be, an ongoing issue in definitions of homosexuality; that the breadth of the term and its imprecision contribute to the negative connotations it still has in many contexts.

Moreover, from a Foucauldian perspective, we might argue that its imprecision and breadth have granted the term a wide efficacy in regulating the behaviours of anyone who strays in any way from the heterosexual norm. That is, if the connotations of the term 'homosexual' are so negative, then it was all the more useful as a threat. This is the kind of threat identified by the term 'homophobia'.

Homophobia is often taken to mean a negative view of or bias against homosexuality, and specifically against people who are identified as homosexual. Often homophobia is experienced in exactly that way, however, in view of the arguments above, we might consider a slightly different understanding of it. Given the role of heterosexuality in producing the accepted versions of masculinity and femininity, so allowing men and women to identify as male and female subjects, any threat to heterosexual identity can be read as a threat to not only an individual's sexuality but also to their gendering, and so to their status as viable or acceptable social subjects. Homophobia can then be seen not only as a hatred of homosexual subjects, but also as a disciplinary strategy employed against *all* social subjects.

G.K. Lehne wrote in his study of masculinity that 'homophobia is a threat used by homosexist individuals to enforce social conformity in the male role, and maintain social conformity' (Lehne, in Marshall, 1993, p. 154). In this formulation, homosexist refers specifically to anti-homosexual attitudes and homophobia to the threat to transfer the negative connotations of homosexuality to any individual/man who refuses to conform to compulsory heterosexuality (as interpreted by the homosexist).

Homophobia is not only a hatred of homosexual subjects, but also a disciplinary strategy employed against *all* social subjects to ensure that they comply with society's preference for heterosexuality.

Conformity, therefore, means not just the refusal of same-sex sexuality, but an embrace of the (sexual) masculinity and (gendered) maleness sanctioned by heterosexuality; in other words, conformity to the abuser's conception of maleness, which is quite likely to be a patriarchal masculine stereotype (see Chapter 4). Lehne (in Marshall 1993, p. 154) notes that homophobia is used 'against the 49% of the population which is male', not primarily against homosexuals, because its function is to enforce 'certain types of male behaviour and to define the limits of "acceptable" masculinity'. Homophobia depends for its effect on the negative construction of homosexuality and the maintenance of heterosexuality as a guarantor of acceptable gendering. So Lehne notes that homophobia is mobilised consistently against *all* men as a mechanism of social/sexual control.

Homophobia is also experienced by homosexual women or lesbians (see the section entitled 'Lesbian') as a more or less explicit construction of them as outside normal femininity – as unwomanly – and so as unacceptable female subjects. Anti-lesbian homophobia receives less attention in the press and public forums because it seems less often to result in overt violence against lesbians, and its deployment as a threat against heterosexual women is also less overt. Lehne (in Marshall 1993, p. 154) notes that the taunt, 'What are you, a fag [or pansy or poofter and so on]?' is commonly used as a disciplinary mechanism with men. Among women the gendering is sometimes less overt, for example it may refer to a woman's inability to get or keep – or even want – a male partner, or it may be directed at a childless woman. Essentially, however, the threat – of exclusion from correct gendering – is the same and it proceeds from the same homophobic premise.

Lesbian

One of the terms used to describe women who are perceived in heterosexist culture as not correctly gendered is 'lesbian'. While the word has an older use as the adjective derived from the name of the Greek island of Lesbos, its use in the context of gender and sexuality is relatively recent. The *SOED* gives as its secondary meaning 'Lesbian vice, Sapphism' and records its first use as 1908. The term 'Sapphism' is defined in the *SOED* as 'Unnatural sexual relations between women' and is traced to 'the name of *Sappho* (see SAPPHIC), who was accused of this vice'; the dictionary records its first use as 1890. The value judgements implicit in the use of terms such as 'unnatural' and 'vice' are quite clear. When used pejoratively (and its definition suggests that it is implicitly pejorative), lesbian does not simply refer to sexual difference or homosexual specificity; it is used to attack the woman's womanliness – her gendering as a viable social subject. A woman who is a lesbian is, under this (heterosexist) regime, not a woman.

While there are now many projects devoted to reconstructing lesbian history and identity, it is also the case that the contemporary heterosexist conception of lesbian is relatively recent. As the discussions of homosexual and homosexuality (above) indicate, contemporary understandings of gender, sex and sexuality can be traced to the nineteenth century and the production of a heterosexual discourse which pathologises non-heterosexuals. Nineteenth-century writings about lesbians tended to favour the term 'invert' (see above), which continued to be popular well into the twentieth century: for example, it is the term used by Radclyffe Hall in *The Well of Loneliness* (1982, first published 1928) to describe the sexuality of her protagonist, Stephen Gordon. However, as noted above, invert carries the negative connotations reflected in its more usual, everyday meaning: to turn upside down. An invert, then, is one in whom the normal is turned upside down – a definition which conserves, rather than challenges, the social practice of heterosexuality. That is, by representing inverts as having upside down sexuality, the term 'invert' preserves the idea that heterosexuality is the norm from which non-heterosexuals stray, by choice or (un)natural inclination.

The Well of Loneliness, Hall's anguished examination of lesbian life, continues to be a very popular novel; it was recently reissued in a new edition by Virago Press. In view of the public censure against homosexuality, this seems rather surprising and it speaks to the ambiguities within which lesbianism operates. On the one hand, it might be argued that lesbians have never suffered the same degree of overt persecution as homosexual men, who are also ungendered by heterosexism. The instances of legal persecution of lesbians as lesbians seem to be confined to situations in which women masqueraded as men, committed sexual misdemeanours as men (for example using a substitute penis), or somehow gained benefits as if they were men (for example pensions). In other words, the sexual behaviour of lesbians seems not to be an issue in a heterosexual order which defines sexuality in terms of male sexual performance. On the other hand, it may be that the persecution of lesbians is more covert, that it is implicit in the culture of heterosexism. Without arguing a parallel, we might suggest that it would be naive to think that in a white supremacist society, a black person can only be seen as persecuted if or when legal sanctions are used against them. Instead we have to recognise that discrimination and harassment often takes place at an almost subliminal level – through what people say or don't say, through assumptions made and by various behaviours. Lesbians experience covert discrimination of this kind, as well as institutional discrimination in a whole range of areas, including banking, credit, adoption, child custody, travel allowance, immigration, health care, insurance, wills and taxation. So, on these grounds alone, it seems invalid to do as many studies have done, which is to regard lesbians as just like homosexual men, except that they are women (Faraday 1981).

In her analysis of social science research about lesbians, Annabel Faraday criticises the assumption that lesbians and gay men share certain characteristics because of their same-sex relationships:

> What is *not* recognized is that while both lesbians and gay men are not 'heterosexual', heterosexuality itself is a power relationship of men over women; what gay men and lesbians are rejecting are essentially polar experiences. (1981, p. 113)

From this perspective, lesbians commit the unforgivable crime of not being attracted by and to men as both sexual partners and the locus of power and authority, whereas homosexual men do, at least, appreciate the appeal of the masculine. Along with writers such as Rich and Wittig, Faraday argues for the specificity of lesbian experience; that is, that it must be seen as an experience specific to women.

Adrienne Rich, in her well-known essay, 'Compulsory Heterosexuality and Lesbian Existence' (1993a), makes the same point that to 'equate lesbian existence with male homosexuality because each is stigmatized is to erase female reality once again' (p. 239). Rich uses a number of terms in this essay to describe lesbian and/or female reality, which have had a continuing influence on attempts to (re)conceptualise lesbian experience. For example, the term 'lesbian existence' is used to describe both 'the historical presence of lesbians and our continuing creation of the meaning of that existence' (p. 239). In other words, Rich acknowledges that lesbian is a term in a contemporary debate about female existence, for which she also provides a historical trajectory not determined or limited by heterosexual assumptions. Another term, 'lesbian continuum', is used to describe a range of what Rich terms 'woman-identified experience', which may or may not include sexual experience with another woman. The notion of the lesbian continuum is a controversial one in both lesbian and heterosexual communities. For conservative, heterosexual women, it suggests a sexualisation of their female friendships which is threatening and disruptive; for some lesbians it suppresses the specificity of their non-heterosexual experience and sexuality. However, it may be that both lesbian continuum and woman-identified experience derive their power and value as much from their rejection of heterosexist constructions of femininity as from their description of particular female friendships or experiences.

A common heterosexual characterisation of women is that they are engaged in an ongoing war among themselves over men. So women are seen as incapable of sustained friendships, gossiping about each other and being generally nasty to each other, especially when men are around. Novels such as Marilyn French's *The Women's Room* (1977) explored this construction in some detail, noting its disastrous effects on women who were thereby silenced and prevented from forming mutually supportive groups and communities. The counterstrategy of many feminists in the 1960s and 70s was to encourage women to share their experience of heterosexist society, including their relationships with men, in order to provide a supportive environment in which to explore the nature of contemporary society. Rich's ideas of the lesbian continuum and woman-identified experience continue this interrogation of heterosexuality and its constitution of the feminine.

Rich's essay might also be seen in the context of the 1970 essay, 'The Woman-Identified Woman' (Radicalesbians 1973) in which a group of lesbian feminists, identifying themselves as Radicalesbians, argue that what identifies the lesbian is her rejection of the female role as constituted for her by her society. Subsequently, the term 'woman-identified woman' has been used to refer to a woman whose frame of reference was not that of the heterosexist feminine, but who may or may not be a lesbian. That is, it describes the woman who refuses the stereotypical femininity assigned to women by compulsory heterosexuality – competitive (with other women), gossipy (about other women), nasty (to other women). Conversely, the term 'male-identified woman' is used to refer to women who adopt stereotypical (patriarchal or heterosexist) feminine behaviours.

The use of a term developed by lesbian feminists to describe the experience of both lesbians and women who do not identify as lesbians indicates the social critique implicit in any rejection of stereotypical femininity; both non-stereotypical heterosexual women and lesbians make a socially critical choice to behave as woman-identified. As Rich's lesbian continuum suggests, the experience of heterosexual women and lesbians cannot be separated as clearly as heterosexist discourse claims. This interrelationship reinforces the notion that lesbianism is a specifically female experience, not just a female version of male homosexuality; however, it does not help to explain the specificity of lesbianism.

Acknowledging the work of Rich and others in deconstructing the assumptions of what she calls 'heteropatriarchy', Shane Phelan (1994) writes that lesbianism is less a state of being than a becoming. As we discussed above in relation to homosexuality and heterosexuality, identities based on a particular conceptualisation of sexual behaviours and relationships are based on an implicit acceptance of the parameters of the definition which constitute one position (heterosexual) as normal and others as aberrant. Although taking pride in one's aberrant positioning may be a form of rebellion (see 'Gay' below), it can also be read as preserving the normal versus aberrant schema (which Rich's continuum, for example, works against). For this reason, Phelan (1994) argues against fixed notions of lesbian identity, which tie lesbianism into heterosexuality as its defining opposite. She suggests that an individual 'becomes lesbian or not with the choices one makes' (p. 52), noting that these choices are essentially about recognising the sociocultural specificity of heterosexuality and choosing whether or not to comply with it. She argues for a politics in place of an identity: 'I do not need epistemology to justify my desire, my life, my love. I need politics; I need to build a world that does not require such justifications' (p. 55). Phelan quotes Teresa de Lauretis' description of lesbianism as 'a space of contraditions, in the here and now, that need to be affirmed but not resolved' (p. 56); from affirmation may come the strategic alliances which enable the rigorous interrogation of heterosexuality, but not the resolution which implicitly affirms the position of (heterosexual) normality.

Gay

One such strategic alliance of homosexual men and women in the twentieth century was formulated around the identity, gay. Gay has had a number of meanings and mapping them is an interesting deconstruction of its contemporary usage. Its earliest use is defined as 'full of or disposed to joy' (*SOED*), describing a particular attitude or temperament. This was also glossed as 'airy, off-hand', not quite so positive a term, and later (in 1802) was also 'applied to women, as a conventional epithet of praise' (*SOED*). The gendering of the word seems significant here, given the binaristic logic which has characterised thinking about men and women, and about masculinity and femininity. If a term is conventionally applied to women, we might wonder what is its conventional masculine opposite. The trajectory from joyful to airy and off-hand to a conventional feminine epithet is a negative or downward one, from a state suggestive of spiritual exaltation to one of cynicism or moral vacuity to feminine vagary. This seems to accord with another early meaning (from 1637): 'addicted to social pleasures and dissipations' and 'of immoral life' (*SOED*). So gay carries the apparently contradictory meanings of joyful exaltation, on the one hand, and immorality and sensuality, on the other – along with a gendering which reinforces that contradiction. That is, in a society and language characterised by the negative definition of the feminine (in contrast to the positive definition of the masculine), a quality associated with the feminine is immediately suspect; if not indicative of spiritual, ethical or intellectual weakness, it will certainly be associated with the physical, and perhaps with the sensual or carnal. It is not surprising to discover, therefore, that in the nineteenth century gay was used to refer to immoral women – prostitutes and other fallen women. So the other secondary meanings of gay such as 'bright or lively looking', 'showily dressed' and 'brilliant, attractive' can also be read ambiguously as either positive or negative, depending on the context of use.

By the early twentieth century, gay had accumulated a number of meanings with nuances ranging from the spiritual to the ethical and intellectual to the sensual. It was also (conventionally) gendered to reflect that spectrum of nuances, with the negative aspects of the word associated with the feminine. Yet it was used quite unselfconsciously well into the twentieth century to reflect a sense of spiritual uplift and personal well-being, which suggests that its euphemistic references to immorality were not well known and so did not compromise its use.

The non-technical terms used to refer to homosexuality by the early twentieth century included gay, but it was not so commonly used, especially among the heterosexual community. The more common terms were 'queer' (see Chapter 2), 'fag', 'faggot', 'fairy', and so on, all essentially terms of abuse outside the homosexual community. Terms such as these were used throughout the twentieth century, which was a time of great persecution of homosexual people. The Laboucherie Amendment discussed above lay the groundwork for a series of scandals in the late nineteenth century, culminating in the trial of Oscar Wilde, which had interesting parallels with the trial of Socrates – both reviled as corrupters of youth, both actually guilty of an acute analysis of their own society. The legal persecution of homosexuals, defined by that trial, continued throughout the twentieth century, which also saw the Stalinist persecution of homosexuals in Russia and the Nazis' imprisonment and brutalisation of homosexual people in their notorious death camps. In the camps, homosexual prisoners were identified by the wearing of a pink triangle, which now is often used as a symbol of gay pride and rebellion. After World War II, during the McCarthyite period in Western societies (the 1950s and early 1960s) when those suspected of Communist sympathies were hounded from their jobs and homes (in the USA by a Senate subcommittee presided over by Senator Joseph McCarthy, in other countries by conservatives who followed that lead), homosexuals were also targeted as a potentially subversive group and persecuted on those grounds.

During this time societies and organisations were formed to provide support for homosexual people and fight against this persecution: for example, the Scientific-Humanitarian Committee was founded in Berlin as early as 1897 (later suppressed by the Nazis). The production of the category homosexual was, therefore, not only an occasion for public identification of homosexuals by others, but of public self-identification of homosexuals by themselves. This recognition of identity can be seen both positively and negatively; positive in that it enabled homosexuals to work together against social alienation and persecution, negative in that it was an implicit acceptance of the categories of heterosexual and homosexual (see 'Queer (Non) Identities' in the next chapter). Still, at a time of public persecution, mutual support was obviously more important and empowering for individuals than esoteric discussions about the power of categorisation.

Where such discussions became important was in the internal politics of homosexual organisations, as they debated how to relate to the newly defined heterosexual mainstream. The Mattachine Society (named after a medieval court jester who expressed unpopular truths from behind a mask (Adam 1995, p. 67)), established in Los Angeles in 1951, had intensive internal debates about the relation between themselves and the non-homosexual community. This society had a clear agenda of support and education:

- 'TO UNIFY' those homosexuals 'isolated from their own kind ... '
- 'TO EDUCATE' homosexuals and heterosexuals toward an ethical homosexual culture ... paralleling the emerging cultures of our fellow-minorities – the Negro, Mexican, and Jewish Peoples ...
- TO LEAD: the 'more ... socially conscious homosexuals [are to] provide leadership to the whole mass of social deviates' and also
- TO ASSIST 'our people who are victimized daily as a result of our oppression'. (Adam 1995, p. 68)

Yet under the stress of the McCarthyite period, Adam reports that the leadership of the Mattachine was to adopt an assimilationist politics which 'insisted that gay people are just the same as heterosexuals except for what they do in bed' (Adam 1995, p. 69). This politics moves away from the liberationist strategy suggested by the society's original 'missions and purposes'. And it was not until the police raid of the Stonewall bar in Greenwich Village, 27–28 June 1969, that gay pride was able to be openly demonstrated.

Throughout the twentieth century, homosexuals had been harassed in public places, either openly by police raids of gay bars or by covert entrapment practices (in which police officers posing as homosexuals invited sexual advances which then became the basis of prosecutions). The raid of the Stonewall bar was just another example of police harassment, except that this time the bar's clientele fought back. Various accounts of the events of this evening exist, but the salient point is that the people in the bar refused to be intimidated by the police action. Several days of police harassment in the area followed, which was met with collective – sometimes violent – resistance from the gay community. In the months following this pivotal incident, gay took on its most popular contemporary meaning, which unites the sense of joyous exaltation with an acknowledgement of social disapproval. Rather than being overwhelmed and defeated by that social disapproval, as in pre-Stonewall times, homosexual activists wore that disapproval as a badge of honour, because it was also an exclusion from the oppressive and authoritarian forces in society which codified and repressed not only homosexual citizens, but the *whole* of society.

Gay liberation was a powerful voice in the 1970s, arguing against conventional views that defined sexuality by reference to heterosexuality and the monogamous, heterosexual marriage. Adam explains that, for gay liberation, 'there was no "normal" or "perverse" sexuality, only a world of sexual possibilities ranged against a repressive order of marriage, oedipal families, and compulsory heterosexuality' (Adam 1995, p. 84). In other words, the gay liberation movement of the 1970s worked from a similar premise to many contemporary gender theorists in that they recognised in the definition or delineation of normal sexuality, the means by which men and women are both gendered and judged socially acceptable, or not.

Since the 1970s the gay community has gone through periods of relative quiet and through renewed activism around the issue of AIDS, demanding funding for research into the disease and help for those who contract it, as well as attempting to combat the homophobia which pervades many discussions of the AIDS virus in the West. The gay community has also been through periods of intense self-examination in relation to its own politics, and this will be discussed more fully in Chapters 2 and 4. In defining the history of the term gay it is important to note the context in which the word acquired the meanings it has today, and it is also important to note that those defined by the term are a heterogeneous group.

Historical research shows that, within the homosexual community itself, gay has had particular nuances, depending on its social context. So while it was used widely in the 1950s in the US homosexual community, in the UK gay had a specific class inflection; it referred to the upper socioeconomic bracket; a gay club was seen as classier than the queer pubs associated with those from lower socioeconomic groups. At the same time, 'queer' was a term widely used in the non-homosexual community, almost always with negative connotations (see Chapter 2). The use of the term 'gay', therefore, is an implicit rejection of the labelling applied by the heterosexual community, basically by those whose own socioeconomic status empowered them to take such a stance. At the same time, however, it signifies that the homosexual or gay community is as varied, by class, ethnicity, race, age and so on, as the heterosexual community.

'Gay', then, is the term around which members of the homosexual community choose at times to make strategic alliances in order to fight for common causes. An analogy might be drawn with the use of the term 'Christian'. There are very many different kinds of Christians, from different backgrounds and cultures, following different churches, who may at times choose to forget their differences in pursuit of a common goal. In fact, the gay community is rather less internally divided than the Christian community. However, these differences exist, with gay often still used primarily to refer to the more affluent and socially mobile members of the homosexual community. This acknowledgement should not weaken the notion of a gay community, but rather should prevent any heterosexist attempt to lump all gay people together as a homogeneous group, as a function of their (heterosexually defined) sexuality. The obvious analogy here is with sexist descriptions of women which identify all women as a function of their biology, ignoring differences of ethnicity, race, class, age and so on. As noted above, the terms which are used within and without the gay community to describe individuals – such as 'gay' and 'queer' – historically had different class connotations. To these might be added differences of gender, race, ethnicity, age and so on, for example gay is less likely to be used to refer to lesbians (see above) than to male homosexuals. So while gay is a signifier of shared concerns and interests, it does not signal a community any more homogeneous than the heterosexual community.

Identity

In the discussion of the word 'gay' and the ways in which it has been used strategically by people choosing to identify as being gay, we have opened up the question of what identity is. The concept of identity, like that of the subject and subjectivity which we discussed early in this chapter, has undergone something of a major revision in our postmodern times. Earlier views of individuals as self-determined, integrated beings have been replaced by a more complex notion of individuals as multiple subjectivities, sometimes described as fractured or split (to make the difference from the earlier concept clear). In this postmodern revaluation of the concept of subjectivity, we might question the fate of a concept related to both subjectivity and experience – identity.

As we have seen in our discussion of the production of the homosexual as a negative classification, identities can sometimes be turned around, and mobilised for positive political ends. For many people identity has been a very useful concept in that it enables them to discuss their common experience of the world with others whom they regard as like them; that is, others who share what they see as crucial features of their social positioning (such as gender, sexuality, ethnicity, class and so on). The example of being gay has been extensively outlined above. This has been particularly important for those whose experience has been devalued by normative or regulatory notions of experience derived from the interrelationships of one or more groups privileged (by access to institutional power and/or force) within society. For those excluded from influence and so from the validation of their experience, the notion of shared identity – and hence shared experience – enabled them to move beyond an internalised sense of inferiority; a notion that they did not have the normative experiences (and behaviours, feelings and thoughts) because they were *personally* inadequate. Instead it acknowledged that they shared their difference with many others, who were not personally inferior, but who had a different set of interrelationships with the world. Their experience was different (from the normative) and so their world was different (from the normative), because they were different (from the normative). Their experience was not valued *not* because it was inherently inferior, but because they were socially and politically less powerful. By providing such groups with a way of sharing experience and discussing their differences from the norm, identity was an extremely powerful social and political tool.

Cultural critic bell hooks (1990) has written of the anxiety felt by some African-Americans, therefore, at the deconstruction of identity which has accompanied the postmodern interrogation of subjectivity. She reports the response: 'Yeah, it's easy to give up identity, when you've got one' (p. 28). And she comments that African-Americans might be wise to question the deconstruction of subjectivity and identity when it occurs just as they are achieving a socially acknowledged subjectivity and identity for the first time. Nevertheless, hooks goes on to argue for a postmodern concept of identity, one which is not based in a unitary or monolithic concept of subjectivity and so an essentialist notion of identity:

> Such a critique allows us to affirm multiple Black identities, varied Black experience. It also challenges colonial imperialist paradigms of Black identity which represent blackness one-dimensionally in ways that reinforce and sustain white supremacy. (hooks 1990, p. 28)

That is, hooks recognises in essentialist notions of identity a regulatory or normative force, even where the identity being addressed is not a socially influential one. Class theorists have noted the same problem with essentialist concepts of class. If working-class identity is equated with a particular set of characteristics, is there a point at which an individual is effectively debarred from working-class identity (for example through education or employment)? And if education and employment can be seen as determining class identity, then does that not paralyse working-class culture, producing the kind of one-dimensional identity that hooks notes as a feature of colonialist views of black identity?

Another important feature of postmodernist (multiple, split, fractured) identity relates to its political function, and is perhaps the way past the concern that postmodernist interrogations devalue shared experience and shared identity: 'Postmodern culture with its decentered subject can be the space where ties are severed or it can provide the occasion for new and varied forms of bonding' (hooks 1990, p. 31). If identity is seen as fluid, rather than fixed, but as capable of points of (temporary or conditional) stasis, then its political force is not lost, but enhanced. So, for example, a working-class Anglo gay man might be able to form a temporary or conditional identification with a middle-class Asian gay man on the grounds of shared sexual identity (and despite differences of class and ethnicity) for the purpose of shared social, cultural and/or political communication and activity. The identity here is conditional, in that both individuals will be aware of their differences (of class and ethnicity), yet it enables kinds of sharing and activity which less flexible notions of identity would tend to devalue. In the postmodern scenario, identity is not an essentialist attribute of an individual but a strategy which individual (complex, multiple) subjects can use to create new and varied alliances.

The concept of the 'nomad' is used by philosopher Rosi Braidotti (1994) to explore this strategic use of identity. The nomadic subject, says Braidotti, is a fiction which enables her to think about and beyond well-known categories such as class, race, ethnicity, gender, age and so on, without being confined or limited by those categories. It enables her to think of the individual subject in relation to many of these categories at once, even where they sometimes contradict; as she says, 'blurring boundaries without burning bridges' (Braidotti 1994, p. 4). This concept of the nomad is also prominent in the work of the philosophers Gilles Deleuze and Felix Guattari (1983, 1987) where it argues for the strategic alliances made possible by self-aware, conditional, socially grounded interrelationships. In other words, they argue that such alliances are only possible when people do not deny or refuse to acknowledge their differences, as normative identities would demand, but instead make the combination of differences and commonalities a positive and powerful feature of a conditional, temporary alliance.

The anxiety reported by bell hooks is still there as an echo in these arguments. Is there a danger that this strategic sense of identity might be romanticised in such a way that the history and actual experiences of (some of) those involved may be lost? If that happens, is it not likely to be the experiences of those who have least social influence? An example of this kind of problem arose within the feminist movement when it was found, after the euphoria of the 1960s, that the experience and history of women who were not Anglo, not middle class and not heterosexual (among other things) was not voiced and not validated in feminist theory. Strategic alliances had been formed often by women from varied backgrounds, but those differences had not been acknowledged. As a result, the only experience and history which was theorised was that of the socially powerful groups within the movement – predominantly Anglo, middle-class heterosexuals. The consequences of such exclusions become clear when the theory is translated as policy and the women's movement became preoccupied with issues which related solely to the experience of that (socially privileged) group. This important issue will be taken up in Chapter 2.

Identity is a concept which enables groups to come together around the articulation of shared experience.

Experience

Now that we have set out how our understandings of identity have changed, we need to discuss the underpinnings of experience. If identity is something that we actively produce, not something which is given to us, then experience too may be something which we produce, not something which merely happens to us. Experience then is like identity; it seems a simple term, a description of what makes up our everyday life. Experience is what we do and feel during our encounters with other people and things. It is essentially a relational concept; that is, experience occurs in relationship with others or with objects or activities of some kind – real or virtual. It impacts on us bodily, even if we exhibit that impact primarily in how we think and feel.

In relation to the discussion of the modern subject above, we might say that experience is what turns the abstract concept of subjectivity into a real-life concept. As individuals experience the world, they develop a repertoire of subjective positions or subjectivities, each of which is appropriate to a specific situation. They learn to do this through their experience of that type of situation; by learning what is effective and ineffective behaviour in that situation – by experience.

This all seems fairly straightforward; however, looking more closely, we discover that some basic issues have not been raised. We might begin by exploring the relationship between the individual and experience: is there a preformed individual who has experience, or is it experience which forms the individual? Teresa de Lauretis (1984) writes of experience as 'the process by which, for all social beings, subjectivity is constructed' (p. 159). She explains further that it is by being immersed in the realities of social life that the individual 'perceives and comprehends as subjective (referring to, originating in oneself) those relations – material, economic, and interpersonal – which are, in fact, social, and, in a larger perspective, historical' (p. 159). That is, the individual's interactions with material, economic and interpersonal realities are transformed by her/him as subjective experiences, originating in and/or referring to her/himself and in the process constitutes her/himself as a subject. De Lauretis also notes that the relations which the individual perceives as personal are actually or also social and historical, although this broader perspective may be missed by the individual. So, through her/his experience of the social world, the individual becomes a subject, not vice versa.

Agreeing with de Lauretis' view, Scott (1992) writes about the commonplace uses of the term 'experience' which locate it outside the individual. She says that such usages

> preclude inquiry into processes of subject construction; and they avoid examining the relationships between discourse, cognition, and reality, the relevance of the position or situatedness of subjects to the knowledge they produce, and the effects of difference on knowledge. (p. 28)

This is a complex deconstruction which begins with reference to the area of subject formation. Like de Lauretis, Scott notes that the commonplace use of experience isolates it from its intrinsic part in the constitution of individuals as social subjects. Scott then adds other factors to her analysis. She argues that commonplace uses of experience also obscure the relationships between the ways we formulate our understandings of and attitudes towards issues and social practices (discourse), the ways we think (cognition) and the material world we encounter in our everyday lives (reality). That is, they do not ask how our attitudes towards and understandings of issues and events shape and are shaped by the ways we think; nor how the ways we think shape our encounters with the everyday world; nor how our basic attitudes and understandings shape our encounters with the everyday world.

This relationship is particularly important when the experience of individuals is used to validate a particular understanding of the world, as it is in the work of some contemporary historians and critics. In this context it is sometimes referred to as 'the authority of experience' and Scott challenges its use in this way. Her point is that, in order to do so, the experience discussed is usually unproblematically equated, in an essentialist way, with a particular social subject or identity. There is some sympathy for this viewpoint; it does recognise that different people experience the world differently, so that experience is not a universal – with the further implication that the experience of an elite few cannot be used as any kind of measure for the experience of others. Nevertheless, as Scott argues, the end point of this analysis is often a kind of essentialism, which militated against the interrogation of identities. For example, consolidating working-class identity around the notion of working-class experience works against a systemic challenge to the production of class. We are led to observe the fact that people from different class backgrounds have different experiences of the world, rather than to ask why these different classes exist at all.

In order to avoid this kind of essentialising of experience, and identity, Scott argues what is a typically poststructuralist demand for the specific location of the experience and its associated identity. In other words, she argues for 'the relevance of the position or situatedness of subjects to the knowledge they produce' (Scott 1992, p. 28). Scott glosses this by reference to the work of Gayatri Spivak and Stuart Hall, quoting from Hall's discussion of the identity, black: 'Black is an identity which had to be learned and could only be learned at a certain moment. In Jamaica that moment is the 1970s' (Hall quoted in Scott 1992, p. 33). An unselfconscious use of the concept of experience would locate in the attested experience of black subjects what it means to be black – without ever asking how and when the identity black developed and to whom it is applied in the generation of black subjects. Because it does not challenge the situatedness (development, being, function) of the specific identity, this unself-conscious usage naturalises it; that is, makes it seem natural or uncontrived. In the case of black identity, we are made to feel that the identity is natural in that we can identify those individual subjects who are black. Yet research shows that black is an identity which has changed radically in the last two centuries (Hall 1992; Michie 1992; Cranny-Francis 1995). In England it has meant the Irish, later those from Africa and the Indian subcontinent, and more recently West Indians. So how do we identify those who are black? As Hall observes, the identity black is the product of a particular set of forces at a particular time and place: 'It, too, is a narrative, a story, a history. Something constructed, told, spoken, not simply found' (Hall quoted in Scott 1992, p. 33). In naturalising the identity of Jamaica as a black society, the unselfconscious use of experience takes what Hall reveals as a 1970s' construction and makes it seem self-obviously true, natural and transhistorical. This not only conceals the position or situatedness of those black Jamaican subjects (that this is a sociocultural and political identity, not a natural one), but also the position and situatedness of those who have generated the identity of black Jamaica. This identity construction is part of a knowledge about the world which positions subjects in specific ways – with more or less social status, for example – so that concealing the processes by which it takes place not only validates or autho-rises that specific, constructed view, but also makes it seem natural and, there-fore, not open to question. In this way, the knowledge itself is protected from interrogation, along with the identities it generates. Scott notes that there 'is no power or politics in these notions of knowledge and experience' (p. 28); that is, the power and politics involved is not acknowledged.

Scott's point about the 'effects of difference on knowledge' (p. 28) takes up this question of the power and politics involved in the production of know-ledge. The notion of difference is discussed in Chapter 2, but suffice it to say here that recognising difference is about recognising the grounds by which different identities – and therefore different experiences – are generated; it is not about accepting that certain differences naturally occur. This inevitably leads us to challenge our knowledge: Whose knowledge is it? What social, cultural, political, economic practices does it validate? Who does it empower and who does it disempower? Scott concludes:

> Experience is at once already an interpretation *and* is in need of interpretation. What counts as experience is neither self-evident nor straightforward; it is always contested, always therefore political. (1992, p. 37)

The concept of experience has great value for us, although not perhaps always in the ways assumed. It is not that we can simply (and simplistically) use a recitation of someone's experience of the world to give us a different view. After all, as Carolyn Steedman notes in *Landscape for a Good Woman* (1986), the alienness of that different experience often precludes understanding. Steedman tells the story of Henry Mayhew, the nineteenth-century social observer, who is totally unable to comprehend the narrative of an eight-year-old watercress seller as she attempts to explain her life to him. The pride she takes in helping to support her family by her very hard work is read by him as pathetic and tragic, since he hears her from the position of a middle-class man with quite specific assumptions about childhood. Mayhew has sympathy for the girl, from the perspective of his own class, yet this is a sympathy which neither comprehends her life with its joys and griefs, nor is prepared to deconstruct the class system itself. However, experience can be the means by which we explore the ways in which we construct our world and the people in it. By seeing experience as a discursive construct, recognising its role in the production of subjects (rather than *by* subjects), and analysing its role in the generation of knowledges about the world, we can use it to explore the relationships between individual subjects and the society and cultures within which they operate.

Experience is the process where a subject interacts with material, economic and interpersonal realities and transforms them into subjective experiences, interpreting and creating her/himself in the process. It is a doing and a becoming.

Summary

Throughout this chapter we have traced the history and meanings of many of the words which are currently used in the analysis of gender. One of the most striking findings of this study is the extent to which we are forced to re-examine our assumptions and preconceptions about sexuality and gender.

Terms such as 'heterosexual' which we might assume to be quite old terms, on which terms such as 'homosexual' are based, prove instead to be relatively recent. And, in fact, it seems that the term 'heterosexual' could not be coined before the concept of 'homosexual' was formulated in order to operate as its other or defining term. Similarly, while we might trace a history of homosexual and lesbian activity and embodiment back to the beginnings of Western society, it is also surprising to note how relatively recently it was formulated in those terms. This might prompt us to question the investment in terms such as hetero- and homosexual: What is their function and purpose? How do they operate to constitute and regulate contemporary society? How do they constitute and regulate individuals?

Defining lesbian and gay raised a number of issues about the nature of identities based on sexuality, not least of which is the extent to which current conceptions are inevitably based on a rejection of heterosexist versions of identity, which move beyond sexuality to gender. That is, the debates about what constitutes lesbianism demonstrate the extent to which the gendering of all women takes place in relation to heterosexist norms, which assume a compliant femininity devoid of autonomous sexual desire. The early gay movement is shown battling with this same regulatory function of heterosexual society, calling for the liberation of all to practice whatever sexuality they wished, not just the versions officially sanctioned by heterosexual discourse, under its cheeky revision of the term 'gay'. All these terms are part of our vocabulary of gender, the terms in which we think and formulate and enact what we understand as our own gendered subjectivities. In the next chapter we examine the politics of identity, and some of the current responses to the shifting meanings of the categories of man and woman.

Recommended Reading

Abelove, Henry, Michèle Aina Barale and David Halperin (eds) (1993) *The Lesbian and Gay Studies Reader*, Routledge, New York.

Butler, Judith (1990) *Gender Trouble: Feminism and the Subversion of Identity*, Routledge, New York.

Hall, Stuart (1996) 'Introduction: Who Needs "Identity"?' in Stuart Hall and Paul du Gay (eds) *Questions of Cultural Identity*, Sage, London, pp. 1–17.

hooks, bell (1990) *Yearning: Race, Gender and Cultural Politics*, South End Press, Boston.

Jaggar, Alison M. and Bordo, Susan (eds) (1989) *Gender/Body/Knowledge: Feminist Reconstructions of Being and Knowing*, Rutgers University Press, New Brunswick, NJ.

Mansfield, Nick (2000) *Subjectivity: Theories of the Self from Freud to Haraway*, St Leonards, NSW, Allen & Unwin.

Scott, Joan W. (1992) 'Experience' in Judith Butler and Joan W. Scott (eds) *Feminists Theorize the Political*, Routledge, New York, pp. 22–40.

Exercises

These exercises are designed to help you put the ideas in the chapter into practice.

1. How do you 'do' gender? What things do you do to your body to claim a gender (for example think of hair, clothing and so on); how do you interact non-verbally (for example how do you sit, eat, move); verbally (for example interrupt, level of voice, and so on); and what activities do you engage in (for example watching football = doing masculinity and so on)?

2. How is sexuality policed in your community? Imagine three or four different events, public and private – a religious ceremony, dinner party, home and school meeting, office party, and so on – where everyone is heterosexual; where one person is the lone homosexual; where most people are homosexual. How does this change the planning for the event or the event itself?

3. In what ways do people begin marking a child's gender after its birth? How soon does this take place?

4. How would you specify your own identity? What features of your background, education, physical presentation, work experience and so on do you think are important in specifying that identity? How do different situations in which you are involved influence your expression of that identity?

2

Ways of Thinking

What we hope you will have gained from Chapter 1 is a healthy caution concerning the naturalness of what it is to be human. Time and again analysts remind us that gender is constructed, or not natural, but produced. How it is produced is the question that this chapter will address. We will look at several thinkers and analysts who try to understand how the subject is produced, and how gender is constructed. We will also examine some of the political and theoretical implications of the constructedness of the subject. If there are no natural categories of man or woman, how do we begin to talk about our experience, or make plans for political action? These are important questions, and we will trace out some of the lines of thought that have been followed in looking for answers to them. The final sections of this chapter will look at some of the work which has followed the questioning of the category woman, such as queer theory and the idea of embodiment.

As we discussed in Chapter 1, 'subjectivity' and 'the subject' are terms that have generally replaced the terms 'selfhood', 'the self' and 'the individual' when talking about who we are and how we got to be that way. Where terms such as 'the self' suggest rational, coherent, autonomous beings fully present to themselves and in control of their actions, thoughts and meanings, the terms 'subjectivity' and 'the subject' suggest less powerful, more tentative beings who are subject to forces not entirely within their control or comprehension. These forces are both external – historical, economic and cultural – and internal – bodily energies or drives, their psychic representations, unconscious fantasies and repressed thoughts. The terms 'subjectivity' and 'the subject' are reminders that each of us is born into a particular historical moment, a particular social class and a culturally specific place with its own systems of meaning, coherence and value. Even the language we learn is encoded with predetermined values and insights. Many of the thinkers who, following Freud and Marx, rejected the rational individual as a model for the subject, turned to linguistic theories to develop their own models of the formation of the subject.

Models of Subjectivity

In this section we will examine twentieth-century ways of thinking about the subject by thinkers as diverse as Louis Althusser, a political theorist; Michel Foucault, a historian and social critic; Luce Irigaray, a feminist psychoanalyst; Julia Kristeva, a linguist and semiotician; and Jacques Lacan, a psychoanalyst, as their work has been taken up repeatedly in gender studies. To begin, we will look more closely at the work of Freud from which so many twentieth-century ways of thinking about subjectivity have been derived.

Freud undertook a detailed elaboration of the functioning of the human mind and the mental apparatuses it develops as it encounters the external world. One of his most important insights about the human mind is that there is a part of it which is not accessible to consciousness. The mind's perceptions and behaviour are affected by unconscious material. The unconscious consists of material that is either too exciting or too painful to be allowed into consciousness; this material is repressed but nevertheless continues to affect the thinking and behaviour of the subject. The unconscious is the repository of repressed material, such as infantile desires and aggressions, conflicts, traumas and fixations. Through trial and error, Freud developed the practice of psychoanalysis, or the talking cure. The patient would talk to an attentive listener (the analyst) and, through the process of free association and the analysis of dreams and fantasies, bring repressed or unconscious material into consciousness. As a result, Freudian theory is very much caught up in the question of language because language is part and parcel of the material of the analysis in psychoanalysis.

The cornerstone of the psychoanalytic model is the idea of the unconscious. Freud studied the thinking processes which take place as the infant and later the child and the adult become adapted to the world. He soon speculated that mental life, or the psyche, could not be reduced to what subjects experience consciously and that the psyche is full of active yet unconscious ideas which show up in various ways. For example, you're on your way to work and try to put your house key into the car door lock; perhaps you'd rather be staying at home. This classic Freudian slip is an indication of the unconscious at work. Although they are often quite creative, sometimes these signs of the unconscious at work are highly neurotic or aggressive. Freud was arguing then, that such mad behaviour was not due to physical predispositions to madness, but to repressed childhood trauma, repressed aggression or desire. This insistence on social and personal sources for madness was quite courageous·at the time; the prevailing wisdom of Freud's day believed in biological causes for madness, such as hereditary degeneracy or merely the possession of a womb.

In his psychoanalytic practice in Vienna at the turn of the nineteenth century, Freud saw many patients whose symptoms of repression put them on the margins of society. Their lives were disturbed by physical (somatic) and psychic symptoms of repression: repeated gestures, disturbing dreams, slips of the tongue, nervous tics, delusions, hallucinations and so on. For Freud, the unconscious has its own logic far removed from conscious thought; unrecognised wishes and desires constitute the unconscious, but because they have been repressed, their content is inaccessible to consciousness. This forms the material which psychoanalysis attempts to decipher. Freud embarked on a therapy of interpreting these symptoms, to try to discover the childhood traumas which were being held back by the psyche, which were forcefully repressed. In psychoanalytic practice, the illness and the symptoms become signs which need interpretation, they are caused by and connected to unconscious drives and desires.

The unconscious is a crucial concept for Freudian psychoanalysis, in which it is understood as the repository of the fears, desires, traumas and conflicts too difficult for the conscious to manage. Although this material cannot be directly accessed, it can be engaged through an analysis of the practices – linguistic, visual and behavioural – through which it is expressed.

In one important case (Freud 1905, 1925), after attempting to use hypnosis as a therapeutic method, and not having much luck, Freud's colleague Josef Brener decided to let his patient just talk, while he listened attentively to her hysterical invented language. The patient in question, whose pseudonym was Anna O., called this treatment 'the talking cure', which has become a nickname for psychoanalysis. The act of talking proved to be of great therapeutic value, because the act of speaking creates a theatre in which deeply unconscious, traumatic material is performed again. The shift from hypnosis to the talking cure as a psychoanalytic therapy has various important implications for the status of psychoanalysis within gender studies.

In psychoanalytic practice, speaking starts the process of transference. Transference indicates a mainly unconscious process through which the patient comes to identify the analyst with important figures from her or his childhood. This enables the patient to experience something of the unconscious trauma again, and thus gain access to the material at the source of the psychic problem. The analyst functions as a screen for specific projections. This position allows her or him the possibility to turn the transference into a therapeutic tool. Freud was not always good at this: in several cases he mishandled the transference and, as a consequence, the therapeutic process broke down. He had to learn the hard way that transference functions both ways: the unconscious of the analyst is also mobilised in countertransference (the analyst projects desires onto the patient). Later, analysts would point out that Freud's own views on sexuality and gender made it difficult for him to work with the unconscious material produced by several young women (for feminist discussions of these important cases see Bernheimer and Kahane 1985; Showalter 1985b; Hunter 1989; Braidotti 1995).

Freud was also interested in the processes by which people became social beings. In order to explain the way that a child learns to take his or her place in society, Freud proposed the Oedipus complex. Adapting the story of Sophocles's Oedipus who (unknowingly) kills his father and marries his mother, Freud proposed the idea of an Oedipus complex (1931). It suggests that the child's growing awareness of its position in a triangular relationship – the mother, the child and the father – is one of the major mechanisms in the formation of subjects. Through the process of changing identifications from an infant fantasy of complete oneness with the mother, to a conflicted identification with either the father or the mother (depending on whether the child is a boy or girl) the child moves from being an infant in a kind of corporeal fantasy land to a socialised child. The triangle, in which the father represents a third party to the mother/child dyad, challenges and prevents the child's symbiosis with the mother. We will discuss this at greater length later in this chapter.

The Linguistic Subject

The French linguist Emile Benveniste (1971) argued that 'It is in and through language that man constitutes himself as a *subject*'. For Benveniste, subjectivity is assumed only in the act of saying 'I'. When we say 'I', we invent ourselves both through the very language we use and the ways language uses us. That we can use only certain pronouns – I, you, he, she, we, they – and not others assigns us certain kinds of place within language.

In the twentieth century, the study of language became central to several disciplines concerned with understanding subjectivity, history and social functioning. Writers and theorists have re-examined Freudian theory in the light of early twentieth-century work on linguistics which emphasised the inextricable links between language and subjectivity. Among those thinkers who have rewritten Freudian and Marxist terms from a language-oriented perspective are Jacques Lacan, Louis Althusser and Michel Foucault.

Jacques Lacan

We have already mentioned how the struggle to understand the unconscious made Freud pay close attention to his patients' use of language. In his reworking of Freudian theory, psychoanalyst Jacques Lacan (1977a) saw

Freudian material in linguistic terms. He argued that 'The unconscious is structured like a language', that is, the unconscious is determined by the dominant system of signs of the social order which Lacan called 'the Symbolic' (1977a). In Lacan's version of the Oedipus complex (1977a), the child represses the desire for the mother through the acquisition of language. By learning to speak, the infant must renounce a special corporeal oneness with a fantastical, all-powerful mother that it imagines, and become a child who takes up language – with its already inscribed system of sexual difference. (We can talk about an infant as 'it' but it seems very strange not to speak of a child as 'he' or 'she'.)

Lacan reinterpreted one of Freud's studies, in which Freud had observed his grandson (age one and a half) playing with a wooden reel attached to a string; the child would throw the wheel out of his cot exclaiming 'There' and then pull the reel back into his cot exclaiming 'Here'. Freud referred to this as the *Fort! Da!* game (*fort/da* means here/there in German) and surmised that the *Fort! Da!* game, the child playing 'gone' with his toys, enabled the child to cope with the idea of absence. From the *Fort! Da!* game, Freud formulated a more general hypothesis, 'the compulsion to repeat', a behaviour which may give the subject an illusion of mastery but which also may lock him or her into destructive and non-adaptive behaviour. Lacan added a linguistic dimension, speculating that the verbal ability to symbolise absence by words such as 'here' or 'there' is an apparatus for surviving the pain of slowly dawning self-awareness and the sense of being alone that is dependent on this. Language covers the pain of separation, of the breach of the bond with the mother. In this way of looking at things, society does not simply influence autonomous individuals but actually comes to dwell within them at the moment of the appropriation of language (Turkle 1992, p. xxv).

So Lacan emphasised the symbolic network into which the child is incorporated with the acquisition of language and through which his or her subjectivity is constituted.

For Lacan, language structures not only our conscious social life, but our unconscious life as well. By studying a subject's dreams and speech patterns, one can illuminate features of the split in the subject's imaginary register.

It is through substitution, through an endless metonymic chain of language, that the subject seeks to evoke the presence of the absent (m)Other or the object of desire. The social and the individual psyche are here welded together in a way that seems quite foreign to the model of the subject as an individual. We will take up these ideas again in Chapter 4.

Louis Althusser

We will now look briefly at the work of the Marxist political philosopher Louis Althusser who was influenced by Lacan's rewriting of Freudian and Marxist theories of the subject. The Marxist subject is defined primarily by its relation to the mode of production. Marx argued that a worker's self was defined by their relationship to their work, and the ways in which the worker could carry it out, whether they worked in a factory or on a farm, whether they participated in the ownership of that factory or farm and so on. Because few people work alone, Marx imagined that subjectivity would be developed collectively; who you were was also in important ways defined by the people you worked with. When a subject defined their own interests against other workers and with people who did not share the same relationship to the means of production, this was termed 'false consciousness'.

Althusser (1971) takes this model up, but he adds to it some of the linguistic models of the day. He argues that institutions, what he calls 'ideological state apparatuses' – such as the family, schools, the government, church, the media, sports and so on – interpellate (or address, call out to) individual subjects. Althusser gives the example of a policeman who shouts out in the street: 'Hey, you!' Everyone in the street turns around and immediately questions themselves. 'Have I done something wrong?' 'Is the policeman addressing me?' 'Who is the bad guy?' The policeman's calling out makes everyone within earshot feel that they've been found out, called to account, addressed by an authority figure. In that sense, they have been interpellated into the system. Althusser thought that institutions were constantly calling out to us, demanding that we respond to their call.

Althusser believed that we are all necessarily part of the system of ideology in which we live; that is, we are interpellated by ideology.

In this way, because such institutions speak to us, neither false consciousness nor ideology is something which is forced down our throats, but rather something that makes up our daily lives. In this sense, the subject is never outside ideology, the system of culture, government, church, schools, media and so on which makes up our view and experience of the world. The subject's daily life and thoughts are directly affected by social institutions such as the government, the administration, the army, the police, the courts, the prisons, what Marx called 'repressive state apparatuses' which function by violence in the public domain. Moreover, the daily practice of the subject is also affected by the various world outlooks of the ideological state apparatuses (religion, education, the family, the political system, the legal system, the trade unions, media, culture and so on), which function in the private domain through ideology, which Louis Althusser defines as 'a "represent-ation" of the imaginary relationship of individuals to their real conditions of existence' (1971, p. 152). Althusser argues that ideology and subjectivity are inextricably connected and that no one is outside ideology, although one of the effects of ideology is that it appears natural and inevitable ('ideology never says, "I am ideological"'). Hence the subject unreflectively accepts his or her subjection to ideology and is interpellated into the system 'in order that he shall make the gestures and actions of his subjection "all by himself"' (1971, p. 164).

For Althusser the individual can never be outside ideology, since it is through interaction with ideology that the individual subject comes into being.

The result is the relatively smooth functioning of society. The idea of the modern subject, the collective subject, which we identify with Marx, and which we discussed in Chapter 1, is reproduced not only through a relation to our working life, but also through the way language and culture transmits and reproduces subject positions.

Michel Foucault

The third writer we are going to discuss briefly is Michel Foucault. Foucault argued that discourses – such as medicine or psychiatry – yoked together power and knowledge, and then subjected individuals to them, subjected subjects if you like. A discourse such as medicine defines a position that someone can hold – patient or doctor – and the power or lack thereof avail-able in that position. The subject is not something that exists in advance, but is produced through the operations of discourses. This is a fluid model of the way the subject and the social field interact.

Foucault conceptualises the subject as produced by and in the negotiation of discourses that constitute our (social) life.

Michel Foucault was interested in the processes of power and subjection that run through a particular social institution, such as a prison, a hospital and so on. Throughout his work Foucault argues that the general social body is permeated by relations of power which, at the same time, characterise and constitute that particular social body. To understand subjectivity we need to understand how these relations of power operate on the individual – constituting our bodies, the way we behave, even our body language. In Foucault's words, the individual is

> an effect of power, and at the same time, or precisely to the extent to which it is that effect, it is the element of its articulation. The individual which power has constituted is at the same time its vehicle. (Foucault 1980, p. 99)

Common to all these theories is the view that the human subject is never in a pure state of nature but is always being operated on and influenced by social codes and institutions. When you realise that free will, the autonomy of the subject is compromised, then the question of how someone can act, the issue of agency, becomes very important. How can the subject effectively make decisions and act in the world in ways that might be oppositional to the dominant shaping forces? The contemporary emphasis on the compromised autonomy of the subject does not mean that we must view humans as prisoners of predetermined systems, deprived of agency or choice. These theories provide insight into the nature of the structures that must be challenged in order to work towards social and personal change.

Gender and Subjectivity

The theories of Marx, Althusser and Foucault which we have just reviewed outline, by and large, a neutered account of subject formation, but that has not prevented other analysts from taking them up and altering them to investigate the formation of a gendered subject.

Femininity and masculinity are ideologies in the Althusserian sense, discussed in the last section, and operate in such a way that they appear natural and inevitable. The process of forming the subject as masculine or feminine starts early. A pregnant woman will often be told that she is carrying high, a sure sign of a boy child, and any feisty kicks will be then read as a confirmation of the child's gender. Behaviour, being, gender are linked together before an infant draws its first breath. Boys are likely to be rewarded for vigorous, aggressive activity, while girls are likely to be discouraged for the same behaviour. The conditioning begun in infancy and continued in school carries over into relationships and the workplace. It is played out in the media, in talk-back radio, current affairs programmes and mainstream films. Australian sociologist Bob Connell (1987) uses the phrase 'gender regime' to refer to the gendered social practices characteristic of various institutional sites (family, school, workplace) in which one lives out one's daily life. In this, he is drawing on both Marxist and Foucauldian thoughts on subject formation.

Teresa de Lauretis, a feminist film critic, has drawn on the work of Althusser, and particularly Foucault, to describe what she calls a 'technology of gender' (de Lauretis 1987). She makes four very important points. First, gender is a representation; it is semiotic. It works through discourse, images and signs which only function in relation to one another. Gender is not something which exists in bodies but is, in Foucault's words, which she quotes, 'the set of effects produced in bodies, behaviours, and social relations' by the deployment of a 'complex political technology' (1987, p. 3) and she sees this construction of gender, this set of effects, as reproduced through what Althusser called the 'ideological state apparatuses', the media, schools, the courts, the family and so on.

Moreover, de Lauretis sees herself involved in reproducing gender, in constructing it herself, by theorising about what it is. The construction of gender is, in her view, *'the product and the process of both representation and self-representation'* (1987, p. 9, italics in original). This means, as Althusser pointed out, that no one is outside ideology. What goes on in the intellectual community, in avant-garde artistic practices or local feminist politics is involved in dismantling and simultaneously constructing gender. And the question which de Lauretis asks is one which is very important to feminism: *'If the deconstruction of gender inevitably effects its (re)construction, the question is, in which terms and in whose interest is the de-re-construction being effected?'* (1987, p. 24, italics in original). This is a question which working-class women and women of colour have asked of second-wave feminism. It is a question that we take up in the section on critiques of identity politics. So, in de Lauretis' writing, the influence of the major theorists discussed earlier in this chapter can be seen, inflected specifically for the study of gendered subjectivity.

While many of the major male theorists of subjectivity suppress the issue of gender, theorists such as Teresa de Lauretis employ the same negotiative model of subject formation to explore gender as both representation and self-representation.

Psychoanalysis and Gender

While many theories of subjectivity pay little attention to the productive role of gender in the formation of the subject, psychoanalysis, for all its limitations, has always been interested in gender as primary in the production of subjects. Freud articulated the Oedipus complex to understand the process of becoming a subject, of taking up gendered subjectivity, or, put more simply, the road to becoming a woman or a man. For Freud, this complex is a useful story to explain how an infant comes to deal with its incestuous desires – both erotic and destructive – for its parents. The Oedipus complex plays a fundamental part in the structuring of the personality, and in the orientation of human desire.

Freud imagined the libido (human desire) as a great reservoir of psychic and sexual energies which were channelled through particular drives (sometimes called 'impulses' or 'pulsions'). Like many writers of his day, he used modernist metaphors of industrial production in his theories; Freud's libido resembles a hydraulic power plant which sends out and receives great flowing gushes of libido. These metaphors of hydraulics outline how the flow of sexual energy is regulated through apparatuses, production processes and mechanisms (Ferrell 1996). Through a process called 'cathexis' we channel our libidinal energy to one object or another; we choose the object of our affections and direct the flow of our desire to it, him or her. This process of object choice is crucial to Freudian theory, as it is one of the mechanisms that seems to explain the operation of compulsory heterosexuality at an individual and unconscious level.

Freud argued that infant sexuality is unchannelled and 'polymorphously perverse'. Its 'libidinal economy' is unstructured. That is, the infant loves everything and everyone: grabs all fingers; enjoys farting; believes that breasts are part of the giving universe; plays with him/herself; thinks peeing is fun; and, generally, is not quite sure where his or her own body leaves off and others begin. Breasts, fingers, toes – these are all part of the extension of the infant's body. In other words, many ('poly') forms ('morph') of pleasure (perverse) appeal to the infant. How then to turn this squeezing, farting, peeing good-time baby into a proper girl or boy and, subsequently, a heterosexual, 'well-adjusted' adult?

The Oedipus complex describes the psychic operation of a complex of attraction, desire, love, hatred, rivalry and guilt that the child feels towards his or her parents. It takes place around the age of three to five years and explains how the child comes to identify with the same-sex parent.

In classical Freudian theory, the Oedipus complex comes in two flavours, one for boys, one for girls (Freud 1925, 1931). Both are outlined below.

In the pre-Oedipal phase children of both sexes are one with their mother. In this state of 'polymorphous perversion' there is no formation yet of sexual desire; the child experiences primarily oral and anal drives (impulses, forces of desire, needs and wants). When the child separates from its mother and breaks out of this close unity with her, the path for each gender differs.

The little boy takes the road through the positive Oedipus complex, where he desires his mother and identifies with his father. (At the end of a positive Oedipus complex the love object is the opposite sex; the negative Oedipus complex produces a same-sex object of desire. The normative beliefs of his society operate in the names Freud gave his complexes.) Freud speculates that when the boy child becomes aware of sexual difference, he is concerned with the mother's lack of a penis and assumes that she has been castrated by the father (the castration complex). According to Freud, because of its visibility, the penis is the most important reference in the organisation of sexuality; in contrast, the female genitalia lie hidden, which is the cause of male castration anxiety: 'the fear of nothing to see'. The young boy goes through a twofold motion: he discovers the absence of the penis and consequently fears that the father will punish him for his forbidden love for his mother by taking away his penis, too. He gives up his love for the mother, and his rivalry with the father, and identifies with his father, thereby taking on a masculine identification. By repressing his desire for his mother, he forms a strong and strict superego. His drives change from oral and anal to phallic or genital drives. Freud posited this story as a way of explaining how the boy child grew psychically and consolidated the functions of the ego and superego.

The little girl takes a different route after the pre-Oedipal stage; she too enters the genital/phallic stage in which she loves her mother actively. In this stage her drives are focused on the clitoris, which is considered by Freud to be an inferior sort of penis. When the young girl makes the dramatic discovery that she has no penis, she develops a castration complex, which involves self-hate and resentment towards the mother. The castration complex results in penis envy, which forces the girl to enter the positive Oedipus complex. According to Freud, the girl substitutes a yearning for a baby for this penis envy. For the girl, the Oedipus complex involves giving up the fiercely desired penis and replacing it with the desire for a baby; to do this, she redirects her desire towards her father. Freud adds that only by bearing a (male) child does a woman achieve full access to mature femininity.

Freud argues that the route to femininity is more tortuous; the little girl is initially a little man but becomes passive when she discovers that she is castrated. Feeling wounded and resentful at her lack of a penis, she turns away from the mother as a love object and towards the father with the desire to bear a child of her own to compensate for her lack of a penis. In the Oedipal stage, then, the young girl has to make two libidinal shifts: she replaces the erotogenic zone of the ('phallic') clitoris with the ('female') vagina, and she shifts the object of her love from the mother to the father. For the girl, the psychological consequences of the Oedipus complex are permanent: penis envy gives her a sense of being castrated and therefore injured. The psychological scar of this wound to her self, this narcissistic wound, will leave the girl with a permanent sense of inferiority.

Because the girl's Oedipus complex is not destroyed by castration anxiety as it is in the young boy, the Oedipal stage is never wholly resolved and, as a consequence, the girl has a weaker need for repression. As a result of this, says Freud, the girl scarcely develops a superego and remains morally defective. Repression leads the subject to the need for sublimating his/her drives, just as artists sublimate their desires and aggression through the creation of works of art. Castration anxiety is a precondition for sublimation which, according to Freud, explains the limited participation of women in culture.

More Than One Freud

It is important to note that there is more than one way to read Freud. People taking up Freud's ideas have turned them to their own uses. Generally, different psychoanalytic theories mobilise different concepts and often different assumptions – there is no unified body of thought called 'psychoanalytic theory'. With its link to clinical practice, it is a body of writing that is very much caught up in changing personal, cultural and social stories. This gives it a provisional quality – a 'let's see if this works' aspect – and keeps psychoanalysis from becoming fixed in a disciplinary regime. This is one of the reasons why it is difficult to study; there are many forms of psychoanalytic thought.

For now, let us mention a few of the more important versions of psychoanalysis for considerations of gender. It makes a big difference to the account of subjectivity whether you choose a theorist who emphasises the mother (Klein 1963; Winnicott 1975; Chodorow 1978a, 1978b) or one who emphasises the father (Freud, Lacan). The early female analysts used their own mothering experience and that of their patients to lay stress on the interpersonal factors which modified the instinctual drives. They pointed to processes of identification (Deutsch 1944), internalisation and projection (Klein 1963), maternal separation and loss (Anna Freud 1967), the influence of the social (Horney 1973) and intersubjectivity (Benjamin 1988).

Gender as a category in feminist psychoanalytic discourse circles around the question of how and where to formulate the problem of cultural construction. There are three major strands of this debate: one comes from Lacanian psychoanalysis; another from the school of Object relations; and the third, radical gender and queer theory, comes through in the reworkings of gender by women such as Gayle Rubin and Judith Butler. We will hold off on this third strand until later in this chapter and Chapter 4. The strand of psychoanalytic theory known as Object relations theory is associated with a group of writers and analysts following the work of Melanie Klein: for example, Winnicott (1975) in Britain, Chodorow (1978a, 1978b) and Guntrip (1968, 1971) in the USA. Whereas the focus of classical Freudianism was primarily on the

conflict between instinctual drives and the frustrations of external reality
which produce repression, Object relations theory focuses more on the child's
relations with its real or fantasised others. It provides a more intersubjective
and socially oriented account of psychic reality. Nancy Chodorow's (1978b)
book *The Reproduction of Mothering* is generally seen as part of this strand; it
has been one of the most influential psychoanalytic texts for women in the
United States. Jessica Benjamin (1988) is another contemporary theorist who
adopts this more intersubjective approach, and there is currently a great deal
of interest in her work.

Dorothy Dinnerstein (1976) and Nancy Chodorow (1978a, 1978b) take up
work by Melanie Klein and argue that the cultural institution of women's
mothering is the key factor in gender development – since children of both
sexes inevitably identify with their first carers. According to these theorists,
children consolidate a core gender identity in the first two years of life, well
before the Oedipus complex articulated by Freud. This research demonstrates that maternal identification is the initial orientation for children of
both sexes. However, the girl sustains the primary identification with the
mother, while the boy repudiates maternal identification in favour of identification with the father. These analysts point out that under gender arrangements in which the mother is often trapped in the home as the primary carer,
the child perceives the mother as extraordinarily powerful and not lacking,
as Freud would have it. In this context, the father represents to the child the
possibility of separation from the mother and progress towards individuation. However, in a society in which the genders are not equally valued,
the repudiation of the mother becomes a repudiation of the qualities associated with her (relation, connection, nurturance) and with femininity in
general. According to Jessica Benjamin (1988), an identification with the
father becomes a denial of dependency. We will look at the impact of these
ideas a little later in the chapter when we discuss difference, and the relations
between Self and Other.

Freud's theories of the psyche, subjectivity, masculinity and femininity
made the impact of the unconscious all-pervasive. So all-pervasive is it that
even rational science has been affected, and acquired an unconscious. For if
all meaning-making processes are thus caught up in the unconscious, this
would include, of course, forms of knowledge. It would include, in fact, the
very science of psychoanalysis which Freud was developing, and as Freud
himself showed so clearly, the formation of the unconscious and sexual difference are bound up together. Writers such as Luce Irigaray put psychoanalysis
on the couch, and analyse its own unconscious (1985a). However, we can't
embark on a psychoanalysis of psychoanalysis until we know a bit more
about it. We will discuss this at greater length in Chapter 4.

Rethinking Gender: Feminisms and Identity

What is clear from the preceding two sections is that understanding how subjects are formed is a crucial question to understanding how gender functions socially and psychically. What modern theories of the subject offer people studying gender is the idea that identities are not fixed. Freudian theory gives us a sense of how conflicted and precarious our hold on gendered subjectivity is. At the same time, work by Foucault and Althusser reminds us how interested institutions are in fixing our identities, to further their own purposes. Having examined the question of the subject quite closely, we can see why the politics of identity are so crucial to gender analysts. Understanding the ongoing processes of subject formation shows us that the very categories of man and woman are constructed. Recent feminist writings in other arenas have also grappled with the concept of identity and the category of woman; these writings are concerned with how women can both recognise their differences and form alliances across those differences. They give us another view on the question of gendered subjectivity, on what a woman is.

The Question of Identity Politics

For women of colour, working-class feminists and lesbian feminists, the major feminist theories failed to provide a voice, as did the major conservative discourses and social practices in which these women were involved or embedded. Put most simply, the major strands of feminist thought, as it was being constructed at the time (Marxist, liberal, socialist feminism), all tended to assume that they spoke for *all* women, and they could do that because they were generated by women.

> The feminist theorists whose work constitutes the female liberation movements spoke to a universal sisterhood of women and *for* that universal sisterhood. They consistently failed to recognise that there were crucial differences between themselves and many of the women for whom they spoke; primarily between themselves and the women who had very different life experiences and backgrounds from them.

Not surprisingly, many of these theorists were white and middle class – women from privileged backgrounds who were in a position to write and publish theory. The problem was not that they did so, but that they failed to see that their experience – and subsequently the theory based on that experience – was specific to women of their own background. The further problem with that failure of recognition was that it constructed a universal woman who effectively disenfranchised, silenced, those women who did not fit her description.

Barbara Omolade, for example, wrote in 1985 about the failure of white feminists to include the 'history and culture of women of color' in their writings. She writes:

> We assert simply that Black women are not white women with color but are women whose color has obscured their historical and cultural experience as Africans, as chattel slaves and as more than half the population of the black community. (Omolade 1985, p. 248)

Omolade traces the differences in the experiences of black and white women over several centuries, noting, for example, that in the Middle Ages when the social position and status of Western European women was very poor, black women enjoyed 'high status, and the civil and human rights accorded all tribal members' (p. 247). Also, between 1500 and 1700, while in Europe tens of thousands of women were burned at the stake as witches, 'female organisations in Western African tribes flourished and were responsible for educating women about sexuality, obstetrics and gynaecology' (p. 249). Closer to the present day, Omolade records the leading role that black people had in the fight against slavery in the United States, another fact largely ignored in official histories. She notes also that contemporary feminist organisers, too, have largely ignored the skills of black women and their input to the feminist struggle. Instead they have defined the aims of feminism in terms such as 'employment opportunities and changing sex roles' which, Omolade notes, 'ignore the history of Black women as workers in Africa and this country, which have proven that economic independence from men is not liberation' (p. 255). In some of the basic principles of feminist politics there are established cultural differences between white and black women which feminism has ignored: for example for many (white) feminists, child-bearing is a sign of 'oppression and restriction' yet 'Africans viewed motherhood as an honour necessary for the tribe's continuance' (p. 249). In other words, there are very concrete differences in the experiences of black and white women which Western feminism has ignored. Not only has this greatly impoverished feminism as a politics, but it also has contributed to the silencing and negating of racism which is the history of African-Americans.

Audre Lorde's letter to Mary Daly after the publication of her book, *Gyn/Ecology* (1978) makes the same point (Lorde 1984). As she read through Daly's stories of the goddess, Lorde notes, she asked herself: 'why doesn't Mary deal with Afrekete as an example? Why are her goddess images only white, western european, judeo-christian?' (Lorde 1984, p. 67). Her first thought was that Daly was only dealing with the ecology of Western European women, in which case her choices were valid. However, she subsequently found that the book does deal with non-European women 'but only as victims and preyers-upon each other' (p. 67). So by selectively not citing the cultural heritage of non-European women who do, after all, feature in the study, Daly makes that heritage invisible. The consequence is

> the assumption that the herstory and myth of white women is the legitimate and sole herstory and myth of all women to call upon for power and background, and that nonwhite women and our herstories are noteworthy only as decorations, or examples of female victimization. (Lorde 1984, p. 69)

Because of its universalising strategy, Daly's book is part of the silencing of black women's history, and so part of the oppression of black women.

In her essay 'Third World Diva Girls', bell hooks begins by noting that 'no one really speaks about the way in which class privilege informs feminist notions of social behavior, setting standards that would govern all feminist interaction' (hooks 1990, p. 89). So hooks argues that standards are set for appropriate interaction between women without any recognition of the fact that such standards derive from a particular class and the interactions which characterise it. hooks writes about the assimilationist drive within any institution which coerces all working within it to act in a way which accords with its cultural history: to 'talk the right kinda talk'. Her response is to reject that coercion because of how 'radically disempowering it is for people from underprivileged backgrounds' (p. 90). In other words, hooks does not simply fake it and act like she belongs, but maintains the signifiers of her own class background. This has disadvantaged her in many ways as an academic – because her writing is perceived as less theoretical and so less valuable than that of others, and because she does not engage in the same bourgeois competitive behaviours as her colleagues. Equally disempowering is the fascination she detects in white feminists as they observe dissent among black feminists which, in them (black women), is perceived not as laudable competitiveness (as it is among white women/feminists), but as affronting good taste – the standards of scholarly debate. In other words, classism and racism combine to produce an environment which is radically disempowering for many black women.

Working-class white women report similar problems with early feminisms: the demands that they should speak openly in contexts which were alien to them not only because they were women, but also because they were working class and so voiceless in that context; the denigration of motherhood to women from a culture in which motherhood held high status; the drive for career advancement in a competitive environment for women whose acculturated (working-class) drive or desire is to/for solidarity rather than competition and individuation. Again such class-blind standards for feminist women alienated many working-class women, and also failed to use their wisdom.

Pamela Farley Tucker also writes about the exclusions within feminism by noting that, apart from male–female difference, 'other differences, such as those of color and sexual identity, which are also used oppressively, are simultaneously glaring and invisible' (Farley Tucker 1985, p. 267). For many lesbian feminists, the assumption of heterosexuality in a lot of feminist writing was problematic not only for its failure to recognise that not every woman shared this sexuality, but also because it ignored the misogyny which fuels homophobia (you might refer back to Chapter 1 here). That is, the taboo against lesbianism is a reflection of the social constitution of femininity: '*the dependency of "men" upon "women" is a great secret of History*' (Farley Tucker 1985, p. 271, italics in original). Ignoring differences in sexuality, then, contributes to the maintenance of conservative (patriarchal) society.

These criticisms of feminism are not raised simply in order to denigrate feminism. By focusing on the role and status of women they began our contemporary reassessment of all aspects of gendering. However, while providing much useful commentary on and theorisation of gender, these feminisms often also tended to universalise the experience of oppression. In doing so, they unwittingly contributed to the strategy of Othering, which is fundamental to the conservative gender politics against which they struggled. As Audre Lorde notes, 'Institutionalized rejection of difference is an absolute necessity in a profit economy which needs outsiders as surplus people' (Lorde 1984, p. 115). The distinction Lorde draws here is between the notion of 'Other' (outsiders) and that of 'difference'. Lorde identifies here the institutional strategy of creating Others, people who are alien to everything a society and its citizens represent: these Others are, literally, non-citizens. The binary they inhabit is: citizen/non-citizen. They have no independent, autonomous existence as 'different from' US citizens: there are only US citizens or non-US citizens. From Lorde's perspective, this is because the capitalist economy needs a supply of expendable people, who can be treated as non-citizens and given no rights. She goes on to note that there are many differences between us – 'of race, age, and sex' – but that these differences are not what separate us: 'It is rather our refusal to recognize those differences, and to examine the distortions which result from our misnaming them and their effects on human behavior and expectation' (p. 115). So, she notes of class difference, that 'unacknowledged class differences rob women of each others' energy and creative insight' (p. 116) and of race:

> As white women ignore their built-in privilege of whiteness and define *woman* in terms of their own experience alone, then women of Color become 'other', the outsider whose experience and tradition is too 'alien' to comprehend. (p. 117)

Difference

'Difference', for Lorde, is a concept which allows the recognition of another's specificity. It works against the silencing impulse of Othering and its refusal to accept the Other as autonomous, but different. Difference encodes a recognition that universalism is a strategy of the victor, not an egalitarian gesture; the only people who can write as if their experience is shared by all are those who are in positions of social dominance.

So difference can be a powerful strategy, deconstructing binaristic thinking. Trinh Minh-Ha also writes that 'Difference is not otherness'. She goes on:

> Difference always implies the interdependency of these two-sided feminist gestures: that of affirming 'I am like you' while pointing insistently to the difference; and that of reminding 'I am different' while unsettling every definition of otherness arrived at. (Trinh 1991, p. 152)

For Trinh, Lorde, hooks and others, difference provides a basis for the simultaneous recognition of similarities and the acknowledgment of difference – for sharing but not suppressing. It has become an indispensable conceptual category for contemporary gender theorists.

> The concept of 'difference' is a way of acknowledging difference while also recognising similarities, unlike the notion of 'otherness' which suggests total incompatibility. It enables conditional alliances to be made on the basis of shared purpose, without suppressing the differences between those involved.

Hélène Cixous, in the opening section of 'Sorties' (Cixous 1981, pp. 90–1), revisits the list of binaries we quoted in Chapter 1 – binaries such as man/woman and father/mother are equated by Cixous with others such as activity/passivity, culture/nature, intelligible/sensitive, logos/pathos and sun/moon. Cixous explains the significance of this binary by noting how it appears throughout Western literature, philosophy, representation and critique as a central and structuring metaphor. She then goes on to suggest a way in which they can be undone – not by reversing or revalorising them (making some of the terms currently not valued seem valuable, and the reverse), but by an explicit acknowledgment of their hierarchical nature. What she means by this is that the terms of the oppositions in her list, such as sun/moon and man/woman, are not equal; instead one dominates the other. The oppositions are hierarchical. Sun and moon are not equal and different, nor are man and woman. In this metaphorical way of thinking that characterises Western societies, the first term in the opposition dominates the second. The simple step of recognising that these oppositions are hierarchical was a major break-through in our study of social, including gendering, practice.

The French philosopher Jacques Derrida (1978) also wrote about the priv-ileging of one term in these oppositions – the equivalent to Cixous's hier-archy. Derrida explained that not only is one term privileged above the other, but that the secondary term in the binary is central to the definition of the privileged term. The first term could not exist or function without the second unprivileged term. The secondary term is therefore permitted no autonomy but derives its meaning purely through its opposition to the nature of the privileged term. Its only functional role seems to be to act as a support to the meaning of the primary term. So, in an opposition such as man/woman, the term 'man' is privileged; it exists as the dominant term in the hierarchy, man/woman. Also the term 'woman' has no independent existence, no autonomy; it exists as the negative or opposite of the primary term, 'man'. Man is defined as what woman is not – activity, sun, culture, father, head, intelligible, logos. So when Freud charted the semiotic (meaning-making) practices of his own time, it is not surprising that he recorded that woman has no autonomy, sexual or otherwise. She is simply the 'other' of man. In the terms Freud recorded at the beginning of the twen-tieth century, man/woman did not equate with penis/clitoris (or clitoris + labia), but with penis/no penis; that is, woman is sexually a void, a recep-tacle of sexuality that is essentially male.

Lorde and others use a similar deconstructive practice; rather than reverse the opposition, instead they reveal how the hidden secondary term is pivotal for the meaning of the primary term and deconstruct its position as primary. The other term in the binary is recognised as a construction that defines, by opposition, the dominant term. In this sense, there is no other term (that is, man/woman is, more correctly, man/not man; there is no woman). As Lorde says, it is ignored; we refuse to recognise it. A politics of difference, on the other hand, is based on a foregrounding of that recognition. It demands relational, rather than oppositional, thinking. By placing the secondary term of the binary at the heart of the dominant term, this relational thinking decon-structs not only the power relation in which the terms are engaged, but also the meaning of each term – the dominant term (why is it defined in certain ways?), but also the absent secondary term (who does this term refer to? how is it related to their actual conditions of being?).

This relational thinking had many ramifications for feminists. For example, the notion of 'patriarchy' came under challenge since it assumed that male or masculinity inevitably equated with power and privilege. Yet, it was clear that to be male and black did not automatically equate with privilege in every situation, nor did male and working class. So the simple category man was seen as not sufficient when a particular situation or event or individual was considered. It contributed to the working out of power relations in the situation or the event or person, but it was not the sole determinant. So, gender was seen to be just one factor operating in the production of an event or an individual subjectivity, and it needed to be considered in relation to other factors, such as class, ethnicity, sexuality and so on.

Psychoanalysis and the Other

It is obvious that psychoanalysis too will have a great deal to offer in terms of thinking about the relations between selves and others. Probably most important to thinking about the question of the Other in feminism and psychoanalysis are the revisions to the classic Freudian story of the Oedipus complex, and the various feminist challenges and reinterpretations of it. Psychoanalysts of all kinds are interested in how those others outside us are drawn inside of us; how our 'others' come to reside within us. Both the French feminists and Object relations theorists are keenly interested in the relations between the Self and the Other.

We mentioned earlier the work of Dorothy Dinnerstein and Nancy Chodorow: they elaborate on early work by Melanie Klein (1963) on mothering as the key factor in gender development. Dinnerstein and Chodorow are interested in the way children consolidate a core gender identity in the first two years of life, long before the moment where Freud imagined children entered the Oedipus complex. These theorists put the emphasis on the importance of the mentally healthy child's integration of the various love objects into his or her ego, and stress that the power differential in current parenting arrangements makes it unlikely that a healthy, balanced ego will be produced. The close union with the mother is repudiated, in part because of her devalued status, and the child turns to the father for a source of identification. As we said earlier in this chapter, this psychoanalytic approach provides a more intersubjective and socially oriented account of psychic reality.

Jessica Benjamin (1988) has argued that the devaluation of the need for the Other becomes the touchstone of adult masculinity. She further argues that Western culture has privileged and institutionalised the masculine ideal of separation, autonomy, self-reliance and individualism as the model for subjectivity, and relegated the qualities associated with the feminine, such as connection, relation and nurturance, to the private sphere. Her point is that all people regardless of gender need to balance agency and mutuality, self-assertion and recognition of the other, in order to achieve maturity and individuation.

French feminist psychoanalysis, which is associated with writers such as Luce Irigaray (1985b), Julia Kristeva (1982) and Catherine Clément (1989), has a different approach to this question of the Other. They have retained and developed Freud's ideas of drives, for they are very interested in different mechanisms of desire – drives, impulses, object choices and so on. Their approaches stress the internal splitting and division of the self, where Object relations theory is more likely to stress the integration of different parts of the self in healthy development, with splitting (disavowal) seen as a mark of pathology.

To understand what French feminism means by splitting, we must return to Lacan's theory of the infant's move into the Symbolic order. Earlier we discussed Lacan's argument that the unconscious is structured like a language. He also argued that language acquisition marks the child's break with the mother and his or her socialisation into the dominant social order, which Lacan called 'the Symbolic order'. Lacan characterises the symbolic order as a patriarchal order dominated by paternal law, which he called *le nom du père*. In Lacan's original French text, this is a play on words. The *nom* means name and refers to the father as head of the household, the social system of patrilineality. But it also sounds like *non*, no in French. Father says No! While Freud speculated that the father is the third side in the triangle which prohibits union with the mother (incest prohibition), and breaks up the happy couple of mother and infant, Lacan used a paternal metaphor, an idea of the fundamentally patriarchal nature of symbolic systems as the agent that prohibits or renders impossible the complete fulfilment of the child's wishes and fantasies.

So this outsider, this 'other' which is language begins a process of loss. The child will try to get back what the *nom* of the Father has taken through language. Lacan saw the operation of Oedipus as an example of metonymy. Metonymy is like metaphor, except that instead of making meaning through association, metonymy makes meaning through substitution. The classic example of metonymy is 'all hands on deck'. Read literally, it conjures up a picture of a galleon with fifty sailors with their hands flat down on the deck like a maritime game of Twister. Read figuratively, metonymically, it is understood that it means all fifty sailors should be standing on the deck, ready for the captain's orders. Language will substitute for the loss the child has suffered.

The Other Within

So, with the no of the father, the infant starts to separate from the mother, and transfers its desire for its mother to an Other. But how does this Other come into being? Lacan devised the idea of the 'mirror stage' to explain how the infant begins the process of emerging from the symbiosis with the mother (1977a). Sometime between the ages of 6–18 months, he says, the infant is able to recognise its own image, its own physical unity in a mirror or through an external relation. In the mirror stage, the infant ascribes to this Other of itself, this mirror image, the same all-powerful status that it imagines its m/Other to have. The infant has also been developing a notion that there is a being who is all-powerful, as is indeed the case in early life. Mother controls food and comfort, and until the infant confronts castration, it will start to hypothesise the existence of a supremely powerful being. The infant begins to separate from the m/other, seeing her as a whole being separate from itself, and then, in a flash, seeing itself, also as a wholly separate being. In the moment this realisation takes place, the infant installs within itself a fantasy of itself as all-powerful, holding on to the first notion that it had of the omnipotent carer in its universe. It installs an Other within itself.

To add a Freudian spin to what we explained about the operation of gender in Chapter 1, one is a man to the extent that one does not desire other men, but desires only those women who are substitutes for the mother; one is a woman to the extent that one does not desire other women and desires only those men who are substitutes for the father. And this is how Lacan imagines that the Oedipus complex generates these identifications and new desires: as a system of substitutions, exchanges, of one love object for another. So in other words, in order to become a subject, the principle of otherness must be internalised. It desires a fantasy, a fantasy of itself as whole, complete, omnipotent. In Lacan's version of Oedipus, both men and women are deprived of the phallus, both are castrated in the sense that both have lost the sense of plenitude and the fantasy of omnipotence experienced in early symbiosis with the mother. For Lacan the acquisition of language is the moment of castration.

Lacan's 'Lack' and the Power of the Phallus

Through the mirror stage, language and law impose themselves on the body like images. It is through substitution, through an endless metonymic chain of language that the subject pursues the ever-elusive object of desire. It is through language that the subject seeks to evoke the presence of the absent Other or the object of desire. Whereas in Freud the sight of an absent penis initiates the flight from the mother, the castration complex and the Oedipus complex, in Lacan, there is no penis. Lacan speaks instead about a 'Phallus'.

> For Lacan, the phallus is not the penis, but the universal signifier of loss. No one, anywhere, has the phallus.

It is not a little flap of flesh. The phallus stands in a series of substitutions that give voice to lack or loss, what Lacan calls *manque à être*, a fundamental lack or absence which can only be fulfilled by the forever unattainable object of desire. It hearkens to plenitude, unity, wholeness, before separation from the mother, outside mortality. The all-powerful mother which is fantasised is sometimes called a 'phallic woman'. Lacan also calls the phallus, the principle of loss which underlies the Symbolic (which, in turn, underlies language and culture) the 'transcendental signifier'.

This lack can be either masculine or feminine. Lack is what makes the subject decentred for Lacan. Unlike the efforts of Object relations theorists, who hope that a whole subject can eventually produced, in this theory, there can be no unified subject, only the imaginary fantasy of one. Threatened with castration, the boy can sidestep into identifying with the father's imaginary potency, but the girl does not have this access to phallic power open to her, unless she is willing to become masculinised (a phallic woman), or to imagine that her mother is hiding a penis (fetishism).

Critiques of 'The Phallus'

While it is certainly possible to imagine that the phallus is not a penis, that the phallus is an attribute of power that no one, neither men nor women have, it still remains the case, as many gender analysts such as Jane Gallop (1982) have argued, that the phallus and the penis, in the current political climate, can be conflated or confused. And once confused, it will seem that Lacan's ideas about the phallus, his 'transcendental signifier', will support a social structure which assigns power to men rather than women. As Gallop (1982) has noted:

> And as long as psychoanalysts maintain the separability of 'phallus' from 'penis', they can hold on to their 'phallus' in the belief that their discourse has no relation to sexual inequality, no relation to politics. (p. 97)

How much easier it would have been had Lacan called this universal signifier of loss the navel. It could signify the separation from the Mother, and the inscription on each body of the idea of mortality and loss (Bronfen 1989).

To return at last to the French feminists, and 'splitting', we now know what is meant by this word. Splitting is the installation of the principle of the 'Other' at the heart of the subject.

For French feminists, such splitting, or disavowal, in the subject is not curable. The self is always seen as a decentred subject for French feminists.

Splitting is the installation of the principle of the 'Other' at the heart of the subject.

Julia Kristeva and Abjection

Julia Kristeva (1982) developed the idea of the 'Other' at the heart of the Subject with her discussion of abjection. In the process of learning to draw the boundaries between what is proper to 'me' and what is 'not-me', the subject develops a disgusted fascination with the abject products of the body (blood, sweat, urine, mucus, faeces and so on). This fascination is one with boundaries, the borderlines of the self.

The concept of abjection derives from the disgusted fascination with products expelled from the body, which mark the boundaries of the body and the subject.

The reaction of disgust is due in part to how tenuous, how porous this boundary between outside and inside, between Self and Other, can be. In Chapter 5, we will discuss how Iris Young has used this idea to develop an understanding of the social unconsciousness of racism, sexism and other rejections of Other – she sees a psychoanalytic explanation as useful for understanding the very viscerality of such rejections. We will also see, in Chapter 4, the split between Self and Other called upon to explain the pleasure people take from watching films, or looking at fashion photography.

We have barely scratched the surface of these psychoanalytic theories, which no doubt seem quite complex. We will show in the next chapters how different writers have used them to understand particular cultural productions, and in this way, they should become easier to grasp. The one idea which is particularly compelling about Lacanian-based theories of the subject is the installation of a fantasy of omnipotence, of phallic potency, at the base of all subjects. While we might certainly want to question the timeless inevitability that seems to go along with this theory, an unconscious desire for complete oneness and self-sufficiency at the base of individual subjects, and at the base of symbolic systems of language and culture, might go a long way to understanding the way the Western world functions. In the next section, we will be looking again at this question of power, but from a Foucauldian perspective.

Difference and Power

One of the significant changes which accompanied the reassessment of binary thinking was a new way of thinking about power. In major nineteenth- and early to mid-twentieth-century social and cultural theory, power is usually described as a characteristic of some group in society – men, the middle classes, whites. The issue then is how to resist that power when it is exercised against us or others. This way of thinking about power is still very common; how often do we blame things which happen to us or our society on some invisible 'they'? It is also the kind of thinking which is spoofed and parodied in television programmes such as *The X-Files*, which constantly discover ever-more obscure cadres of bad guys (all male) who secretly control not only the USA, but the whole world (via the metaphor of alien invasion). Every now and then *The X-Files* turns the parody back on itself and deconstructs the top-down view of power on which many of the stories are based, for example when the cigarette man reveals that it was actually he who shot JFK.

For Marxist theorists, for example, the middle classes are in the position of Self, the dominant position – and they maintain that position by a systematic repression of the working classes. In this view the working classes are both repressed and powerless. This view of bourgeois society does explain some social behaviours and situations. However, it has a number of negative consequences. First, it constitutes the working classes as victims and makes it very difficult to imagine how they might ever improve their social situation – except perhaps by the goodwill of the middle classes. Second, it does not provide a way of understanding how it is that working-class people do exercise power, both to resist bourgeois demands and in their social and personal relationships.

Some feminist theorists took a similar position in relation to men and women. For them, men have all the power and they maintain it by a systematic repression of women. Again, however, this view has a number of negative consequences. Women are constructed as victims, structurally incapable of improving their social positioning other than by the goodwill of individual men. Also, this view does not explain how women do exercise power, both in their working environment and in their social and personal relationships.

One way of rethinking power is to see it as relational, rather than hierarchical (as we rethought the binaries discussed earlier). Instead of power being seen as a repressive force that some people have access to and others don't, power can be thought of simply as enabling; power enables things to happen. Foucault uses the metaphor of the matrix to describe power. The matrix is constituted in two ways: first, by many different relations of force – cooperative, resistant and transformative – that operate in a given sphere of activity, and second, by the strategies by which they operate (that is, that organise those lines of force in effective and enabling patterns or vectors). This matrix in operation, and not simply repressive force, is what Foucault describes as power:

> power is not an institution, and not a structure; neither is it a certain strength we are endowed with; it is the name that one attributes to a complex strategical situation in a particular society. (Foucault 1981, p. 93)

> For Foucault, power is not inherently *in* particular institutions or situations or individuals; rather, it is our perception of the matrix of forces in operation that we recognise as power.

Foucault also notes that an important implication of this view is that the operations of power can be grasped at a local, not only global, level: 'it is the moving substrate of force relations which, by virtue of their inequality, constantly engender states of power, but the latter are always local and unstable' (p. 93). This understanding is critical for the development of gender studies because it essentially confirms the value of the study. After all, if gender relations are conceived as universal and immutable – and as hierarchical and irresistible – then any study of them seems pointless. However, if instead, that immutability, universality and irresistibility are reconceived as strategies that are part of the operation of power, then it becomes crucial to study the minute operations of these matrices of power, in order that their strategies may be understood and the power relations themselves disrupted. That is, if power is manifest in these local strategies, then disrupting the local force relations can disrupt the entire matrix of power itself, since it can lead us to the strategies which organise the matrix to produce global/ising effects to which we object. These strategies include the very notion that particular ideas and relations are immutable, universal and irresistible.

Another important corollary of Foucault's model of power is that power is seen as pervasive: 'Power is everywhere; not because it embraces everything, but because it comes from everywhere' (p. 93). This means that we are all implicated in the operations of power. No particular group can absent itself from the operation of power because no group exists in isolation. Even within the most isolated group, power will operate. In Foucault's terms, lines of force will run through that group which will operate strategically at certain points to produce effects.

So, if power is relational, and we are all involved in it, then it becomes very difficult to hold to a position that simply attributes power to any one group in society. This is not the same thing as saying that some groups are not potentially privileged by their position within mainstream society; for example women of colour remind white feminists not to ignore their 'white skin privilege' that sets them apart from non-white feminists. However, it does argue against simplistic structural models which hold that all men are abusive and all women are victims. In a real sense, it opens the way for more complex studies of gender relations and the way those relations are articulated and reproduced.

Partial Identities and Provisional Positions

The development of a notion of identity as multiple and fragmented, rather than essentialist and unitary, has been critical for contemporary feminisms. This multiple subjectivity is a way of thinking about the differences among women, and also recognising what women share – their embodiment as women. Donna Haraway (1991, p. 155) writes: 'Identities seem contradictory, partial, and strategic.' Her formulation recognises that a subject negotiates a range of roles and positionings so that it is never wholly focused on any particular positioning (partial); that some of the positionings the subject negotiates may be in conflict (contradictory); and that the subject positions her or himself at any specific moment in relation to the context in which she/he finds her/himself (strategic). Therefore, this subject is able to negotiate strategic alliances with other women and with men at particular moments or locations to achieve an end – rather than identify her/himself always with one specific political end or process.

This strategic nature of contemporary feminism is what has given rise to the claims that we are in a postfeminist era. For many women, this seems a silly claim since it suggests that gender relations and gender identities are no longer problematic, and they know that is not the case. However, another way of reading the term 'postfeminist' is more like 'post-second-wave-feminist': that is, it is a challenging of earlier feminisms which locked women into silences and repressions of critical aspects of their subject positionings (for example non-white, working class, lesbian). 'Postfeminism' is one term for the freeing of women from the ideological straitjackets imposed by some feminisms, enabling them to recognise their differences from other women and so to eradicate the silences within feminism; to form new, respectful alliances with women different from themselves, and to learn from those women; to position their own feminist critique specifically in relation to their own cultural background (and its implicit beliefs, values, behaviours and desires).

Contemporary feminist theory and practice is extraordinarily diverse. Perhaps the essence of what separates these contemporary versions from earlier feminisms is their response to the demands for a politics of difference. The focus on difference and the concept of multiple subjectivity that expresses the many different positionings available to the individual had two responses: a greater focus on the individual, and a greater focus on the strategies for collective action. The attention to difference and specificity led to an intense investigation of the production of individual subjectivity which, for some, meant a greater focus on aspects other than gender which generate individual identity, for example class, race, ethnicity and sexuality. Non-white and working-class and lesbian feminists articulated their concerns as women of colour, as working class, as lesbian, enabling them to form alliances with women from similar backgrounds, ethnicity and sexuality. Such alliances were strengthening and enabling for those individuals, and for the voices they were increasingly able to generate. The other response – to focus on collective action – mobilised feminists to explore the nature of both their differences and similarities and work towards the elimination of inequities that separate women – racism, homophobia and classism. For many feminists this involved a complete rethinking of their own positioning, a revaluation of their own social roles to account for the way in which racism, homophobia and classism are essential to the maintenance of those roles. It also involved a revisioning of their own theories and practices to eradicate those elements, along with a recognition of where and how their own specific positionings are inscribed in those theories and practices.

Feminist Standpoint Theory

Several strands in feminist theory and practice which show clearly the gradual positioning of feminist knowledge are sometimes grouped under the umbrella term 'feminist standpoint theory'. This phrase pulls together disparate thinkers and trends in feminist thought (see the special issue of *Signs* (1997) as a good starting point). Out of second-wave feminism's emphasis on relying on the experience and consciousness of women as a starting place for analysis came the articulation of knowledge as located and situated. This work also emphasised that reality, rather than being available to a neutral observer, is socially and materially constructed. As Dorothy Smith has pointed out, a variety of philosophers and researchers, particularly those working in the social sciences, became concerned to identify, highlight and subvert, where possible, the 'embedding of the standpoint of white men as hidden agent and subject' (1990, p. 394). What developed gradually in the 1970s and 80s were several related methodologies which relied on valorising the experience of women, as subjects in research and knowledge, a political methodology which had been foundational to the women's movement.

For the social analysts shaped by these foundational ideas, it was important to connect everyday life with the analysis of social institutions that shape life (Hartsock 1983). Social analysts came to see local practices as knowledge. How and where to go shopping; how to read a book; or how to get on a bus and go to work; local competencies such as these were seen as a kind of knowledge. And if the practices which people acquire through their experience are seen as knowledge, they themselves can be seen as knowers, and able to share their knowledge. It is important to point out here that while the slogan 'the personal is political' has been interpreted in myriad ways, most feminist standpoint theorists were referring to the reconstruction of the standpoint of historically shared, group-based experiences. As Patricia Hill Collins argued: 'Groups have a degree of permanence over time such that group realities transcend individual experiences' (1990, p. 375). Similarly, Hartsock (1983) would stress a Marxist subject: the subjects who matter are not individual subjects but collective subjects, or groups. These methodologies and theories argue against 'the view from nowhere', the belief in a disembodied objectivity that Cartesian thought instituted.

In short, feminist standpoint theory:

- defines knowledge as particular rather than universal
- rejects the neutral observer of modernist epistemology
- defines subjects as constructed by relational forces rather than as transcendent.

The first articulations of feminist standpoint theory are generally taken to be typified by the work of Nancy Hartsock (1983). Her argument, which was clearly caught up in the liberatory discourses of second-wave feminism, argued that one location, that of the standpoint of women, was privileged because it provided a vantage point that reveals the truth of social reality. That is, that some perceptions of reality are partial, others true and liberatory. So, even though feminist social scientists wanted to highlight the limits and specific shape of the white-bourgeois-male view from nowhere which had become embedded in empirical social science, the belief in a liberatory standpoint of women was based on a certain essentialism and lingering beliefs in the universality of knowledge. What some theorists wanted to do was make a leap directly from the experiential knowledge we garner from our social life to claims to universal knowledge – that these particular knowledges could write the script to make us all free. The essentialism that was part of some of these attempts to change the shape of what knowledge was assumed to be, often constructed the category woman and the social group women as a unified and totalisable whole.

But as became clear with the participation of women of colour in these epistemological debates in the 1970s and 80s, this essentialist category left little room for the consideration of the impact of race on such investigations into the status of knowledge. Patricia Hill Collins in *Black Feminist Thought* (1990) argued that if the differences between women were to be taken seriously and the conclusion that women occupy many different standpoints and thus inhabit many different realities, this thesis that the standpoint of woman is liberatory must be re-examined. Yet many thinkers were not sure how to continue imagining a knowledge and categories in that knowledge that were particular, and which would allow change. If we abandon the monolithic concept of 'woman', some asked, what are the possibilities of a cohesive feminist politics? Various issues were raised. If there were a variety of women's standpoints, would coherent analysis become impossible, because there would be too many issues to take into consideration? And if these multiple realities are acknowledged, how can one choose between them? What or who would legitimate knowledge? How to choose? These were questions that came predominantly from white middle-class thinkers in feminism, and show lingering traces of the presumption of a central viewpoint, the 'god trick' that was so disdained in 'malestream' thought. Imagine a black woman rising in the morning, thinking, 'Now which shall I wear today, the breasts or the skin?' For many feminists, these difficulties of choosing between multiple perspectives or issues were not new.

Fractured Identities

The response to this question of how to give up the essentialist and universal categories, which had structured the pursuit of knowledge and theories of revolution, came through a growing recognition of the importance of coalition – of choosing a unity based on affinity not identity. Chela Sandoval's (1991) notion of the importance of strategic identity for women of colour represents an important advance in understanding this process, as does her development of the notion of oppositional consciousness. She points out that the category 'woman of colour' is not one which is based on some natural biological indicator, such as skin, or sex, or blood, but is rather a group which is united by affinity, by the decision to come together against a common cause.

Sandoval argues that what she calls US Third World feminism can function as a model for oppositional political activity. She proposes that we view the world as a kind of 'topography' that defines the points around which 'individuals and groups seeking to transform oppressive powers constitute themselves as resistant and oppositional subjects' (1991, p. 11). She holds that once the 'subject positions' of the dominated are 'self-consciously recognised by their inhabitants', they can be 'transformed into more effective sites of resistance' (p. 11). What we can see developing here in standpoint theory is the idea of the standpoint as conscious decision and intervention in the construction and reconstruction of our lives. As Kathi Weeks (1996) puts it: 'A standpoint is a project, not an inheritance; it is achieved not given' (p. 92).

Cyborg Feminism

One exciting voice in this contemporary feminist debate is Donna Haraway (whose work on identity was referred to earlier). In her essay 'A Cyborg Manifesto', Haraway (1991) used the concept of the cyborg, the hybrid being with no natural origin or identity (for example Frankenstein's Creature, the androids of *Blade Runner*, the cyborgs of *Star Trek*), to deal figuratively with the development of new technologies and their impact on human society – both the material transformation of the workplace and the sociocultural trans-formation of individual subjectivities. It also enabled Haraway to address the need for feminists to think strategically in the way Sandoval suggests.

Haraway acknowledges the negative potential of these new technologies and their workplace consequences – the creation of a disempowered, vulnerable and culturally impoverished – feminised – workforce. She also records the 'high-tech gendered imaginations', the militarised imaginary which characterises the video game culture (Haraway 1991, p. 168). However, Haraway's response is not a quiescent one. Rather than retreat from this domain, Haraway engages with it, reworking its imagery – its own mythical history – with the Frankensteinian figure of the cyborg.

Shelley used her cyborg figure, the Creature, to critique the society of her own time; Haraway does the same thing. Haraway uses the notion that the cyborg is a human, not natural, creation, combined with the perception that the development of twentieth-century information technology had made all of us cyborgs, to suggest that we are all human, not natural creations. So any notion of identity based in some natural or essentialist category (race, ethnicity, class, gender) is doomed to failure, since all of those categories are also human creations.

This perception is crucial for all gender theorists. Haraway writes of its impact on white feminists: 'White women, including socialist feminists, discovered (that is, were forced kicking and screaming to notice) the non-innocence of the category "woman"' (Haraway 1991, p. 157). In other words, there is no neutral (innocent) category 'woman' to which an individual can claim identity, because the question of what constitutes woman is itself implicated in the power relations of those controlling the definition. That is, the definition of woman will always be decided by those with the power to do so, and that definition may well be blind to factors in the lives of the non-powerful, including cultural imperatives and material conditions. So, for example, if the definition of woman included an assumption that a woman will naturally want to stay at home with her young children, how might that impact on the lives of those women who are economically unable to do so, even if they want to? By that definition, those working women are less womanly than more affluent women. The definitions – the identities – can themselves operate, as the criticisms by women of colour had pointed out, as silencing and oppressive, not liberating, categories. 'Cyborg feminists have to argue that "we" do not want any more natural matrix of unity and that no construction is whole' (Haraway 1991, p. 157).

Haraway refers to the work of Chela Sandoval who identifies herself as a US Third World feminist; that is, a feminist living in the USA from a social and cultural group which is oppressed within US society. Haraway found a model for her own notion of cyborg feminism in Sandoval's notion of 'oppositional consciousness'. She glosses Sandoval's own argument about what constitutes the identity 'US women of colour' in this way:

> This identity marks out a self-consciously constructed space that cannot affirm the capacity to act on the basis of natural identification, but only on the basis of conscious coalition, of affinity, of political kinship. (Haraway 1991, p. 156)

This notion of strategic alliance on the basis of shared ideas and ideals is the basis of cyborg feminism.

Sandoval (1995) later responded to 'The Cyborg Manifesto' in an essay which clarifies the critique of institutionalised feminism, but also extends her vision of strategic alliance. She notes the institutional use of Haraway's work to appropriate the critical theories and methodologies of those from non-traditional disciplinary and sociocultural positionings; US Third World feminist criticism is now read, Sandoval argues, as an example of cyborg feminism, rather than the reverse. However, Sandoval goes on to applaud Haraway's ongoing struggle to break down disciplinary boundaries and gain recognition for the work of 'the different social subject', such as women of colour or US Third World feminists.

> This challenge to feminist theory – indeed, we can read it as a challenge to all social movement theory – represents a powerful theoretical and political shift, and if answered, has the potential to bring feminism, into affinity with such theoretical terrains as post-colonial discourse theory, U.S. third world feminism, postmodernism, and Queer Theory. (Sandoval 1995, p. 415)

For Sandoval, too, then the recognition of difference (see above) and the rejection of essentialist notions of identity (which have, ironically, allowed middle-class white feminists to speak for – and silence – all other, or different, women) will enable feminism to form strategic alliances with trans-disciplinary studies ('theoretical terrains') which will inform feminist theory and practice. In particular, as Sandoval's own work shows, this cross-fertilisation of critical theories and perspectives has meant that gender itself is recognised as just one factor influencing the lives of individuals in our society; class, ethnicity, sexuality and age are just some of the other factors which determine the experience of the individual at a specific location and time. In the next three sections – Queer Identities, Masculine Identities and Embodiment – we will be looking closely at three areas where contemporary writing is coming to terms with the impact of difference, the particularity of the subject and new meanings of gender.

Queer (Non) Identities

Among those many factors which help to determine the kind of life an individual experiences, sexuality is most obviously linked to the individual's constitution as a gendered subject. As we discussed in Chapter 1 compulsory heterosexuality not only constructs a view of acceptable or viable sexuality, but also uses this view as the basis of its gendering practice, constructing acceptable or viable genders on the basis of compulsory heterosexuality. So any individual who is not heterosexual is not only unacceptably or non-viably sexed, but also unacceptably or non-viably gendered. And because we relate an individual's subjectivity to their gender, then such a person is not a viable or acceptable subject. In the terms of the old Soviet regime, she or he is a non-person. For those who identify as non-heterosexual, then, gender is a major issue, and theorists writing from the perspective of a non-heterosexual subject have contributed greatly to the development of gender studies.

As we discussed in Chapter 1, when identity is fixed as an attribute of individuals, it inevitably involves the (self-)recognition of certain defining characteristics. Gender activists and theorists at times found themselves confronted with versions of gay and lesbian identity which they did not recognise; for some the version of gay identity with which they were asked to identify was too middle class; for some lesbians that gay identity was predominantly a white, male, middle-class identity, and the inclusion of 'lesbian and ...' in many publications and activities was simply an afterthought; for others gay identity was too restrictive in terms of its permitted range of sexual activity and/or self-presentation. In other words, queer was one response to the restrictions which attend the naturalisation of any notion of identity, whereby the identity is no longer recognised as a strategy or political practice, but is naturalised as an attribute of individuals themselves. When this happens, individuals are positioned by the discourse which supports and reinforces that identity to be judged and regulated. Queer was/is used to challenge that naturalisation or essentialising of identity.

According to the *SOED* (3rd edition), queer means 'Strange, odd, peculiar or eccentric, in appearance or character'; it also means 'Not in a normal condition; out of sorts; giddy, faint or ill'. Another use is 'Bad; worthless'. As a verb, it is used to mean 'To quiz or ridicule; To impose upon; to cheat; and 'To spoil, to put out of order'. In the Addendum to this edition of the *SOED*, queer is also defined as meaning 'A homosexual'. Jeffrey Weeks, writing about the transformation in meaning of the word 'gay', notes that '"Queer" was the universally used word, the definition of the oppressor, and the term symbolising the accepted oppression' (Weeks 1977, p. 190). This use of queer to refer to a homosexual person, then, brings with it the derogatory meanings which accrue to the word in other circumstances – not normal, bad or worthless, cheat, spoil. As Weeks notes, this is the judgement of the heterosexist order on the individual who refuses to comply with compulsory heterosexuality; furthermore, it comprises the set of negative terms which constitute one part of the binaristic construction of heterosexuality – as normal, good, worthwhile, true, pure. Interestingly, in England at least, queer also had class connotations – as discussed above in relation to gay. While gay was associated with apparently opulent venues (classier clubs) frequented by the wealthy, queer was used to refer to the gathering places of the workers (queer pub or cottage) (Weeks 1977, p. 190). So queer has been used to refer to homosexual people; it was – and is – often derogatory, and in England it has also been classed.

In the early 1990s, however, queer was redefined. We discussed earlier how the term 'gay' was adopted by many people in the 1960s and 70s as a positive term of (self-)identification. Recently, queer has been given a new set of meanings by some gender-based political activists and some gender theorists. Of course, the immediate difference we might note is that the term 'gay' has always had some positive connotations, whether in its more banal usage as airy or off-hand (as in expressions such as 'gay blade', meaning, ironically enough, a carefree young heterosexual man), or as a positive attribute of (heterosexist) women. These ambiguities and the general sense of light-heartedness associated with the term make its choice as a term of positive self-identity and community formation very attractive. Queer, on the other hand, does not have the same kind of semantic history. It has almost always been abusive and its connotations, as noted above, are mostly negative. So we might wonder why it has been adopted so readily by some as a useful term. And note that the qualifier 'some' is used earlier in the description of its supporters (some ... activists; some ... theorists) to indicate that this is a controversial usage.

One reason for concern about the use of queer derives from the fact that, as do many poststructuralist theorists, queer theorists and activists challenge the very idea of identity. (You might want to refer back to early sections of this chapter for a review of the current poststructuralist writing on identity.) So, for example, some gay theorists and activists are concerned that using the term 'queer' means the loss of the identities gay and lesbian and the positive sense of (self-)identity and community they have engendered. Their concern echoes the complaint reported by bell hooks: 'Yeah, it's easy to give up identity, when you've got one' (hooks 1990, p. 28). Having fought for that identity and the benefits it offers, they argue, why give it up? And the queer response, like that of bell hooks, is to challenge the mechanism of identity as a regulatory force: as Annamarie Jagose notes: 'queer marks a suspension of identity as something fixed, coherent and natural' (1996, p. 98). For hooks the critique of identity enables an affirmation of 'multiple black identities, varied black experience'; at the same time it 'challenges colonial imperialist paradigms of black identity which represent blackness one-dimensionally in ways that reinforce and sustain white supremacy' (hooks 1990, p. 28). In the same way, queer activists use the concept 'queer' to affirm multiple non-heterosexist identities and varied non-heterosexist experience. They also challenge the construction of a one-dimensional version of lesbian and gay identity which reinforces and sustains heterosexism. And it is worth noting that this one-dimensionality has often meant the supression of lesbian identity and experience. What remains is a notion of gay which is the defining 'other' of heterosexual. How ironic, then, that one of the earliest uses of the term 'queer' in academic circles (by Teresa de Lauretis (1991) in a copy of the feminist cultural studies journal, *differences*) was written as a protest against the suppression of lesbian identity and experience in much contemporary writing on homosexuality.

Interestingly, de Lauretis herself rejected her own term, because it 'has very quickly become a conceptually vacuous creature of the publishing industry' (de Lauretis 1991, p. 6). Here de Lauretis refers to a use of queer also cited by theorist Annamarie Jagose when she writes: 'Often used as a convenient shorthand for the more ponderous "lesbian and gay", "queer" is a boon to sub-editors' (Jagose 1996, p. 97). Jagose goes on to quote from Rosemary Hennessy's (1994) argument that the queer project marks

> an effort to speak from and to the differences and silences that have been suppressed by the homo-hetero binary, an effort to unpack the monolithic identities 'lesbian' and 'gay', including the intricate ways lesbian and gay sexualities are inflected by heterosexuality, race, gender, and ethnicity. (p. 99)

Hennessey's argument reflects de Lauretis' original paper, as reported by David Halperin:

> both *to make theory queer*, and to *queer theory* to call attention to everything that is perverse about the project of theorising sexual desire and sexual pleasure ... to introduce a problematic of multiple differences into what had tended to be a comparatively monolithic, homogenizing discourse of (homo)sexual difference, to offer a way out of the hegemony of white, male, middle-class models of analysis, and to resist intellectual domination by the empirical social sciences. (1996, online)

In other words, the strategy of de Lauretis and other theorists in using the term 'queer' was to challenge the mechanism of identity and its inevitably regulatory and delimiting function.

Queer challenges the concept of identity and the binaristic (self/other) thinking it encodes. It rejects the binaristic definitions of gender and sexuality that construct heteronormative descriptions of male/female, masculine/feminine, heterosexual/homosexual.

It may be useful at this point to note also the activist derivation of queer. The emergence of the HIV/AIDS epidemic necessitated a range of responses which challenged established notions of identity. For example, the need to contain the epidemic meant that safe-sex education had to be directed to all whose sexual activities might put them at risk. At first, this was assumed to mean gay men only, but research soon showed that sexual behaviour is far more complex and far less normative than heterosexist discourse allowed. As researchers soon discovered, there are heterosexual men who have sex with other men, but do not consider themselves gay; there are heterosexual couples who engage in sexual activities which might formerly have been considered gay male practices. The only solution was to focus the educational material not on sexual identity but on sexual practice. However, since heterosexist discourse assumes a transparent, naturalised relationship between identity and practice, this move was fundamentally disruptive of notions of identity and, therefore, of heterosexual discourse itself. Equally the activism around the epidemic which united gays, lesbians, bisexuals, transsexuals, sex workers, parents and friends of AIDS sufferers, and people with AIDS suggested a new definition of identity, based not on some essentialist quality but on a mutual interest; a strategic sense of identity and community. So the lived experience of AIDS and activist responses to both the epidemic and the homophobic hysteria it raised in the heterosexual community also led to an interrogation of the concept of identity.

As both de Lauretis and Jagose have noted, however, queer has also been used in ways that have tended to corrupt that critical function. Or as Halperin writes, once queer theory became Queer Theory: 'Far from posing a radical challenge to current modes of thought, queer theory is in the process of becoming a game the whole family can play' (1996, online). Halperin's observation succinctly captures the potential and the problem with current formulations of queer. On the one hand, queer offers a challenge to current ways of thinking via its problematising of the concept of identity, and this challenge extends beyond the parameters of gender. As Sandy Stone (1991) predicts in her 'Posttranssexual Manifesto' and Rosemary Hennessey (1994) in the statement quoted above ('an effort to unpack the monolithic identities "lesbian" and "gay", including the intricate ways lesbian and gay sexualities are inflected by *heterosexuality, race, gender,* and *ethnicity'*), queer is not necessarily confined to the interrogation of gender or sexual identities, but can also be used to explore the ways in which individuals experience identity across a range of signifiers (for example race, ethnicity, class). On the other hand, queer's deconstruction of identity is experienced by some as destructive of lesbian and gay identities and community/ies. Its apparent failure to limit membership, to act as an identity, is seen as facilitating the heterosexist assumption of gay and lesbian identity; the troublesome, dangerously embodied terms 'gay' and 'lesbian' disappear in favour of the queer who can be anyone who fancies her or himself outside the boundaries of (normalising) heterosexism. So queer itself becomes a kind of fashionable non-identity, which is an identity.

This debate continues today, and it may be argued that this attests to the value of queer as a concept – that it provokes debate, destabilises identities and challenges attitudes and values. Furthermore, it should be noted again that queer accords with poststructuralist understandings about the nature of subjectivity – that it is a process of constant negotiation, not of stable identity, and so challenges stereotypes of gender and sexuality.

Bisexual Identities

Another positioning which is often seen as fundamentally interrogative of categories of gender is bisexuality. Like transvestism and transsexualism, bisexuality disrupts the social categorisation of male and female, heterosexual and homosexual as binary opposites. For some bisexuals the gay liberation movement of the 1970s had a negative side in that a normative notion of gay identity began to evolve; gay men do not have sex with women; lesbians do not have sex with men. Bisexuals, who have sex with both same-sex and opposite-sex partners, found themselves excluded by both homosexual and heterosexual society. Garber notes in her study of bisexuality *Vice Versa: Bisexuality and the Eroticism of Everyday Life* (1995) that bisexuality is:

> a sexuality that undoes sexual orientation as a category, a sexuality that threatens and challenges the easy binaries of straight and gay, queer and 'het,' and even, through its biological and physiological meanings, the gender categories of male and female. (1995, p. 65)

Her study encompasses many well-known figures such as Oscar Wilde and Virginia Woolf, whose bisexuality has often been suppressed in the analysis of their sexual ambiguity or social aberrance. She also explores the extensive politics of the bisexual movement which was organised to combat the exclusion of bisexuals from what they saw as essentialist sexual movements and categorisations – which included both heterosexuality and homosexuality. Perhaps the most important observations about bisexuality are those offered by Garber in her introduction to *Vice Versa*: 'Why, instead of hetero-, homo-, auto-, pan-, and bisexuality, do we not simply say "sexuality"? And does bisexuality have something fundamental to teach us about the nature of human eroticism?' (1995, p. 15).

Like transvestism and transsexualism, bisexuality disrupts the social categorisation of male and female, masculine and feminine, heterosexual and homosexual as binary opposites.

Masculine Identities: The Men's Movement and Men's Studies

The questioning of the category woman has not surprisingly been accompanied by a questioning of the category of man. Another contributor to the development of gender studies as an interdisciplinary site is the men's movement. This is a relatively recent formation, comprising men's groups with a number of different – sometimes conflicting – perspectives and agendas in relation to gender relations and gendered identities. The history of these groups tells us a lot about why they are so diverse. Some men's groups, for example, developed alongside feminism and in support of it. Men in these groups usually accepted feminist analyses of social practice and gendered experience and worked to minimise their own involvement in the oppression of women. Other men's groups developed out of men's frustration with what they saw as anti-male prejudice in society, particularly with issues such as childcare and child custody after divorce. For others again dissatisfaction with the roles allocated them in society was the impetus to gather together and explore unconventional options; while others embraced the conventional and worked to reverse many recent social changes, particularly those related to gender. As this thumbnail sketch indicates, with such different histories these groups cannot be said to have a single voice, and some voices are directly contradictory. It may be useful, therefore, to spell out in some more detail what the major groupings are, and what are their concerns.

David Throop (1996) divides the contemporary men's movement in the United States into five distinct strands. Writing of the movement in Australia, Michael Flood (1996) locates four strands, with the major difference between the two being Throop's inclusion of a Christian strand. Throop notes of the Christian strand that it is generally anti-feminist, disapproves of homosexuality and favours traditional gender roles. There is a tendency for Christian men's groups to regard men as innately violent and to see it as society's role to control that violence. The violence of contemporary (US) society is, for them, proof of social failure and disintegration, which they relate to the breakdown of the family (which in turn is often traced to the influence of women's liberation movements). For them the answer lies in fundamentalist Christianity, with its narrow conventional views on gender. Those conservative Christian views on gender are the rationale for a gendered division of labour in the home and outside, and for a masculinity characterised by authority and control.

Flood and Throop both list as another strand the anti-sexist or feminist men's movement. Men in such groups share feminist perspectives on the oppressive nature of many social institutions, and particularly of conventional gender roles. They do not see men as innately violent, but as having been conditioned to be violent by their society. They generally mistrust social institutions which they see as perpetuating this conditioning. Some men in this strand are also active politically in support of women, as in the Men Against Sexual Assault groups in most major Australian cities. Flood also traces two distinct groups within the anti-sexist men's groups, one of which he relates to radical feminism and the other to liberal feminism. The former focus on the 'organisation of masculinity and men's lives as privileged over women's and as violent and aggressive', while the latter 'give greater emphasis to the ways in which both men and women are constricted by gender roles, and some say that men, like women, are "oppressed"' (Flood 1996). The major concern of anti-sexist or pro-feminist men is to battle sexism wherever it appears.

Flood adds to his list of strands the category, men's liberation, which might be thought of as the male analogue of liberal feminism. For men's liberationists, conventional gender roles are destructive of men, rendering men's lives 'alienating, unhealthy and impoverished' (Flood 1996). As Flood notes, this perspective is shared by men in many of the strands of the men's movement, although their major concerns and/or political strategies may differ. Men's liberationists are particularly concerned, for example, with the socialisation of men and boys which produces the damaged, angry and violent men they see around them. In this group we might include the work of many educationists and educational sociologists (such as Paul Gilroy and R.W. Connell) who have studied the ways in which the education system contributes to the production of specific kinds of gender identities and gender relations for boys. Those identities are overwhelmingly conservative, with boys consistently positioned to adopt stereotypically masculine identities and modes of behaviour. The new lad movement might be seen as another example of men's liberation, with young men encouraged to examine their own gendering – both how they enact gender and how gender has operated in their lives.

The 'mythopoeic men's movement' listed by both Flood and Throop is concerned with men's personal liberation from restrictive social roles, usually via the medium of myth or spirituality. The focus of this group is on the inner life, and participants refer to a range of spiritual influences including native American and Aboriginal Australian cultures. These groups are often critical of conventional male roles, substituting a number of alternatives ranging from the 'warrior within' archetype to the notion that men have been alienated from their feminine side and need to re-establish contact with that lost part of themselves. Men from this movement may translate their inner work into a political critique on issues such as feminism, environmentalism, pacifism, anti-racism and anti-militarism. Flood notes that the movement 'is more symbolic than literal, more therapeutic than theoretical' (Flood 1996, online); however, anecdotal evidence suggests that this mythopoeic approach to gendering is often combined with more grounded social analysis to generate new ways of thinking about gender. A close analogy may obviously be drawn with the goddess movement in which many women are involved. The goddess and her different manifestations are used to explore different kinds of femininity from the stereotypical submissive feminine, and also to express pride in femininity. The mythopoeic men's movement may operate in a similar way, using positive masculine images to reconceptualise masculinity and generate a pride in masculinity. The concerns of many women and men about this movement are about the nature of these positive images, such as the warrior; whether they displace or simply reinforce stereotypical masculine images.

The final strand of the men's movement nominated by both writers includes the fathers' rights groups and men's rights groups. The fathers' rights groups have a specific interest in the rights of men during divorce and custody hearings. These groups were formed as a result of a perceived court bias towards awarding women custody of children. Men in these groups are often very hurt and very bitter – and often anti-female or specifically anti-feminist. Their analysis of the reasons for this inequity of custody is rarely very thorough and tends to focus on notions of women's power and men's silent victimhood – sometimes allied with virulent attacks on feminism, which some men see as responsible for the custody inequities. Different groups vary widely in their political perspective, however, some leaning to Christian fundamentalism and others closer to men's liberation. The men's rights groups overlap with the fathers' rights groups in being critical of the social roles available to men, and in blaming women – or feminism – for their victimhood. They argue that men are forced into limited and damaging social roles, as are women; men are success objects as women are sex objects. Accordingly, even powerful men are seen as victims. These groups are often viewed as the backlash against feminism because of their anti-feminist perspective.

As this summary indicates, the men's movement has contributed to the debate about gender roles, although primarily with 'an overriding emphasis on personal growth and healing' (Flood 1996). However, Flood also writes that:

> more and more men are realising personal growth and the reconstruction of individual masculinities are useless without an accompanying shift in the social relations, institutions and ideologies which support or marginalise different ways of being men. (1996)

Contemporary men's studies engage with most of these positions adopted by the men's movement. It includes sociological studies such as those discussed earlier into the socialisation of boys into men, as well as cultural studies of the gendering practices which boys and men encounter in their everyday lives. These include the representations of masculinity which men encounter and which model masculinity for them – in film, on television, in newspapers, novels and opera, in business and at leisure. It also includes the homophobia to which men are exposed and which operates primarily as a gendering practice (see Chapter 1), as well as the masculine behaviours which they are expected to display and which offer them pleasure and power, but also grief and powerlessness. The interest shared by all strands of men's studies is the delimitation of men by compulsory heterosexuality, although their responses to the question and the assumptions from which they proceed differ widely. For gender studies this is the principal contribution of men's studies – that it does, in its very different ways, highlight the constructedness of contemporary gender roles, and so acknowledges gender as a social practice rather than a natural attribute. From this basic position a number of different kinds of studies emerge – historical, sociological, cultural, philosophical, ethical, psychoanalytic – tracing the ways in which a particular version of gendering (compulsory heterosexuality) has operated in Western society, how it is maintained in and through institutional practices and cultural productions, and how it influences the subjectivity (emotions, beliefs, values, perceptions) of individual men.

Some might see men's studies as a kind of counterpart to feminism (feminism with a scratchy face), however, this assessment does not take account of the kinds of philosophical and critical change which have enabled such a study to develop. Here it may be useful to recall the work of Foucault discussed earlier in this chapter and its effect on our understanding of difference and power. If power is reconceptualised as relational, as a matrix of relationships in which we are all involved and not as a characteristic of individuals or institutions, then the perception of men as inherently powerful must change. Which is not to say that men are not often positioned in a matrix of relations in such a way that they are able to make things happen – to wield power. What it does, rather, is to suggest that we are studying a far more complex phenomenon than might once have been allowed, when men were considered in essentialist terms as emotionally disengaged, physically aggressive and spiritually obtuse. That construction of masculinity might instead be seen as a product of compulsory heterosexuality, with its homophobic training regimes and essentialist categories.

The contribution of men's studies to contemporary gender studies encompasses both the deconstruction of specific kinds of gendering (for example men in contemporary heterosexual societies) as well as a reconsideration of gender itself as a locus of power.

Embodiment

'Embodiment' and 'the body' have become key terms in recent writings on subjectivity and identity, at least partly because they provide a way of exploring differences. In the discussion of experience at the end of Chapter 1, it was noted that 'experience' is a relational term describing the interrelations of individual subjects with other people and with things or activities; those interrelations having a bodily impact. So the body is seen as the site at which experience is realised. That experience might be interpersonal or institutional; it might be physical or symbolic; the result of actual material practice or the consequence of ideas and value systems. For Braidotti (1994) the body is 'a point of overlapping between the physical, the symbolic, and the sociological' (p. 4) and also 'a layer of corporeal materiality, a substratum of living matter endowed with memory' (p. 165). The second definition is reminiscent of an episode of *Star Trek: The Next Generation* in which the android first officer, Commander Data, was threatened with being dismantled – disembodied – for purposes of scientific research. In Data's defence, Captain Jean-Luc Picard cites a shameful human history of slavery – of appropriating the bodies of others for purposes of labour and/or pleasure. Perhaps this is where the discussion of embodiment and the body should start.

Embodiment can be seen as an incorporation of the interrelationships which constitute experience into the constantly evolving body. That incorporation may be primarily physical or emotional or psychological or intellectual or spiritual – or a combination of these. When individuals were stolen from their homes and families and taken to be slaves, they did not experience this violence only intellectually or only physically, but as a combination of all the factors cited above. Their bodies became that experience and the experiences which followed: that is, that incorporation of experience became an integral feature of their corporeality. Less traumatic experiences also have an effect: young girls are taught by experience to modify their behaviour so that they do not appear too masculine, and young boys are taught to modify their behaviour so that they don't appear too feminine. The result of this learning (acculturation) is to produce their bodies in particular ways – creating certain postures, mannerisms, physical abilities and limitations, which *are* their bodies. So it is not that they have a real body underneath crying to get out; but that the body they develop is the result of their acceptance and/or rejection of a range of learning experiences. They have *embodied* a range of social and cultural demands related to gender. Sometimes those demands are complied with – many girls stop being so physically active in adolescence while boys continue or become more so; at other times the demands are rejected – some girls continue their physical activities while some boys refuse to be coerced into displays of physical strength – although not without consequences. In each case, however, the demand is experienced and action is taken, with the

resultant effect on the individual's body. Perhaps the most surprising consequence of this understanding of embodiment is that there is no such thing as
a natural body. Every/body is socially and culturally produced.

In the 1930s, sociologist Marcel Mauss (1992) observed the ways people
from different cultures walk; in particular, he compared US and French
walking and he noticed that, as US films became more available in France, the
French began to walk in the same way as US screen idols. To begin with, they
may simply have copied the walk but soon that American walk *became* their
walk. He went on to examine different modes of walking in a range of societies and concluded: 'There is perhaps no "natural way" for the adult' (Mauss
1992, p. 460). Nothing about the body is 'natural', in the sense that it is a consequence of a non-acculturated interface with people or things or activities.

Another example might be found in the attribution of body colour to individuals as a marker of race. British cultural theorist Stuart Hall (1992, 1996b)
and others argue that this is a colonialist concept – a way of signifying otherness by the colonial ruler – and is not transparently related to any aesthetic
conception of colour. So, in England, Caribbean-British are black, whereas
Anglo-Saxon-British are white. However, Indian-British and Pakistani-British
are also black, although they apparently share few cultural characteristics with
the Caribbean-British. And in the nineteenth century the Irish were black –
although again sharing few cultural features with Caribbean, Indian or
Pakistani citizens. The property, black, then seems not a material attribute –
actually related to a physical property such as skin pigmentation – but a signifier of social and political positioning. At the same time, through its symbolic
significance and the association of that with particular physical characteristics,
those characteristics are aligned in commonsense knowledge as black – and
the people who are then identified as black come to experience themselves as
black. This can be painful and traumatic if the individual also internalises the
negative attitudes associated with being black. However, Stuart Hall (1992,
p. 308) points out that, since the mid-twentieth century, Caribbean-, Indian-
and Pakistani-British have subsequently used their identity as black as an act
of political solidarity and subversion. It is subversive of the colonialist attitude
which would tend to isolate them as inferior non-whites, rather than as
autonomous, strong, independent (black) citizens, and as a result functions as
a strategy in the political battle against colonialist and racist attitudes. Again
the point is that, for socialised, acculturated human beings, there is no such
thing as a natural body.

Finally, it is instructive to consider why embodiment became such a
popular topic that it made it into the script of *Star Trek: The Next Generation*.
This was because the notion of a natural body had made the body theoret-
ically invisible. In other words, if the body is conceived as natural, then there
is no point theorising about it, discussing it, arguing about it; it just is. Except
that it isn't. As many critics began to point out, this untheorised acceptance of

the body meant that there was a body assumed in theoretical accounts of life, subjectivity, experience and identity, and, on closer analysis, that body was male, white, Anglo, middle-aged or slightly younger, middle class; not natural or impervious to specification, but a very particular embodiment. Which meant that when issues to do with equal opportunity in employment were made into policy with *this* concept of the natural body, there was no provision for pregnancy, childbirth, nursing, menstruation, menopause, and all of those feminine events were pathologised as aberrations, as illnesses. Embodiment became an important concept because it expresses the *unnatural* state of the body, the notion that the bodies in which we live are formed through our experiences of the world – inscribed by those experiences (Algerian writer Frantz Fanon (1967) describes his pain as a child on discovering that his (North African) body was regarded as ugly in mainstream European discourse) and formed within those experiences (as the French patterned their walking gait on that of US film stars).

Embodiment can be seen as an incorporation into the constantly evolving body of the interrelationships which constitute experience.

Summary

Contemporary gender studies, then, is a very complex field to which many different discourses contribute. Feminism, men's studies, gay, lesbian and transgender studies, queer studies, all bring different perspectives to the issue of gender: how it is theorised as a concept; how it operates in the lives of individuals; and how it functions as a social practice via institutional and cultural technologies. As we begin the twenty-first century, the ways we have of thinking about gender have been enriched by recent work from a variety of critical and political sources: critiques of feminisms by women of colour and working-class feminists; the reconceptualisation of power in the work of Foucault; the new understandings of the subject produced by psychoanalysis; the new structural and linguistic ways of analysing ideology and institutions; and the development of concepts such as queer theory and embodiment which enable us to specify how gender is constituted and enacted in a variety of situations. Certain key terms and concepts such as 'identity', 'power', and 'difference' have had a major impact on how gender is conceived, traced and theorised. This chapter has dealt with these terms and has introduced some of those many different perspectives on gender – our contemporary ways of thinking about gender; the following chapter focuses on how to read the action of gender in our lives.

Recommended Reading

Brod, Harry and Michael Kaufman (eds) (c. 1994) *Theorizing Masculinities*, Sage, Thousand Oaks, California.

Bullough, Vern L. and Bonnie Bullough (c. 1993) *Cross Dressing, Sex, and Gender*, University of Pennsylvania Press, Philadelphia.

Case, Sue-Ellen, Philip Brett, and Susan Leigh Foster (eds) (1995) *Cruising the Performative: Interventions into the Representation of Ethnicity, Nationality, and Sexuality*, Indiana University Press, Bloomington.

Cranny-Francis, Anne (1995) *The Body in the Text*, Melbourne University Press, Melbourne.

Creed, Barbara (1993) *The Monstrous-Feminine: Film, Feminism, Psychoanalysis*, Routledge, London.

Flax, Jane (1993) *Disputed Subjects: Essays on Psychoanalysis, Politics, and Philosophy*, Routledge, New York.

Foucault, Michel (1980) *Power/Knowledge*, (Colin Gordon, ed.) Pantheon, New York.

Foucault, Michel (1981) *The History of Sexuality: Vol. I* (trans. Robert Hurley) Pelican, Harmondsworth.

Garber, Marjorie (1992) *Vested Interests: Cross-dressing and Cultural Anxiety*, Penguin, London.

Grosz, Elizabeth (1989) *Sexual Subversions: Three French Feminists*, Allen & Unwin, Sydney.

Hall, Stuart (1992) 'The Question of Cultural Identity' in Stuart Hall, Daniel Held and Tony McGrew (eds) *Modernity and its Futures*, Cambridge, Polity.

Jagose, Annamarie (1996) *Queer Theory*, Melbourne University Press, Melbourne.

Kristeva, Julia (1982) *The Powers of Horror: An Essay on Abjection* (trans. Leon Roudiez) Columbia University Press, New York.

Mauss, Marcel (1992) 'Techniques of the Body' in Jonathan Crary and Stanford Kwinter (eds), *Incorporations*, Zone Books, New York, pp. 455–77.

Pfeil, Fred (1995) *White Guys: Studies in Postmodern Domination and Difference*, Verso, London.

Sandoval, Chela (1991) 'U.S. Third World Feminism: The Theory and Method of Oppositional Consciousness in the Postmodern World', *Genders*, **10**: 1–24.

Sandoval, Chela (1995) 'New Sciences: Cyborg Feminism and the Methodology of the Oppressed' in Charles Hables Gray (ed.) *The Cyborg Handbook*, Routledge, New York, pp. 407–22.

Stoller, Robert J. (1968–75) *Sex and Gender*, Hogarth Press and the Institute of Psychoanalysis, London. (A classic text that has been critiqued often but bears reading.)

Woodhouse, Annie (1989) *Fantastic Women: Sex, Gender and Transvestism*, Macmillan – now Palgrave Macmillan, Basingstoke.

Exercises

1. Think of an example of a Freudian slip you have made. If you think of it as signifying unconscious processes that you might have not felt able to voice directly, what might your particular slip have meant?

2. Apply Althusser's ideas about the connection between ideology and subjectivity to one of the ideological state apparatuses with which you are involved (for example the education system). Are there ways in which you think you resist the coercive power of ideology?

3. How does a focus on the father or the mother in psychoanalytic theory change the ways in which the individual is conceptualised or understood? Applying these different paradigms to your own experience, which seems more productive, and why?

4. How does the concept of 'difference' help you to understand your own experience? How does it expand or enhance the way we think about identity, especially as strategic? Apply this concept of difference to how you understand your own subjectivity and relationships.

5. How are difference and otherness related – or different? Can you give examples of how the two concepts might be employed to conceptualise other people? And how do they function in our understanding of ourselves?

6. Give some examples of how the 'abject', in Kristeva's terms, operates within gendered practices. Think, for example, of the coyness that attends advertisements for tampons. What do you think are the effects of the manipulation of abjection on the individual and social practice?

7. Think of a particular social situation in which you have been involved (for example university seminar, chat with friends or family interaction). Try to specify all the different power relations that have operated in that context. Where do you locate yourself in that network of power relations?

8. Explore the notion of partial or split or multiple subjectivity by specifying what you consider your own identity to be. What different factors are involved in specifying that identity (for example gender, class, ethnicity, age and so on)? Do you enact the same identity at all times, or do you strategically compose your identity to suit the situation in which you are involved?

9. Think of the different sexed identities that challenge stable notions of heterosexuality (for example transvestism, posttranssexualism or queer). Locate one or more instances in which you have experienced this identity (or non-identity) operating – in your own life, in the people around you, in a text. How has it challenged heteronormative conceptions of gender and sexuality? What is your own response to this (you might consider here the role and meanings of abjection)?

10. Do you think men's studies has a major place in gender studies? Explore how different strands of men's studies can be used in the critical analysis of gender by

applying the theoretical perspectives on which they based (for example mythopoeic, Christian and men's liberationist) to specific situations, experiences or texts.

11. Explore the gendering of embodiment by critically observing and analysing the ways in which masculinity and femininity are constituted in our society. You might do this by mapping the embodiment of gender in a specific set of texts (for example soap operas, sports broadcasts, opera or films in particular genres) or you might conduct an empirical study, observing the ways men and women enact their embodiment at a particular site (for example coffee shop, university tutorial, bar, museum or sports event).

3

Ways of Reading

This chapter deals with how we talk about the ways we read gender in texts – ways of reading. It also looks at how our reading practice positions us to think about and understand – and sometimes to talk about – gender in certain ways. It is this reciprocity – we not only read texts, but are positioned by them – which has made reading a focus for gender theorists. Understanding this inter-relationship of reader and text not only enabled theorists to posit readers as active participants in meaning-making, rather than just as passive recipients of textual messages; it also made it essential to understand the reading process and how it might be used as what Teresa de Lauretis (1998) called a 'technology of gender'. That is, reading might be seen as a practice by which certain views about gender are incorporated into the thinking of readers and viewers.

Note here that we use the term 'reading' not only in relation to both readers and viewers, but also in relation to written texts. It might be useful at this stage to clarify the terms we use to talk about reading, beginning with 'text' itself.

Text

Text has many complex, technical definitions, but the essential features are these: a text is a combination of signs (Thwaites et al. 1994, p. 67); a text involves an act of communication; in the process of communication a reader or viewer activates those signs to produce or generate meanings. We might summarise this as follows:

> A text is a sign-based communicative practice that involves readers or viewers activating signs to generate meanings.

In stressing the productive or generative nature of the text, we are referring back to the writings of linguist and cultural critic Roland Barthes (1977), who described the move from 'work' to 'text': a move away from the notion of the literary or artistic work existing in isolation; preserved by its brilliance; and whose meaning did not change from generation to generation (if only we could work out what that meaning is). Instead, Barthes proposed the notion of text to express the culturally enmeshed practice of the artistic or literary production: existing within a particular context of production and consumption; reinvented by successive generations to explore their particular problems; and meaning not one but many different and often contradictory things, according to the ways in which the meanings are generated.

So you might think of the plays of William Shakespeare which are now enmeshed in cultural meanings for us, including the idea that Shakespeare is the world's greatest playwright – a historically and culturally specific idea, with which not all societies and cultures would now agree and which has not always been the case in English literary opinion. Shakespeare's work exists for us as the product of a specific culture and time, to which we often refer in an attempt to locate meanings in the plays (context of production). It is also a contemporary theatrical – and filmic – practice, and contemporary audiences bring to their watching or viewing of the plays (and films) meanings or ideas drawn from their own education and experience (context of consumption). Shakespeare's plays are reinvented in successive productions which sometimes quite overtly relate them to specific contemporary experience: for example Baz Luhrmann's *William Shakespeare's Romeo and Juliet* (1996) characterised the feuding Capulet and Montague families as Anglo-Celtic and Hispanic and located them in a version of contemporary Los Angeles. And many different and conflicting meanings may be generated from the one play: for example Romeo might be seen as pitiable because of his thwarted love for Juliet or as socially irresponsible for placing lives in danger to gratify his own desires; at the same time, the play might be seen as a meditation on the nature of institutional power and influence and the way that it is enacted in the everyday lives of individual subjects – a reading which might have us once again pity Romeo, even if we find his actions culpable.

In a sense this represents a dethroning of the literary work; it is no longer seen as the sole source of transcendent meanings which we mortals need to seek out. Yet it does not deny that a particular combination of signs was originally put together by someone who understood at least part of the potential of that combination to generate meanings, nor does it deny the power of particular combinations to generate in and through readers or viewers new insights about the nature of themselves and their world. Instead it argues against the notion of fixed meaning, and for the idea that meanings are generated partly by features outside the work itself: for example contemporary social, cultural and political practice and the reader's familiarity with other cultural stories and artefacts. So someone familiar with the practice and history of an art form such as opera might well generate different meanings from a particular operatic work than a novice; similarly, someone conversant with the history and practice of blues music may understand a contemporary blues song differently from the casual listener.

For those involved in the study of concepts such as subjectivity, identity and embodiment, the value of this definition of 'text' is that it opens up one of the mechanisms by which, as Hall (1996b, p. 4) notes, the individual constitutes identity and through which the body is constantly reformed; by enabling us to see a way in which fundamental issues such as gender, sexuality, class, race and so on are re-presented, resisted and incorporated. In the texts of a culture, meanings about some or all of the fundamental issues of identity may be generated by the reader, viewer or listener. In this way the reader explores that issue – relates it to her or his own experience and identity, sometimes overtly, at other times subliminally. Sometimes we walk out of a film thinking 'I didn't like that movie', without specifically formulating our reasons. But when we put in the work to do so, we often find it is not only the splatter effects or the sentimentality which made us squeamish, but the kinds of value espoused; ideas about gender, sexuality, class, ethnicity or other things which we find fundamentally offensive. And often we also feel irritated at the skill of the film-maker who can have us go along with those values as we watch the film, so that we also feel coerced into something we disagree with.

The notion of text enables us to stand back from a film – or a song, book, advertisement, conversation, television programme (any combination of signs) – and analyse how we are positioned by that particular combination of signs. Further, we might ask if there is a way of reading that combination which enables us to resist being positioned in ways which are offensive to us, and we might also then question the way institutions operate to make one reading or meaning seem correct and others either less correct or plain wrong.

Texts, Bodies and Identity

Stuart Hall (1996b, p. 11) observed that the body has served as a kind of suture, pinning back together the fragmented postmodern subject; the body holds together in one space/time location the many different subject positionings of the postmodern subject. For Hall, even the work of Foucault, which demonstrates the ways in which the bodies of individuals are disciplined by the regulatory practices of their society, is problematic since it does not address the ways in which those bodies incorporate the discipline or how bodies resist; the body, for Foucault, is the passive recipient of any and all social and cultural influences and pressures. One of Hall's responses to this problem is to explore the ways in which individuals formulate themselves in relation to the narratives and representations which characterise their society;

how the individual constructs her or his own personal narrative in relation to those cultural constructs. This narrative (not the passive, disciplined body) enables the fragmented, multiple, contemporary subject to survive, rather than to fragment into incoherence (although that sometimes also happens). It is, if you like, the story of the nomadic journey which constitutes the individual subject and, like all stories, it is a transformation of the many other stories which constitute its cultural context(s).

One way in which the individual encounters these stories is through the texts of a society and its constituent cultures. Hall (1996b, p. 4) notes that identities are 'constituted within, not outside representation'. The problem with the dominance of heteronormativity in the cultural productions of a society is not simply that it misrepresents the composition of a society, but rather that it offers the individual subject such a narrow range of representations with which to interact in the formation of her or his subjectivity and identity. Of course, the individual can adopt a combative stance each time and formulate a subjectivity in opposition to the majority of these cultural products (as many do), but that is a very difficult road, and it will not be without casualties. If every cultural product (from advertisement to poem, blues song to opera) assumes patriarchal heterosexuality as the norm, then it is not surprising that someone who cannot accept that position comes to feel that they are abnormal. For the student of gender studies, then, cultural texts and representations are an important site at which to explore the possibilities available to individuals in their constitution of themselves as gendered subjects.

Again it might be useful at this stage to reiterate that the term 'text' is used very widely to mean any combination of meaning-making signs, and those signs might be written, verbal, visual, musical, gestural, olfactory and so on – in other words, signs which are ways of appealing to our senses in systematic or systematised ways. This means that the analysis of texts extends beyond written texts in specific genres such as novels, poetry and plays to any of the myriad ways we have of communicating meanings to one another in society: casual conversation, film, television, advertising, newspapers, visual arts, novels, drama, service encounters, parent–child interactions, legal documents, parliamentary papers, historical documents, photographs and so on.

In order to deal with such a wealth and complexity of material, it is useful to have terms which are transdisciplinary, which do not focus solely on a specific genre or medium of text. One term which is used in this way to discuss the meanings generated by a wide range of texts is 'discourse'.

Discourse

A discourse can be most simply described as a way of talking about an issue or practice. Yet, if we consider the ramifications of that simple statement, we can see that it is more than just a kind of arbitrary theorising. Our ways of talking about issues are also our ways of thinking about issues, and further, they tend to determine how we act. So discourses are part of who we are (how we experience ourselves) and how we think, speak and act (how we experience the world). Foucault stated that:

> Discursive practices are characterized by the delimitation of a field of objects, the definition of a legitimate perspective for the agent of knowledge, and the fixing of norms for the elaboration of concepts and theories. (Foucault 1977, p. 199)

In other words, discourses operate not only by defining their field of interest, but also by establishing what is a viable perspective on this field and also by defining the ground rules about what kinds of theory can be regarded as legitimate in relation to this field for a theorist operating from this perspective. Gunther Kress (1985) put this very simply when he wrote that discourses 'define, describe and delimit what it is possible to say and not possible to say (and by extension – what it is possible to do or not to do) with respect to the area of concern' (p. 7). Kress uses as his example the discourse of sexism. Sexist discourse, he explains, 'specifies what men and women may be, how they are to think of themselves, how they are to think of and relate to the other gender' (p. 7). Kress notes further that sexist discourse specifies

> what families may be, and relations within the family ... It reaches into all major areas of social life, specifying what work is suitable, possible even, for men and for women; how pleasure is to be seen by either gender. (1985, p. 7)

A discourse defines a way of talking, thinking, acting and feeling about an idea, issue or area of concern. It may be generated and experienced verbally, visually, aurally or in any of the sign systems operating within a culture.

The 1987–97 US television show *Married With Children* makes sexist discourse its main topic. Sexist discourse is constantly articulated and enacted by the characters in the programme, whose failures operate as deconstructions of that sexism (although some viewers might argue about the role of class in this programme). The point is that to be sexist means men and women must think and talk and act and be in certain ways. Any deviation is a resistant act. The US sitcom *Roseanne* also addresses sexism, often by the taboo act of speaking what sexist discourse attempts to silence. So when Dan says he will do something for Roseanne, and she asks him if what he is doing is telling her that she is too weak or silly or incompetent to do it for herself, Roseanne is deconstructing that sexist discourse. Roseanne is a very resistant subject.

So discourses operate by marking out or colonising a field of interest and then determining how that field can be legitimately experienced and recreated. This is a very powerful strategy as it allows no legitimacy to any perspective other than its own. Furthermore, discourses tend to work by constructing their own perspective as natural or inevitable. For example, sexist discourse generally works with very conservative definitions of masculinity and femininity and so claims that it is natural that men do the dirtiest jobs in a society because women don't like to get dirty (tell this to a mother with a young baby). Bourgeois discourse, with its roots in the social Darwinism of nineteenth-century capitalism, claims that it is natural for men to struggle against each other competitively to improve their lot in life and so argues for a free-market system, while massively subsidising all sorts of industries in order to maintain a home advantage.

Discourse is an important conceptual tool for gender theorists because it is a way of understanding and reconceptualising these 'tactical elements or blocks in the field of power relations' (Foucault 1981, p. 101). Foucault wrote that the work of Freud and Marx has the quality of discourse. Both attempted to provide an explanation of the phenomena they studied and both offered legitimating categories for the theorist by means of which his or her work will be acknowledged as a contribution to knowledge. As a result, the writings of both Marx and Freud have been used to qualify and disqualify the theories and observations of subsequent generations of theorists. For gender theorists, the term 'discourse' enables Freud's work to be studied as a complex set of theories and acute semiotic observations, rather than as a set of facts. For example, penis envy is not read literally as a practice whereby little girls walk around wishing they, too, had a penis; but rather is seen as an acculturated desire for the power which the phallic order makes available to male subjects. Similarly, a whole range of different views of masculinity and femininity can be isolated for analysis, rather than subjected to some kind of quasi-scientific truth test. The claims that many of these discourses make for a biological imperative (it's just natural that ...) can then be seen as part of the rhetoric which makes them so effective and so powerful.

Discourse is also a means by which power is distributed in the matrix of force relations which constitutes society. A discourse can be seen as providing a trajectory for these force relations; that is, channelling those forces to produce certain effects which we experience as power. Being able to deconstruct discourse – to determine what knowledge is propagated by a particular discourse, what values are embedded in it, the rhetoric it uses – is simultaneously a way of analysing the operations of power in society, specifically those relevant to the field of concern of the discourse. Gunther Kress suggests beginning an analysis of the discourse operating in a particular situation with three questions:

1. Why is the topic being written about?

2. How is the topic being written about?

3. What other ways of writing about the topic are there? (Kress 1985, p. 7)

These three questions take the analyst directly to:

1. the strategy involved in generating a particular discourse

2. the rhetoric it uses

3. the alternatives suppressed by this discourse.

A discourse defines the way that power is distributed in the matrix of social relations that operate around an issue, idea or area of concern. Analysing that discourse is a way of exploring the power relations it mobilises, identifying the distribution of power and making it available for critique.

In Chapter 1 we defined the meaning of institution as 'a set of relationships and/or practices which are expressions of mainstream social values and beliefs, and have the support – explicit and implicit – of other social and cultural institutions'. Discourse is a useful term to use in describing the nature of an institution. For example, there are a number of different discourses circulating about the nature of the family, not all of which accord with the institutional definition of the family. However, if we want to describe the institutionalised family, we might talk about a discourse which is heterosexist and bourgeois. Both of these terms is a discourse in itself, in that it colonises a specific area of experience or interest (for example heterosexist discourse refers to the area of human sexuality), determines what perspective on this area is valid (for example heterosexist discourse regards opposite sex relationships only as valid), uses a specific rhetoric (for example a selective reading of biology), and effectively suppresses – or pathologises – other ways of conceptualising the family (for example extended families, group households and homosexual families). When the terms operate together, they construct that institutional conception of the family. So, using the notion of discourse, it is possible to unpick that institution, revealing its strategic production of knowledge, its rhetoric and its suppressions.

Analysing Gendered Discourse

Discourse analysis is used in a variety of disciplines to analyse the ways in which ideas about gender are generated in texts. At this point it might be useful to demonstrate this analysis by reference to a variety of different kinds of text.

The role of conversation in generating meanings about gender is doubtless apparent to all of us, if only because of the uncomfortable ways we often have to negotiate the gendered meanings generated by everyday conversation. For example, in situations where our understanding of gender relations differs from that of the person we are speaking with, we are often faced with the decision of whether or not to express our disagreement. For example, consider the following exchange:

A: My little boy has started turning all his toys into guns.
B: Yes, well, boys will be boys!

If we begin with the assumption that speaker A was actually intending to express some concern about her or his son's activity, specifically because it is so heteronormative, then speaker B's response is problematic. B is not sympathetic to A's concern about gender stereotyping, but accepts it as natural or at least inevitable. We might posit that A's statement was generated by a feminist discourse, which rejects the conventional patriarchal association of masculinity with violence and aggression, whereas B's response articulates, through its implicit acceptance of such behaviours, the patriarchal discourse which concerns A. There are many ways in which this conversation might proceed, all of which involve the speakers in negotiating the differences in the gendered discourses they have articulated. For example, speaker A might decide this is a no-win situation and not pursue the point:

A: My little boy has started turning all his toys into guns.
B: Yes, well, boys will be boys!
A: Ummm …

Of course, this raises all kinds of interesting questions about how a transcript of this exchange might be read subsequently. Superficially, a discourse analysis of this text could be read as a simple confirmation of patriarchal discourse, generating conventional patriarchal notions about masculinity, particularly if the reader ignores the ambiguity in the 'ummm …' response. Returning to our speakers, however, we might equally imagine a number of different ways in which the conversation might proceed, including ways which might specify the gendered meanings of the different speakers. So, rather than obscuring her or his response (perhaps in order to avoid conflict) as above, speaker A might have gone on to specify the concern:

A: My little boy has started turning all his toys into guns.
B: Yes, well, boys will be boys!
A: But I don't want my son to be that sort of boy – to feel that the only option he has is to grow up being violent and aggressive.

By responding in this way, speaker A has clarified the gendered meanings she/he intends, and in the process has articulated a discourse which is clearly in opposition to the patriarchal discourse on boys and masculinity.

We might continue this exercise at some length, exploring the ways in which the speakers negotiate this situation and the meanings about gender it produces. From our viewpoint, the important point to note is that such simple everyday interactions are crucial sites for the production of meanings about gender, and we can understand and analyse these texts as the negotiation of different discourses about gender, rather than as simple differences between individuals. In this example, of course, the conversation deals fairly obviously with meanings about gender; we need also to consider situations in which the meanings are not so explicit.

Another spoken genre in which discourses about gender are often quite explicit is the service encounter, in which one person obtains a service of some kind from another person. Most people have encountered service situations in which the gendering of the encounter is problematic: women treated like children and told to consult with their (assumed) husbands before a purchase; men assumed to be incompetent to deal with purchases related to feminine tasks such as childcare. In one of her books on pregnancy and childbirth, Sheila Kitzinger (1998, p. 145), British midwife and educator, discusses the following encounter, transcribed and sent to her by one of her readers:

Doctor [reading case notes]: Ah, I see you've got a boy and a girl.
Patient: No, two girls.
Doctor: Really, are you sure? I thought it said ... [checks in case notes] Oh, no, you are quite right, two girls.

Kitzinger uses this incident to warn readers about the necessity to choose doctors very carefully. For the theorist of gender, however, the encounter is interesting because of the way it generates a particular discourse about gender. We might use the three questions suggested by Gunther Kress (see above) to work out what is happening in this interaction, which constructs the patient as not knowing the gender of her own children. One set of answers to the discourse analysis questions are as follows:

1. *Why is this topic being written about – or, here, talked about?*
A. Because the patient is about to undergo a medical examination.

2. *How is the topic being talked about?*
A. The patient is regarded as lacking in knowledge, if not rationality. This is a very conservative way in Western medicine of positioning the patient.

3. *What other ways of talking about the topic are there?*
A. To respect the patient's knowledge; the approach taken by holistic medical practices and practitioners.

So our discourse analysis might suggest the operation here of medical discourse which positions the patient as subordinate to both the doctor and the case notes; in fact, one might argue that the patient is positioned as barely sane – unable to recognise the gender of her own children. It is also a discourse which positions the doctor as subordinate to the case notes; that is, he is guided more by the case notes than the interaction with the patient. This is a very conservative, scientistic medical discourse, which positions any direct human opinion as subordinate to written texts (ironically, of course, produced by the same fallible humans). Still, this one discourse doesn't seem sufficient to explain the assumptions in this text – a patient who cannot identify the gender of her children and a doctor prepared to make this kind of assumption. We might ask these questions again of this text:

1. *Why is this topic being written about – or, here, talked about?*
A. Because the female patient is about to undergo a medical examination by her male doctor.

2. *How is the topic being talked about?*
A. The patient is regarded as lacking in knowledge, if not rationality. The construction of women as irrational is a feature of patriarchal discourse.

3. *What other ways of talking about the topic are there?*
A. The male doctor might respect the female patient and so challenge his own recall rather than suggest that his patient is capable of such an error.

So we might suggest that another discourse, related specifically to gender, is operating in this text. In this discourse, the male doctor is positioned as sufficiently authoritative that he is able to challenge the rationality of his female patient. The discourse which operates in terms of such a binary – male = authoritative, powerful, rational; female = without authority, powerless, irrational – is patriarchal discourse. So, in this example, two discourses operate to reinforce each other: a conservative medical discourse (rather than, for example, a holistic medical discourse) and patriarchal discourse (rather than an egalitarian, non-sexist or feminist discourse). As a result the absurd encounter transcribed can occur. Furthermore, such encounters do occur regularly and their effect on both parties to the encounter is to engage them in the mutual negotiation and production of gender discourses, which are incorporated by those participants into the production of themselves as gendered subjects.

In the book in which Gunther Kress discusses discourse (above), he also provides some examples of discourses operating in written texts. One example he quotes (Kress 1985, pp. 6–7) is an extract from the Australian women's magazine, *Cleo*, in which women are offered advice about how to be successful:

Miss Mouse

This type is a dead give-away. The first thing you notice is her posture – rounded shoulders, hands in lap, head cast down and she's fidgeting, always fidgeting. She would never initiate a conversation and if asked a question, she's likely to whisper a non-committal response or just shrug her shoulders and smile wanly. Her clothes are neat but she doesn't have much sense of style …

Miss Mouse should always try to sit up straight (even if it is a strain) and find a magazine to read in waiting situations (thus fidgeting would be unnecessary). Clothes: check out magazine fashion pages for some ideas on how to inject touches of colour to an outfit without compromising style, and consider a brighter lipstick to liven up your face.

Kress performs his own analysis of this piece, reading its purpose as 'to instruct women about how to see themselves, and to tell both men and women what type of women to value' (Kress 1985, p. 8). He identifies the way in which the topic is being spoken about as sexist. Other ways of writing about the topic, he suggests, are through 'extensive analyses, particularly by feminist writers, of sexist discourse' (p. 8). Although Kress does not specify the reasons for his identification of the discourse as sexist, we might argue that the very question itself, as proposed by the magazine, is sexist, in that it positions women to discipline and regulate their own behaviours in ways which are intended not to challenge sexist constructions of the feminine, but rather to make themselves more attractive to look at. So Miss Mouse is not helped to understand why it is she feels so shy and withdrawn, perhaps through an analysis of patriarchal discourses which consistently position women as inferior and inadequate. Instead she is advised simply to make herself look more attractive within a certain framework, one in which women must sit straight, not fidget, and be colourful to the eye. This is a discourse in which woman is produced as spectacle, as the subject of the (male) gaze (we deal at length with this critical notion of the 'gaze' in Chapter 4). In this way the text (and the magazine in which it appears) generates a sexist discourse.

There are many other examples of such discourse being constructed in and by texts of all genres – fictional, factual, spoken and written, visual and verbal. Kress's definition of discourse and his three questions are useful tools for gender analysts in that they help in the task of identifying the kinds of discourse operating in a text, and how those discourses operate. It is also important to keep in mind why analysing gender in texts is such a useful project. As Stuart Hall (1992, 1996b) noted, individuals produce themselves as gendered subjects in relation to, or through a negotiation of, the narratives and representations which characterise their society. Texts are not just interesting cultural objects in and of themselves; they become part of the embodiment of the readers and viewers who encounter them. As noted earlier, for this reason Teresa de Lauretis (1987) refers to texts as 'technologies of gender'. Texts are not only gendered, but are actively engendering.

Texts as Engendering Practices

This active role of texts in constituting the gendered subjectivity of their readers or viewers is also a concern of literary critic, Catherine Belsey (1980, 1985). She refers to the germinal work of Louis Althusser in his essay, 'Ideology and Ideological State Apparatuses' (1971). For Althusser, texts are among the many social practices which operate as ideological apparatuses, interpellating individual subjects with particular ways to think and act. In particular, he was concerned with how such practices produce and reproduce individual subjects in Western societies as bourgeois subjects, diverting their disruptive impulses into desires and fears which reinforce the bourgeois state. Althusser has since been criticised severely for the determinism of this essay, which many people read as suggesting that individuals have very little freedom to think or act outside official state policy and practice. It might be argued that, given his premise, his own essay could not be written, or at least that it simply serves the needs of the bourgeois state and so is fundamentally contradictory. However, as Belsey notes, there is an important truth in Althusser's work: our interactions with texts might not be as deterministic as Althusser suggested, but they are nevertheless crucial in our self-production as gendered subjects. The title of one of Belsey's essays, 'Constructing the Subject, Deconstructing the Text' (1985) makes this point; the reason for deconstructing texts is so that we understand how they construct subjects.

Teresa de Lauretis has worked consistently on the ways in which filmic texts operate as technologies of gender. As viewers watch a film, she argues, they are positioned in certain ways, not only by the story itself but also by the way that the story is told, to accept particular ideas about gender. In Chapter 4, Ways of Seeing, you will read about the 'gaze' and how the implicitly male gaze in film has consistently constructed woman as spectacle. De Lauretis was concerned both with the implicitly (patriarchal) male gaze of many film texts and the patriarchal narrative so many of them reproduced. She writes: '*The construction of gender is the product and the process of both representation and self-representation*' (1987, p. 9; italics in original). So the construction of gender takes place both in representation and the self-representation of individuals, which is itself constructed in relation to, or through negotiation of, representations. De Lauretis notes:

> *The construction of gender goes on through the various technologies of gender (e.g., cinema) and institutional discourses (e.g., theory) with power to control the field of social meaning and thus produce, promote and 'implant' representations of gender. But the terms of a different construction of gender also exist, in the margins of hegemonic discourses. Posed from outside the heterosexual social contract, and inscribed in micropolitical practices, these terms can also have a part in the construction of gender, and their effects are at the 'local' level of resistances, in subjectivity and self-representation* (1987, p. 18; italics in original).

We will return to de Lauretis' last point later when we talk about the different, resistant ways people have of reading texts and so of intervening in their gendering. In relation to her first point, about the role of texts in 'implanting' particular discourses about gender, it may be useful here to consider some examples.

This example is a conversation text recorded by a student for an exercise in analysis. The student was asked *not* to specify the gender of the speakers, so that students might then try to work out from the text what their gender is. Of course, we are reading a text here which is isolated from some of the factors which comprise the meaning-making signs of everyday conversation, such as gesture, body language and so on; however, this exercise is nevertheless useful in isolating some of the ways in which gendered meaning is produced in this kind of text. Note that, where consecutive lines are underlined, speakers spoke at the same time and that the speakers are all of a similar age and socioeconomic and ethnic positioning.

A Did er … Wayne and Heather's … house go on the market?   1

B I haven't seen them but … er

C   as far as I know

B Wayne was … said it … was going to, yeah.

C Must not be worrying about it   5
  cause when they got home the first Saturday Kerry was there
  and then when they came back … um …
  Heather's Mum and Dad were there.

A Umm <u>trying</u> to talk em out of it ... you reckon?

B   <u>Umm</u>   10

C Must be a big panic now
   <u>trying to talk em out of it</u>

B <u>Must be</u> ... yeah

C Heather's getting upset
   cause people keep on asking her ...   15
   'What are you going to do for a job?'

B For employment
   <u>Yeah</u>

A <u>Well that's what I was thinking today</u>

C <u>'Where are you going to get your money from?'</u>   20

A <u>What's Wayne going to do?</u>

C <u>That's probably the biggest ...</u>
   That'd be the biggest problem of the lot.
   Where are they going to get money from?

A Umm   25
   I mean if Wayne gives up his job
   how's he going to get another one?
   I mean <u>what</u> ... ?

C <u>but it's</u> not only that ...
   The only money they're going to have is what ... umm ...   30
   Is left over from the house ...
   They're not going to have a lot of money.

A Umm ...
   <u>But</u>

C <u>They've gotta</u> be able to buy things   35
   They're not going to be able to support themselves on
   <u>that size block</u> of land

B <u>thin air</u>
   yeah

C Specially when half of its still rain forest   40
   and he wants to keep it that way ...
   so he's probably only got three acres <u>to use anyway</u>

B   <u>And and the way</u>

they've been talking about ... um ... things up there
like they're really worried about the dog getting ...   45
worms? round worms ... and this sort of <u>stuff</u>

C   <u>Ticks</u>

B Weren't they?
and ticks are really bad up there apparently
<u>and things like this</u>   50

C <u>yeah especially ticks</u> up there
cause it's a rain forest

B Um[1]

This conversation has been discussed elsewhere (Cranny-Francis 1992) but it is interesting to our analysis because here the gendering is not so much a result of a discussion, more or less explicit, about gendering practices, as of the ways in which the participants to the conversation interact. Linguists such as Cheris Kramarae (1980, 1981, 1988 and in Kramarae et al. 1983, 1985), Cate Poynton (1985), Deborah Cameron (1985, 1990, 1995), Deborah Tannen (1990, 1993, 1994) and Jennifer Coates (1996) and Coates and Cameron (1989) have all explored the gendering of conversational texts through a number of non-subject-related features such as:

● *interruption* – who is prepared to interrupt other speakers in the course of a conversation;

● *backchannelling* – noises such 'ummm' and 'hmmm' and terms such as 'I see' and 'Yeah' which enable the conversation to continue without necessarily intervening in the subject under discussion;

● *hedging* – terms which suggest tentativeness – 'I *think* I'll go', 'Could you *possibly* do this for me?';

● *verbal dominance* – who takes up most verbal space in conversations;

● *pausing* – how long the pauses are after certain people speak;

● *topic rejection* – who is prepared to reject a particular topic and move to another one.

By considering the kind of femininity made normative by patriarchal discourse, it may not be difficult to predict that, in terms of the features listed above, in mixed-sex conversations men are found to interrupt more, women to backchannel more, women to use more hedges, men to speak more, longer pauses to occur after men speak, and men to reject women's topics more often than women reject men's. Tracing the contour of those choices provides us with discursive outlines of the constitution of patriarchal femininity and masculinity through conversational interaction. Interestingly, it differs in interesting ways from the patriarchal rhetoric about femininity and masculinity.

When first-year students are asked to decide who is male and female in the conversational text reproduced above, the most common response is that C must be female because she talks so much, and because she often talks over other people. The students refer to a common patriarchal stereotype of the feminine as gossipy and likely to dominate conversations, although they explain their reasoning in naturalised terms: 'women talk more'. In other words, their analysis is itself an articulation of patriarchal discourse. In practice, patriarchy produces the opposite effect: men, constructed as the more dominant and intellectual gender, tend to dominate mixed-sex conversations and talk over women and other men in pursuit of this dominance. And, in complementary fashion, women tend to speak less, allow themselves to be spoken over, be supportive (through backchannelling) and tentative, and rarely dismiss topics introduced by men. In so doing, both men and women enact a gendered discourse which positions them as patriarchal subjects, identified by their embodiment of a particular version of masculinity or femininity. Exploring the conversation above can be a useful exercise in identifying both the conversational strategies of women and men and the stereotypes which we may unwittingly bring to our own readings of them. It is these strategies and the stereotypes they enact which constitute such everyday conversations as engendering practices. As with the first conversation analysed above, the participants face a number of choices at each point in the conversation, some of which are to do with how they are perceived as a gendered subject by the others involved in the conversation and by themselves (representation and self-representation). It is in the making of those choices that the practice of gendering takes place.

In the conversation text above, all three speakers enact a patriarchal discourse, using the kinds of strategies identified by the linguists cited above. The male speaker, C occupies more verbal space than either of the female speakers, A and B. He also speaks over other speakers more consistently, and then carries the conversation onto the topics he has introduced. A and B both provide a lot of backchannel support to the conversation; they allow the initiative to be taken away by C; and they express their ideas more tentatively than C. In other words, the three speakers constitute themselves, through this conversation, as patriarchal subjects – the women as conventionally feminine, the man as conventionally masculine. This conversation both contributes to and reinforces the conventional (en)gendering of the participants.

Advertisements have long been analysed for their constructions of gendered subjects, particularly the feminine. And again it is useful to make explicit the reasons for the concern about the kinds of representation which advertisements generate. Although there is now a body of material which challenges the deterministic response to advertising (for example Bray 1994; Lumby 1997) – that is, the notion that individual subjects are simply brainwashed by advertising into accepting certain ideas about gendering – it is still reasonable to posit that advertising has some effect on viewers; the money spent on advertising attests to this. Advertisements, like all texts, are negotiated or processed by those who read or view them and in the process those readers or viewers make choices, implicitly or explicitly, about the gender discourses they carry. Consider, for example, the advertisements for margarine and butter which show smiling women in domestic situations pulling trays of scones or biscuits out of ovens, to the tune of jingles such as: 'You ought to be congratulated!' Those advertisements most obviously refer to a 1950s stereotype of the woman as domestic worker, the effect of which is a normative view of femininity as home-centred, private (rather than public), nurturing, caring, happy and selfless. Just asking the question – congratulated for what? – is disruptive and transgressive in this context; the point about the jingle is that it does not, must not, be challenged. Viewers negotiating this advertisement must deal with the representation, of femininity it 'produce[s], promote[s] and "implant[s]"', to use de Lauretis' formulation. Of course, viewers may reject this representation, yet this act of rejection is an active negotiation of their own gendering in response to the engendering practice of the text. Readers and viewers of advertisements constantly negotiate their own gendering in relation to these texts, just as actively and consistently as do the participants to everyday conversations.

> Texts are engendering practices to the extent that they position readers or viewers to accept a particular view about gender in order to read or view the text. However, readers may engage with the text in ways that do not comply with that positioning, and so may resist that engendering practice; that resistance also constitutes an engendering practice.

Analysing Textual Practice

In order to analyse the means by which texts instantiate discourses about gender, it is useful to be able to refer to terms which are applicable to texts across a range of media and disciplines. The use of such terms enables the analyst to isolate the means by which texts position their readers or viewers and so to intervene in that process; to make the engendering practice of the text visible and so open to critique. One term which can be particularly useful in understanding textual practice is 'genre'. We also need to consider the complexity and diversity of texts, which often carry contradictory meanings about gender as well as about a range of other issues and ideas. Finally we need to consider the role of readers in relation to texts, and whether different readers might make different meanings from texts.

Genre

Genre has proved a useful concept for many theorists (Derrida 1980; Jameson 1981; Morson 1981; Todorov 1984; Kress 1985; Rabinowitz 1987; Cranny-Francis 1988, 1990), as it operates as a point of mediation between text, reader and society. This understanding of genre is based on the work of Russian linguist Mikhail Bakhtin and is more than just the formulaic description of different kinds of writing found in much literary criticism. Todorov explains Bakhtin's view of genre very clearly when he writes: 'Genre is a sociohistorical as well as a formal entity. Transformations in genre must be considered in relation to social changes' (1984, p. 80). So genre is about, although *not* only about, form or textual practice – the features which identify a particular text as a novel, poem, play, film, legal document, photograph or painting. It is also about how those features articulate or represent the sociohistorical context in which the particular text was constituted. Furthermore, these two features are completely inextricable: changes in a genre can only be understood in relation to changes in the society within which a particular generic text is composed. This deceptively simple formulation involves the analyst in a complex set of analytical practices: identifying the conventions which characterise a particular genre at a specific time and place (recognising that genres change with social change); identifying the social and cultural assumptions implicit in those generic conventions; and relating those assumptions to the discourses circulating in the society in which the text was composed. For the gender theorist this way of analysing a text can be very useful, as it enables the gendered assumptions which are embedded in textual conventions or strategies to be identified and made available for critique. This is particularly useful with conventions which might otherwise appear to be gender neutral or natural.

Genre is a concept that relates the way a text works as a set of signs to the culture(s) within which it is produced and consumed. It enables the gender analyst to trace how and why particular textual practices are gendered.

Writer Marele Day opens *The Life and Crimes of Harry Lavender*, her first detective novel, with a conventionally tawdry first-person narration from her detective:

I woke up feeling like death. Ironically appropriate, given what the day held in store. White light poured in, even before I opened my eyes and a variety of sounds all too loud. Someone was pounding my brain like a two-year-old who's just discovered a hammer. In between blows I managed to prise open the eyes. Close by the bed was a bottle of Jack Daniels: empty. And an ash tray: full. ... As I got out of bed I realised I wasn't the only one in it. There was a good looking blond in there as well. (1988, p. 5)

Day constructs her detective in line with the conventions of hard-boiled detective fiction, the fiction which produced characters such as Philip Marlowe and Sam Spade. Conventionally, this detective is a hard-drinking, smoking, hard-living man who uses women either as sexual objects (the blonde) or as support mechanisms (usually the secretary who is secretly in love with him). He is, however, ethically true to himself, incorruptible within his own terms of reference and contemptuous of authorities and the wealthy whom he perceives to be corrupt. In other words, this character, arising at a particular time and place (United States, early to mid-twentieth century), embodies a particular discourse about masculinity – essentially patriarchal but non-bourgeois. The femininity articulated in these texts is also patriarchal, but borders on the misogynistic. As John Cawelti notes, 'the hard-boiled formula very often adds one central role, that of the female betrayer' (1976, p. 147). This conventionally blonde and big-breasted female betrayer often carries the major burden of evil in the plot:

> danger and betrayal emanate from the city and are most often manifested in an ambiguously attractive and dangerous woman who sets out to seduce the hero in order to prevent him from discovering that she is the murderess. (Cawelti 1976, p. 156)

As engendering practices, then, this enormously successful genre seems to have little to offer a feminist writer. Day continues her opening section:

> The coffee revived me a little, a hot then cold shower even more. The blond slept on, unperturbed by my rummaging through the clothes on the floor looking for something suitable to wear. Thank God the black suit was hanging in the wardrobe neatly pressed. ... As long as I didn't start haemorrhaging from the eyes things would be all right. I grabbed the dark glasses. Just in case.

> 'Time to go sweetheart,' I whispered into the blond's aural orifice. Not a flicker of an eyelid or a murmur. Next time I shook him. 'C'mon mate, wake up. I've got to go to a funeral.' (1988, p. 5)

By reversing the expected gendering of detective and blonde, Day opens up the gendering practice of the text and the genre; she not only signals that her own text constitutes gender differently, but she also makes visible the implicit gendering of all other texts in this genre. The surprise experienced by many readers on reaching the end of paragraph three of the book is confirmation of the extent to which the gendering practices of a genre are embedded in readers' expectations. This suggests that the patriarchal discourse conventionally articulated by the genre is tolerated by, if not wholly acceptable to, many readers. So that, as an engendering practice, this genre might be seen as reinforcing conventional patriarchal constructions of masculinity and femininity. Marele Day is one of a number of writers (others include Marcia Muller, Sarah Paretsky, Sue Grafton, Katherine Forrest, Julia Smith, Claire McNab) who have challenged the patriarchal gendering of the genre, not simply by a kind of gender reversal, but through a detailed reworking of all associated generic conventions which sustain the conventional gendering (for example the use of violence, the characterisation of evil, the nature of sexual encounters). Using the notion of genre with which we started, we must trace this transformation of a literary genre to social change, and the most obvious change articulated through the gendering of the detective and so the reworking of gendered practices in these texts is the increasing visibility of feminist or non-patriarchal discourses in society. Not that the patriarchal discourses have vanished, but other discourses about gender are also present.

The same kind of analysis might be carried out with every genre of text. To mention another brief example, consider the practice of renaming the role of the person chairing committee meetings. The recognition of the chairman and his role was a convention of the genre of meetings. That convention was changed some time ago, with the renaming of the position as chairperson and the change of direct address to mister or madam chair (depending on the incumbent). It might also be posited that certain other conventions associated with this position changed, along with its explicit recognition of female incumbents. Again, the social change this convention reflects or expresses is an acceptance of women in positions of public authority, which indicates the operation of non-patriarchal discourse. Hence, of course, its fierce opposition by some people whose own gendering (self-representation) is conducted in terms of the more conventional patriarchal discourse. For them, too, this change to the genre means their exposure to texts in that genre (that is, meetings) where the engendering practice (non-patriarchal – at least, in terms of this one convention) is deeply disturbing to them.

Understanding the genre of a text, therefore, enables us to understand how its conventions situate readers discursively (by identifying the discourses which motivate textual conventions), to place the text sociohistorically (by identifying how this text fits into the history of this genre and whether it transforms the genre in any way), and to situate it in relation to social change (by identifying how the discourses generated textually relate to the discourses circulating in society). For gender theorists this can be an extremely useful tool for understanding why certain texts (and their genres) are very successful; why changes to texts (and genres) take place, and why those changes can be so disturbing for some readers; and how to change texts and genres, and their engendering practices.

Complexity and Disjunction

It is worth noting also that texts at times carry quite different and sometimes conflicting meanings about gender; for example the same text may articulate both patriarchal and feminist discourses. The reason for this might be understood in this way: just as societies are complex and contain different and sometimes conflicting voices, so too do the texts which are generated by those societies. Referring back to the work on genre, we might see this complexity and diversity in the different conventions which characterise a specific genre. Some of those conventions may articulate a particular discourse about gender; others its opposite. In the meeting genre discussed above, the change to the naming and role of chair may articulate a non-patriarchal discourse about gender, one which recognises public authority as an acceptable feature of femininity (as patriarchy does not). However, it would not be surprising to discover that other conventions of this genre or that features of specific meeting texts (instances of the genre) articulate conservative, patriarchal discourse – either because of the persistence of those attitudes in society as a whole or because of their persistence in the individuals who are part of the constitution of a specific meeting. For example, we would not be surprised to discover that men in meetings employ some of the textual strategies discussed earlier in relation to mixed-sex conversation (verbal dominance, interruption, speaking over, topic shifting) as a way of establishing themselves and their opinions as part of that meeting. In the process these men are gendering themselves as patriarchal subjects, and the specific meeting text accordingly articulates that discourse. So an analysis of a meeting in which such behaviours take place, which also features a female chairperson, can be seen as articulating both non-patriarchal and patriarchal discourses. It is highly unlikely, in fact, that texts of any kind will carry just one discourse about a particular issue or concept, again because texts (and genres) articulate the ideas and behaviours of complex and diverse societies and groups of individuals.

The same kind of analysis can be used with fictional texts. Consider a well-known text such as *Star Wars*. In the 1970s, when this film was made, the character of Princess Leia was seen as extremely forthright and assertive; Leia's character was seen as an articulation of contemporary feminist discourse. Yet, at the same time, Leia spent the whole film dressed in an ungainly white dress and with her hair braided in a style which seemed adapted from illustrations to fairy tales. She was also, literally and metaphorically, the princess of fairy tale and romance narrative – a role which is an embodiment of a patriarchal fantasy of the feminine. So, in Leia's character and representation alone, we can identify two different and conflicting discourses about gender – feminist and patriarchal. Generic analysis suggests that the reason for such a contradiction lies with the gendering practices of contemporary 1970s' US society, in which a vocal feminist movement existed in tension with equally vocal patriarchal attitudes. In the film, Leia's conventional narrative role, supported by her costume and make-up, constitute patriarchal femininity. On the other hand, her verbal assertiveness and physical activity transgress this conventional role, transforming it for the 1970s and constituting a feminist version of the feminine. The engendering practice of this film extends beyond the characterisation of Leia, of course, but this analysis alone suggests how discursively complex the film is.

Many films, books, magazines and texts of all kinds are complex in this same way and one reason for this diversity is the complexity of the audience at which they are directed. With the *Star Wars* example, we might ask why the makers of the film were not prepared to present Leia simply as a female leader; for example why did they need to modify her assertiveness by dressing her as they did? The answer might well be a recognition on the part of the film-makers that their audience comprises both patriarchal and feminist subjects – or more and less conservative viewers. The contradictory image of Leia is a simultaneous appeal to the broadest possible audience, which might be seen as a cynical financial ploy and/or an appreciation of audience diversity.

The film *Alien* has often attracted attention for a similarly contradictory treatment of its main female character, Ripley. Barbara Creed (1990) published a subsequently much-cited article on the constructions of the feminine in this film, both through the character of Ripley and the egg-laying mother-alien. She concludes her article with a reading of the final scenes of the film, which have always disturbed feminist viewers. Having survived the alien attacks with courage and tenacity, Ripley is then shown undressing on camera. Ripley also rescues her cat, a move which contradicts all her previous concerns about quarantine. Creed concludes that the questions about why such scenes are included can only be explained by reference to 'a phallocentric concept of female fetishism' (p. 140):

> Compared to the horrific sight of the alien as fetish object of the monstrous-feminine, Ripley's body is pleasurable and reassuring to look at. She signifies the 'acceptable' form and shape of woman. In a sense the monstrousness of woman, represented by Mother as betrayer (the computer/life-support system) and Mother as the uncontrollable, generative, cannibalistic mother (the Alien), is controlled through the display of woman as reassuring and pleasurable sign. The image of the cat functions in the same way; it signifies an acceptable, and in this context a reassuring, fetish object for the 'normal' woman. (p. 140)

So while the active, courageous Ripley articulates a feminist discourse, the film ends with a reassuring (for some), recuperative, conventional patriarchal discourse in which woman (represented by Ripley) features as spectacle and as desirous of the phallus. Again we might ask whether such contradictions in the gendering of a text reflect social diversity in its makers or a keen financial eye; the answer is probably both – given the complexity of the film-making process, involving not just writers and directors but also producers, financiers, studio representatives and so on.

> A particular text may communicate different, and sometimes conflicting, meanings about gender, reflecting the complex discursive environment in which texts are produced. Analysing the generic operation of a text enables the reader or viewer to identify those different meanings and how they are conveyed.

The final point to note here is that individual texts may carry traces of several different genres. Derrida's (1980) claim that 'one can never not mix genres' attests to the fact that texts seldom fit neatly into one textual category. Even the most orthodox of texts will often borrow conventions from other genres, perhaps in the process of transforming the dominant genre in its make-up, or perhaps as part of its articulation of a particular event or practice. This is not to devalue the use of genre in analysis, since most texts signal their membership of one dominant genre as part of their communication with readers or participants. However, the mixing of generic conventions can be a useful way of making new meanings. Consider, for example, the mixing of science fiction and romance elements in the fiction of prolific writer, Anne McCaffrey. In the first half of the twentieth century, science fiction did not deal sympathetically with interpersonal relationships. Its preoccupation with hardware and technological accomplishment not only reflected the war-like nature of the first half of this century, but also the development of nuclear weapons and a range of other technologies. It was sometimes known as 'toys for the boys SF' and, as the phrase indicates, articulated a phallocentric gender discourse. Many feminist SF writers reworked the conventions of SF in the 1970s to voice an opposing feminist discourse: see anthologies such as Pamela Sargent's *Women of Wonder* (1974) and *More Women of Wonder* (1976). Anne McCaffrey dealt with SF's inability to deal with the personal by blending romance conventions into her texts: see, for example, the *Dragons of Pern* series and the *Ship Who* series. In these texts she uses science fiction to set up an alternative world premise and then plays out romances which are more or less conventional (depending on the individual text), opening up to scrutiny the narratives by which the gendering of intimate encounters is related. Generic mixing may not necessarily signify that gendering practices are under scrutiny, but it often does, and can reveal the struggles of a society negotiating changes in its discursive constructions of gender.

Most texts carry traces of more than one genre, even if they are usually perceived as belonging to one specific genre. This generic mixing has creative potential, enabling new and different meanings to be made. It can also be a site at which debates about gender are articulated.

Complex and Diverse Readers

The other way in which different meanings are generated from texts is through the reading practices of different readers. The rest of this chapter deals in some detail with the terms which are used to describe a number of different reading practices, so here we simply introduce this notion that different readings of the same text are not only possible, but virtually inevitable.

In the first half of the twentieth century, differences in reading practices were not encouraged; in fact they were actively suppressed. Using the textual genres of a society, which often meant the genres used by its dominant cultural group, was seen as a prerequisite to full participation in the society. These included written genres, verbal genres, audiovisual genres and visual genres. A sign of this normative process was the construction of various canons of cultural production such as literature and painting. Certain literary works were 'canonised' as representing the highest achievement in literature and readers were taught to read them as such. If a reader did not read them that way, would not or could not appreciate their greatness, then that reader was considered ill-informed, uneducated and uncultured. Interestingly, one of the most radical rejections of the literary canon came from feminist literary critics who challenged the predominance in that canon of male writers and the concomitant universalisation of male experience in the texts of the canon. Critic Elaine Showalter argued that women 'are expected to identify with a masculine experience and perspective which is presented as the human one' (1971, p. 856). The canon, feminists argued, was an engendering practice enacted through specific readings of a selection of texts characterised by the dominance of dead, white males:

As readers and teachers and scholars, women are taught to think as men, to identify with a male point of view, and to accept as normal and legitimate a male system of values, one of whose governing principles is misogyny. (Fetterley 1978, p. xx)

A recent list of the 100 greatest novels of the twentieth century chosen by US critics has now extended that canonisation process to a dominance of live, white males. For feminist critics, the fact that so few women writers were and are included in literary canons points not so much to the inadequacy of female writers as to the acculturated and gendered prejudices of those making the choices. Virginia Woolf expressed this in simple terms in *A Room of One's Own* (1977) when she noted: 'Speaking crudely, football and sport are "important"; the worship of fashion, the buying of clothes "trivial". And these values are inevitably transferred from life to fiction.' The result is that the literary canon operated as an engendering practice, which constructed the masculine in conventional terms as intellectual, rational, courageous and, most importantly, as universal – the norm against which other experience was to be evaluated (and found lacking). This construction of the masculine is actualised not only in the subject matter of the books on the list but also through its selection of writers. The rejection of this canon by feminist critics was, therefore, a rejection of this engendering practice, not only a demand that the authority of women as writers be recognised, but also a rejection of this universalisation of masculine experience and its concomitant relegation of feminine experience as 'other', ephemeral, unimportant and trivial. As the recent list of 100 greatest novels shows, however, the debate continues.

This canon debate (which subsequently spread into an examination of the canon as not only gendered but also classed and raced) is one example of gendered differences in reading practice. Myriad examples occur with texts every day. One oft-quoted example concerns the science fiction writer, James Tiptree Jr. For years Tiptree remained incommunicado, sending work for publication but never allowing face-to-face contact. When rumours began to circulate that Tiptree might be female, editor and writer Robert Silverberg wrote a vigorous defence of his writer, claiming:

> Tiptree's stories don't bore. They are lean, muscular, supple, relying heavily on dialog broken by bursts of stripped-down exposition. ... His work is analogous to that of Hemingway, in that Hemingway preferred to be simple, direct, and straight-forward, at least on the surface. ... There is, too, that prevailing masculinity about both of them – that preoccupation with questions of courage, with absolute values, with the mysteries and passions of life and death as revealed by extreme physical tests, by pain and suffering and loss. (1975, p. xv)

While it is fascinating to consider the discourse about femininity implicitly constructed by Silverberg in this statement, it is equally revealing to discover that Tiptree was the pen name of Alice Sheldon. In other words, Silverberg's reading of Tiptree's work is constituted in terms of a discourse about masculinity to which he aligns Tiptree's writing, regardless of the actual gender of the author and the gendering which other readers associated with her work.

Readers of textual practice are drawn from a variety of different socio-cultural backgrounds, and they bring to their reading some of the values (and their constitutive discourses) of that background. Of course, readers also learn, implicitly and/or explicitly, the conventions of the texts with which they engage, and to some extent their reading and participation is guided by those conventions. Nevertheless, alternative readings are possible – just as feminist critics came to see the suppressions which constituted the literary canon or as Silverberg read ineluctable masculinity into the work of Tiptree. For gender theorists, reading differently has become a major way of exploring the construction of gender in texts and in the cultural assessments of texts, and hence of the ways in which these texts operate as engendering practices.

Ways of Reading

We noted earlier the definition of text as 'a combination of signs' to which we added 'which are activated by a reader or viewer to produce or generate meanings' as a recognition of the role of the reader. We also noted that this combination was generated originally by someone with a specific meaning or set of meanings in view – although this original intent or purpose does not in itself close down the meaning-potential of the text. So we might say, therefore, that the writer (artist, director and so on) originally produced this combination with the reading (viewing, listening and so on) skills of an audience in mind; skills which would (re)produce from the text a particular meaning, or set of meanings. The product of that set of reading skills – the set of meanings – is what we call a 'reading'. At the same time, however, a critic with a repertoire of skills for generating meanings from texts might make a different reading of the same text, and that, too, would be a reading. One reading is not necessarily more valid than the other; the readings have different purposes, different social functions.

For gender theorists, this recognition that the same text can generate a number of different readings was critical to their analysis of reading as an engendering practice. It helped to explain the practice of reading as a conservative gendering practice: for example the way in which the teaching of canonical literature was a crucial way in which a woman was taught to adopt a masculine way of reading, and so of thinking about herself and the world. In Elaine Showalter's words:

> By the end of her freshman year, a woman student would have learned something about intellectual neutrality; she would be learning, in fact, how to think like a man. And so she would go on, increasingly with male professors to guide her. (1971, p. 855)

Of course, as discussed earlier in this chapter, this engendering practice is not just a feature of the literary canon but occurs with every kind of text. As a sociocultural practice, then, reading can propagate conventional, patriarchal attitudes to gendered subjectivity and relationships. However, different readings might challenge this conventional gendering practice of the text, just as the feminist critics quoted above challenged the (patriarchal) literary establishment by producing readings which not only contradicted the conventional, patriarchal readings, but also located the assumptions on which those readings were based. Around this notion that reading is an active social and cultural practice have evolved a range of concepts for describing readings.

Mainstream or Compliant Reading

It might be best to begin this discussion of mainstream readings by noting Annette Kolodny's point that 'reading is a *learned* activity which, like many other learned interpretive strategies in our society, is inevitably sex-coded and gender-inflected' (1980, p. 588). A mainstream (or compliant) reading is commonly defined as a reading which complies with and is defined by the reading practice which is considered typical of mainstream literacy in that society. It is the reading which might be expected of a literate member of that society. Note that this might not be the same as the reading for which the text was originally designed or configured, if that text was composed in a different time or a different society. So the mainstream or compliant reading is a sociohistorically specific concept. Still it can tell us a great deal about how a specific text is likely to be used; the kinds of meanings which it can be expected to generate.

A mainstream or compliant reading of a text is the reading expected from a literate member of the reader's society. It does not describe the reader's or the text's politics, but the politics of reading in the reader's society.

A typical screen romance, for example, will tell us the story of a man and a woman who seem destined to be together but who, when they meet, are involved with others; the narrative of the film is the story of their eventual relationship – often ending in marriage. A mainstream or compliant reading of the narrative follows them through conflict to reconciliation and consummation (resulting in a warm inner glow for the reader – the embodied expression of this narrative). Their final coming together is a confirmation of the social and cultural values represented by their story. However, if this is a story from which you are excluded – perhaps your sexuality means that you cannot present yourself as a member of the required heterosexual couple or your attitudes to masculinity and femininity may find their common narrative representations (men as strong, powerful, but childlike and vulnerable; women as emotional and/or zany, and desirous of a strong, powerful man) offensive – then you may have no warm inner glow, or it may not be a soft pink glow, but an angry red one. That is, you may be able to make the compliant reading but nevertheless find it unsatisfying.

The important point for the gender theorist is, of course, the pervasiveness of these mainstream readings as learned activities which reinforce and reproduce conventional patriarchal gendering practices. While the feminist debates about the literary canon might seem, at some level, rather removed from the concerns of everyday life, it is important to ask how often does the same principle apply to the texts which we encounter and enact every day, including non-fictional texts. For example, the conversation text about Wayne and Heather discussed earlier in this chapter is an example of participants enacting a mainstream reading of a text, the effect of which is to engender them in conservative patriarchal terms. What we see in this text is that the participants have learned the (generic) rules of the conversation which include features such as turn-taking, backchannelling, topic choice, interruption, verbal dominance and so on. Furthermore, they have learned these rules as gendered practices: in mixed-sex conversation, men interrupt, choose topics and dominate verbally; women backchannel and accept male dominance of topic choice and time. That conversation text could be classified as mainstream because no one in the conversation challenged the conventions in any way – there is a great deal of social pressure not to do so. We might consider, for example, the consequences of a choice to reject the gendered practices of a particular genre. In conversation, for example, women who refuse to accept male dominance and interruption are commonly referred to as pushy or difficult. This is a form of social discipline or regulation, the purpose of which is to pressure women into accepting their designated (conventional feminine) role. Responses to feminist critiques of the canon and the patriarchal reading practices which are the mainstream in our society elicited similar disciplinary responses from conservative (mostly male) critics. For example, Dale Spender quotes a review of Kate Swift and Casey Miller's *Handbook of Non-Sexist Writing*:

> From the photograph supplied of Mss [sic] Casey Miller and Kate Swift, I should judge that neither was sexually attractive … a sense of grievance can often bring out the worst in people, and there is no reason to extend our sympathy where the motives of these disgruntled feminist agitators is simply to make a nuisance of themselves. This would appear to be the inspiration behind Swift and Miller's *Handbook of Non-Sexist Writing*. (1989, p. 68)

This personal attack on the writers is enlightening because of its focus on their femininity; the rules they are breaking in publishing such a volume are not only generic but also gendered. It is perhaps not surprising that this mainstream reading practice is sometimes also called the 'compliant reading' because not only does it reflect a willingness to comply with contemporary (generic and gender) rules; it also represents a capitulation to the pressure to conform – to comply with both generic structures and their conventional gendering.

Many people encounter the pressure to conform generically (and in gendered terms) to contemporary reading practices: the secretary asked to perform domestic tasks outside her job description and which construct her as non-professional; the lawyer positioned not to challenge the implicit masculine address of a legal document; the television viewer presented with yet another conventional fairy-tale narrative, in a sitcom or news programme. It is not surprising that many people capitulate to the pressure not to resist (at least openly) this reading, because reading is a social practice with a big stick attached. The cost of resistance can be public humiliation as 'neurotic', 'irrational', 'a humourless feminist', 'a wimp'. Another way in which people are pressured into not resisting the mainstream reading is by the construction of any resistance as taking away the fun. The response that analysing a text destroys the reader's enjoyment in it is so commonplace that we would be right to question its propagation. In fact, as Catherine Belsey (1980) argued in her book *Critical Practice*, common sense is very often where the ideology of a society is most effectively encoded. Again, the unspoken question 'why would understanding how a text works take away the fun?' is a useful deconstructive move. There are not many areas of life in which people profess a preference for ignorance and allow themselves to be manipulated; why should reading be a site for ignorant, uninformed and compliant behaviour? We might argue, in fact, that the repetition of this attitude in the press, through everyday conversation, by students in classrooms, on talkback radio and other sites suggests an unstated recognition that people can and do resist mainstream readings and positionings, and their conventional gendering. The repetition is an attempt to reinforce the mainstream reading practice by projecting any other practice as unrewarding for readers. Nevertheless, people continue to make those different readings and in the remainder of this chapter we discuss these readings, how they operate and the terms used to describe them.

Resistant Reading

Readers who produce a reading of a text which resists the compliant or mainstream reading, and its positioning of the individual as a subject who accords with the values it articulates, are often described as making a 'resistant reading'. Here resistant refers not (or not only) to social values in themselves, but (also) to the reading practice in which they are encoded.

A resistant reading of a text rejects the mainstream or compliant reading, and instead performs a reading that implicitly or explicitly challenges that reading and the meanings it generates.

So the feminist readers of the literary canon were often referred to as resistant readers because they not only rejected some of the meanings which were seen as represented in the texts of that canon (for example the equation of masculine experience with universality), but also the conventional reading practice which located and valorised those meanings. One of these critiques, by Judith Fetterley, is called *The Resisting Reader* (1978). There are different ways in which readers can be seen as producing a resistant reading. One is by a critical reading of the text.

Resisting the Text

In gender terms, this is a reading in which the reader identifies and resists the ways in which gender is textually articulated as a relationship between individuals or as a relationship between individuals and their society. One very basic example of this resistant reading is the rejection of the generic 'he'; that is, rejection of the idea that the masculine pronoun he can be used (generically) for both men and women as a universally inclusive pronoun. The reasoning behind this resistance is that such usage establishes the masculine as universal and the feminine as other (the same reasoning that feminist critics applied to the conventional construction and reading of the literary canon). The corollary of the generic 'he' is that the feminine 'she' is the marked position (the 'he' is unmarked), and so is the site of specificity, ephemerality and triviality. Given that this universal 'he' appeared throughout Western written and verbal texts – from the most private, as in conversation, to the most public, in legal and judicial documentation – what it signified was a pervasive sociocultural bias against the feminine, identified by many critics as phallocentric. This resistant reading practice has had great social influence and the official policy now in many Western countries is to avoid the use of the generic 'he'.

We discussed briefly above the work of feminist critics which has been particularly influential in the development of this concept of resistant reading. In 1980, for example, Rosalind Coward published her essay 'Are Women's Novels Feminist Novels?' in which she observes the feminist challenges to conventional reading practices: 'where critics have championed

D.H. Lawrence for his honest accounts of sexuality, feminists have exposed these accounts as phallocratic and degrading representations of women' (1985, p. 227). She goes on to argue that:

> As feminists we have to be constantly alerted to *what* reality is being constructed, and *how* representations are achieving this construction. In this respect, reading a novel can be a political activity, similar to activities which have always been important to feminist politics in general. (1985, pp. 227–8)

For many feminist critics since the 1970s, reading has been a political practice by which the conservative, engendering practice of a wide variety of texts has been exposed. Kate Millett's (1970) resistant readings of the work of writers D.H. Lawrence, Norman Mailer, Henry Miller and Jean Genet in her book *Sexual Politics* were crucial to the development of feminist literary criticism, as was Germaine Greer's ironic reassessment of Lawrence and Hemingway as 'sexual romantics', whose work she likened most closely to that of the *grande dame* of romance fiction, Barbara Cartland: 'Their vocabulary is larger than Cartland's but the structures of titillation are the same, provided we accept the fuck as the end of the story and not the kiss' (Greer 1970, p. 185). The importance of this work is that it disrupted the institution of literary criticism, by revealing the discourses which it articulated. Reading, it demonstrated, was not a value-free, neutral, objective activity guided simply by taste, sensibility or even a keen appreciation of literary convention. Instead it was a political activity, through which certain meanings and values (including patriarchal or masculinist ideas about gender) are propagated and established as socially correct or normative. With that assumption exposed and any concept of neutrality or objectivity repudiated, it was thereafter possible to argue for different readings or interpretations of texts.

A text which has inspired a host of resistant readings is the 1991 film *Thelma and Louise*. The film is a female buddy film, a road movie with female characters. On a night out together Louise shoots and kills a man who is attempting to rape Thelma, starting the two on a flight from (patriarchal) masculine authority as embodied, on the one hand, by the police force and, on the other, by Thelma's husband and, less threateningly, by Louise's caring boyfriend. It culminates in a stand-off on a desert mesa; Thelma and Louise in their pink Cadillac must choose between submission to the authority of the police force or drive their car over the cliff in an attempt to reach the next mesa and so the Mexican border. In the version of the film released to the public, the film ends with the car inscribing an arc through the clear desert air. Critics have worried at length at this ending. Its obvious narrative reading, that Thelma and Louise must die for their affrontery in challenging masculine authority, is challenged textually by the fact that the viewer does not hear a crash or see the car burst into flames. Nevertheless, a mainstream reading precludes their escape, since the gendered narrative constituted by this ending – that women can escape their patriarchal gendering – is too threatening and socially disruptive. This was confirmed by the preview process, in which audiences were shown different endings to the film; the escape ending was not popular and has never been released.

In a sense, then, this was a film which invited resistant readings and there have been many. One example is the reading made by Marleen Barr (1993) in her study *Lost in Space*. She reads the final scene as a 'plunge into a magical space of nonhuman signification; they enter an alternative text', in the process becoming 'fantastic, magic, surrealist' (p. 28). And Barr notes that the car does not fall over the mesa: 'it flies' (p. 28). For Barr, Thelma and Louise triumph because 'they desert patriarchal reality, leave it behind in the dust' (p. 28). With this reading, Barr resists the narrative generated, and road-tested, for the conventionally gendered audience, choosing instead to read the ending from another perspective which confirms, rather than undermines, the challenge to patriarchal constructions of femininity which is constituted by other aspects of this film.

Jonathan Culler (1991), in his influential essay first published in 1982, 'Reading as a Woman', surveyed the impact of one strategy used by feminist critics, which is to read as a woman. He writes:

> Criticism based on the presumption of continuity between the reader's experience and a woman's experience and on a concern with images of women is likely to become most forceful as a critique of the phallocentric assumptions that govern literary works. (p. 511)

Since then much critical effort has been put into analysing the images of women in literary texts, advertising, legal documents, newspapers, the visual arts and so on, with the finding that these images are almost invariably constituted in terms of patriarchal stereotypes – woman as weak, helpless, caring and nurturing, or alternatively as betraying, vicious and corrupt.

One regrettably rich source for such representations is fairy tale. Jack Zipes, in his book *The Trials and Tribulations of Little Red Riding Hood* (1983), traces the variations to the tale of Little Red Riding Hood and so demonstrates the way in which the tale has been constantly rewritten to articulate the gender discourses of its authors. In another study of the tale published in the collection *Don't Bet on the Prince* (1986), Zipes makes his own resistant reading of the major written versions of Little Red Riding Hood:

> In the [patriarchal] male imagination it was the woman who was devious, sinful, and subversive; her sexual appetite interfered with male institutionalised relations; she was an instigator, in league with the devil, that is, with wolves or male heretics, who represented sexual play, amusement, gathering flowers in the woods. So, by

the nineteenth century Little Red Riding Hood and the wolf had become primarily responsible for the violation of bodies, for chaos, disorder, and sin …

Ultimately, the male phantasies of Perrault and the Brothers Grimm can be traced to their socially induced desire and need for control – control of women, control of their own sexual libido, control of their fear of women and loss of virility. (pp. 255–7)

Fairy tales can also be examined for the kinds of gender identities they project for male readers. Again the predominance of patriarchal gendering is most apparent: the male as sexual predator (wolf), or as patriarchal father (hunter/woodsman) (Cranny-Francis 1992).

Interestingly, resistant readings of this kind, which locate gendered identities which are very conventional and sometimes misogynistic in texts, have recently been attacked for their tendency to construct the (compliant) reader as victim. Girl power is a catch phrase used to describe an international trend to reject such readings in favour of an attitude that women can handle all kinds of constructions of themselves, even the most apparently negative, since such images nevertheless grant women a kind of power. It is this power that Zipes (1983) sees the 'male phantasies of Perrault and the Brothers Grimm' as designed to control. Obviously, this is a complex question, which involves issues of socioeconomic power, literacy and independence as well as a reassessment of the role of power in securing autonomy and choice. It is perhaps interesting to contrast it with the new lad movement which argued for male power from a similar perspective, and yet might arguably be seen as having involved primarily a restatement of conventional gendering practices.

Finally, it is worth returning briefly to the factor which Culler (1991), revisiting the work of Showalter, Fetterley, Baym, Kolodny and others, recognised as critical to the making of these readings: the experience of being a woman. He quotes Showalter's identification of feminist critique as being concerned 'with the way in which the *hypothesis* of a female reader changes our apprehension of a given text, awakening us to the significance of its sexual codes' (p. 513). Here, we might recall the earlier commentary on Teresa de Lauretis' analysis of film in which she discussed the position of the female viewer, confronted by a narrative, filmic construction of woman, which did not at all coincide with her own experience of being a woman. It is the disjunction between the two – the patriarchal feminine woman and the experience of being a woman – which de Lauretis identifies as the source of women's resistant readings.

For gender theorists, therefore, resisting the text can be seen as arising from a number of practices, many of which were pioneered by the feminist critiques from the 1960s and 70s. Those practices include analysis of the gendered representations which occur within a text; analysis of the gendered assumptions which structure the text (for example the equation of masculinity with universality); and the comparison of both gendered assumptions and representations with the actual experience of the reader, male or female. The latter point is especially useful in understanding resistant responses which can be as basic as 'yuch'; which is to say, not necessarily an argued critique but a perception of invalidity or bias which may arise primarily from a reader's implicit contrast of the truth of gendering practices, as she/he knows them, and the discourses constituted by the text.

Rewriting the Text

Another way in which readers have been identified as making resistant readings is in their production of texts which are based on genres, or even specific texts, with well-established cultural meanings, but which change or subvert those meanings. We might consider, for example, the early performance practice of Madonna, in which her name and the religious iconography she used constituted a rewriting of the meanings of those symbols – from the conventional gendering with which they are usually associated to a new and powerful femininity which confronts the submissiveness and passivity of conventional femininity. Similarly, Madonna's early video *Material Girl*, in which she dresses and performs as Marilyn Monroe singing Diamonds are a Girl's Best Friend in the film *Gentlemen Prefer Blondes*, confronts the conventional feminine identities evoked, and arguably also confronted, by Monroe in that performance: woman as dependent; woman as materialistic; woman as betrayer. Where Monroe expresses the feminine reality of gendered relationships with the line, diamonds are a girl's best friend, Madonna deconstructs the nature of her society: 'We live in a material world/And I am a material girl.' Through her revision of these texts and their constitutive images, Madonna constructs a resistant reading which exposes their conventional engendering practice.

Another example is the use of the term 'Ms' as a form of address for women. This term necessitated a revision of conventional modes of address used in English. Linguist Susan Ervin-Tripp's (1971) exploration of the conventional system of address in the USA reveals the reasons for the invention of this term. Ervin-Tripp's work shows that the whole system is based on a recognition only of masculinity; male is the normative identity from which all identities are derived. Significantly, a man may be married or not and his title – Mr – remains the same. A woman, identified in this system as not-male, may be married in which case she is addressed as Mrs, or unmarried in which case she is addressed as Miss. This example suggests very clearly that this is a society based on an exchange of women who must, therefore, be identified as available (unmarried) or not. Furthermore, the exchange value only of women is confirmed by the fact that the system has no space for an autonomous female identity. The title Ms, which is used only for women and does not specify marital status, disrupts this conventional system and the assumptions on which it is based. It is not surprising, therefore, that it attracted so much conservative criticism when first used. Effectively we might say that this term, and its subsequent disruption of the conventional system of address in English, was generated by a resistant reading of that system of address.

Another set of texts which are based on resistant readings of familiar texts are the revisions of fairy tales. In her article 'Stoning the Romance: Girls as Resistant Readers and Writers', Pam Gilbert (1989) discusses versions of fairy tales written by some ten-year-old girls. One of the stories she examines is called 'The intelligent princess'; it tells of a princess who rejects the passivity of the conventional feminine and goes off on her own to find a prince. After various adventures, during which she looks after herself very well, she eventually does find a prince – a little boy. Zillah, the princess, looks after him and makes him croissants while Glen, the travelling companion she has picked up along the way, makes the boy a beautiful cushion. In various ways, as Gilbert points out, the sexual politics of the story are conventional, particularly as the princess only escapes her predestined princess role by becoming a servant to a royal brat. Nevertheless, she does not become what the stereotype demands, a passive object valued only for her beauty. Gilbert points out that resistant readings such as this one are often produced without a great deal of technical knowledge or critical insight. Those girls are exhibiting their resistance to the conservative discourse about gender and its constitutive representations, even if they are coerced by the (textual) conventions into producing something like the traditional tales. Gilbert notes that:

> such resistance is frequently not noticed. Instead of being used to foster further resistance, and to make girls explicitly aware of convention and the breaking of convention, these stories are often read in quite different ways by teacher readers. (1989, p. 78)

There are also a number of resistant fairy tales produced by adult readers. One of the most entertaining is a version from 1939 by James Thurber which tells the story of a little girl confronted by a wolf in a nightgown who claims to be the girl's grandmother. In this account:

> She had approached no nearer than twenty-five feet from the bed when she saw that it was not her grandmother but the wolf ... So the little girl took an automatic out of her basket and shot the wolf dead.

And he adds:

> *Moral: It is not so easy to fool little girls nowadays as it used to be.* (1983, p. 210, italics in original)

Thurber's version exposes not only the conventional representation of the girl in the story as gullible, childish and incapable of independent action, but also, through his explicit inclusion of the moral, reminds the modern reader that the fairy tale is indeed a morality tale, used to propagate specific discourses about gender (among other things). Jack Zipes (1983) includes in his study of Little Red Riding Hood an oral version collected in France in the late nineteenth century which gives the tale a wholly different meaning. In this version, the girl is inveigled into bed by the wolf but, when he announces his intention to eat her, declares that she needs to go to the toilet. Although the wolf urges her to do it in the bed, she insists on going outside. The wolf ties her ankle with a rope and attaches this to the bed. Once outside, however, the girl unties it and ties it to a tree. By the time the wolf realises what has happened, the girl has managed to run home safely. Zipes concludes that the tale is a sort of coming-of-age story in which girls are instructed how to take care of themselves, even in the most perilous of situations, by using their intelligence and being assertive – a very different use to which the tale was put by many of those who wrote it down.

The science fiction novels of James Tiptree Jr (Alice Sheldon) are another example of resistant reading manifested as the inventive rewriting of a familiar genre. In one of her most disturbing stories, 'The Screwfly Solution', Tiptree (1981) reveals many of the premises at the basis of patriarchal fantasies about women. In this story aliens have decided to take over the earth but, rather than engaging in a messy war, they seed the earth with chemicals which cause men to become overtly sexually aggressive towards women. Once all the women are dead, the men will die out, and the earth will be there for the taking – well-composted. The story is based on biological control strategies used against insects such as the screw-fly. In the process of storytelling, however, Tiptree includes some savage indictments of the misogyny enacted in (patriarchal) male fantasies:

A terrible alarm bell went off in his head. Exploded from his dream, he stared around, then finally down at his hands. *What was he doing with his open clasp knife in his fist?*

Stunned, he felt for the last shreds of his fantasy, and realized that the tactile images had not been of caresses, but of a frail neck strangling in his fist, the thrust had been the plunge of a blade seeking vitals. In his arms, legs, phantasms of striking and trampling bones cracking. And Amy –

Oh God, Oh God –
Not sex, blood lust.

That was what he had been dreaming. The sex was there, but it was driving some engine of death. (1981, pp. 67–8, italics in original)

In reporting the response of the Catholic Church to this widespread murderous misogyny towards women, Tiptree reports an actual early (pre-1000AD) Church opinion that: 'the Scriptures define woman as merely a temporary companion and instrument of man. Women ... are nowhere defined as human, but merely as a transitional expedient or state' (1981, p. 65). The story thus deals in the most graphic fashion with the history and contemporary manifestations of misogyny, in a genre which, for the first half of the twentieth century, had tended to reflect this same misogyny.

Sonya Dorman, in her story 'When I Was Miss Dow' (1978), turns science fiction to similar ends. In this story, a shape-shifting alien assumes the character of research assistant Miss Dow in order to explore human interactions. The alien discovers that gendering is an essential feature of human existence, and finds itself experiencing both patriarchal femininity (in its own form) and masculinity (through its interactions). The story demonstrates a number of the ways that patriarchy operates: constructing certain behaviours as acceptable which the alien finds extraordinary (the way the scientist treats his assistant); the construction of complementary masculine and feminine patriarchal identities (the alien starts to assume a patriarchal feminine identity as it is subsumed into the patriarchal framework of the human colony); and the coercive power of the discourse (again, as the alien transforms into a patriarchal feminine subject). In fact, as mentioned above in the section 'Analysing Textual Practice', the 1970s and 80s saw a flowering of feminist science fiction which has transformed the genre, with texts such as Ursula Le Guin's *The Left Hand of Darkness* (1981), the stories of James Tiptree Jr and the Pamela Sargent anthologies mentioned earlier. All these texts are written as resistant readings of a twentieth-century science fiction preoccupied with technology, weaponry, colonialist adventure or xenophobic defensiveness.

Just as feminist writers have transformed the genre of science fiction, they have also transformed a series of other literary genres, including detective fiction, fantasy, romance, the 'literary' novel, performance drama and poetry. Adrienne Rich's poetry, for example, represents a resistant reading of the romantic and modernist poetry with which she had been raised, with its focus on 'universal' (masculine) concerns and written from a masculine viewpoint, for a masculine reader. In her essay 'Blood, Bread, and Poetry', Rich writes:

> To write directly and overtly as a woman, out of a woman's body and experience, to take women's existence seriously as theme and source for art, was something I had been hungering to do, needing to do, all my writing life' (1993c, pp. 239–52).

And yet, as she notes, such a stance meant *'the breakdown of the world as I had known it, the end of safety'* (p. 249, italics in original).

This feminist resistance to the gendering of cultural production has been a source of regeneration for texts in all these genres, but also for the visual arts, sound arts, television and film. Consider, for example, Cindy Sherman's famous photographic texts in which she poses herself as either a well-known feminine fantasy figure, such as Marilyn Monroe, or as a *film noir* character in order to expose the constructiveness of the gendering of those images and their coercive force as engendering practices. Then there are Barbara Kruger's collage texts, such as 'Your gaze hits the side of my face' – cut-out words pasted over a classical statue of a woman – which not only deconstruct the male gaze, but also indicate the essential violence of that gaze. Another example is the futurist science fiction film *Born in Flames*, by Lizzie Borden, which takes the major step of addressing the viewer as female. Resistant reading has transformed practices we encounter in everyday life – such as service encounters (the woman quoted by Kitzinger earlier in the chapter did not return to that doctor), everyday conversation (arguably people are more aware of the gendering practices they employ in everyday conversation than they were some thirty years ago), and forms of address – as well as the cultural practices by which our society reflects on itself and its discursive and material practice.

Rewriting the Reading

A final form of resistant reading, which had a major role in both the resistant practices described above, is the reading which challenges the ways in which texts are conventionally read; the address is to the text via its commentators. This practice involves locating the conventional reading of the text, which inevitably suppresses some of the meaning-making possibilities of the text, and explicating some of those meanings to produce a different understanding of that text. We have already referred to this practice in the work of the feminist critics who challenged the authority of the canon. A specific example occurs in Elaine Showalter's (1985a) essay 'Towards a Feminist Poetics', when she re-reads the critical study by Irving Howe of the opening scenes of Thomas Hardy's *The Mayor of Casterbridge*. She quotes Howe's evaluation of this scene in which central character Michael Henchard sells his wife and infant daughter at a fair:

> To shake loose from one's wife; to discard that drooping rag of a woman, with her mute complaints and maddening passivity … to wrest, through sheer amoral wilfulness, a second chance out of life – it is with this stroke, so insidiously attractive to male fantasy, that *The Mayor of Casterbridge* begins. (1985a, p. 129)

and then comments:

It is obvious that a woman, unless she has been indoctrinated into being very deeply identified indeed with male culture, will have a different experience of this scene. I quote Howe first to indicate how the fantasies of the male critic distort the text; for Hardy tells us very little about the relationship of Michael and Susan Henchard, and what we see in the opening scenes does not suggest that she is drooping, complaining, or passive. Her role, however, is a passive one, severely constrained by her womanhood, and further burdened by her child, there is no way that *she* can wrest a second chance out of life. (p. 129)

Thus Showalter begins a critique of the novel which leads her to quite a different critical assessment of its meanings to the usual. Her opening argument is worth quoting at length, however, because it demonstrates Culler's point quoted earlier that analysis which is based on 'reading as a woman' – which, in Western societies, still mostly means reading resistantly – is likely to be 'most forceful as a critique of the phallocentric assumptions that govern literary works' (Culler 1991, p. 511). Showalter, reading as a woman and a critic, is able to locate – by her exclusion from it – the phallocentric reading of this text. That reading, as Showalter, Rich and many others attest, is the basis of a reading practice which is also powerfully engendering: it constitutes the (patriarchal) masculine position as the universal and women as the excluded 'other'. And this reading practice is demanded of both men and women. By exposing that reading practice, as noted above, Showalter was in the vanguard of the feminist critics who led the assault on the masculine literary establishment and its construction of its own viewpoint as the universal, objective and desirable one. That challenge subsequently enabled an extensive revisioning of the critical judgements on a variety of textual genres.

One genre which received such attention is the nineteenth-century sentimental novel. Jane Tompkins engaged powerfully with the debate over the sentimental novel through an analysis of Harriet Beecher Stowe's *Uncle Tom's Cabin*, of which she writes: 'Expressive of and responsible for the values of its time, it also belongs to a genre, the sentimental novel, whose chief characteristic is that it is written by, for, and about women' (1985, p. 83). That characteristic is also primarily responsible for its relegation to the critical wasteland, as Tompkins argues:

Stowe's novel and the tradition of which it is a part ... have for too long been the casualties of a set of critical attitudes which equate intellectual merit with certain kinds of argumentative discourse and certain kinds of subject matter. A long tradition of academic parochialism has enforced this sort of discourse through a series of cultural contrasts: light 'feminine' novels versus tough-minded intellectual treatises; domestic 'chattiness' versus serious thinking; and summarily, 'the damned mob of scribbling women' [Nathaniel Hawthorne] versus a few giant intellects, unappreciated and misunderstood in their time, struggling manfully against a flood of sentimental rubbish. (1985, p. 83)

Tompkins' analysis of academic parochialism has been extended to reading practice in general, across a range of media. Tania Modleski (1984), Ien Ang (1985), Janice Radway (1984, 1986) and Carol Thurston (1987) transformed the ways in which we think about the literary genre of romance and the television genre of soap opera, by challenging the critical judgements made about them based on the kinds of cultural contrast which Tompkins identifies. Modleski, for example, took the innovative step of treating female viewers and readers as rational, desiring social subjects and explored what the genres offered them, rather than assuming that the genres are trash and treating their audience accordingly. As a result, she and many subsequent analysts of these genres (see, for example, Modleski 1986; Gledhill 1987; Gamman and Marshment 1988; Brown 1990; Lewis 1990) have found that viewers read these texts not only compliantly but also resistantly, locating in their utopian depictions of gender relationships a critique of contemporary gender relations and expressing through their complicity with the male characterisations their desires for a different kind of (non-patriarchal) gendering. Teachers anecdotally report schoolgirls using romance and soap opera in the same ways. The girls evaluate the behaviours of the boys, girls, men and women they encounter against the ideal described in the romance and ask why the discrepancy occurs. They also explore the effect of such apparently unrealistic representations on their lives and ask what needs to change in contemporary gendering practices for the ideals to be achieved.

Following these feminist interventions, commentators have challenged the gendering of reading practice across a wide range of media. Sue Best, for example, challenges the conventional judgements of art history:

Art history repeats the same story, women artists 'depend' on male styles – they do not have styles of their own. His style is original, authentic; her style is but an imitation, unauthentic, a masquerade – she merely plays at having the phallus. By borrowing the style she is said to pay homage to the phallus. (1994, p. 154)

The resistant reading of art history typified by this passage is the critical equivalent of the visual work of artists such as Barbara Kruger, Judy Chicago, Rose Garrard, Monica Sjoo and others, whose work directly addresses issues of representation and its domination by a (patriarchal) masculine viewpoint. The result is that the visual arts, as mediated by contemporary art history and art criticism, act as a conservative gendering practice – in the same way as does the literary canon and its academic apologists.

Another canon and its institutional establishment which has recently been subjected to a gendered critique is the musical canon. Both Susan McClary

(1991) and Marcia Citron (1993) challenge the conventional gendering of music by its performers and critics. Both note the similarities between the role of canon formation in literature and music, although Citron adds: 'Literary critics ... tend to subject the texts to cultural analysis as a matter of course ... traditional musical analysis had remained mostly within formalist discourse' (1993, p. 37). McClary and Citron, therefore, take the musical establishment to task over the gendering of specific formal aspects of music (the 1970 *Harvard Dictionary of Music* includes the following entry: 'A cadence or ending is called "masculine" if the final chord of a phrase or section occurs on the strong beat and "feminine" if it is postponed to fall on a weak beat' (quoted in McClary 1991, p. 9)), but they also attempt to move beyond this limited scope. As McClary notes, in a radical divergence from formalist musicology:

> Meaning is not inherent in music, but neither is it in language: both are activities which are kept afloat only because communities of people invest in them, agree collectively that their signs serve as valid currency'. (1991, p. 21)

From this point, she and Citron proceed to subject music – as a canon and an institution – to the kinds of criticism pioneered by literary critics, discovering in the process the many different ways (textually and institutionally) that music is gendered, and operates as an engendering practice.

The major point to be drawn from all these examples is that resistance to the gendering practice of reading often begins with an analysis of conventional reading practice, as much as it does with the text itself. Those conventional reading practices are powerful technologies for maintaining and reinforcing the dominance of a particular (gendered – and classed and raced) view on the proper or correct way to read a text or genre. At the same time, they conceal or suppress meanings and readings of a text or genre which would contradict that view. They are, therefore, essential sites for analysis by anyone wanting to challenge that view and its engendering of readers.

Tactical Reading or 'Textual Poaching'

Resistant readings are text-centred readings in that the text remains the focus of attention for readers, who may deconstruct the text and/or use it as the basis of another and different text and/or deconstruct the conventional readings made of specific texts and genres of text. However, for some readers, the text is less a focus than a point of trajectory; meanings generated by a reading are extrapolated beyond the text into a reading/meaning-making practice which states and reinforces the attitudes and values of that reader. This kind of reading practice is referred to as tactical reading, and it is often defined as a reading which, at some level, empowers the reader. It is not necessarily a socially critical reading, and it is not necessarily a reading which accords with mainstream reading practice. Instead the reader generates a set of meanings which supports her or his own values and attitudes, no matter what meanings the work itself would seem to indicate.

Referring back to the earlier example of the conventional love story, a child might make a tactical reading of this narrative by finding the attitudes and posturing of the lovers ridiculous, supporting the child's view that adults are often irrational and behave absurdly. This reading empowers the child by making her or him feel superior to adults. A (mainstream) response to this might be that the child simply does not understand the reading practice required, and so cannot follow the story. This may or may not be true; a literate child may still find the story ridiculous. What marks the reading as tactical is that it originates in the child's perception of her or his own subject positioning and in the determination to strengthen that positioning. So the child does not allow her or himself to feel excluded by this story, to feel inadequate because she or he is not old enough to take part in such a story. Instead she or he retells the story in terms which enhance her/his own positioning – as wise enough to see the folly in the behaviours and attitudes dramatised. And, in this as with many tactical readings, a non-mainstream perspective might be seen as revealing elements of the story which the mainstream reading works to conceal.

A tactical reading (also called textual poaching) uses the text as a point of departure for a meaning-making practice that empowers the reader; it does not present itself as a coherent and consistent explanation of textual practice.

The notion of tactical reading originated with the work of sociologist Michel de Certeau (1984), who examined the ways in which people resist the mainstream institutions of their society. In his study, de Certeau argues that if we accept Foucault's argument about the pervasiveness of disciplinary apparatuses in our society, we then need to explain how 'an entire society resists being reduced to it, what popular procedures ... manipulate the mechanisms of discipline and conform to them only in order to evade them', which necessarily involves understanding the 'microphysics of power' (Foucault's term) used by consumers to resist the coercive force of disciplinary practices which maintain the socioeconomic order (de Certeau 1984, p. xiv). In other words, if the pressure to be a particular kind of subject – for example patriarchal, consumerist – is conveyed throughout a society, in its cultural productions, material practices and interpersonal relationships, how do individuals resist this pressure? And de Certeau begins his analysis by recognising that such resistances do happen; he then theorises the mechanism of this resistance. He uses the terms 'strategy' and 'tactics' to refer to the relationships of force employed respectively by mainstream institutions and individuals acting within/in their influence, on the one hand, and resistant individuals on the other. De Certeau explains this further by noting that while a strategy is 'a victory of space over time', the tactic 'depends on time' (p. xix); that is, the strategy uses institutional power and influence to negate the transformative power of time and establish a space within which particular rules, regulations, values, attitudes and practices are normative, while tactics only have time through which to accomplish their 'microphysical' assaults on hegemonic institutions. The tactic is a momentary victory over the strategic power of institutions, which those institutions will inevitably regain, although not without the transformative incursion having taken place. The graffiti artist, for example, achieves a momentary victory over bourgeois society by transforming a site with mainstream institutional purposes to another use – to articulate his or her marginalised voice. The act of graffiti is soon recuperated by mainstream discourse which constitutes it as vandalism – or occasionally as high art – and so silences that marginalised voice. However, the graffiti has been seen, and often remains visible for some time, which means that the trace of its resistance remains.

Cultural critic John Fiske (1989) uses de Certeau's concept of tactics extensively in his own work on reading. In his book *Understanding Popular Culture*, Fiske defines his use of the concept tactical reading as 'meanings produced *from* the text, not *by* it' (p. 57). Fiske gives as one example a reading of the film *Rambo* by a group of Australian Aboriginal people. While he had expected them to be affronted by Rambo himself and to see him as representative of white racism – a reading based on a mainstream reading of the narrative – this audience made quite a different reading, and set of meanings, from the text. Ignoring the mainstream reading, instead they configured the narrative as a conflict 'between Rambo, whom they saw as representative of the Third World, and the white officer class – a set of meanings that were clearly relevant to their experience of white, postcolonial paternalism', and Fiske notes that this identification 'may well have been functional in helping them to make a resistant sense of their interracial relationships' (p. 57). This alternative reading protected its readers from the racism which would be generated *by* the text, and instead generated *from* the text an anti-colonialist discourse with which readers could identify. The Aboriginal audience thereby transformed the text into a set of meanings which reinforced, rather than undermined, their own subject positioning.

In other situations, however, the beneficial result of tactical reading is more doubtful. For example, activities such as shoplifting (Fiske 1989), truancy and playground rebellion (Hodge and Tripp 1986) have also been read as tactical responses to institutions such as consumerism and liberal education. In these cases, it is imperative to consider what might be the result of such tactical responses for the individual. It might be argued that some of these tactics are self-defeating; that, if staying away from school is seen as a tactical response to a system of enforced education, it may not be a very useful tactic for the individual in the long term. However, it should be noted that the term 'tactical' does not employ a value judgement; it simply records the fact that individuals find ways of resisting social and cultural pressures. Truancy and playground rebellion are tactical responses to the liberal education system in Western societies. They may not have beneficial effects on individuals in the long term; however, they do locate the sites at which individuals feel under pressure. Thus tactical reading has a diagnostic value, as well as a momentarily empowering effect for the individual reader.

One set of tactical readings which has received considerable critical attention are made from the four television series, *Star Trek*, *Star Trek: The Next Generation*, *Star Trek: Deep Space Nine* and *Star Trek: Voyager*. The original series *Star Trek* was notable for the size and nature of the fan base it generated. Not only were – and are – there millions of fans all around the world for this series, but also these fans have addressed the object of their interest in ways which the shows' producers sometimes find quite transgressive. Some time ago it became widely known that fans of *Star Trek* were publishing for themselves stories which were based on the characters in the series, and some fans (for example Jean Lorrah, Sondra Marshak and Myrna Culbreath) went on to have novels published by commercial publishers. These stories range widely in their relationship to the original text: some are adventure stories not unlike the series; some focus more on individual characters and begin to fill out a life history for the character; while others focus on the erotic possibilities suggested by the characters. In his book-length study of fans' appropriations of textual fiction, *Textual Poachers: Television Fans and Participatory Culture*, Henry Jenkins (1992) refers to another term used by Michel de Certeau – 'poaching':

> De Certeau gives us terms for discussing ways that the subordinate classes elude or escape institutional control, for analyzing locations where popular meanings are produced outside of official interpretive practice. De Certeau perceives popular reading as a series of 'advances and retreats, tactics and games played with the text,' as a type of cultural bricolage through which readers fragment texts and reassemble the broken shards according to their own blueprints, salvaging bits and pieces of the found material in making sense of their own social experience. (p. 26)

Jenkins goes on to discuss the ways in which fans have poached the *Star Trek* texts in order to produce work which articulates their own concerns or desires; concerns and desires absent from or silenced by the original text. He and critic Constance Penley have shared an interest in *Star Trek* fan writings, including a set of texts – known as K/S (Kirk/Spock) or 'slash' fiction – which focus on a homoerotic relationship between main characters Captain James Kirk and his First Officer Mr Spock (see, for example, Jenkins, 1991, 1992, 1995; Penley 1991, 1992, 1997). Both writers seem to have been motivated by the popularity of the series with female fans, despite its objectification of women and delimitation of the roles of female characters. What they find in the fan writing, and most strikingly in the slash fiction, is an attempt by female fans (who produce over 90 per cent of media fan writing (Jenkins 1991, p. 178)) to rework *Star Trek* to articulate a specifically feminine voice and specifically female desires. Jenkins writes of fan writer Jean Lorrah's novels and stories about the relationship between Mr Spock's Vulcan father, Sarek, and his human mother, Amanda Grayson (played by Jane Wyatt), that 'the alienness of Vulcan culture becomes a metaphor for the many things that separate men and women, for the factors that block intimacy within marriage' (1991, p. 189). And Penley writes of the apparently contradictory heterosexual masculinity of the lovers Kirk and Spock, that these stories are about '"retooling" masculinity itself, which is precisely what K/S writing sets out to do' (1991, p. 155). Jenkins likens fan writing to the

> privately circulated letters and diaries and ... collective writing projects which Cheris Kramarae noted were some of the ways in which women 'express themselves outside the dominant modes of expression used by men'. (Jenkins 1991, p. 180)

In other words, this fan writing constitutes a tactical reading of the *Star Trek* series, from which female fans elaborate their own desires for new kinds of masculinity and femininity.

To make explicit the kind of reading entailed here, consider one of the stories written by Jean Lorrah, *The Vulcan Academy Murders* (1984). As the title suggests, this text is a curious mix of science fiction and detective fiction, in which Captain Kirk and Mr Spock investigate a murder on Spock's home-world, Vulcan. This murder plot serves as a backdrop against which Lorrah describes the telepathic bonding which accompanies Vulcan marriages and which reaches across human–Vulcan differences, as in the marriage of Sarek and Amanda Grayson, Spock's parents. The murders have, in fact, been perpetrated by Eleyna Miller, a young human woman who is desperately in love with Sarek. So the murder mystery, too, is intricately tied into the conceptual focus of the novel – an exploration of interpersonal intimacy. For Lorrah, the telepathic bonding of the Vulcans is a metaphor for the absolute commitment and loyalty which is the rhetoric, but rarely the practice, of bourgeois love. The novel continually probes the meaning of such holistic love – through the story of Sorel and T'Zan, the Vulcan pair who are separated when T'Zan becomes the first murder victim; through the story of another human–Vulcan pair, T'Mir, Sorel's daughter, and Daniel Corrigan, her father's human partner; and through the story of Sarek and Amanda, which is threatened

when Amanda undergoes a medical procedure which makes her vulnerable
to Miller. By contrast, the flirtatious relationship between Kirk and Eleyna
Miller demonstrates how shallow and self-serving human relationships can
be, particularly as Miller flirts with Kirk specifically in order to conceal her
murderous behaviour and then to attack him (Cranny-Francis 1997).

So there is a sense in which this is a *Star Trek* novel primarily because the
characters are *Star Trek* characters, rather than because it typifies the science
fiction stories of the television series. Instead the series provides her with a
starting point *from* which she tells an entirely different story from that which
preoccupied most episodes of the series. Her tactical reading of the series
enables her to explore a different kind of gendering from that articulated by
the series. Jenkins writes of Lorrah's stories of Sarek and Amanda that they:

> represent a painstaking effort to construct a feminist utopia, to propose how a trad-
> itional marriage might be reworked to allow it to satisfy the personal and profes-
> sional needs of both men and women. (1991, p. 189)

This topic, even the notion of sexual equality, is not one which the original
Star Trek series approached very seriously. In fact, the outright sexism of many
episodes and the costumes of female characters date the series for contemporary viewers. Perhaps it might be argued that the imaginative brilliance of the
original series provided something of the energy required by fan writers to
transform the patriarchal, patronising and often misogynistic product into
something quite different. Most importantly, however, the concept of tactical
reading enables the analyst/reader to negotiate the complex of gender
discourses, including some very conventional gendering of Sarek and
Amanda's relationship: for example, before she goes into hospital, she makes
lots of dinners and puts them in the freezer for him. To a critic working with
conventional and even perhaps conventional *and* resistant reading strategies
in mind, this text can be read as essentially conservative. It is only when a
reader seriously considers that textual strategies such as the mind-meld might
have a tactical function related not to the *Star Trek* universe, or to the genre of
science fiction, but to some other meaning that the writer is attempting to
articulate that a new reading becomes possible – one which is able to locate
the disruptive (en)gendering practice of this text.

Another reading practice which is sometimes seen as tactical and other
times as resistant is 'queer' reading. We have already discussed the meaning
of 'queer' as a critical stance and non-identity (see Chapter 2). A queer
reading, then, is one which is produced by non-mainstream readers from a
text; a reading which supports the queer perspective of those readers. In
terms of gender, a queer reader may choose to read the elaborately posed
photographs in fashion magazines as about female strength and beauty,
rather than as about consumerism and woman as spectacle. They may choose

to read fashion photographs of two women together as being about the beauty of lesbian relationships, rather than about selling clothes through a more or less implicit suggestion of same-sex sexuality. There are queer readings of *Star Trek* which identify certain characters as gay or lesbian and complicate their relationships with other characters. In the Boston area of the USA, a group called the Gaylaxians specialise in such readings, with the ditty: '2, 4, 6, 8, how do you know Kirk is straight?/ 3, 5, 7, 9, he and Spock have a real fine time!' (Jenkins 1995, p. 237). As a critical stance dedicated to challenging the coercive force of mainstream social (including textual) practices in any genre or media, queer inevitably contributes to both resistant and tactical reading practices. As groups such as the Gaylaxians demonstrate, queer reading can also be a powerful technology for building a new understanding of self and society, because it not only resists mainstream positioning, but also enables the reader to elaborate something different – rather than simply be relegated to the position of 'other' by a patriarchal and heteronormative discourse.

It is worth reiterating, in finishing off this section, that the concepts of tactical reading and tactical action developed from a respect for the resistant practices used by people in their everyday lives to resist social regulation. Sometimes those resistant responses make no sense to the analyst; they seem unconnected to the literate or normative reading of a text or situation. The response of the rule-governed critic is to devalue that response as aberrant, uneducated, meaningless or destructive. And public examination systems, for example, demonstrate that same normative response in practice. However, given that the tactical reading is an articulation of the subject's perception of their own positioning, an understanding of the tactical response can be an important tool for the analyst in understanding that subject's self-perception, and in making a different perception available to the analyst which reveals the (mainstream) assumptions governing her/his own positioning. Of course, tactical readings often locate non-mainstream elements within texts which the mainstream reading tends to suppress. So, for example, the slash readings of *Star Trek* can be seen as locating a homoerotic element within these texts which is suppressed by the patriarchal discourse they articulate. School truancy or playground misbehaviour might be telling us something critical about the education process – its subject matter, disciplinary practices, student–teacher relationships – if only we are prepared to listen. Queer readings locate the suppression of different gender identities and discourses within and by patriarchal discourse, and begin to elaborate a place for that difference. For gender theorists, an understanding of tactical reading can lead to valuable insights into the ways in which conservative gendering practices are resisted and transformed, which might in turn provide models for the reconceptualisation of gendered relationships and identities.

Summary

Without readers there are no texts; a set of signs without a reader to activate them is a voiceless, meaningless object. Therefore, the ways in which we read texts must be recognised as equally important as the texts themselves in determining the meanings which texts generate. This chapter has dealt in some detail with the ways we have of talking about the ways we read texts. By text, we mean cultural production and communication in all media and genres – including everyday conversation, service encounters, terms of personal address, bureaucratic exchanges, legal documents, historical manuscripts, novels, plays, films, television programmes and so on. With the aid of critical concepts such as 'discourse' and 'genre' which can be used with all these different kinds of text, we explored how a text can operate as both a gendered and an engendering practice. That is, we looked at how texts articulate certain attitudes and values – discourses – about gender, and how they position readers to accept these discourses. We then went on to examine how this positioning of readers takes place and how readers resist that positioning.

Some of the most influential work on reader resistance of textual positioning was seen to originate with the feminist deconstructions of the literary canon. Having challenged normative reading practice in their analysis of the literary canon and its accompanying critique, feminist readers turned their interest to other kinds of text. Their resistance to the engendering practice of texts took several forms: analysis of the discourses articulated in specific texts and genres of text, with particular attention to the gender discourses and their positioning of readers; production of their own texts, based on a resistant reading of more conventional texts and genres; and analysis of conventional (gendered) reading practices, again for how they position (and engender) readers. In each case we looked at examples of these resistant practices and how they have enabled readers to understand how specific texts and genres operate as engendering practices, as well as to generate texts which produce new and different discourses about gender.

Finally we looked at tactical reading, a reading practice characterised by its focus on the reader rather than the text. In tactical reading, the text is the starting point rather than the focus of an analysis which is concerned primarily with articulating the reader's sense of their own positioning. Of course, it might be argued that all reading can be described in this way. However, in tactical reading, little attempt is made to tie this articulation of discourses back to the originary text. Tactical reading is a particularly useful concept for the analyst, as it allows her or him to understand readings which are otherwise inexplicable; which operate neither as mainstream nor resistant readings. Furthermore, because these readings focus on an individual's social self-perception, they provide intriguing insights into how individuals experience the engendering (and other) practices of their society, and how they move beyond those practices in search of new and more satisfying gendered identities and relationships.

Recommended Reading

Cranny-Francis, Anne (1992) *Engendered Fiction: Analysing Gender in the Production and Reception of Texts*, New South Wales University Press, Sydney. (This book has a longer analysis of the transcipted conversation text discussed above.)

Creed, Barbara (1990) 'Alien and the Monstrous-Feminine' in Annette Kuhn (ed.) *Alien Zone: Cultural Theory and Contemporary Science Fiction Cinema*, Verso, London.

de Lauretis, Teresa (1984) *Alice Doesn't: Feminism, Semiotics, Cinema*, Indiana University Press, Bloomington.

de Lauretis, Teresa (1988) *Technologies of Gender: Essays on Theory, Film and Fiction*, Indiana University Press, Bloomington.

Fiske, John (1989) *Understanding Popular Culture*, Hyman Unwin, Boston.

Gilbert, Pam. (1989) 'Stoning the Romance: Girls as Resistant Readers and Writers' in Frances Christie (ed.) *Writing in Schools*, Deakin University Press, Geelong, Victoria, pp. 73–80.

Jenkins, Henry (1991) 'Star Trek Rerun, Reread, Rewritten: Fan Writing as Textual Poaching' in Constance Penley, Elisabeth Lyon, Lynn Spigel, and Janet Bergstrom (eds), *Close Encounters: Film, Feminism, and Science Fiction*, University of Minnesota Press, Minneapolis.

Jenkins, Henry (1992) *Textual Poachers: Television Fans & Participatory Culture*, Routledge, New York.

Sinfield, Alan (1994) *Cultural Politics – Queer Reading*, Pennsylvania University Press, Philadelphia.

Thwaites, Tony, Lloyd, Davis and Mules, Warwick (1994) *Tools for Cultural Studies: An Introduction*, Macmillan Education Australia, South Melbourne.

Zipes, Jack (1983) *The Trials and Tribulations of Little Red Riding Hood: Versions of the Tale in Sociocultural Context*, Heinemann, London.

Zipes, Jack (1986) *Don't Bet on the Prince: Contemporary Feminist Fairy Tales in North America and England*, Gower, Aldershot.

Exercises

1. Apply Kress's questions about discourse to some very different texts: for example an advertisement, a newspaper or magazine article, a poem or a film. What sorts of discourse do you find operating in those texts?

2. Collect an example of conversation – something you overhear and jot down, a taped conversation or something videotaped from a TV or radio chat show. Analyse the discourses operating in this text (as for question 1). Now transcribe all or part of the text, without identifying the participants as female and male. Ask someone else to read the text and try to work out the sex of the speakers, and then explore the expectations which that reader brings to the text.

3. Choose a text from any source and then explore the text generically: locate the genre(s) which structure the text; explore the genre(s) in terms of their social function and meanings (this will require some historical research on the history and development of the genre as well as some contemporary work on the meanings and uses of the genre); finally, relate this research to the specific text in order to understand how the text has made use of the genre(s) in its production of meanings. In the process, pay particular attention to the gendering practice of the genre(s); that is, how they position or construct female subjects.

4. Identify a text which you consider very sexist. Locate the reasons for your judgement, by reference to the discourses operating in the text, the genre(s) used and the meanings it/they carry and so on.

5. Choose a text from any source and then perform a number of different readings of the text, focused around issues of gender. Your readings might include a mainstream reading, a resistant reading, a tactical reading and a queer reading. How do you need to shift your own reading position or perspective in order to make these different readings?

6. Try rewriting a popular story – perhaps a fairy tale – by changing the gendering practice of the text (which might mean changing characters in particular ways and/or changing the ways in which characters act and interact). Try the same thing with a newspaper article. What does this tell you about how texts work as gendering practices?

Note

1. This conversation text was supplied by linguist Cate Poynton, from a class exercise, with permission of the student.

4

Ways of Seeing

In Chapter 3, we introduced you to some tools and concepts which we hope will allow you think about how texts make meanings and how you make meanings generally. In this chapter, we will take that analysis further by looking at how seeing, in particular, is caught up with producing identities and meanings. We will focus on reading fashion photographs and film, and on the way reading visual material is caught up in visual pleasures which structure the social and subjective psyche. We also look at the idea of performing gender, and examine some of the terms which are important to thinking about how people have treated gender as something to be staged. We begin this chapter on ways of seeing by looking at stereotypes – how they function, how they can be resisted – and how this way of seeing is one which is still operating in the fabric of daily life.

In John Berger's book *Ways of Seeing* (1972) he wrote:

> Men act and women appear. Men look at women. Women watch themselves being looked at. This determines not only most relations between men and women but also the relation of women to themselves. The survey of woman herself is male: the surveyed female. Thus she turns herself into an object – and most particularly an object of vision: a sight. (p. 47)

In this chapter we will look closely at the question of representation, paying particular attention to the visual register. We will be looking at the ways we see, and the ways we see others and others see us, from within the frameworks of gender. Some of the major issues we will be dealing with are the processes of stereotyping; the formation of identification and desire through seeing; the processes of looking at cultural texts such as fashion magazines, photography and films; and the question of gender as a performance or masquerade.

For the second-wave feminists of the early 1970s, the politics surrounding images of women were extremely important. It was through a politics of changing representations that many second-wave feminists felt the lot of women could be changed. If women were no longer seen as objects, if they could control the images made of them, or even make their own images, then they believed that they could be liberated from the cages to which oppressive images consigned them. Yet it soon became apparent that getting a clear picture of woman was not as easy as it initially sounded. For one thing, the one-to-one correspondence between images and social structures did not seem to correspond to practice. Nor did it always turn out to be the case that images produced by women were free from what viewers might interpret as sexism. The same issues that came up in the discussion of reading as a woman in Chapter 3 could be raised here, in relation to seeing as a woman. The politics of gender and vision are complex.

Stereotypes

The word 'stereotype' comes to us from the technology of printing presses, where it refers to the metal plates used to make exact and multiple copies. Before stereotyping was used, printers had to set each letter one at a time, line by line, in big wooden frames. These forms could be changed, and the letters reused for other publications. A stereotype is a poured metal plate, and once the metal is poured, the plate can't be changed. Before the digital age, the newspapers that thousands of households received every morning were made from stereotypes. The origin of the word in this description of its technology tells us a great deal about what a stereotype is when ascribed to people. It is fixed, and can't be changed. It is used to produce multiple copies of the same thing, over and over again. It is a visual metaphor, which reminds us that when a stereotype is applied to a person, it is frequently done so on the basis of their appearance.

Stereotypes function by simplifying, by reducing classes of people to a few characteristics by which they are generally said to be identifiable. The easiest way to think about this might be to return to the public toilet doors we invoked in the first chapter. The reasons the icons on the toilet doors function – a woman in a skirt/a man with trousers – is that it is assumed there is a visible and identifiable difference between men and women. In this example, the skirt is standing in for the secondary sex characteristics (breasts and sexual organs) that are usually invoked as the obvious indications of difference between men and women. These visual differences which can be detected in groups of people and are said to be natural (for example race, gender) are then yoked to a few simple characteristics or types of behaviour. In a vicious circle, the visual differences then serve as proof for the reductive character profile. Through several structural mechanisms (science, medical research, economic structures), the sight of difference and the meanings of difference are welded together and serve to support each other. Such a process generally happens from outside the group in question, although people from stereotyped groups can be involved in the maintenance of stereotypes.

A stereotype is a radically reductive way of representing whole communities of people by identifying them with a few key characteristics. Individuals from the group who don't fit that stereotype are then said to be atypical.

Stereotypes permit people to immediately recognise and classify others by processing a few simple visual clues – whether they are dark skin or long hair. It is important to the smooth functioning of stereotyping that these clues be unambiguous. And if, as you yourself may have noticed, the stereotypes are often inaccurate, it is because they are usually produced from outside the group in question: limited knowledge and restricted contact enable the extremely simple character profiles to be produced in the first place. Moreover, one person cannot produce and circulate a stereotype all alone; stereotypes function within groups of people as knowledge which is shared, a kind of cultural databank. Importantly, they are usually produced by people who are positioned to circulate their ideas widely, so that even the group stereotyped may then come to take on this simplified bit of visual shorthand as a kind of fact (Perkins 1979). Using stereotypes short-circuits critical thinking; how effective a stereotype is depends on the willingness of the cultures using it to take the short cut that stereotyping involves.

Not only does stereotyping categorise groups of people according to natural, highly simplified or reductive characteristics, it also employs a mechanism of separation. Stuart Hall calls this a 'strategy of "splitting"' (1996a, p. 258). What this means is that the process of stereotyping doesn't just use visual clues welded (naturally of course) to cultural characteristics to distinguish one group from another; it also divides the normal from the abnormal, the acceptable from the unacceptable. Stereotypes exclude or reject everything which falls out of its definitions, everything which is different. It sets up symbolic boundaries and then provides the mechanisms of cultural production for people to police those boundaries. People use stereotypes to determine who should naturally belong to one group or another. Hall writes:

> Stereotyping … is part of the maintenance of social and symbolic order. It sets up a symbolic frontier between the 'normal' and the 'deviant', the 'normal' and the 'pathological', the 'acceptable' and the 'unacceptable', what 'belongs' and what does not or is 'Other', between 'insiders' and 'outsiders', Us and Them.' (1996a, p. 258)

A stereotype is a political practice that divides the world into like and unlike, self and other.

Inequalities of Power and Access

If these natural visible differences which divide people into one category or another only served as a harmless cultural shorthand, then it is unlikely that books on gender or race would be particularly interested in them. However, the final attribute of stereotyping that we will discuss is its relationship to the maintenance of certain relations of power. As we mentioned above, one group, which doesn't have much contact with the group it stereotypes, constructs a stereotype and circulates it, partly in order to maintain its own access to power. And the first kind of power to which constructing a stereotype provides access is, in fact, the power to name. Already the fact of creating and widely circulating a stereotype means that one group has the power to circumscribe the other – how it will be seen, how it will see itself.

Joined to this power of naming are structural forms of power that maintain stereotypes in relation to the major groups which suffer this kind of representational violence in our societies – blacks, women, gays and others. A stereotype, because it rests on the assumption of a natural and visual difference, hides the operation of inequalities in power distribution – the racist stereotype of black men being less intellectually capable explains the fact that there are so few black CEOs in companies; they are seen as naturally unsuited to such positions. The mechanisms of exclusion which have worked to keep them out of the schools and networks which might position them to take on such roles are thus hidden from view. Laws, traditions and institutions structurally support stereotypes; stereotypes enable institutions and laws to continue to function and maintain themselves.

Stereotypes apply not only to marginalised groups but to all groups. While marginalised groups receive negative stereotypes; powerful groups are endowed with positive stereotypes. Thus the stereotype of a white professional man may be that he is intelligent – clever rather than an intellectual – and reasoned, reasonable and cool, unlikely to show emotion. If a white, able-bodied, middle-class man does not fit this stereotype, he may indeed come in for some serious criticism. In this way, such positive stereotypes function as the norm, while at the same time securing access to power for those who fulfil them. Understanding how stereotypes around masculinity or whiteness or being able-bodied function is just as revealing as understanding how negative stereotypes operate.

Stereotypes conceal the operation of power within society by characterising inequalities as natural differences of ability or inclination.

Examples of Stereotypes

Let us look now at a few examples of common stereotypes and how they illustrate the points that have been made about stereotyping so far. Black men and women are generally associated with primitiveness, which translates into several characteristics – a heightened sexuality (although diminished potency in black men), brute force or strength, aggressiveness and a diminished capacity for rational thought. These stereotypes developed during the period of European imperialist colonialism. As European countries such as England, France, Belgium, the Netherlands, Spain and Germany explored the New World (North, Central and South America), the empty land of Australia, exotic Asia and the dark continent of Africa, frequently dispossessing the indigenous inhabitants as they moved through, they developed a number of stereotypes to bolster and legitimise their activities. They convinced themselves that black peoples were naturally less intelligent, less rational, more aggressive, more sexually active and so on than they were. Skin colour was linked to cultural characteristics which permitted the horrors of imperialism to be perpetrated – plantation slavery, widespread territorial dispossession and genocide. In the nineteenth century, as the sun was setting on several European empires, European science's attempt to prove the validity of its stereotypes mounted into a kind of frenzy. Medical research undertook to measure various parts of the bodies of black people – the size of their brains, their sexual organs and so on – to prove that they were all that Europeans claimed them to be – primitive, aggressive, irrational and undeveloped.

Such stereotypes continue to function today, reinforcing the structures that position most black people in the labour market as unskilled workers. Nor has the attempt to prove that physical and racial characteristics will naturally produce cultural effects ceased. For example, it is currently found in a great deal of the popular reporting on genetic research. We can see that the stereotype of black primitiveness follows the general lines of the functioning of stereotypes which we outlined above. It provides a short cut in thinking – black = primitive. It associates a natural and visible marker with a cultural construction, and it functions in conjunction with institutions, laws and traditions (for example plantation slavery, apartheid, Jim Crow laws (legislated segregation), labour market segmentation and so on).

Let's go on to look at a gender stereotype, before looking at a few specific examples of stereotypes in action. Women have come to be seen as naturally nurturing, sensitive, emotional and deferring. The fact that women have a womb is linked to these characteristics. Women are seen to be natural mothers, in the sense that by having a womb they also are possessed with patience, a natural predisposition towards children, a nurturing, affectionate nature and so on. The womb also predisposes women to madness, according to a certain stereotype; to be a woman, visibly, physically, is to be predisposed to a heightened emotional nature which can turn to madness. Indeed, the word 'hysteria', which has always been seen by the medical and psychiatric professions as a woman's disease, comes from the Greek word for 'uterus'.

The overrepresentation of women as mentally ill is a phenomenon that gender analysts have studied extensively (Showalter 1985b; Smith-Rosenberg 1972). For example, in her book *The Female Malady: Women, Madness and English Culture, 1830–1980*, Elaine Showalter (1985b) documents in great detail the way notions of gender influence the definition and treatment of mental disorder, in particular the construction of madness as a female malady. She examines the representation of the madwoman in legal, medical and literary texts, and in painting, photography and film, seeing these images as 'part of the fundamental cultural framework in which ideas about femininity and insanity were constructed' (p. 5). She examines three historical phases of English psychiatry and culture: psychiatric Victorianism in which public asylums were filled predominantly with women in the hopes that 'homelike mental institutions' would both 'house feminine irrationality but also ... cure it through paternalistic therapeutic and administrative techniques' (p. 17); psychiatric Darwinism during which 'the female nervous disorders of anorexia nervosa, hysteria, and neurasthenia became epidemic' – at precisely the time when middle-class women were beginning to organise for 'higher education, entrance to the professions, and political rights' (p. 18); and third, psychiatric modernism during which the World War I brought 'the urgent necessity of treating thousands of shell-shocked soldiers – male hysterics' (p. 19).

The natural association of women with characteristics such as madness, irrationality, nurturing and natural sensitivity is structurally reinforced by medical and psychiatric institutions (as we have seen above), but also by economic structures which look at women as a reserve pool of labour. Ensconced in the home, they are naturally happy raising their children and providing a soothing environment for their husbands who are out being buffeted by the rigours of the world of work. At the same time, they can be held in reserve for labour in the modern workforce. The period around World War II is quite interesting for the way it mobilised and demobilised certain stereotypes around women's natural capabilities for work. During the war, when large numbers of able-bodied working-class men had been drafted into the armed forces, women were induced to work in munitions and other factories. The poster girl 'Rosie the Riveter' – an attractive young woman, hair tied back in a bandana, engaged in manual factory work – encouraged women to work in the factories.

The trend of women working outside the home had already begun before the war, but increased during this period. However, after the war, when significant numbers of men returned to the workplace, a great deal of propaganda took up the stereotype of the nurturing mother, the happy housewife, in order to encourage women to leave the public realm and return to private, domestic bliss. Such propaganda (posters, films and articles in newspapers) is largely responsible for the picture that we have of women in the 1950s. Mrs June Cleaver, the aproned mother in the television show *Leave it to Beaver*, (USA 1960s) was more wish fulfilment on the part of industrialists and government officials trying to control labour flows, than a representation of the actual state of affairs. This example illustrates the boundary-policing activities of the functioning of stereotypes.

Against the way women are stereotyped as emotional, men are seen as removed, rational and authoritative. In keeping with the second point we noted about stereotyping, that it polices rigid boundaries, we might consider some stereotypes of white middle-class masculinity. Some of the effects of masculine stereotyping, which constructs men as all-powerful, emotionless and authoritarian, include higher levels of suicide, drug and alcohol abuse and addiction. Many men experience the stereotype of Superman as a kind of prison or poison (Horrocks 1994, p. 145). This prison is difficult to escape and stereotypes of men who don't fit into the categories help to police those boundaries. Take the stereotype of the male buffoon. A man who does not fit in with the emotionless and authoritative hypermasculine stereotype is a figure to be mocked, and the process of laughing at wimps admonishes men to make sure they stick to the straight and narrow of masculinity. Among the popular figures who play with these strictures of masculinity are John Cleese's portrayal of Basil Fawlty in *Fawlty Towers* or Rowan Atkinson's *Mr Bean* in contemporary British TV comedy. In the USA, Jerry Lewis and Woody Allen made the emasculated buffoon a comedy art form. Woody Allen put it succinctly when he announced: 'I'm the only man I know with penis envy' (quoted in Horrocks, 1994, p. 149). These caricatures function to mark the uneasiness around the failure of stereotypes successfully to herd white men into the strong, silent type.

Stereotypes in Conflict

Of course, having conjured up briefly a few stereotypes with which we are quite familiar – the nurturing, emotional woman and the primitive black person – now it will be useful to look at the way that some stereotypes continue to operate, even when they are blatantly contradictory. Black women, for example, are enlisted under the nurturing, naturally caretaking characteristics of the stereotype for woman but also are associated with primitive brute strength through the stereotypes of racism. How to reconcile that a black woman can be both naturally suited to working in the fields (or a similar urban equivalent – industrial cleaning) and, at the same time, warm and nurturing, the Aunt Jemima stereotype who fixes hot breakfasts for sleepy children? We have already mentioned that stereotyping in fact short-circuits critical thinking. It is entirely possible for the media, the courts or cultural institutions to use two contradictory stereotypes simultaneously, because of the short cuts in thinking which stereotyping represents. Moreover, keep in mind that stereotypes are usually maintained and developed by people who have little contact with the group being stereotyped; this makes it easy for contradictory stereotypes to operate simultaneously. It does not, however, make it easy for people to live inside those simultaneously contradictory stereotypes.

> Different stereotypes applied to a particular social group or community may attribute to them conflicting characteristics. This apparent contradiction reveals the fact that stereotypes are (a) generated by those outside the group and (b) are part of a political strategy for managing that group or community.

Equally important is the point that many theorists of masculinity have made, such as Fred Pfeil (1995) in *White Guys: Studies in Postmodern Domination and Difference*, and that is that challenging the monolithic positive stereotypes applied to white men as a homogeneous group can reveal many of the contradictions at the heart of ideas of patriarchal masculinity, or beliefs in racial superiority.

The Ormond College Case

Cases of sexual harassment cause intense media anxiety, unleashing powerful if contradictory stereotypes regarding appropriate gender behaviour for women. In a case of sexual harassment in Australia, in which two residential women students successfully brought a case of sexual harassment against the Master of Ormond College, the media displayed a volatile mix of stereotypes to report the affair. The young women were stereotyped as seductresses, man-hating harpies, bitches, monsters, feminazis, Furies, lesbians and victims; the women who supported them were feminist ideologues, feminist conspirators and Puritan feminists. The issue of sexual harassment almost disappeared. Media representations of the young women became so vitriolic that one of the newspapers implicated in the coverage published an editorial to the effect that it was little wonder that the young women wished to remain anonymous (Mead 1997, p. 28). Later, one of the young women wrote in *Bodyjamming* that:

> During the height of media interest I watched the stories and misrepresentations unfold with horrified fascination ... I had somehow contrived to become simul-

taneously frigid, slutty, lesbian, sexually irresistible, terrifying, puritanical, man-hating, vengeful victim. (Mead 1997, p. 54)

It was altogether, she writes, 'a frightening portrait of young, powerful women capable of destroying innocent men's lives in the wake of their evil pursuit of vengeful feminism' (p. 56). She concluded from the media representation that 'The message was that women who make a fuss are dangerous. University educated women are dangerous' (p. 58). The point here is that stereotypes, even collections of contradictory stereotypes, attempt to police people into adopting certain behaviours.

The Hill/Thomas Case

The importance and function of stereotype in the playing out of social reality was also dramatically illustrated in the Anita Hill/Clarence Thomas affair (see Morrison 1993a for an excellent collection of essays). In 1991, George Bush Senior, the US President, nominated Clarence Thomas, a conservative black judge, to the Supreme Court. A black woman law professor challenged the presidential decision and brought forward allegations of sexual harassment against Clarence Thomas. In the US Senate hearings, which were broadcast on national television, the deployment of powerful racial and gendered stereotypes substantively contributed to the outcome of the hearings – including the ratification of Thomas's appointment to the Supreme Court and the disempowerment of Anita Hill by the Senate, the White House and the popular press. There were many doubts as to Clarence Thomas's qualifications and suitability for the position. He had consistently demonstrated his lack of perception and sympathy regarding systemic discrimination and its impact on the lives of black men and women in the United States, including that of his own sister, whom Thomas had earlier publicly castigated as a 'Welfare Queen'. When he was chairman of the Equal Employment Opportunity Commission, he refused to enforce anti-discrimination laws and publicly opposed affirmative-action programmes.

Despite his disdain for affirmative action, in the Senate hearings that occurred to test the importance of Anita Hill's allegations, Thomas asserted that he had become the victim of a high-tech lynching, thus shifting the subject of inquiry from sexual harassment to racial victimage. Thomas, who considered his adversaries to be white feminists and black civil rights advocates whining about racist oppression, told the Senate that he had become 'the victim of a high-tech lynching'. (The intensive national TV coverage could indeed lead one to believe in a high-tech lynching but, given the outcome, the victim ended up to be Hill, not Thomas.) In this scenario, Anita Hill became a woman who was in league with white men and women to persecute

Thomas (Painter 1993, p. 208). Because of the power of stereotyping, its functions in policing and simplifying identity categories, both black and white audiences found it difficult to comprehend Hill's identity as a highly educated, ambitious, black, female Republican. While Thomas was able to adopt the figure of the southern black lynch victim, Anita Hill had, in Painter's words:

> no comparable tradition of a stereotype that had been recognised, analysed, and subverted to draw upon ... Mammy, welfare cheat, Jezebel, period. These were the roles available to Anita Hill. (1993, p. 210)

And none of these stereotypes had undergone a sufficient questioning to offer an alternative stereotype to 'Black Lady', 'Welfare Queen' or 'Jezebel' for Hill to use to attempt to mobilise media support. As Wahneema Lubiano points out, few people would have been persuaded by Thomas the corrupt judge or bigot, but

> for Thomas the Black male victim of 'Sapphire' – Black female emasculator and betrayer of Black men and carrier of Black family pathology – well, the African American legions would and did rise to battle, against her. (1993, p. 345)

The existence of those stereotypes – black lady and welfare queen – literally saved Thomas's name and his nomination to the Supreme Court.

Resisting Stereotypes

What is evident from the discussion thus far is that contesting stereotypes is not easy. But it is tempting to do so, for different stereotypes inscribe different levels of access to power and prestige. It is obvious that a group which is trying to change its structural position within society will focus on stereotypes as a point of protest about the status quo and its own position. Some groups might be tempted to try to reverse a stereotype, or to take on the opposite groups positive stereotype. This would be the case, for example, of the white professional woman trying to break the glass ceiling by adopting the stereotype of the white male professional. Several recent films take on this subject.

Stereotype Reversal

In the 1993 erotic thriller *The Last Seduction*, Bridget Gregory (played by Linda Fiorentino) is a superwoman executive who plays all situations to her own financial and sexual advantage. She is a master of seduction who uses men as sexual objects to fulfil her voracious desire. In this film it is the men who complain that 'we never talk' and whine about communication and meaning. Bridget is completely successful; she secures all the money from the drug deal which she organised in which her husband almost lost his life, she manipulates her lover to murder her husband (although she finally has to do the deed because he is too squeamish) and frames her lover for her husband's murder. She gets away with murder, leaving all the men utterly confounded. Unfortunately, the reversed stereotypes (the masculine woman, the predatory woman and the career woman) play into the stereotype that women who attempt to enter the male bastion of the business world are threats to civilised society. Each positive stereotype carries with it complementary stereotypes which are dependent on essential characteristics. If someone tries to break one stereotype, another related stereotype quickly becomes available. This is what happens in the discussion above, where people have tried to break the bond between certain groups' essential natures and their characters. So, in this example, a woman should be nurturing. Instead she is ruthless. When she acquires the positive characteristic of the businessman (after all, when applied to him, it permits him access to wealth and power), it becomes negative. Moreover, she no longer has access to the limited benefits of her positive stereotype as nurturing female. She is doubly damned.

The penalties for trying to challenge stereotypes include recuperation into this double negative net of stereotypes. Or, when periods of change create the conditions for the radical challenging of stereotypes, new stereotypes are sometimes created in an attempt to contain social movements and the change they herald. We can see this in the hysteria generated by the idea of political correctness – which itself has become a stereotype signalling that feminists (or blacks, lesbians or Asians … insert appropriate noun here) have gone too far. The denigration of political correctness is an attempt by a dominant group to silence an oppressed group's attempt to change its social status and counter the negative stereotypes which contribute to its oppression – the name-calling, stereotyping, shunning and moral pressure that kept women, wogs and weirdos in their place. As Meaghan Morris (1997) points out in 'Sticks and Stones and Stereotypes', even the idea that there is a coherent politically correct movement – a visible group of people who stomp on every expression of what they see as prejudice – is a stereotype. It short-circuits critical thinking, and enables the dominant group to reaffirm rather than rethink its stereotypes about oppressed groups. Penalties for contesting stereotypes can go beyond the production of more stereotypes. The laws, traditions and institutions which maintain stereotypes can step in and put a halt to any tampering with the status quo.

When the Australian edition of *New Woman* first appeared on newsstands in 1990, it promised to challenge the traditional women's magazine mix of diets, man-catching and beauty tips. However, when editor Cyndi Tebbel featured a size 16 model on the cover of *New Woman* in April/May 1997, and ran anti-dieting articles, advertisers were upset. In an interview, Tebbel stated that her decision to use the attractive but far from skeletal Ms Aronson on the cover 'so alarmed advertisers' that they began to voice concern about 'the direction of *New Woman*. There was a real fear that *New Woman* would now be known as "the fat woman's magazine"' (*Sydney Morning Herald* 1997). Ms Kirsten Burgoyne, spokesman for the Sydney marketing consultancy Desire Brand Management, said that cosmetic advertising was designed to be 'aspi-rational' because 'that's what everyday women want' (*Sydney Morning Herald* 1997). Tebbel was advised to look at more 'how to find a man and keep him stories', which she found objectionable in the light of the positive feedback she received from the 'big issue'. As a result of her anti-stereotype efforts, editor Cyndi Tebbel was soon out of a job.

One final possibility for contesting a stereotyped 'regime of representation', as Stuart Hall calls it, is through parody, or irony. By creating a new image which tries to play games with the stereotype itself, but from within the context of a social movement, sometimes a new content is created (Hall 1996a, pp. 269–73). An example here might be the way some lesbians have appro-priated the image and demeanour of the popular television personality of *Zena Warrior Princess* (US) and her sidekick and close friend Gabrielle.

This section has dealt extensively with processes whereby stereotypes are produced and reproduced, and has outlined some of the issues raised by attempts to resist stereotyping. If the options for resisting stereotypes do not seem very promising, perhaps it is time to look at some other ways that people acquire images of themselves. In the next section, we will be exam-ining how the visual intersects with the process of subject formation. How do seeing and subjectivity connect? Stereotyping seems to be a process which assaults the subject with an image produced in the social realm. However, not all the ways we have of seeing ourselves are produced at such a distance. Sometimes seeing others and others seeing us is an intimate aspect of how we become who we are. Stuart Hall made the point that stereotyping involved a strategy of splitting, a process of internalising the normal and abnormal, lodging within us social boundaries at a psychic level. How does this process of splitting work? How do we effectively 'other' ourselves? What do we need to know about the processes of identifying with images on a more intimate psychosocial level?

Identification

In this section we will elaborate some of the Freudian-derived theories on identification we introduced in Chapter 2. The process of identification is not the same thing as having an identity. Theorists such as Diana Fuss (1995), for example, would argue that not only do we have an identity, something rather fixed, but that we are also constantly caught up in processes of identification, of negotiating our relations to others and our selves, a movement which starts with our earliest childhood experiences.

> Identification is a process of constant negotiation between self and other, inside and outside, between our unconscious desires for Others (to have and be like them) and cultural and social demands; it threatens to unseat our stable sense of self.

Freudian psychoanalysis provides feminist and gender analysts with other frameworks for thinking about the processes whereby we integrate images into our identities and our desires. For Freud, and the theorists who have taken up his work, such as Julia Kristeva, Jacques Lacan and Melanie Klein, the pleasure of looking, what is called 'scopophilia', is key to who we are and how and who we love. It is part of the process of both identification and libidinal structures. Forms of scopophilia, these writers argue, continue to structure how we work, how we make art and how we make friends, long after childhood is over and we are adults.

> Scopophilia is defined as the pleasure derived from looking. This concept can be used to explore the desires of individuals and whole communities by identifying and analysing their presentation of what is desirable to look at – their scopic regimes.

To look at how Freudian-derived theories of identification are useful to gender analysis, we will discuss some of the basic terminology associated with this area of Freudian speculation on the formation of identity. We have discussed Freud's idea of the Oedipus complex in Chapter 2, and you may want to return to it to refresh your memory of that topic. Along with the narrative of the Oedipus complex, through which every child passed, Freud posited that children went through different stages of libidinal development, that is, children focus their love and desires and wants in different ways at different stages of their development. They are the anal phase, the oral phase, the phallic stage, the latent stage and the genital stage. Just as children went through various stages of libidinal development before arriving at the genital stage, at the same time they shifted the focus of their desires – from autoeroticism in infancy before the id/ego is formed, through to a narcissistic love object, followed by either the homosexual choice, or the heterosexual one. This shifting from autoeroticism to a love object is very much caught up in visual pleasure.

Narcissism

First we must recall the ancient Greek myth of Narcissus. In almost all versions of the myth, Narcissus was a beautiful young man who spurned the sexual love of others and died as a result. In the Roman poet Ovid's retelling of the myth, many nymphs and girls fell in love with Narcissus but he rejected them. Echo, one of these nymphs, was so distraught over this rejection that she withdrew into a lonely spot and faded until all that was left was a plaintive whisper. The goddess Nemesis heard her prayers for vengeance and arranged for Narcissus to fall in love with his own reflection. He stayed watching his reflection and gradually died.

Freud believed that different forms of narcissism, of self-love, were key in the trajectory which children followed when becoming subjects. For Freud, different things could go wrong on the road to this visual development of object love, resulting in various kinds of perversity – voyeurism, narcissism, and fetishism. You may recall from the discussion in Chapter 2, how Freud imagined the libido (that is, psychic and sexual energy) through a hydraulic metaphor, and talked about it in terms of it flowing from one place to another. It could get dammed up, or diverted down a strange channel. A healthy person turns his or her libido outwards; in narcissism, there is a damming up of libidinal energies. For Freud, deriving pleasure from looking becomes part of the drive formation of the subject; the subject's self-awareness of looking becomes part of the drive. Freud posited the idea of primary narcissism as a primitive state characterised by the total absence of any relation to the outside world, in which there is no differentiation between the id (sexual instinct) and the ego, and for which intrauterine existence, that is, life in the womb, is the model. In other words, primary narcissism is an infant fully turned in on itself, and turning all its desiring energies onto itself. Eruptions of this infantile self-regarding narcissism structure our culture's visual organisation of gender.

Because this particular kind of blocked-up desire, this perversion, is so taken up with the visual, it will be useful for us to have a closer look at it. Equally important to note, is that narcissism, the stage in which the subject has not yet moved to an object choice, is said to be typical of women – once again, women are coded as being naturally perverse. The stalled development of self-love that is narcissism has been linked by some to the various shopping disorders that seem to plague only women, for example kleptomania and compulsive buying habits (Nava 1992; Camri 1993; Lieberman 1993; Reekie 1993; Kaplan 1997). A part of these arguments suggest that the pleasure to be had from the endlessly repeating images of the shopper which the omnipresent mirrors and plate-glass windows of shopping malls and high-class shops provide is a perverse one, to which women in particular are drawn, because they often have difficulty traversing the psychic terrain which leads to normal heterosexuality. Given what we have discussed about the coerciveness of heterosexuality under patriarchal structures, it is no surprise that some analysts, such as Louise Kaplan in *Female Perversions*, conclude that:

> every perverse scenario is intimately related to the social and economic structures of our westernised industrial societies [and] the social gender stereotypes that are expressed in the perversions ... are the reflections of those structures. (1997, p. 523)

Other aspects of consumption are associated with narcissism and stalled development. The endless repetition and reliability of brand-name goods can be linked to a buried fantasy of the full and plentiful maternal object who never refuses any demand – an image introjected in infancy and not quite dislodged. Or perhaps we might see in the beautiful showiness of packaging the recovery of that complete, original ideal. Although it might seem absurd to connect the pleasures of consumption with psychological processes, it goes some way to explaining why some people continue to shop and consume in ways that have little to do with provisioning the family cupboards. Or it may demonstrate why understanding the social framework for particular acts that have negative consequences can be improved and changed through an understanding of the psychological and unconscious motivations for certain behaviour.

We have looked closely at one particular stop in the forms and routes the libido takes, its libidinal economy (economy means something like structure here), to give a sense of how important the visual register is to Freudian theories of subjectivity. We would like to go a little further now, and look at how visual metaphors are used in two theories of the development of the subject. We haven't picked just any two theories: these two writers are particularly interested in the ways in which the relationship between the Self and the Other develops, and their theories both rely on seeing. We will be looking at Melanie Klein's work on introjection and projection, and looking more closely at Lacan's idea of the mirror stage. (This idea was introduced in Chapter 2.)

For Freud, narcissism is a stage in infancy before one's affections turn out towards external objects (like parents). This inward-gazing self-love allows us to develop a healthy self-image. However, a narcissistic adult fails to recognise the difference between self and the world.

The Other in the Self

This process of internalising external relationships, of embedding images of Others into the Self in formation is prominent in the work of psychoanalyst Melanie Klein (1963, 1975a, 1975b). Klein conducted analysis with very young children, devising a play technique in which the child was able to express the primitive and aggressive material behind his or her disturbance. From this work, Klein gained insight into earlier stages of development than those considered by Freud; she argued the pre-Oedipal importance of the mother to the development of the fantasy life of the infant.

Klein's babies are aggressive little creatures who both envy the mother and want to harm her and rob her body of its contents. The aggressive impulses of the infant lead to a fear that the mother will retaliate – a fear which is internalised as a vengeful superego. The task for the child is to learn to distinguish the internalised image of the mother and his or her actual relation to the mother. This very early relation becomes the model of all other relations as the child learns to distinguish between the inner and outer worlds. This image of others – or 'imago' as it is also known – becomes important to the way the subject has of understanding others and it is built up through the real and fantasised relationships that the subject has within the family environment.

Introjection and Projection

Klein emphasised two processes – introjection and projection. Introjection is the fantasy in which the subject transposes objects and their qualities from outside to the inside of the self by modelling their behaviour, incorporating them, or identifying with them. Projection is where qualities or feelings which the subject refuses to recognise in himself or herself are pushed outside the self and projected onto other persons or objects. Although this description may seem technical, such processes are encountered in everyday life. If someone reacts unnecessarily harshly to a suggestion we make – about fixing a car, or cooking a dish – we may say that they are 'projecting' on to us; they're screening an unresolved and internal conflict with a parent or sibling onto our relations with them.

How is this work relevant to our exploration of selfhood and identification? If we follow Diana Fuss's notion that identification is 'a question of *relation*, of self to other, subject to object, inside to outside' (1995, pp. 2–3), then the relevance of these concepts can be seen. Unlike other ideas about the constitution of identity such as role modelling, this notion of identification suggests that the process of incorporating or *introjecting* a certain relationship is not one which brings into the self a perfect and complete model – the process of introjection and projection is always unfinished business, and the child become adult is always repeating the process of identification. Thus, it is not the same as stereotyping, which produces fixed characteristics which are associated with natural essences. The process of identification is something which will depend on who we meet, what our culture is, what our history is. It will depend on our unfinished business with our mother, or even traumatic moments that happened so long ago in infancy we cannot call them up in conscious memory. Such an idea of identification is a good deal less assured.

Lacan and the Mirror Stage

The way that Lacan integrates the visual register into his own version of the process of subject formation is also interesting. We discussed in Chapter 2 how the story of Oedipus that Lacan develops includes a mirror stage: sometime between the ages of 6–18 months, the infant develops a fantasy of its own wholeness, its own unity. It is able to do this by recognising its own image in a mirror or through an outside relation with someone (usually a carer such as its mother).

> The mirror stage is the stage at which the infant develops a fantasy that it is a unified and complete whole, separate from the rest of the world.

This is when the concept of an I, an ego, a sense of self-awareness is formed. This process seems very close to Klein's idea of incorporation. The 'Other' which becomes part of the new subject is not just an image of the carer, but a fantasised idea about the self, which the infant imagines as perfect and omnipotent (which is how babies imagine their carers in the early months). The little person then misidentifies the 'Other' – that which has been incorporated through the mirror stage as the object of desire. It falls in love with a fantasy of itself/its other. In other words, in order for the ego to be a subject, it must internalise a principle of otherness as a consequence of its own desire to desire.

Narcissistic pleasure can also be understood through the concept of the mirror stage from Lacanian psychoanalysis. A child forms her or his ego by identifying with the perfect mirror image. According to this psychoanalytic idea, looking and knowing that you might be looked at (to-be-looked-at-ness) originates outside the child in something that is obviously other. In looking at something, whether it be an apple, a film or a man, the looker is stitched or sutured to the image. In the Lacanian model, there is a struggle between looking and being looked at; the gaze splits us. While it would seem that the one who looks is in control of the situation, all of us depend on being looked at and acknowledged in order to exist. The gaze involves power and the contesting of positions to determine who has the right to look, the right of inspection and who is to be looked at.

Lacan emphasises that just as humans are inserted into systems of language and discourse that precede their existence, so they are inserted into systems of representation, fields of visuality, which influence their perceiving.

In that sense, what we look at looks back at us. Film and visual theorists have adopted and politicised these insights, pointing out that in Western society to be looked at has generally been the fate of women, while the act of looking has been associated with men.

Why pause over such seemingly arcane speculations? Because it may help us in understanding the relationship between gendered subjectivity and the visual. To put it more simply: Why do women read fashion magazines? Why do they buy *Vogue* or *Gloss*? Shouldn't the analysis of the social implications of the beauty industry have removed these pleasures from them? Perhaps trying to understand the social unconscious will provide some explanations.

Fashion Photography and Sexuality

If readers of fashion photography know consciously that they can't have Elle's perfect body, then what pushes them to continue flipping the pages of the magazines? Is it the compensation of the luxury items that accompany the woman in the photo ('I can't have the body, I'll take those gorgeous red boots!') Are we making up for some loss – in identity, in the fantasy of power? The loss we might be trying to remedy would be, in Freud's terms, a penis; for Lacan, it's the phallus. Could the unconscious processes of Oedipus at work? Perhaps this is why commodity fetishism functions so effectively.

One of the questions that has fascinated cultural analysts is that of why women enjoy looking at the high fashion photographic images of other women. Is it a question of aspiration? Are they identifying with these women? Or is it a question of repressed desire? When women gaze at these images in a voyeuristic fashion, are they looking as lesbians? Of course, it seems likely that the fashion industry would prefer that women look as straight women – the industry would probably sell more products if they did. But it is still a conundrum. What kind of relationship is produced when women gaze at high fashion photos? Does fashion photography provide an image and a socially acceptable activity which provides for its audience not an object of desire, but rather a subject to emulate? And if this kind of role modelling has been roundly criticised for making people slaves to consumerism and dangerous beauty practices, why do perfectly intelligent women still snap up their magazine as they leave the checkout counter at their local supermarket?

What if the operation of identification between viewer and representation had more in common with the tenuous one we discussed above in relation to Lacan and Klein? Perhaps it is not a case of emulation, but rather a kind of disturbing fascination. This is one option that has been discussed with relation to fashion photography (see Fuss 1992 for a full discussion of these arguments). It may be that the kinds of image that fashion photography produces remind us of stages in the Oedipal journey. Our fascination may come from an early moment where the infant experiences the body as fragmented. Perhaps the headless torsos, long gloved arms, truncated hands modelling red nail polish, or close-ups of beautifully sculpted faces re-image the body image of the infant, its amorphous and polymorphously perverse self. Before the Oedipus complex begins, the infant has no sense of the boundaries of its body; it thinks the mother's breast is part of it, but somehow becomes detached from time to time. We might imagine that a hidden pleasure of some of these photographs is a reminder of those polymorphously perverse moments in infancy, before we take the route which has us discovering that mother is lacking, she's missing a penis, and we daughters might just as well have a baby to make up for it all. Thus these photographs would serve as a reminder to the woman who looks at them of her fetishisation, of the disavowal of her mother's castration, of the mother's fall from grace, from power.

But perhaps these perfect images are not there for women to emulate, but rather to draw from us a little shiver, a moment of hesitation. The sight of so many close-ups of women's faces recalls the mirror stage, well after we have passed through it, and the moment of loss of unity that it conjures up. There in the gauzy perfection of the woman from Elizabeth Arden or L'Oréal, her face framed by perfect colour, lighting and pose, is a reminder of the process of introjecting the (m)Other. Perhaps we are not certain on some level that we made it through the Oedipal path and that our subject formation is stable? After all, do not women have to go through a double renunciation to enter heterosexuality? First they have to renounce their desire for their mother, and then displace their desire for the father. Perhaps it didn't quite take.

Julia Kristeva and the Semiotic

Theorists such as Diane Fuss (1992) have made use of psychoanalyst Julia Kristeva's notion of the homosexual–maternal facet to suggest that what is at play in the consumption by women of fashion ads is female homosexuality. It is female homosexuality that Kristeva believes is fundamental to the daughter in her pre-Oedipal identification with the mother, that moment which Klein posited and studied as introjection. Kristeva took Klein's idea further, and suggested that this oceanic, chaotic indistinct moment/site before the splitting into subject/object, self/other, mother/child still irrupts into the subject's daily life, through something called the 'semiotic', or the chora. The semiotic for Kristeva is that perfect union, and it is sometimes reconstituted in the flow of poetry, or images. She balances it against the 'Symbolic', Lacan's word for the realm of language and culture through which we become subjects, this idea of the 'Semiotic'. (Kristeva's use of the word 'semiotic' does not have much to do with the more common use of the adjective 'semiotic' which refers

to relational systems of meaning.) Perhaps then, the secret pleasure of flipping through fashion magazines is a pleasure of reconstituting the mother's
face, and recapturing a moment before the subject/object split. Of course, this
would put us on the brink of a site and moment where all oppositions disappear, where self and other merge, where in fact the subject disappears.
Fashion photographs might be providing the pretext for fantasised evocations
of a pre-subjective choric union with the mother, and a return to the
homosexual–maternal continuum. This may sound progressive – a kind of
woman-identified psychoanalytic reading of why it's fun to read *Vogue*. The
problem here is that returning to that moment of oneness with the mother,
particularly for infants who become daughters, means returning to a narcissistic moment. For Freud, Lacan and Kristeva, the homosexual–maternal
connection is a regressive one. It is an effect of the Imaginary, and could be
read as a symptom of woman's predisposition to narcissism, to a desire for
herself. After traversing the mirror stage, the Oedipus complex, the healthy
woman has achieved two goals – she has identified with the same sex, and
learned to desire the opposite sex. To go back to a moment before this is
successfully instituted is to return to a moment where there are no boundaries, to what Kristeva calls 'abjection', a threat to stable identity which can
lead to madness. Perhaps this reading of viewing fashion photography is not
entirely as progressive as it may seem at first glance.

In 'Fashion and the Homospectatorial Look', Diana Fuss (1992) has
suggested a third option to the question of whether the beautiful women in
fashion ads are there to be emulated or desired. She speculates that perhaps

> the female spectator's fascination with her etherealised image in fashion photog-
> raphy operates not as an Imaginary effect of primary narcissism but as a Symbolic
> defence against it – against all the terrors primary identification with the mother
> holds for the always imperfectly oedipalised woman. (p. 72)

Fuss suggests that the images of beautified faces may serve to stave off, to
disavow, the instability of identification, the irruptions of the semiotic or the
chora into our lives. We are not reading images of a choric union, but
memorials to a union that is past and dead. The overly made-up, perfect
images of women in fashion photographs are mementos of a homosexual
moment past. The viewer, according to Fuss, doesn't actually purely desire, or
entirely identify with the Other woman pictured in fashion photos; she views
them by flipping between the two options, in a situation which desiring to be
like that other woman draws support from a subterranean desire to have that
other woman.

In this section on fashion photography, we concentrated by and large on
the position of women as viewers of women, and on one specific form of
perversion, narcissism. In the next section, we will be looking at men viewing

women and at women viewing women, but this time, in the movies. We will also be looking at other forms of perverse pleasures – fetishism, voyeurism, as well as narcissism – which are encountered in analysing the processes of identification and subject formation in visual culture.

Going to the Movies

Much of the first two decades of feminist film theory developed in reaction to a key article called 'Visual Pleasure and Narrative Cinema' written by Laura Mulvey in 1973, and published in the journal *Screen* in 1975. In the next few pages, we will go over her main points and discuss the issues surrounding women, men and the movies. Her aim was to understand how film created and reinforced social formations in the individual psyche, through its unconsciously constructed pleasures. She was interested in exposing the psychic unconscious of patriarchal society in film form.

Mulvey, who was writing well before films such as *Thelma and Louise* or *My Brilliant Career*, wondered why women went to films such as Hitchcock's *Vertigo* or *Marnie*. (If you have not seen one of Hitchcock's classic films, it will help you understand this section and Mulvey's ideas if you were to try to see one.) It seemed to Mulvey that these films were set up for male viewers. The ideal spectator for the kind of realist narratives produced by Hollywood was male, as far as Mulvey could determine, and she set out to understand why this was so. At the time Mulvey was writing, most theorists working from psychoanalytic premises saw the movies as compensatory, as making up for something that was missing for the viewing subject, something he or she lacked, that would be too traumatic to face. Mulvey drew on this tradition to argue that the visual pleasures of narrative film were constructed to reassure male subjects of their integrity when confronted with sexual difference. She also used the idea from Lacan that looking at something stitches or sutures you to it; watching films, the specific technological organisation of film watching patches us into certain processes of identity construction. To make this clearer, let's look closely at the argument on her now well-known concept of 'the gaze' or 'the look'.

The Gaze

The concept of 'the gaze' or 'the look' derives from an analysis of the way in which cinema stimulates scopophilia, the pleasure of looking.

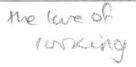
the love of looking

Mulvey links the gaze in classic Hollywood cinema to male voyeurism, fetishism and sadism. The film involves a triple look; the look of the camera; the look of the male character in the film at the female character; and the look of the spectator who, through the look of the camera, identifies her/himself with the main character. Mulvey also argues that the way this male gaze functions is through the conventions of realistic narrative cinema. The look of the camera is never made explicit; a great deal of elaborate photographic work ensures that we feel we are watching a film through our own eyes. The work or the look of the camera as intrusive, is covered over. Nor is the look of the spectators mentioned in the film. Our presence as spectators is never referred to explicitly in the images or in the story on the screen. Unlike a Woody Allen film, where he turns to the audience and talks to them (or even walks in and out of the audience – as in *Purple Rose of Cairo*), narrative Hollywood cinema pretends the spectators do not exist. It is the look of the male characters, the actors in the film, which are primary and which subordinate the other two.

Voyeurism, Sadism and Fetishism

In the dark of the cinema, although you are surrounded by other people, it feels as if you are in your own little world, that you are watching a film in private. This sets up the experience of watching a film as a voyeuristic one, where the spectator takes pleasure at peeking into the lives of other people. There are other sources of psychic pleasure for the men in the audience linked to voyeurism. The action of being filmed (Mulvey calls this the 'pro-filmic event'), although technically seeming neutral, can be seen as inherently voyeuristic (the camera as a kind of peeping Tom) and is coded as masculine (and is almost always undertaken by a male cinematographer).

The man watching the film, argues Mulvey, is viewing the playing out of the active-male/passive-female dichotomy. The actresses in the film connote 'to-be-looked-at-ness'. The male spectator derives enjoyment from looking at the female form displayed for his enjoyment. He also derives pleasure from identifying with the male protagonist, the actors in the film. In realist narrative films, where the story line awards the guy with the girl, the male spectator can fantasise that, like the actor in the film, he is rewarded with the beautiful woman at the end of the story. Thus the woman or women in the film operate on two levels, according to Mulvey: as an erotic object for characters, and as an erotic object for the spectator. In other words, how the woman is represented in the Hollywood films that were available in the 1970s depends explicitly on the ways that men can look at them – either directly as erotic objects or from within the narrative, as available for control and possession through shared identification with the actors. This is where sadism comes in. The control and/or possession of women which classic film stories from Hollywood (and elsewhere) frequently play out is a form of sadism, a kind of narrative violence. As Mulvey puts it, 'sadism demands a story'. This inscribes heterosexuality into not only what is being represented – the story, the couples on the screen – but in the how of being represented – the way men and women watch films. The question of how women watch these films is a tricky one, and one which Mulvey didn't deal with particularly well. But it is an important question to which we will return.

Sexual Difference and Visual Pleasure

These forms of scopophilic pleasure which are available to the male spectator are not without a price. This triple pleasure which is afforded by the viewing of a representation of woman is also threatened by her presence, for she also represents the threat of castration. Voyeurism, sadism and fetishism are perverse pleasures produced through confrontation with castration in the Oedipal drama. In voyeurism, pleasure is gained and the threat of castration is contained, by re-enacting the original trauma (getting to the bottom of the mystery of woman – why has she been castrated?) and then, when all has been revealed, she is either punished or saved – the only sensible strategy when faced with such obvious guilt. This is the classic form of the *film noir*, where a mysterious and somehow still powerful woman (like the mother) is eventually controlled and contained either through marriage, motherhood or death. The second avenue of escape is fetishism, a perverse over-the-top pleasure derived from a particular object; in this case, the erotic objects that women represent in such films. Her castration is completely disavowed, by substituting a fetish object or turning the represented figure into a fetish so that it reassures rather than threatens. But what does that mean in plain English? That the prominence of film stars, the perfect woman and those long, loving close-ups are psychic defences against the terror that the castrated woman represents for male viewers.

This threat that the female image inserts into films, this constant reminder of sexual difference, the struggle of Oedipus and the threat of castration is an undercurrent to the film, always threatening to break through the story and its world of illusion. The fetishised focus on the woman's face, or her legs, works with a story which tries to contain the woman, and these two psychic strategies function to produce most of the films and the way they are watched by men. Or so Mulvey argued in 1973.

Feminism and Film-making

Mulvey's programme to remedy this situation called for revolutionary feminist film-making. As we said, the three kinds of looks which make up the
male gaze are embedded within one look – that of the audience. Mulvey
believed that if you could remind the audience of its presence and its own
activity in watching films and if you could create films which testified to the
work of the camera, films which showed the very material and technology of
camera work, then the visual pleasure which made women into erotic objects
and men into consumers of these objects would be destroyed. For Mulvey, the
destruction of the pleasure of the male gaze (by analysing its role in consumption, and laying bare the device of the camera) was the only option, a stoic
one, and a brutal prescription of self-discipline.

   Coinciding with Mulvey's article was a great push by feminist film directors to try to enact these revolutionary new ideas. Yvonne Rainer's *Film About
a Woman who ...* (USA 1974), in its self-conscious use of intertitles, its refusal
of narrative and its suspension of identifiable familial relationships, broke
from realist Hollywood practices, and used filming techniques which offered
room for critical analysis. Mulvey's own film *Riddles of the Sphinx* (UK 1976
with Peter Wollen) uses a direct address to the camera, and special panning
shots, as well as montage to try to shift narrative perspective to the mother in
the Oedipal triangle. Lizzie Borden's *Born in Flames* (USA 1983) draws upon
the science fiction genre, decentres narrative and explores the function of
representation in constructing political subjectivity. Other films well worth
exploring include Lizzie Borden's *Working Girls* (USA 1986); Trinh Minh-ha's
Reassemblage (USA 1982) and *Surname Viet, Given name Nam* (USA 1989).

The Woman as Spectator

Mulvey concentrated in the 1970s on the male gaze and masculine investments in cinema. In the 1980s and 90s the question was asked: What about
women watching films? Where was the woman spectator in all of this? Is
popular culture a dead end for women? In one of the first articles to attempt
to defend the pleasures of the popular film for women, Ann Kaplan asked 'Is
the Gaze Male?'(1984). How *do* women watch films? Would women want the
gaze? What does it mean to be a female spectator? What might be the female
subject of desire? If we assume that women aren't sitting in the audience
gazing up at the fetishised stars with long eyelashes, who are they identifying
with? The male characters? The story line? When women are in the dominant
position, are they in the masculine position? Or can both genders occupy
either position?

To illustrate this question of whether the male gaze can be reversed, we might look at a scene from a film by a woman director, *The Piano* (Jane Campion 1993). In it, the camera at one point lingers on the protagonist's naked male body as he moves around the piano (which artfully covers up his genitals). The scene is very sensual, and Harvey Keitel, hardly a stereotypical beefcake actor, is rendered as an erotic object. The piano and the actor both become fetishes in this scene. Is this the sign of changing times? Are men becoming fetishised? Or is this scene the exception that proves the rule? On this point, Sally Ann Doane argues:

> The male striptease, the gigolo – both inevitably signify the mechanism of reversal itself, constituting themselves as aberrations whose acknowledgment simply reinforces the dominant system of aligning sexual difference with a subject/object dichotomy. And an essential attribute of that dominant system is the matching of male subjectivity with the agency of the look. (1991 p. 21)

How many female directors are there, how many female cinematographers? Can there be a female gaze as long as the very machinery which makes films (the camera) is coded as a masculine technology (the process of filming is often seen as intrusive, penetrative and voyeuristic in and of itself)? Does the woman in this film advance the action? Is she active rather than passive? How does the film end – with marriage, mayhem or motherhood?

Another challenge to the problem of the male gaze comes as a challenge to the idea of the male gaze itself. In the reversal that is performed in *The Piano*, the character played by Keitel is a white man gone native. He has Maori tattoos, and is closer than most whites to the local Maori community. His brush with the primitive has made him more sensitive, more intuitive. To feminise Keitel as an object of the gaze, some questionable racial stereotypes are invoked (see bell hooks' (1994) excellent analysis). This dovetails precisely with some of the critiques which analysts later made of Mulvey's male gaze. Some critics argue that black men seldom enjoyed the same kind of freedom to look as did white men, and that this would create different structures of looking. In fact, up to the early or even mid-twentieth century a black man in the southern states of the United States who was perceived by a white man to be looking at – deriving scopophilic pleasure from – a white woman was in danger of excessive racist violence.

> The male gaze is not a universal given but is negotiated through whiteness: the Black man's (sexual) gaze is socially prohibited. Racial hierarchies in ways of looking have created visual taboos, the neglect of which reflect back on film theory. (Gaines 1988, p. 13)

Another difficulty we have in imagining the source of pleasure in cinema for women comes from the fact that, as Mulvey put it, 'sadism demands a story'. If the process of telling a story always puts women in the situation of being contained, or disposed of, how can any narrative in film please a woman? She can, of course, masochistically identify with the heroine and her containment. Teresa de Lauretis (1984) in *Alice Doesn't: Feminism, Semiotics and Cinema* worked her way around this barrier by looking at narrative theory and suggesting that the sadism of the story is available not only to men, but that the active masculine position is one which women can take up. They too can identify with the hero and his bold exploits. And because it is doubly difficult for women to traverse successfully the Oedipal terrain, the possibility of women occupying both the position of the object of desire and the masculine actor of desire is entirely possible. The problem for Freud, in his attempt to account for how compulsory heterosexuality installed itself in the girl, had always been the sexual mobility that seemed to be a distinguishing factor in the construction of femininity. So such a double identification is certainly perverse, but possible.

The difficulty with trying to reverse the gaze is that the forms of pleasure which cinema affords are, according to Mulvey's argument, distinctly male. Voyeurism, sadism and fetishism are the little boy's responses to the fear of castration and the route to identity through the Oedipus complex. For women, narcissism, hysteria and masochism are the pit stops on the road to a successful resolution of the Oedipus complex (if it can ever be successfully resolved). To lapse into narcissism, to gaze at the woman on the screen, would not be an exercise in fetishism for the woman, but a return to a period before she consolidated her identity, the period before she broke away from her mother, and entered into the Oedipus complex. This is a dangerous kind of pleasure for the woman spectator, one which borders on the loss of identity, of ego formation, but it is a powerful attraction. The loss and separation entailed by the acquisition of language and the entrance into fields of visual representation – looking, being looked at – lead both the male and female child to desire the mother. The girl then directs her desire to the mother, as we said in Chapter 2, in what is called the negative Oedipus complex.

For Kaja Silverman (1988), it is important to recognise, as this can only happen *after* the pre-Oedipal stage, that there must be distance from the mother in order for her to become an erotic object for her daughter. It is only after the event of the castration crisis, that is, the dramatic onset of sexual difference, that the girl enters the positive Oedipus complex and learns to direct her desire to the father. For the rest of her life the female subject remains split between the desire for the mother and for the father. But the reason Silverman emphasises that the daughter's love for the mother happens after the pre-Oedipal stage is that this happens after the entrance to language. In situating the girl's desire for the mother in the negative Oedipus complex,

Silverman rescues female desire for the mother as fully Oedipal, that is to say, as being within the symbolic order, within language and signification. This means that the female subject can also represent her desires.

So what would happen if the story changed, if, as Teresa de Lauretis put it, when the hero arrived to claim his prize he discovered that Alice doesn't live here anymore? What if Alice, fed up with hanging around waiting to be the beaming bride, went off on some other adventure, made a different kind of film, and invited all her friends to come see it? Some of the popular films produced in the 1980s and 90s might fall into this category. Films such as *Thelma and Louise*, or the *Alien* films have been analysed as offering other potential readings (see Chapter 3 for a discussion of some of these). Other films such as *Girlfriends* (Claudia Weill, USA 1977), *My Brilliant Career* (Gillian Armstrong, Australia 1979) and *Desperately Seeking Susan* (Susan Seidelman, USA 1985) also offer some challenges to the traditional stories of Hollywood and the traditional spectator invited to enjoy them. In fact, we might argue that the feminist critique and remaking of movies has started to have an impact on the popular culture produced be men directors as well. Films such as *My Best Friend's Wedding* (USA 1997) and *Muriel's Wedding* (Australia 1994) by P.J. Hogan offer alternative spectator possibilities from within the film.

Muriel's Wedding, for example, features an insipid young woman who comes from a dysfunctional family in an Australian town. Muriel can't seem to hold down a job and lives in a fantasy world, surrounded by photos cut out from bridal magazines. The movie opens at her high school friend Tanya's wedding; Muriel is wearing a dress she has shoplifted. After stumbling upon the groom making out with the bride's best friend, unlucky Muriel is spotted by the shop detective from the very store where she stole the dress. Her father, a corrupt local politician, has a word with the police, and Muriel manages to avoid arrest.

In the next scene, we see Muriel and her four friends in a bar. Tanya has cancelled her honeymoon when her husband admits to infidelity (but not with Tanya's best friend). Her friends console her, and she announces that she will take them on her honeymoon trip. Muriel is eager to go, but they snub her as too nerdy. Muriel takes this badly, but manages, by stealing a sizable sum of (embezzled) money from her father, to fly off to the honeymoon island.

There, before she can meet up with the stuck-up crowd, she meets Rhonda. Muriel invents a fiancé (Tim Sims) and Rhonda is led to believe that Muriel is having one last pre-wedding fling. Rhonda confronts the clique bitches and sticks up for Muriel, and then, in a parody of a drag contest, Muriel and Rhonda win a talent contest lip-synching to Abba's hit song 'Waterloo'. The two become good friends, but Muriel eventually must fly home, only to be confronted by her father. Muriel flees to Sydney, the big city, where she tells Rhonda she's avoiding the imaginary Tim Sims. They share an apartment together, work across the street from one another. She even manages to get a boyfriend. She calls herself Mariel now, as she feels she's a new person. At the same time, Muriel/Mariel continues to live in a kind of fantasy land. She obsessively plays a video of Lady Diana and Prince Charles's wedding in the video store where she works, and she takes to visiting bridal salons, where the assistants take pictures of her for her 'dying mother who won't be able to attend the wedding'.

After an evening out, where Rhonda dates *two* very attractive men and Mariel has her first (hilarious) sexual encounter, Rhonda suddenly drops to the floor, paralysed. She has a tumour on her spine. When Rhonda bemoans having to go back to Porpoise Spit after the operation, Mariel vows to stay and help her. Scenes with Mariel helping Rhonda and cementing their friendship are nonetheless interspersed with scenes of her persistent wedding fascination. She combs mail-order groom catalogues, and comes up with a prospective mate: David van Arkle, a rich white South African swimmer, who needs an Australian bride in order to circumvent the ban on South African athletes participating in the Olympics. She arranges to marry David for $10,000 and organises a big church wedding. Meanwhile, Rhonda's condition has deteriorated, and she is forced to return to Porpoise Spit to her mother's. Mariel later returns to Porpoise Spit when her mother Betty commits suicide. Here she realises she is little better than her embezzling, unfaithful father. She leaves David after the funeral (and the consummation of their marriage), and goes to Rhonda's mother's house. There is Rhonda, suffering through a visit by the four high school 'friends'. Muriel and Rhonda reconcile, and with a few well-chosen words for the group of four, they ride off in a taxi, waving good-bye to the conservative strictures of small-town Porpoise Spit.

What this movie offers in terms of alternative viewing positions is seen through the treatment of the wedding narrative. That patriarchal marriages are anything but fairy tales, and that weddings are a rite of passage into disaster for many women, is a point made repeatedly. Against the Mills and Boon (Harlequin) romance and the mythological perfection of the fetishised bride, we have the failed examples of Chook and Tanya; Bill and Betty (Muriel's parents); and finally David van Arkle and Mariel herself.

Yet doesn't the film's title suggest that there is a wedding for Muriel (not Mariel)? When women occupy the position of active hero in their own narratives, queer things may happen. Perhaps Muriel gets the girl in the end. The final scene with Rhonda and Muriel in the taxi resembles nothing so much as a just married couple waving goodbye to their friends after the wedding. Instead of Rhonda being made to pay for her too active sexuality and exuberance with spinal paralysis and a stunted life in Porpoise Spit, she regains her life through Muriel.

The system of looks that make up Mulvey's male gaze is also broken down in this film. The pro-filmic event, the look of the camera, is not de-masculinised; that is, made less voyeuristic. However, through the repetition of all those bridal dress photographs, the obsessively repeated video of Lady Di, followed by Mariel obsessively replaying her own wedding video, the role of the camera in fixing the woman as an object is made abundantly clear, and satirised. The mechanics of the camera work are laid bare.

The active look of the male characters is displaced; the male characters actually have very little to do in this movie. It is the look of the female characters, the exchanges of looks between Rhonda and Muriel at the end in Porpoise Spit, or in Sydney through the store-front windows where they work, that seems more important in the drive of the narrative. What the look seems to do is establish a visual romance between Muriel and Rhonda. There are parodic scenes such as the postcoital consummation (an exhausted Rhonda and Muriel lay beneath a palm tree under the stars and share a bottle of champagne after they win the talent contest); visual parallels which establish Rhonda as Muriel's partner (when Mariel walks down the aisle after her vows, two people remain seated when the rest of the congregation stands, Brice, the one boyfriend Muriel has had, and Rhonda); and the just married taxi scene. This film, where the falling bouquet tossed by the bride is accompanied by the sound of a bomb dropping, suggests, through the irony created by the clash between the traditional and alternative looks and narratives, that friendship between women may be underpinned by a queer desire. It is hardly surprising that mainstream reviewers just didn't get *Muriel's Wedding*. They thought it an uninteresting story of an unsympathetic character; but among some groups of women, *Muriel's Wedding* was a female revenge of the nerds, and it certainly had an alternative viewing.

One compelling suggestion that *Muriel's Wedding* makes is that being a woman is a question of performance, of masquerade. When Rhonda and Muriel ham it up in the talent contest, they resemble nothing so much as two drag queens. When popular culture starts to produce images of women imitating men imitating women, and stereotyped images of women at that, then the question of the original version of woman, the real woman, is one that needs to be looked into. Such films invoke a gaze that could be called Queer, an issue we will discuss at the end of this chapter. At present, we will question how performance produces masculinity and femininity.

Femininity and Masculinity as Masquerade

In her 1929 essay 'Womanliness as Masquerade', Joan Rivière suggested that genuine womanliness and masquerade are one and the same, that is, that there is a performative, masquerading aspect to the assumption of normal masculine and feminine subjectivity. To some extent, patriarchal femininity and masculinity are masquerades in which both sexes adopt a role which

findings

covers over the ambivalence and anxiety of subjectivity and sexual identity. Rivière's essay was primarily concerned with intellectual women who, in taking on a role more commonly seen as masculine, are driven to 'put on a mask of womanliness to avert anxiety and the retribution feared from men' (p. 35). In her analysis, Rivière argued that these women wish for recognition of their masculinity from men and claim to be the equals of men, or in other words, to be men themselves. However, to alleviate the anxiety of adopting a masculine orientation – specifically the horrible dread of the retribution by the father – they would publicly acknowledge their condition as women, not only in their dress but in 'compulsive ogling and coquetting' (p. 37). Rivière points out that 'in everyday life one may observe the mask of femininity taking on curious forms' (p. 39). She refers to an extremely competent woman of her acquaintance who 'can attend to typically masculine matters'; nevertheless whenever a man is present:

> she has a compulsion to hide all her technical knowledge from him and show deference to the workman, making her suggestions in an innocent and artless manner, as if they were 'lucky guesses'. (p. 39)

At the end of her essay, Rivière somewhat self-consciously points out that 'These conclusions compel one once more to face the question: what is the essential nature of fully developed femininity?' (p. 43). The answer that she gives in the course of the essay is that of the title of her essay: womanliness as masquerade.

Stephen Heath's (1986) comments on Rivière's essay draw out the implications of her notion of gender as masquerade and point to the question of male display, of masculinity as performance and masquerade. Here he cites Virginia Woolf's mocking excoriation of masculine uniforms in *Three Guineas*: 'Your clothes in the first place make us gape with astonishment … every button, rosette and stripe seem to have some symbolical meaning.' Indeed they do: 'All the trappings of authority, hierarchy, order, position make the man' (p. 56).

For all the masquerade of both femininity and masculinity, both are real in their effects. The legacy of Joan Rivière's work forces us to consider the consequences of sexual identity as construction and representation. A prominent theorist in this respect is Judith Butler who, as we mentioned in Chapter 2, questions the need for a stable female identity for feminist theory.

Butler proposes a radical critique of all categories of identity. In her book *Gender Trouble* (1990), she offers an analysis of gender and sex in terms not of inner capacities, attributes and identities, but of a set of repeated performances that congeal over time to produce the appearance of substance, of a natural sort of being (p. 190). According to Butler, gender only exists in the

service of heterosexism; gender identities come a
upon what she calls 'the heterosexual matrix'. Butle

> it is precisely the butch lesbian and the drag queen (a
> and macho gay), whose performances radically pr
> sexuality in their parodic repetition of the heterosex
> sexuality itself is only produced through its connectio
> practices of gender, gay is to straight not as copy is
> 'copy is to copy': In imagining gender, drag implicitly reveals the imitative struc-
> ture of gender itself – as well as its contingency. (p. 191)

It is important to draw out this last point, for it is one which Butler (1993) had
to emphasise again in 'Critically queer', a chapter in her next book, *Bodies that
Matter*. Butler does not think that one decides one bright sunny morning to go
out and become a woman by putting on a dress. It is the accretion of a series
of performances – putting on nylons and high heels or wearing work boots,
day after day – which provides people with their sense of gender and sexual
matrix. In this sense, it is not so much performance, a one-off thing, as performativity. You create yourself by repeating a series of steps over and over
again, and it is the repetition of such a series of steps that produces you. The
rigidity of heterosexuality, the same question which Freud found so strange,
is one which people such as Judith Butler also continue to find curious.
Why indeed would people say: 'I only desire people from such and such a
category.' Butler is convinced that compulsory heterosexuality is not a natural
category but rather a system built up by repeating over and over again a
series of gestures that say: 'I only desire people from category B.' And of
course, basically, this is a rather silly idea. So for Butler, heterosexuality has to
work very hard at keeping the absurdity of such rigidity from breaking
through. Another way of looking at this is that when one says, 'I am this, not
that', the 'not that' comes back to haunt you. When Rhonda and Muriel dress
up as drag queens dressing up as women, they are sticking out their tongues
at the ghosts of conservative femininity that haunt them. But their imitations
of the imitations of women are intriguing. What are the politics of performance and masquerade? To consider this question, we will look closely at some
issues related to 'looking the part' of gender: transvestism and transsexuality.

Challenging the Gendered Gaze: Transvestism to Posttranssexualism

Transvestism is the practice of dressing in the clothes of the opposite sex –
although clothes often includes cosmetics and body language. While some of
the more famous instances of transvestism involve people who self-identify or

identified as homosexual (for example George Sand), it is not
to people of any particular sexuality. Transvestism is not about
ng to be sexually different from what one is, but is rather an interro-
tion of how sexuality itself is determined and made manifest. In other
words, transvestism problematises the notion of what one is, asking what that
'is' refers to and who or what produces the system of sexual classification.
Marjorie Garber writes of transvestism: 'If it is not a critique of gender roles,
that may be because it is a critique of gender itself as a category' (1992, p. 9).

Transvestism is a radical, because visible, deconstruction of the performativity of gender.

Transvestism intrigues people of all sexualities because of its concern with
the borders or boundaries that maintain the sexes in a particular configuration. The fact that it is identified most strongly with the gay community is,
therefore, not surprising, since that is the community whose boundaries
provide the definition of heterosexuality – the norm. Transvestism is sometimes overtly and deliberately shocking because of the way it reveals one of
the mechanisms by which the sexes are constructed – physical appearance
and (self-)presentation. A big hairy man wearing a dress and make-up is not
just a deconstruction of conventional heterosexual femininity, but questions
the ways in which a society chooses to define sex and gender. The shock value
associated with public transvestism derives from its play with the conventions of both sex and gender; the ways in which the institution of (compulsory) heterosexuality sexes and genders individual subjects via social
conventions such as appearance.

It might be worth noting here that male transvestism has a long history in
theatre and performance. In the West it is traced back to Elizabethan times,
when women were not permitted (by the state) to act on stage, so that all
female roles were played by young men and boys. The English pantomime is
well known for its use of transvestite characters, who may be either good or
evil characters. For example, in the pantomime version of *Cinderella*, the ugly
step-sisters who make Cinderella's life miserable are often played by male
actors. In *Peter Pan*, the character of Peter, on the other hand, is usually played
by a female actor. It is interesting to consider what role transvestism occupies
in comic theatre, whose particular audience is children. Children seem to
regard this gender play as comic, but is that comic appreciation deconstructive or does it reinforce social (heterosexual) norms? In other words, if a man
dressed as a woman is presented as funny, does this not reinforce the boundaries within which individuals must live and (re)present themselves if they
wish to be considered not as funny (comic? queer? aberrant?), but as normal?

At the same time, the transvestism may well have a subversive effect, challenging children's expectations of masculinity and femininity. It may well be the first time children see men dressed as women, and so are challenged to think about why different modes of dress and presentation are used for each sex. Equally, with the Peter Pan character, it may be the first time that children see a female actor in an agentive role, which may also lead them to challenge the passivity of most female characterisations. Perhaps the very fact that these texts seem to invite such a range of readings is significant, so that the text becomes a site at which gender is assessed, rather than simply assumed.

This notion of transvestism as radically deconstructive is not limited to the public performance of transvestism, as in the pantomime or drag queen examples above. For the passing transvestite (that is, the transvestite who does not radically announce her/his cross-dressing, by the combination of beard and frock, for example), the challenge to categorisation is equally fundamental. Note here that 'cross-dressing' is the preferred term for many transvestites, since it avoids the connotations of pathology or disorder often associated with the term 'transvestism'. Garber notes that transvestite magazines which advise male cross-dressers on how to pass as female 'point out the degree to which *all* women cross-dress as women when they produce themselves as artifacts' (1992, p. 49). This is reminiscent of Joan Rivière's argument about femininity as masquerade (discussed above). And Garber extends the interrogative function of transvestism beyond the boundaries of gender to include those between one class and another, one race and another, one religion and another, in fact all the binaries which constitute our social sphere – Jew/Christian, black/white, master/servant, working class/middle class, heterosexual/homosexual. In popular representations, such as the films *Yentl* (1983), *South Pacific* (1958), *Some Like it Hot* (1959) and *Tootsie* (1982), for example, transvestism marks the site of anxieties about class, race and religion, as well as about gender: *'transvestism is a space of possibility structuring and confounding culture:* the disruptive element that intervenes, not just a category crisis of male and female, but the crisis of category itself' (Garber 1992, p. 17, original in italics).

Some of the same issues recur in discussions of transsexualism or transgender. Interestingly, the slippage in the terms transgender and transsexual reflects the current theorisation of the relation between sex and gender; specifically, that gender is not simply the social equivalent of natural sex, but rather that sex itself is a social(ised) attribute. For transsexuals this distinction is a critical one and is reflected in the debate surrounding their status: Are male to female transsexuals men or women? Are female to male transsexuals women or men? Are all transsexuals members of a third sex?

Transsexual theorist Roseanne Allucquere (Sandy) Stone traced the debates surrounding transsexuals in her paper, 'The "Empire" Strikes Back: A Post-transsexual Manifesto' (Stone 1991). Stone notes that some feminists have been very concerned about the simple assimilation of male to female transsexuals into the category woman. This sexing – or gendering – seems to be based on biological categories alone, so that a man who undergoes gender reassignment surgery is therefore – unambiguously – a woman. The objections raised to this (re)classification are mostly based on the gendering practices which the transsexual has encountered in his/her lifetime. The argument here is that even if a man has not enjoyed the pressure to be masculine which he has encountered in a heterosexist society, he has nevertheless enjoyed the privileged status of masculinity throughout his pre-operative life. If we accept that sexing and gendering are social processes, how can a surgical intervention be seen as negating years, usually decades, of that sexing/gendering? Will the woman produced by this surgical intervention be simply a man in a woman's clothing, where that clothing now includes skin?

This question takes us directly back to the issue of performativity, as Stone (1991) acknowledges in her brief history of transsexual narratives:

> Besides the obvious complicity of these accounts in a Western white male definition of performative gender, the authors also reinforce a binary, oppositional mode of gender identification. They go from being unambiguous men, albeit unhappy men, to unambiguous women. (http://www.sandystone.com/empire-strikes-back)

For the transsexuals whose narratives she has read, surgery unambiguously transforms them into women, and Stone notes that charm schools or grooming clinics were set up at gender reassignment clinics to assist in that transformation. Transsexuals were to be taught how to dress, walk, act and talk like the sex of their choice. She also notes the power of the medical establishment in determining who was or was not suitable for surgery. The criteria used find an analogue in the charm schools and, in Stone's words, 'constituted a fully acculturated, consensual definition of gender, and at the site of their enactment we can locate an actual instance of the apparatus of the production of gender' (http://www.sandystone.com/empire-strikes-back). In other words, to be gendered as woman, an individual must show he can dress, walk, act and talk like a woman; that is, perform (as a) woman in his society. Not surprisingly, the clinics and their clients developed a self-referential, self-justifying set of practices which enabled the technology to continue: clients learned what was expected of them by the clinics; the clinics judged the clients by the procedures which it had used in the past to determine suitability; which were in turn learned by the clients and so on. Again, as Stone observes, those practices tended to be based on what we might consider a set of heterosexist stereotypes about what constituted woman and femininity. This included a definition of (correct or permissible) sexual pleasure as orgasm achieved by penile penetration; masturbation was prohibited, or at least hidden – unspoken. After all, heterosexist discourse holds that women have no independent sexuality.

In the twentieth century transsexualism was identified with sexual reas-signment by surgical means – the technological transformation of the body to align it with the subject's and/or surgeon's notion of the how the subject's desired sexual morphology looked.

The problem for Stone with these procedures lies not only in their stereo-typicality, but also in their (related) assumption of some kind of (gender) purity. After all, she notes, the aim of most transsexuals is to pass (see above), 'to live successfully in the gender of choice, to be accepted as a "natural" member of that gender. Passing means the denial of mixture' (http://www.sandystone.com/empire-strikes-back). What this means, as Stone observes, is that transsexuals must deny decades of their life experience – lived in what is often referred to as the wrong body. The phrase 'wrong body' already suggests the binaristic thinking which motivates heterosexist notions of gendering; an individual is either male or female and should act accordingly – no negotiation, no spectrum of sexes and sexuali-ties. For Stone, this oppressive regime means that transsexuals must construct their relationships on the basis of a lie (the denial of their former sex). Furthermore, this process of engendering 'forecloses the possibility of a life grounded in the intertextual possibilities of the transsexual body' (http://www.sandystone.com/empire-strikes-back); that is, a life which embraces the different perspectives and experiences offered by the transsexual.

Marjorie Garber supports this position, referring specifically to the trans-sexual experience of the travel writer Jan (formerly James) Morris: 'Morris now believes that the transsexual era may be ending, that cultural change and other things may have obviated some person's need to seek a surgical solution to their gender dysphoria' (1992, p. 15). Garber goes on to identify surgical trans-sexualism as a specifically twentieth-century manifestation of cross-dressing and the anxieties of binaristic thinking. Like Stone, Garber identifies in trans-sexualism 'both a confirmation of the constructedness of gender and a secondary recourse to essentialism – or, to put it a slightly different way, trans-sexualism demonstrates that essentialism *is* cultural construction' (1992, p. 109).

Stone's response as a transsexual is to decide to live openly as what she calls posttranssexual. Stone does not underestimate the difficulty of this choice, particularly the social opprobrium it invites. To openly display sexual ambiguity in a heterosexist society which legislates (medically and legally) for purity is to challenge the mainstream values by which many constitute them-selves as subjects; the result can be fear and hostility. The posttranssexual, perhaps more than any other sex, is an embodied deconstruction of the gendering practices of heterosexist society.

R3 posttranssexual.

> Posttranssexualism rejects the acceptance of sexual binarism (male, female) implicit in transsexualism and calls instead for an acceptance of sexual ambiguity.

The posttranssexual presents to the public gaze an embodiment of sexual ambiguity that can be profoundly disturbing, as it challenges our assumptions about the visual representations of gender and sexuality. It is critical to note here that these representations function as part of a scopic regime that is very powerful in maintaining heteronormative sexuality.

Queering the Gaze

It is probably most appropriate to end with a brief discussion of one of the most recent initiatives in unsettling the heteronormative gaze, the practice of queering. As the name suggests, this practice of looking derives from the ideas associated with queer (as discussed in Chapter 2). Like Stone's posttranssexualism, queer rejects the binarisms inherent in the gendered and sexed identities available in a heteronormative regime. Instead, queer focuses on the ambiguities in texts that can be read as sites of non-heteronormative desire.

Queering the gaze is a play with the normative practice of the gaze, as defined by Mulvey. In place of both the (male) gaze that is often identified as the normative practice in scopic regimes in Western societies, and the oppositional practices of looking that constitute resistances to that gaze (whether advertisers' play with the male gaze in role-reversal images or the attempts of feminist film-makers to displace this regime), the queer gaze works as a kind of tactical reading. It does not focus on how the gendered and sexed images in a text construct the narrative or argument in terms that assume heterosexual desire, although it acknowledges that will most often be the case. The queer gaze identifies moments in the text that unsettle that regime. One famous example occurs in the film, *Gentlemen Prefer Blondes* (Howard Hawks, 1953). This film involves a sustained play with sexed and gendered representation, as Marilyn Monroe and Jane Russell explore the femininities they need to adopt in order to achieve their required end – financial security via masculine patronage. It is, of course, in this film that Monroe sings the deconstructive song, 'Diamonds are a Girl's Best Friend' in a performance later reproduced by Madonna for her *Material Girl* video, in another deconstructive assessment of heteronormative femininity. The film ends with a double wedding, the Monroe and Russell characters with their beaus, but the final shot focuses in on the two women. The intimacy of their look suggests that desire is located in their relationship, not between them and their male partners. And, in fact, throughout this film, as in *Muriel's Wedding*, there are numerous instances of this same intimacy and of a desire that is not contained by heteronormativity.

Another famous set of examples, discussed at length in Chapter 3, involves the television series *Star Trek*, in which the relationship between Captain Kirk of the starship *Enterprise* and his First Officer Mr Spock was and has been consistently read as non-heteronormative; which is not to say that both characters did not also engage in relationships with women. However, the relationship that sustained them was seen (literally) as their mutual love for each other and a palpable desire for each other. Although one of the actors (William Shatner, who played Kirk) and the show's producers disclaimed any such possibility, *Star Trek* has been read this way by fans since the 1960s. Instances of emotional and physical communication between them in the show are read as erotic play, and fans have compiled tapes of the characters engaged in these practices which they cut into very different narratives from those presented in the programmes. The same queering gaze has been applied to many television programmes and, not surprisingly, to many of the subsequent *Star Trek* series, allowing critical viewers to locate similar instances of non-heteronormative desire.

The value of the queering gaze, as of queer itself, is that it works to destabilise divisive regimes based on binaristic thinking and perception; the thinking that constructs male and female as oppositions, masculine and feminine, heterosexual and homosexual. Instead it opens up the possibilities that texts can tell us what we may find difficult to acknowledge; that gender is not a natural given but a performative process. The implication of this is that its binaristic construction is just that – a construction: gender, and the sexuality that we classify on perceptions of erotic gendered relationships, is a sociocultural construction. Individual subjects signal their (self-)positioning in relation to that classification by performing gender is specific ways. By reading these textual performances as ambiguous, open to interpretation, not confined within normative constraints, we challenge (the performance of) gender itself.

Summary

This chapter has surveyed some of the feminist and gender analysis which allows us to think through questions of identity and seeing, of watching and being. By looking at the ways in which stereotypes operate, and the difficulties we have in contesting them, we are able to see how deeply our societies are convinced that seeing is believing, and that essence is a surface that we can read in our daily lives. We then went on to examine how our first steps into the field of representation continue to shape the ways we see ourselves and others. By looking at narcissism, and the question of how women desire, we tried to understand the libidinal economy that structures our ways of incorporating others in our selves and daily lives. We furthered this analysis by looking at the masculine structures of visual pleasure, and how they operate in watching films. We then examined the question of the woman as spectator in films, and looked at her pleasure. This posed questions for us of the fixity of identity, and the idea of gender as performance and masquerade. This idea of the performativity of gender led us to the question of embodiment. Transvestism and transsexualism both play with embodiment, and specifically with the visual understanding of embodiment, as sexed and gendered in specific ways. Both have the potential to deconstruct mainstream gendering, and both can also be conservative. Stone's posttranssexualism directly confronts the conservative potential in transsexualism, to conserve the appearances that validate heteronormativity, and argues for the introduction of gender ambiguity to disrupt conservative gendering. The queer gaze has a similar project, by locating within mainstream texts the contradictions and ambiguities in which the constructedness of gendered norms is revealed. In our next chapter, we will look at some of the debates about how to talk about men, women and the other sexes/genders when the firmness of boundaries has disappeared.

Recommended Reading

Berger, John (1972) *Ways of Seeing*, BBC and Penguin, London.

Butler, Judith (1990) *Gender Trouble: Feminism and the Subversion of Identity*, Routledge, New York.

Doane, Mary Ann (1991) *Femmes Fatales: Feminism, Film Theory, Psychoanalysis*, Routledge, New York.

Gever, Martha, Pratibha Parmar and John Greyson (eds) (1993) *Queer Looks: Perspectives on Lesbian and Gay Film and Video*, Routledge, New York.

Hall, Stuart (1996) *Representation: Cultural Prepresentations and Signifying Practices*, Sage, London.

Mead, Jenna (ed.) (1997) *Bodyjamming: Sexual Harassment, Feminism and Public Life*, Vintage, Sydney.

Morrison, Toni (ed.) (1993) *Race-ing Justice, En-gendering Power: Essays on Anita Hill, Clarence Thomas, and the Construction of Social Reality*, Chatto & Windus, London.

Mulvey, Laura (1989) *Visual and Other Pleasures*, Indiana University Press, Bloomington.

Rivière, Joan (1986)[1929] 'Womanliness as Masquerade' in V. Burgin, J. Donald and C. Kaplan (eds) *Formations of Fantasy*, Routledge, London, pp. 35–44.

Stone, Sandy (1991) 'The "Empire" Strikes Back: A Posttranssexual Manifesto', http://www.sandystone.com/index.html.

Sturken, Marita and Lisa Cartwright (2001) *Practices of Looking: An Introduction to Visual Culture*, Oxford University Press, Oxford.

Exercises

1. Compare two of your favourite TV shows (*Friends, Big Brother, CSI – Crime Scene Investigation, Everybody Loves Raymond, The Guardian, The West Wing*). What roles and stereotypes are related to men and women? Who is portrayed as having the most authority and control at work and at home? In evaluating representations of gender, you need to (i) take into account whether media reports or products include similar images, views, backgrounds of both men and women, (ii) consider how the media represents men and women and what stereotypes it relies on, and (iii) consider the different roles of men and women in controlling the processes of production.

2. Keeping in mind the discussion about viewing fashion photography, give some thought to the function of posters. Can you do a psychoanalytic reading of different kinds of posters? What function, for example, do some political posters serve (for example the icon of the black woman fighting; the working-class woman of the nineteenth century with babe in arms at the front line of striking workers)? What processes of identification are being activated?

3. Notice over a weekly period the displays of the body. How many 'objectified' bodies are displayed for your gaze – on television, advertising billboards, in the newspapers and so on? How many objectified male bodies do you see and how many female? How is the viewer of the display positioned? Is it assumed that the viewer is female, male, straight or gay? How do you think those bodies are being read by contemporary audiences, male and female?

4. Watch a Hollywood film and test out Mulvey's theory of the gaze. Is the woman the object of the gaze? Is the man the bearer of the look? Do you identify with him or with her? How does the camera frame the image?

5. Watch the opening three minutes of the film *Rear Window*. Who is the film addressing and how – through what camera angles, what kind of story, what kind of hero? What will the film be about? Take notes on your impressions and forecasts. Now watch the first 15 minutes of the film. What kind of 'looks' can you identify? Finish watching the film, and check your impressions and predictions against what actually happens.

6. Watch some films in which transvestism features as a part of the story of the film (for example *Some Like it Hot, Tootsie, Shakespeare in Love, The Crying Game*). How does transvestism work in these films to unsettle heteronormative representations of masculinity and femininity? What does it reveal about the performativity of *both* sex and gender.

7. Try performing a queer reading of a film or television programme. Where do you find the text offers opportunities for reading against conservative gendering? How does this reading unsettle the more conventional understanding of the text?

5

Ways of Being

Introduction

This chapter will introduce you to some of the most influential recent writing on gender and bodies. The body has long been a topic in women's studies, and is no less important to the study of gender. We will be looking at how some of the second-wave theories of women's bodies are transformed, resurrected or challenged in the age of newly imagined cyborg and transgendered bodies. An interdisciplinary method to the question of the body seems best, and we hope to provide you with the outline of the major debates from the various disciplines which provide the context for questions about the body. Sociology, which is primarily concerned with institutions and social structure, the constitution of society and social change, has made significant contributions to work on the body, through feminist sociologists in the 1970s and 80s, and more recently by mainstream sociologists who are becoming interested in the paradoxes which the body poses in a world where identity is in flux. If bodies are no longer seen as natural, but rather cultural and social, then they are grist for the mill of all sociologists. Psychoanalysis is important for the debates that it initiated over the relationship between the body, desire and social law. Its contributions to an understanding of the hysterical body at the end of the nineteenth century are important, as are the ideas of narcissism and incorporation, which you have been introduced to in Chapters 2 and 4. Psychoanalytic approaches to the body consider how bodies and the psyche are intimately linked. Philosophy, which has long questioned the relationship between mind and body, is particularly important for this chapter, as feminist philosophers have been leading important debates for some time now about the masculine nature of thought in our modern era. And reading the body calls on the disciplines of cultural studies and history, in order to situate the gendered meanings of bodies in our societies.

By using certain themes to frame our discussions of the latest work on the body, we will trace where gender analysts have turned their attention to embodiment as a useful way of thinking about certain political, cultural and theoretical problems. Some of these questions are: How are bodies marked in relation to systems of social stratification based on gender, race, age, economic class and sexuality? How do bodies inscribe relations of power? Which bodies in particular incite suspicion, scrutiny or desire? Is there a generic human body? The chapter is divided into five sections. After looking closely at the relationship between the mind and the body, and how this intersects with gender, we will be concentrating on four more topics: medicine, beauty, law, and space.

Bodies of Knowledge

We often speak of bodies of knowledge, but to speak of a body that knows runs counter to most of our ways of formulating the relationship between minds and bodies. By and large, the body and the mind are separated insistently, following much the same binary opposition of the traditional gender categories of male and female. In this next section, we are going to look at a few of the ways in which the separation of mind and body has an impact on the way we think, particularly in relation to gender.

We say 'brains and brawn', 'mind over matter', or confess that our 'spirit is willing, but the flesh is weak'. All these common phrases are rooted in the philosophical traditions which underpin Western societies. We'll dwell on two of these for the next section: the idea that the mind and the body are radically separate and, intertwined with this idea, the supposition that to think, one must overcome the body, the flesh. These ideas are rooted in the ancient Greek philosophies of Plato and Socrates and received new form through René Descartes' treatise on scientific method (1979). Descartes, a seventeenth-century French philosopher and scientist, is generally acknowledged in Western thought to be the founder of modern scientific method.

Descartes' famous dictum *cogito ergo sum* – 'I think therefore I am' – establishes the rational individual as the site of a variety of interlocking practices of sanctioned knowing. This thinker is self-defining and self-sufficient.

In Descartes' formulation, the process of thinking precedes the process of being in the world. This means that thinking and being are separate, and that thought has primacy over being – mind over matter. These ideas are no doubt familiar to you by now; we canvassed them in Chapter 2 in the sections on 'Partial Identities and Provisional Positions' and 'Feminist Standpoint Theory'.

The Cartesian method also sees knowledge or science itself as universal, available to all who follow the appropriate rules of investigation and draw on this primary principle of mind over matter. This implies that while bodies are specific, mind can be free-floating, available to anyone, in short, the idea of mind is a disembodied universal. Knowledge, particularly rationality, is imagined as the universal property of human being. Not only does the thinking subject transcend its own corporeality in this model of knowledge, but it also sees itself as a neutral observer (on this, see Haraway 2001). This transcendent subject – the one which establishes itself by announcing 'I think therefore I am' – is also capable of neutral observation. This is the second aspect of the Cartesian method which has a profound impact on the issues of gender and thought. If thought comes before being, then proper thought must remain unsullied by the specificities of materiality, the messy flow of bodily process.

This emphasis on neutral observation as part of the modern world's conquest of the objects of knowledge makes sight the most important of our five senses. Seeing is believing, after all. Yet this most distant of our senses, the one which distances us most from what we sense, entails the separation of the subject from the object and, under our current way of thinking about knowledge, involves a mastering of those objects with the 'mind's eye'. To imagine a knowledge that involves flow, undecidability and a certain messiness is a very recent postmodern endeavour. And if keeping your distance from the research is coded as a masculine rationality, some of the newer emphases on chaos, fluidity, touch and so on might be said to herald a new feminine idea of knowledge. In an essay entitled 'Fluid Mechanics' from her book *This Sex Which Is Not One*, Luce Irigaray (1985b) makes this very point.

In the early twentieth century, a series of discoveries in theoretical physics and mathematics, such as Heisenberg's articulation of the uncertainty principle, or the discovery of the wave/particle duality (which basically argues that whether light is observed as a wave or a particle depends on the method and perspective of the observer), contested this principle of neutral observation. However, these new ideas have yet to make their way fully into the cultural imagination. Despite the considerable changes that followed such discoveries, the assumption that all true knowledge, all true science, is rooted in neutral observation by a disembodied subject is still very much with us. It remains prominent in disciplines as varied as cognitive psychology and cartography. Hence we have the idea that scientists of all kinds – from social scientists to market researchers – are able to conduct tests, experiments, interviews and so on in which their own participation, their own bodily and personal presence, is seldom or not at all taken into account as part of the research. And perhaps most obviously, it lingers on in our cultural imagination.

Descartes' transcendent subject – the neutral human observer – eschews any involvement with the messy realities of corporeal existence. The separation of mind and body, intellect and corporeality, is central to the claim to knowledge of this subject.

In science fiction, or in televised hospital dramas, scientists and doctors draped in white coats, a symbolic invocation of their disembodied and disinterested status, come into conflict as science and politics meet. The premise of these dramas – whether they are 1950s' science fiction B movies such as *Tarantula*, or episodes from the present-day medical drama series *Chicago Hope* featuring a baboon heart transplant – is that when all is preceding normally, the desires, physical frailties, and cultural and ethnic baggage of the scientists does not impede their work. However, forces sometimes conspire to place an ethical conundrum before the doctor or scientist, and so an episode or a drama develops. But off-stage, when the drama subsides, neutrality is reinstated. How he (and sometimes even she) manages to address this unusual situation marks the difference between the happy or tragic ending. In short, the idea that knowers are disembodied, and neutral, is still very much with us.

Of course, not all bodies manage to be rational and neutral in this way: those bodies which are not able to transcend their own material cages are objects of suspicion in this model of knowledge, as not being fully human, or not able to mobilise rational thought. What bodies are we talking about here? As far as the eighteenth and nineteenth centuries were concerned, women, all races not deemed white (which included even the Irish for a while) and the working classes were all suspected of being too close to the body. The separation of mind and body that marked the acquisition of reason was deemed foreign to these people. We might even say that it was believed that they had too much body. Caught in their cages of bone, only with a kind of supreme effort would they be able to break free of materiality and think rationally. This discourse underlies the discussion about the right and left brain capacities of men and women, debates about whether girls can do maths, whether boys can do language, whether black kids will ever do better scholastically than white kids, and so on.

Their identification with the body excluded some people – women, non-whites, working-class people – from the role of neutral observer, and so from the positions of theorist and knowledge-producer.

To gauge how the biological discourse about the capacity for rational thought is still very much with us, you need only nip into your local bookstore and examine some of the titles which position men and women from different planets (Mars and Venus) according to a mysterious biological essence. Moreover, this discourse is undergoing a renewed push from genetics.

Who Knows ... ?

Anyone who has ever seen the musical film *My Fair Lady* (or the play, *Pygmalion*, on which the film is based) will probably have come to the conclusion that to be intelligent, one must play the part. This film shows exceptionally clearly that the sanctioned knower has a certain accent, a certain gender, a certain class, a certain skin colour. When Eliza Doolittle is rescued by two gentleman linguists in late Victorian London from her life on the streets selling bundles of flowers, and taught to talk proper English and dress like a lady, the contrast between the Eliza before and after education is stark. When we first meet Eliza Doolittle, she is virtually hysterical half the time – she's dirty, irrational, a 'baggage' according to the rational, proper, clean gentlemen. Their new scientific methods of language study soon make Eliza over to be virtually unrecognisable; when she attends the ball, her carriage, her dress and her speech all mark her as an educated, well-bred and well-born woman. Throughout the film, although it is Eliza who is doing the learning, she remains an object, part of an experiment which the two linguists are conducting, and not a scholar.

The theme of the working-class woman who uses education to move above her station can be found in several films and television programmes of recent decades. From *Educating Rita* (UK 1983) to the sitcom *Pearl* (USA 1996), the transformation of the ignorant body to a knowing one continues to fascinate. These texts introduce quite easily some of the more common assumptions about bodies that know. For one, the body represented as a knowing one is usually male, middle-aged, white and able. Moreover, other bodies are not merely sidelined from the realm of science, they are constituted as objects to be known. The very idea of knowledge carries with a range of assumptions that produce certain kinds of bodies. So who is positioned as a knower? And who is positioned as an object to be known?

The Gendered Learner

This configuration of gendered bodies and knowledge affects all Western systems of education, at all levels, and there has been a great deal of interesting analysis of the gendering of education. Bob Connell's (1987) work on gender regimes is one good example (Connell's work is also discussed briefly in Chapter 2). He shows how there are various practices that construct different kinds of femininity and masculinity: sport, dancing, choice of subject, classroom discipline, administration and others. He outlines the sexual division of labour between staff, where certain kinds of work were done by women teachers and other kinds by male teachers. But this gendering begins at the door of the kindergarten (Walkerdine 1990).

As Valerie Walkerdine discusses in her book *Schoolgirl Fictions* (1990), early in schooling, genius is configured as natural, not learned. Learning is a rational activity separate from emotion; and mastering subject matter involves taking a distance from the objects of knowledge. Moreover, self-mastery is an important aspect of being a successful learner. Both teachers and learners become entangled in the negative valences of the dichotomies between rote-learning and real understanding, between activity and passivity, between nature and nurture, between rationality and emotion, and these dichotomies are enhanced by gender (as well as race and class). So the very idea of the learner is gendered, sexed, classed and raced from the very beginning of the child's schooling, and to make the circle complete, we can end with that binary opposition we started with, that of the mind against the body.

Feminist Critiques of the Disembodied Knower

Had Eliza Doolittle been picked up by two feminist linguists influenced by these understandings of the pursuit of knowledge, she would have been made a participant in the research process in some way (see Reinharz 1992 for an excellent survey of feminist methods of research). Eliza's relations with the linguists, and with the social communities in which she was situated, would have been made part of the research: indeed, all the drama of *My Fair Lady* – the question of what is to become of Eliza after she's been made too good for her working-class family and community – would have been part of the research question. Finally, our two linguists would have assumed that what they and Eliza learned about switching accents to switch class was not necessarily knowledge that could be transported to different circumstances, yet still hold good.

The body always threatens to break through and disrupt this production of disembodied reason. Resistance to rationality in the form of any expression of conflict becomes an excess, a sickness, but most importantly, it becomes personalised, an aspect of the personality, the psyche. Passion and activity in women, mothers and female teachers becomes something to be cured. Criminal activity, poverty and open rebellion (the stereotypical problem areas of black ghetto schools and working-class teaching environments) are removed from social relations to become established as aspects of the psyche, such as experiences of personal frustration, or bad family environments. These psychic aspects of the gendering of education are taken up through some of the theories of psychoanalysis.

The argument that there was no possibility of a view from nowhere, a neutral Archimedean point outside knowledge, found common ground with the psychoanalytic argument that complete self-possession or self-awareness is impossible, and that the knowing, rational, speaking, subject is dependent on structures outside conscious control which are impossible in principle to grasp in their entirety.

Whereas since Descartes, the individual had been conceived as autonomous, rational and masterful, Freud emphasised the structuring role played by the unconscious. The psychoanalytic concept of the subject, in opposition to the humanist term 'individual', does not collapse subjectivity with the conscious self. For Freud, subjectivity is a laborious and endless process, in which the subject is torn back and forth between desires and drives on the one hand and cultural and social demands on the other. As Rosi Braidotti puts it, philosophy, the love of knowledge, must come to terms with its own unconscious:

> The subject of the unconscious demands that the subject of philosophy ... faces his/her incompleteness, recognises the libidinal bodily roots of intelligences, and accepts the partiality of his/her modes of thinking. (1991, p. 35)

In short, Freudian theory would see the unconscious desires of the researcher and the research subject as influencing thought.

Faced with the insistent separation of mind and body, some feminists have turned to phenomenologists to supply a theory of the subject that does not put mind and body in opposition. The work of Maurice Merleau-Ponty has become increasingly popular, for he posits a subject who knows because the body knows. He locates subjectivity not in the mind, or consciousness, or in the self, but in the gradual accumulation of the body's orientations to its surroundings, its environment, its world of people and things. This reorientation of the question of how one becomes a human, how we relate to the world, has been particularly useful for writers trying to overcome the Cartesian duality of mind/body. It situates subjectivity in the lived body. The body is not an object, an 'it' which arrives on our doorstep, already constituted. I think my body and my body thinks 'me'.

Merleau-Ponty's work rejects the Cartesian duality of mind and body, and its implicit identification of subjectivity with mind, for a notion of subjectivity as the lived body.

To illustrate this, Merleau-Ponty wrote: 'You are your body and your body is the potential of a certain world' (1962, p. 106). What this means is that the relationship between the body and the world is a two-way street – reciprocal. Inasmuch as the body is able to go into the world, approach it, take hold of it, appropriate its surroundings for its own purposes and intentions, then this body/subject has a world, is in the world and of the world. By being oriented towards and acting upon its surroundings, the subject gives meaning to itself and the world. Like the psychoanalytic approach to subjectivity, this phenomenological approach sees the growing infant as embarking on the construction of its subjectivity through its relations with the world. This implies both an openness to the world, an exchange with the world, and an exploration of the ways and limitations on the body's possibilities as the primordial conditions for human existence. It is your experience of the world through your body that provides you with ideas of time and space. Time and space are not some absolute measurements, Merleau-Ponty argues, but are experienced through our bodies. Rather than thinking of time as something which is measured absolutely – as in Greenwich Mean Time – we might think of our bodies as anchoring ideas of here (as opposed to there) and now. Through the repetition of bodily acts we carve out pathways of being for ourselves, ways of acting in the world. Cultural objects – for example cars, chairs, air conditioners rather than horse carts, dry ground and fans – establish relationships between the body, its habits and culture.

This gradual accrual of personal and largely unconscious habitual bodily attitudes towards the world Merleau-Ponty calls the 'intentional arc' (1962) or the 'postural' or 'corporeal schema' (1964). This arc or schema at once organises sense impressions, and structures the meaning of lived experience. We might think, for example, of the phrase: 'It's like riding a bike, you never forget.' Even if it had been a decade since you had last been on a bike, it is likely that you would automatically move your body in the correct way to perform this fairly complicated action. Activities such as this, or driving a car or playing a piano, are kinds of bodily knowledges that can become automatic, but which show the driving forces of desire and purpose. Few of us who drive have not had the experience of leaving work and arriving home without any memory of how our bodies/minds got us there. Through experience we learn a great number of things, both technical and personal which become part of the material experience of living. To take a more gendered example, most women automatically avoid making eye contact with strangers in the street. Knowing how to do such things becomes part of our bodily selves, our embodiment. It becomes crucial to our subjectivity, our sense of self.

The relationship of this kind of subjectivity to other people in its world would then be structured quite differently from the adversarial self/other, subject/object model that is caught up in the Cartesian epistemology. In this conception, the body produces and enables social interaction. Again quoting

Merleau-Ponty: 'It is through my body that I understand other people, just as it is through my body that I perceive "things"' (1962, p. 186).

This idea of reciprocity through the body is in many ways similar to the psychoanalytic idea of incorporation: we become bodily imbued with others – objects and people. (You might want to review the section on 'Psychoanalysis and the Other' in Chapter 2 at this point.) We incorporate them and don't just imitate them. You remember similar ideas of the mirror stage which Lacan develops, or you may think here of Melanie Klein and Object relations theory. By taking others into ourselves, by sharing with them, joining with them, we are able to comprehend their similarities to us, and their differences. What Merleau-Ponty was arguing was that this process is not just or only an intellectual process, but a corporeal one.

While feminists and gender analysts have critiqued some of Merleau-Ponty's ideas (and we will be examining this critique near the end of this chapter), here it is enough to point out how some writers have used these ideas to elaborate more located and corporeal ideas of knowing. Iris Young (1990a) has relied on a phenomenological approach to subjectivity in her work, particularly in her essays in *Throwing Like a Girl* on 'Breasted Experience', 'Pregnant Embodiment' and 'Women Recovering our Clothes'; Catriona Mackenzie has used this approach in writing on the experience of deciding not to be pregnant (1992) and Ros Diprose has outlined how the experience of embodiment is a useful way of thinking about the issues surrounding surrogate mothering (1994).

What this review makes clear to us is that the separation of the mind and the body, and presumption of disembodied objectivity as the *only* form which the acquisition of knowledge can take is waning (see Jaggar and Bordo (1989) for a selection of essays which discuss this idea). The philosopher Lorraine Code (1995) has suggested that it would be worthwhile to argue that empirical methodology, which relies on neutral observation, should be put in its place; that its usefulness in very specific knowledge endeavours be acknowledged, but that at the same time, other knowledges upon which we rely daily for survival (empathy, for example) also be given an important place in our understanding of what knowledge is. Similarly, television programmes such as *Profiler*, *The X-Files*, and *Millenium* in many ways are confronting the inadequacy of this model of knowledge, this epistemology, head on, by mixing the disinterested and highly technical methods of science with the intuitive and interpersonal. *The X-Files* in particular plays havoc with many of the dichotomies which structure our common understandings of what knowledge is: Dana Scully (Gillian Anderson), the beautiful woman, is the rational scientist who is highly proficient in the objective and scientific technologies of the laboratory, while Fox Mulder (David Duchovny), a highly celebrated scientist in his own right, is clearly motivated by personal relationships and intuitive hunches in the hunt to ferret out answers. What such television programmes bring home to us, is not so much that rational is bad and intu-itive is good, but rather that they are not necessarily opposites, and that there may very well be more than one way to know, and different bodies that can know. And so they announce, ironically, that 'The truth is out there'.

In the next four sections, we will be looking at ways in which bodies and gender are configured in specific arenas, such as medicine, fashion, law and out in public. In the next section, we look at how bodies are doctored, how the institutions of medicine produce certain kinds of bodies.

Doctored Bodies

In this section on the medicalisation of bodies, we are going to look closely at some of Foucault's ideas about power, docile bodies and biopower, and the technologies of surveillance and confession that he elaborated to explain their construction. In *Discipline and Punish* (1979, p. 25) Foucault wrote:

> The body is directly involved in a political field; power relations have an immediate hold upon it; they invest it, mark it, train it, torture it, force it to carry out tasks, to perform ceremonies, to emit signs.

Many gender analysts have found his ideas useful, matching up well with their own questionings, and they have taken his initial ideas and developed them in ways that his own work did not pursue. His work is particularly interesting for trying to understand how bodies are produced in the early twenty-first century. As human reproduction is one of the primary sites for examining the intersection of gender and the medicalised body, we will be focusing on some issues related to the new reproductive technologies later in this section.

Many of the problems of modern medicine – dehumanised treatment, over-specialisation and neglect of the mind's healing resources – are traceable to medicine's fundamental belief in the paradigm of mind versus body. We have just discussed how imagining a different kind of knowing body leads to a view of knowledge as situated, and transforms the objects of knowledge into participants in the construction of that knowledge. This epistemological framework is *not* one which is shared by most medical scientists. The kind of science, or knowledge production, governing their work by and large oper-ates within the Cartesian framework: for example in the field of reproductive technology, women and men hoping to become parents are objects of know-ledge, not participants in its creation. This collision of power and knowledge (or power/knowledge) and the body is something which Michel Foucault dubbed 'biopower'.

Biopower: Control of the Body, Control of the Species

In seventeenth-century Europe, about the same time as the Cartesian method was taking hold, what Foucault (1979) called 'biopower' emerged as a coherent political technology, a series of interlocking mechanisms for exercising power. He contrasts biopower with sovereign power, which he argues is the form that power took before this period. Sovereign power was exercised from the top down – the king decrees and his wishes are carried out. Foucault suggests that this form of power became less prominent during the Classical Age, as the fostering of life and the growth and care of populations became a central concern of the state, and a new type of political rationality and practice took form. The modern forms of power we are familiar with are exercised at the micro-level of the body, through discipline and confession rather than top-down oppression. In the nineteenth century, the two poles of biopower – control of the body and control of the species – came together to form the technologies of power which still characterise our postmodern society.

> 'Biopower' is Foucault's term for the institutional control of the body in the modern state, through methods of categorisation, measurement, definition and validation. It includes practices in all institutionalised areas of life (including education, health, work, reproduction, law and order) which thereby generate specific kinds of knowledge about the body – and so produce specific kinds of bodies.

The establishment of biopower through the surveillance of the population, the species, took place during the eighteenth and early nineteenth centuries, Foucault argues, with the development and increasing importance of disciplines such as history, demography, geography, climate study, evolutionary biology, comparative anatomy, epidemiology and so on. Governments and administrative apparatuses needed information that was concrete, specific and measurable (as they still do). With the spread of biopower, social welfare programmes become professionalised. People gradually went from being subjects of the king, juridical subjects, to being the objects of science. The very category 'species' or 'population' only came into existence during this period. The human species increasingly became the object of political attention in a consistent and sustained fashion through the watching eye of scientific surveillance.

First, the body became an object to be manipulated. A new science, or technology of the body as an object of power, gradually formed in scattered places. Foucault labels these developing practices and structures 'disciplinary technologies'. In his study of the birth of the prison in *Discipline and Punish*, for example, Foucault (1979) shows how the architectural design and organisation of a prison such as Jeremy Bentham's panopticon provides a perfect surveillance machine, where prisoners are constantly under the watchful eye of their warders.

In this model prison, the prisoners are constantly in view of a central guard tower but cannot ever be sure when they, specifically, are under surveillance. A prisoner, knowing that he may be watched at any moment, eventually becomes docile; he becomes his own warder, and regulates his own behaviour. Under sovereign power, for example, using torture to extract confession was commonly employed; under biopower, disciplinary technologies aim to produce a human being who would behave as a docile body. This principle of producing a docile, yet productive, body under a watchful gaze was developed through any number of institutions – hospitals, schools, workshops, as well as prisons.

What an elegant solution to the muckiness of exercising power: have biopower produce docile bodies. We don't have to be under the watchful eye of a prison guard to discipline ourselves. Think, for example, of school: how we keep an eye on the clock to be on time for classes. We learn to sit for long periods until the bell rings; we remain at our desks. Our bodies themselves respond to the disciplinary frameworks set out for us. And it is a particularly powerful idea when one thinks of the ways in which our bodies are doctored: how the institution of medicine regulates our bodies and channels them from the moment of conception on. Anyone who has spent any time at all in a hospital has probably experienced that the very building itself is constructed to keep a watchful eye on patients: multi-bed wards, partitioned only by curtains; centralised nursing stations; and machines hooking patients up to central information centres. Hospital procedures outline what, where, when and how you eat and sleep. They tell you what you can wear. The list goes on. Moreover, the information on the patient stays in the hands of doctors, specialists and, to a lesser extent, nurses. The relationship between the doctor and the patient is gendered: patients are feminised through this withholding of information. For example, consider the case of a young professional with rheumatoid arthritis who, in order to save time, insists on arranging for his annual X-rays himself, and taking them directly from the radiologist to the rheumatologist. The fact that he refuses to be passive, femininised, makes him a recalcitrant, bad patient. This production of docile bodies is particularly effective on the poor and the working classes, for they seldom have the resources to struggle against enforced docility.

Medicine produces not only individualised docile bodies, but populations of docile citizens. Hospitals, clinics and private practices produce statistics and information about their patients which is fed to governmental institutions. It seems sensible in our age of epidemics that this would be necessary, but such practices have behind them the authority of science. Medical science operates under the Cartesian framework that we spoke about earlier in this chapter; it assumes itself to be neutral. How neutral its observations are could be judged by the pronouncements that have been made regarding AIDS and HIV over the last two decades, and how medical science initially instituted epidemiological control measures which assumed that the disease was limited to the category of men who were gay. Nor is it that medical science has only recently left behind the purity of neutrality: this is the same branch of science which was measuring the size of brains in the nineteenth century and making sexist and racist pronouncements about intelligence (Stephan 1986). This idea of the docile body is already a powerful one, but it becomes even more intriguing when it begins to take sexuality and gender more fully into account.

The Deployment of Sexuality

Later in his writings, Foucault links this idea of biopower, the dispersed operation of power through individual docile bodies themselves, to the deployment of sexuality. As we discussed in Chapter 3, in *The History of Sexuality*, Foucault (1981, 1986, 1988) argues that 'sexuality' is a concept which came into being during the development of biopower; it came to be seen as the very essence of the individual human being and the core of personal identity. Foucault examines the social construction of the body and suggests that the role of sexuality is not a site of repression but rather one of the most powerful technologies for the production of particular kinds of bodies. In the eighteenth century, Foucault argues, French administrators gradually began to institute procedures of intervention in the sexual life of the population. By the beginning of the nineteenth century, a major shift had occurred; a recasting of discourse about sexuality into medical terms. Through the mediation of doctors, psychiatrists and others to whom one confessed one's private thoughts and practices, it was possible to know the secrets of one's body and mind. This historically specific personalisation, medicalisation and signification of sex is, in Foucault's terms, the 'deployment of sexuality'. Foucault outlines four ways in which sexuality was deployed.

First, the woman's body came to be seen as saturated with sexuality. Childbirth became inherently pathological, a kind of sickness. Women of childbearing age were seen as unreliable, and possibly dangerous. Women's wombs were unruly, but as they were at the service of society, they had to be regulated. Medicine and psychiatry were called in for this duty. To be a woman was to be suspected of disease (Ehrenreich and English 1978). Second, Foucault sees the public fight against masturbation in children as an example of the spread of biopower, as the production, not restriction, of discourse. In other words, these public campaigns produced a lot of talk about what one was *not* supposed to do. This battle was built on the belief that all children are endowed with a sexuality that is both natural and dangerous. The tenuous and incidental pleasures of masturbation were converted to shameful secrets. If we read these efforts as the production of power and not as the restriction of sexuality, then we have to admire how successful they were. The third point Foucault outlines is that the conjugal couple was increasingly given both medical and social responsibilities. The couple, in the eyes of the state, now had a duty to the body politic: they must protect it from unhealthy influences. Maladies or lapses in the couple's sexual vigilance might easily lead to the production of sexual perverts and genetic mutants. (You can see how eugenics and state-directed racism can be taken up here.) The failure to monitor one's sexuality carefully could lead to the dangerous decline of health for both the individual family and the social body. Lastly, sex was constructed as an instinct. This instinctive drive, it was held, operated both on the biological and psychic level. It could be perverted, distorted, inverted and warped; it could also function naturally in a healthy manner. In each case, the sexual instinct and the nature of the individual were connected. Sexual science constructed a vast schema of anomalies, perversions and species of deformed sexualities. 'There were … mixoscopophiles, gynecomasts, presbyophiles, sexoesthetic inverts, and dyspareunist women' (Foucault 1981, p. 43). In establishing these species, scientists imagined they were making the specification and detailing of individuals much easier. A whole new arena was opened for the detailed chronicling and regulation of individual life. For psychiatrists, sexuality penetrated every aspect of the pervert's life; hence every aspect of his/her life must be known. All behaviour could now be classified along a scale of normalisation and pathologisation of this mysterious sexual instinct. Through these four routes, the body, the new sexual sciences of medicine and psychiatry, and the administrative and governmental demand for regulation and surveillance were connected. They were brought together in a cluster by the concept of a deep, omnipresent and significant sexuality which pervaded everything it came into contact with – which was just about everything.

Through the deployment of sexuality, biopower spread its net down to the smallest twitches of the body and the most minute stirrings of the soul. It did this through the construction of specific technologies: the disciplining of the subject through the production of the docile body (which we discussed above) and the confession of the individual subject, either in self-reflection or in speech. Broadly speaking, this technology applied primarily to the bourgeoisie, just as disciplinary technology, broadly speaking, had evolved as a means of controlling the working classes and sub-proletariat. Both the disciplinary and the confessional components of biopower, although differentiated by their class applications, were unified by their common assumptions about the significance of sex. For example, at the turn of the nineteenth century, the incest taboo was scientifically pronounced as the universal law of all societies; at the same time, the administrative apparatus used disciplinary technologies (prisons, schools) to attempt to stamp it out in the rural and working-class populations; and, through psychiatric science, the bourgeoisie convinced themselves that by talking and writing about incestuous fantasies they were resisting repression.

Challenging Reproductive Technologies

It is easy to see how feminists investigating the rise and meaning of reproductive technologies would be drawn to these theories which give such prominence to a denaturalised sexuality, and an idea of power which operates on and through bodies. The pregnant woman's body in our postmodern technological society is the ideal site to test Foucault's ideas about the operation of biopower and the deployment of sexuality. But before we go on to discuss this perspective on reproduction, it is worthwhile outlining a few of the major statements in the debate on reproductive engineering, birthing and mothering, for those who would like to pursue these questions further.

What is known as the FINRRAGE (Feminist International Network of Resistance to Reproductive and Genetic Engineering) position stands in as the anti-technological feminist response: writers such as Gena Corea (1985) have criticised the development and use of reproductive technologies, arguing that they embody and institutionalise the patriarchal domination of women and scientifically managed reproduction. As a counterweight, Michele Stanworth (1990) questions whether this position reflects an overly romantic view of natural reproduction. She wonders whether these technologies, and the scientific knowledge embodied by them, are inherently patriarchal and oppressive of women. Perhaps reproductive technology has different impacts on different kinds of women, she suggests, reminding us that a poor woman with a womb for sale will be in a different position to these technologies than a wealthy woman who at last will be able to bear her own biological child (see also Sawicki (1991) or/and Wajcman (1991) for an assessment of this debate). It is probably safe to say that there is no bottom line to be drawn in relation to these technologies: we will have to content ourselves here with analysing their cultural formations, and cautioning against the danger of an uncritical belief in technological progress.

New reproductive technologies have particularly challenged our ways of thinking about human reproduction. Developments in the scientific management of fertilisation, implantation and pregnancy – a lucrative new industry – herald, in the broader context of the rise of biotechnology, significant economic and policy shifts (see Yoxen 1983; Teitelman 1989; Webber 1990). The role of the expert has passed from those whose bodies carry children, or even those who have raised children, to those who have conducted scientific studies on childbirth. What might have previously fallen into the category of old wives tales (that is, valuable advice for remaining healthy passed from one generation of women to another) has now passed into an increasingly technological realm.

> Modern medicine has now evolved to a point where diagnostic judgments based on 'subjective' evidence – the patient's sensations and the physician's own observations of the patient – are being supplanted by judgments based on 'objective' evidence provided by laboratory procedures and by mechanical and electronic devices. (Reiser 1978, p. ix)

Many feminist writers and gender analysts have used or adapted Foucault's ideas to explore these current trends. The role of scientific experts in contemporary practices of childbirth and reproduction can be seen through the frame of Foucault's argument about the role of disciplines in the surveillance of the population. Part of the historical evolution of medicine as an agent of social control in the field of reproductive technology is the early establishment of obstetrics as the professionalised field with institutional authority over the pregnant woman's body (Treichler 1990). The power struggle between midwives and early doctors over who would be knowledgeable in relation to childbirth reflects the installation of medical science as the gatekeeper of reproduction.

The role of medicine as a form of biopower is evident in the dismissal of the accumulated knowledge of midwives in favour of the development of obstetrics as the socially validated modality for managing the body of the pregnant woman.

The increasing scrutiny of pregnancy by the disciplines of medicine, genetics and biology, from well before conception and implantation to long after delivery, has put parent and infant under a regime of surveillance. The new reproductive and genetic engineering technologies can be seen as disciplinary technologies governing the pregnant woman's body. Through a regular series of office visits, the modern pregnant woman can expect to pass through a barrage of tests, the most routine of which include: hormonal analysis, ultrasound scans, serum alpha-fetoprotein testing (for spina bifida), amniocentesis (for prenatal biochemical and chromosomal analyses), routine obstetric laboratory tests and two-hour postprandial glucose tests for signs of maternal diabetes (Volpe 1987, p. 33). But scrutiny does not stop here. Drawing on Arney's critical account of the history of obstetrics, Balsamo (1996) emphasises the valuable point that not only are pregnant women increasingly monitored but also the rise of new technologies has led to a surveillance of the obstetrician.

> Arney goes on to argue that the increased monitoring of childbirth not only has brought the maternal body and foetus into a broader system of surveillance, but it also functions to control and monitor the obstetricians themselves. (p. 89)

To rely on the woman's own corporeal experience of her pregnancy as a source of information, or even on the exchange between two embodied subjects – pregnant woman and partner/obstetrician – is denied as a reliable source of knowledge by modern medicine.

As part of the deployment of sexuality, Foucault argued that women's bodies were increasingly 'hystericised' – they were turned into walking wombs, and these walking wombs were sick, abnormal and needed to be watched over by medical expertise. New reproductive technologies follow this pattern. The rationalisation of reproduction – egg production, fertilisation, harvesting, implantation, feeding and birthing – promotes the technological isolation of the womb from the rest of the female body. This fragmentation of the female body makes it easier to objectify and watch, while at the same time rendering the entire body as a composite of several separate parts more or less devoted to reproduction.

New technologies which fragment the woman's body in this way provide the opportunity for the medical gaze to evaluate women in terms of their potential physiological and moral suitability as container for the embryo or the fetus. Recent developments in visualisation techniques in reproductive technology also produce a climate of surveillance. Ultrasound technology, which can produce enlarged pictures of the fetus has worked with anti-abortion rhetoric to encourage the personification of the fetus. Lisa Cartwright's book *Screening the Body: Tracing Medicine's Visual Culture* (1995) looks closely at the way in which ultrasound is increasingly carrying this surveillance of pregnancy into the very body. Other works, such as Carole Stabile's 'Shooting the Mother: Fetal Photography and the Politics of Disappearance' (1992) and Rosalind Petchesky's 'Fetal Images: The Power of Visual Culture in the Politics of Reproduction' (1987) also examine the politics of fetal imaging in some detail. This climate of visual, technological surveillance is matched by a climate of public, mass media surveillance of mothering.

Cocaine Mothers and Crack Babies

In the chapter 'Public Pregnancies and Cultural Narratives of Surveillance', Anne Balsamo (1996) shows how, in public policy and in the public eye in general, female bodies are viewed increasingly as if they are all potentially maternal, and maternal bodies as if they were all potentially criminal. Current attitudes and constructions of women and reproduction divest a pregnant woman of ownership of her body, Balsamo argues, as she becomes a servant of society, and her reproductive behaviour is socialised. In the spread of biopower through disciplinary technologies, Foucault noted the development of professionalised social welfare programmes. Balsamo focuses on the intersection of the drug wars in the USA with the rise of public discourses on mothering. The so-called crisis of crack babies is an exemplary demonstration of the degree to which the notion of pregnancy has been deindividualised, to the point where women's reproductive health becomes a matter of *public* health policy. She points to the articulation of four social or political patterns that structure the technological management of the potentially pregnant female body:

1. medical research that establishes a broader list of substances and behaviours that endanger a foetus;
2. an expanded argument about the relationship between maternal behaviour and foetal development;
3. new public health programs that seek to increase minority patient/client participation and institutional/clinic surveillance; and
4. the criminalisation of certain forms of drug consumption in the invigorated 'war on drugs'. (Balsamo 1996, p. 103)

Balsamo concludes that the lack of reliable information on the specific toxicity of cocaine puts the eagerness of these kinds of surveillance technologies into suspicion. As Jana Sawicki (1991) argues, these new technologies have made easier:

the creation of new objects and subjects of medical as well as legal and state intervention ... Infertile, surrogate and genetically impaired mothers, mothers whose bodies are not fit for pregnancy ... mothers whose wombs are hostile environments for foetuses. (p. 84)

These technologies of surveillance are matched by technologies of confession. Discourses on pregnancy and mothering are widespread. Talk shows such as *Oprah!*, the *Sally Show*, *Jerry Springer* and others canvas what seems to be every conceivable kind of parent, or engage audiences in an exercise of passing judgement on what is good mothering. Extensive studies are conducted on the advisability of taking vitamins, using drugs, both legal and illicit (caffeine, alcohol, cocaine, marijuana), eating certain foods, exercising and so on. A fine example of this is the bemusement of the newly pregnant Jamie in the US sitcom *Mad About You* who, when browsing through a bookstore looking for advice on how much to exercise, receives a variety of contradictory opinions. Moreover, her husband Paul's characteristically flippant suggestion that Jamie buy the book which suits their own opinion of how best to do things, runs against an increasing culture of surveillance, where those who are experiencing parenting are strongly channelled to behave in accordance with the advice of scientific experts. Of course, as good prospective middle-class parents, Jamie and Paul's very decision to visit the bookstore and canvass the advice of experts can be seen as an example of the operation of the technology of confession. As proper parents, Jamie and Paul submit themselves and police themselves within the systems of self-regulation. The rest of this episode is taken up with the agonising decision of which paediatrician to sign up with – a decision which shows how the deployment of sexuality is alive and kicking in sitcom New York.

What these Foucauldian-based analyses have helped us see in this section on doctored bodies is how the technology of gender, the deployment of sexuality, the gaze of the public eye and the technological gaze of new reproductive technologies function to produce certain kinds of reproducing bodies. We've emphasised up to this point how the new reproductive technologies and their technologies of surveillance and confession are a continuation of certain discourses and technological approaches which began to be established as early as the seventeenth century in the West.

New Bodies

Microscopic viewing technologies coupled with conservative narratives of mothering have produced new bodies: a group of undifferentiated cells takes on, in the public imagination, all the corporeality of an adult human. In 1989 seven frozen embryos were 'orphaned' by the death of the donor parents in a plane crash. The ruling on whether any subsequent successfully formed children would have rights to their dead parents' estate shows how even a collection of cells can be called 'children', 'little children' and 'little people'. Ellen Goodman (cited in Balsamo 1996, p. 188, n. 33) shows how this ruling by the judge leads to ambiguity in relation to birth control devices such as IUDs, which prevent implantation, but not fertilisation. The elasticity of the cultural imagination here (and certain conservative discourses around reproduction) are responsible for extending the boundaries of the human body. But what about when humans decide to change their bodies themselves? In the next section on fashion and cosmetic surgery, we'll be looking at the new plastic bodies that humans are crafting for themselves, and asking how gender comes into play.

Fashioning Bodies

The efforts which critical thinkers have put into reinvesting thinking with bodies, or embodying thought, parallels the work that has been done to de-naturalise the body. One of the areas in women's studies and gender studies which has consistently attracted the attention of analysts for the last three decades has been fashion, or beauty culture. Early in this chapter, we saw the effort that thinkers have put into contesting a natural opposition between the mind and the body. We can see a similar struggle in the work that has been done on contesting some of the ideas about what is natural when it comes to women, femininity and the body. When it comes to beauty, there is no universal aesthetic as a guide: what is one woman's mutilation is another's decoration.

Analysis of fashion has generally taken two main approaches. In *A Vindication of the Rights of Woman*, Mary Wollstonecraft wrote as early as 1792: 'Taught from infancy that beauty is woman's scepter, the mind shapes itself to the body and roaming round its gilt cage, only seeks to adorn its prison.' This first approach looked primarily at the normalisation of appearance through the beauty system, and its conventions of upper-class, Western femininity. By linking the beauty practices of individual women to the structural constraints of the beauty system, a convincing case was made for treating beauty as an essential ingredient of the social subordination of women. This analysis relied on a top-down model of power: that the beauty system, and patriarchy, coerced women into making themselves beautiful. The second main approach to feminine beauty looks at the question in terms of cultural discourses. The routine practices of beautification which women perform are seen to belong to a normalising regime of body improvement and transformation. These analysts focus on the multiplicity of meanings attributed to the female body, as well as the insidious workings of power in and through cultural discourses on beauty and femininity. By the time we reach the end of this section, we will have considered the emergence of a third option to these two main streams of analysing women's participation in beauty culture.

Femininity, Masculinity and Fashion

If you asked someone on the street, they would probably say that gender difference is revealed through biological markers – whether or not one has a penis or a vagina. Yet in most cultures, fashions in dress, hair, make-up, and even scent, are structured and designed through reference to particularly rigid binary oppositions. Fashions are generally crafted by the social and cultural expectations assigned to each gender. Yet there is no bureau of femininity and masculinity that polices such dichotomies. Rather, individual men, women, boys and girls develop notions of what each gender should properly look like (at any given age and from within a particular class) and maintain themselves accordingly – they fashion themselves a proper look. They become self-controlling, self-regulating subjects. This idea of the self-regulating subject (which comes to us from Michel Foucault) is particularly useful, for example, for thinking about gender and the body. Susan Bordo (1992, 1993a) draws on it when she suggests that women themselves police their own bodies through diet. No one rolls up to their house waving a baseball bat, shouting 'You must become a size ten before dawn or suffer the consequences'. Rather men and women discipline their own bodies voluntarily, through self-normalisation to everyday habits of masculinity and femininity, which are sometimes ridiculous, sometimes damaging, and at times life-threatening.

In this section, we will be concentrating in particular on the discourse of femininity. Yet it is worth noting here that men are not immune to the demands and seductions of beauty culture: for example it is widely reported that the incidence of male anorexia has radically grown over the past two decades, as has the tendency for more and more young men to consume potentially dangerous steroids in order to sculpt the kind of body that is visually constructed as the social ideal. These masculine responses to the beauty regimes of Western society need to be analysed in their own right. Some of the questions we ask regarding appearance and the discourse of femininity apply quite well to masculinity, and others do not. One need only think about the anxiety surrounding male baldness, the success of body-building gyms and the international stir caused by the new impotency drug Viagra for examples of the operation of a discourse of masculinity which is caught up in fashion culture.

Beauty culture's successful operation depends on a discourse of femininity. Popular ideas of femininity circulate, are maintained and are renewed through the texts which give instruction on how to be a proper woman. The discourse of femininity tells women and girls, sometimes directly but usually covertly, what is a beautiful woman. Its instruction manuals come in myriad forms: popular magazines, advertisements, icons, films, window displays, toys and so on. But it does more. It tells us that girls and women should desire to be beautiful women. It tells them to expect to be imperfect and to endeavour to become more perfect. It tells them that beauty comes at a cost (both financial and physical): 'no pain, no gain'. It provides a set of objectives to work towards, and practices, methods, tools and images with which to aid those endeavours. In other words, the discourse of femininity functions in precisely the same way as the discourses discussed in Chapter 3.

Femininity, like masculinity, is a body of knowledges and techniques that organises the structure of beauty and its power relations. It structures not only *how* we do things, it structures *why* we want to do them – it gives us our desires, and the means to (almost) achieve them.

The general principle of the discourse of femininity is intimately tied to a desire that can never be perfectly realised – to be a beautiful woman. Because of this desire, this discourse can operate to organise a whole range of local practices and relations in a variety of different sites/locations. The full-figure girl can be in fashion one decade, and in the next, the waif is 'in'. In both cases, the discourse of femininity continues to operate. A black woman in Washington, DC and an Algerian immigrant in Paris will each use different techniques to attempt to achieve a proper womanly look, but both will be responding to the discursive regulation of femininity. Of course, it will probably come as little surprise that in this century, in most Western nations, the basic primers for the beautiful woman say that she should be light-skinned, slim, work-free, carefree and young.

Victorian notions of feminine gentility persist in contemporary ideas of beauty, and there is a great deal of material which traces the elaboration of beauty culture in the English-speaking West to the Victorian period. The nineteenth-century's 'proper lady' or feminine ideal of fragility and submissiveness has been extensively studied. The corset is perhaps the most powerful symbol of this nineteenth-century imprisonment of women in their bodies (Kunzle 1982), with the breathlessness, fainting spells and shifting organs that resulted from wearing it. Yet it is important to emphasise that white women are drawn into the beauty system in a particular way: the strictures of the corset are matched by the alluring promise that they are special. This in turn inscribes for white upper-class women a vested interest in maintaining the beauty system and upholding the oppressive discourse of femininity that it underwrites. To understand how the discourse of femininity operates, we can examine several sites: the relations between the production and consumption of images of femininity; the organisation of the fashion, cosmetic, garment and body industries; as well as people's local practices in everyday life.

Born to Shop!

While practices, codes and techniques of beauty may differ, the fashion industry puts its efforts into turning these various desires into demands for the commodities it produces. In the nineteenth century, the invention of the department store and the gradual move to the assembly-line production of clothing made fashion available to a wide variety of women. The invention of the camera further turned fashion from the preoccupation of the aristocracy to mass appeal. Laqueur (1990) argues that as the significance of clothing shifted – from marking the difference between classes to marking the difference between sexes – a shift in the organisation of social asymmetries of power took place. This would only be possible with the new methods of mass production of clothing and cosmetics of the nineteenth and twentieth centuries. Both the clothing and the cosmetics industries exploited the universal desire for achieving a standard of feminine beauty, while using different ethnic, racial and class codes to produce and market different ranges of cosmetics and looks (Banner 1983; Peiss 1990).

Femininity in general has come to be associated with consumption. Anyone who struggles through the grocery shopping each week, and hunts down bargains to clothe a family will no doubt be surprised at the association of shopping and consumption with passivity. Yet from common opinion to Marxist theoretical analysis, production is generally configured as active and consumption as passive. Performing the work of adorning the body and the home came to be crucial practices in the contemporary construction of the woman as subject, and these activities were marked as negative. Moreover, the association of women with adornment and appearance confirmed and reinforced early psychoanalytic views of the naturalness of feminine narcissism. In the nineteenth century, with the development of the beauty industry, shopping disorders such as neurotic kleptomania were seen as a specifically feminine problem, and continuous with feminine narcissism and weakness. Such a disorder is really little more than the far end of a spectrum where normal behaviour constructs certain kinds of desire for women, desires which are articulated and reproduced through beauty culture. The twentieth century had its own versions of such disorders (see the discussion in Chapter 4 under 'Narcissism', for example). Some authors argue that in the twentieth century, consumption in general became feminised, and that the new participation of men in beauty culture – the hard bodies promised by gym memberships, hair and pectoral implants, new cosmetics for men – is in keeping with their participation in consumer capitalism. Others might argue that a new mutability in gender roles is producing the participation of men in beauty culture.

The Freedom Bin

Perhaps this discourse of femininity which underpins beauty culture would be reasonably harmless, were it not that it functioned in conjunction with other discourses – such as those of self-mastery and perfect control, racism and eugenics, and conservative psychoanalysis – which maintain certain stereotypes about the weakness and narcissism of women. For this reason, feminists have been involved in critiques of fashion for a long time. In her early feminist work, the influential *The Feminine Mystique*, for example, Betty Friedan (1974) critiqued the lives of suburban housewives as stunted, and their participation in beauty culture as confining, echoing Mary Wollstonecroft's early critique (in *A Vindication of the Rights of Woman*, 1975, first published in 1792). The source of the urban legend that women's libbers burned their bras seems to have been an early second-wave feminist event in the USA where women were encouraged to throw away the confining garments of femininity into a freedom bin.

These common critiques of beauty culture reproduce the alignment of women with passive consumption. Generally, they represent women as fashion victims, as bodies which are seduced by advertising to accept their low self-image and the solutions that products can offer (Barthel 1988); or by the proliferation of perfect body image representations in general which control women and support the entire beauty culture including fashion, law, cosmetic surgeries, dieting, eating disorders, cosmetics and more. Naomi Wolf's (1991) influential book *The Beauty Myth: How Images of Beauty Are Used Against Women* is just one in a long line of feminist critiques of the beauty industry which configures women as docile bodies.

Other feminists have pointed to popular resistance to beauty culture, such as those of US black women in the 1960s and 70s repudiating Eurocentric notions of beauty and celebrating black power and identity through African styles of dress (dashikis) or hairstyles (cornrows). Similarly, punk styles in hair, make-up and dress were reworked by young British working-class women to contest public texts of bourgeois femininity (Rothaus 1983). Penny Sparke, who looked at what the 1950s meant to women as consumers in *As Long As It's Pink* (1995), has contested the active/passive dichotomy in relation to women as consumers. She argues against conceiving of women solely as docile bodies, and points to the activity and agency of women in producing contemporary goods, and modern aesthetics. Other questions have been raised about the understanding of advertising in women's lives: do we consume advertisements only as dutiful students of these instruction manuals for beauty? Can pleasures such as window shopping, and scanning the fashion photography in *Vogue* only be conceived as reading the coercive manuals of instruction for production of sexist versions of femininity? To focus on these questions about the ways feminists have critiqued the beauty industry, and some new ideas about the body, we will now turn to cosmetic surgery, an area of burgeoning interest.

Fashions of the Body

Until recently, the beauty industry has been associated largely with clothing, hairstyles and make-up. But advances in medical procedures and the transformation of medicine into an industry in the 1960s and 70s led to an explosion of cosmetic surgery in the 1980s and 90s. Certainly, practices such as skin-bleaching, hair-straightening and body-building existed before this phenomenal growth, but the way in which the body has become plastic is a particular sign of the times. Madonna's lips (inflated with collagen), or Cher's body shape (the object of numerous operations) and the French performance artist Orlan's publicly screened cosmetic modifications of her body (Orlan Panel, 1998) blur the boundary of what is natural and what is cultural. Like other controversial medical procedures and technologies (in vitro fertilisation, fetal monitoring, organ transplants or even female genital excision), cosmetic surgery is justified and criticised for different reasons.

Plastic surgery developed during the Crimean and World Wars I and II, where surgeons gradually learned to reconstruct the bodies of soldiers damaged by increasingly modern technologies of destruction. Later, reconstructive surgery came to be used for cosmetic purposes, although the line between the cosmetic and the reconstructive is an arbitrarily drawn cultural one. New technologies and procedures have been developed since the early 1960s which belong exclusively to the domain of cosmetic surgery.

Plastic Bodies

The body itself, once natural, has now come to be seen as a kind of cultural plastic. It is no longer imagined as merely an object requiring fixing, but has become a commodity like others – a car, appliances, a house, a personal computer – which needs to be updated and upgraded to reflect changing fashions and personal desires. As Joanne Finkelstein (1991, p. 87) noted:

> The body is no longer simply a dysfunctional object requiring medical intervention, but a commodity ... which can be continuously upgraded and modified in accordance with new interests and greater resources.

This discourse of choice has imbued the body with a certain weightlessness – history, biography, social location – none of these seem to constrain the body and its shape any longer (Bordo 1993a, 1993b). Cosmetic surgery allows us to transcend age, ethnicity and even sex itself. With the use of new computer technologies such as computer-aided design, we are permitted a new imagination of the body. With a few simple keystrokes, we are shown two different screens: here are your breasts before – and here they are afterwards (Balsamo 1996). Nature is no longer seen as a constraint to be overcome with corsets, but something to be moulded and improved upon. The barrier between nature and culture becomes less rigid, more permeable, and the body itself becomes part of the consumer culture, which itself is already feminised.

The new cosmetic surgery boom is fuelled largely by women. Although fewer than five per cent of cosmetic surgeries are performed on men, nonetheless there has been a dramatic increase in the amount of surgery performed on men in the last decade. Men too are increasingly participating in consumer culture, and the belief that the body is a kind of play-dough. Many of the most common procedures – such as face-lifts, breast augmentations, liposuction and body contouring – are performed on women for aesthetic and cosmetic reasons. And most of these operations were performed on white women; in 1990 it was estimated that 20 per cent of the cosmetic surgery patients in the USA were Latinos, African-Americans, and Asian-Americans. Of these, over 60 per cent were women (Kaw 1994). (Note the relatively higher percentage of ethnic men undergoing cosmetic surgery; what does this suggest to you about the intersection of racism and gendered positions?) In the USA, an estimated one million women have had their breasts 'enhanced'; in the UK, it is estimated that 6000 silicon implants are performed each year (Davis 1995, p. 25). Liposuction (where a saline solution is injected into fatty tissue, which is dissolved and then sucked out) is the fastest growing form of cosmetic surgery. Types of cosmetic surgery are also ethnically specific. White women opt for liposuctions, breast augmentations, or wrinkle-removal procedures, whereas Asian women tend to have double-eyelid surgery or nose corrections. The new technological innovations of the late twentieth century echo the discourse of femininity that is strongly marked by the imperialism of the Victorian age: fashion privileges a white, ageless, work-free beauty.

As a practice, cosmetic surgery must be repeated. It is body maintenance, not permanent modification. Face-lifts must be redone, as must collagen treatments. Silicon implants must be replaced after fifteen years. Like hair styles, body modification must be maintained or upgraded. This takes us even closer to imagining the body as a kind of plastic, a material for sculpture.

The cosmetic surgery most commonly performed enacts ideals of beauty that accord with contemporary Western notions of feminine and masculine beauty; it is also (therefore) ethnically specific.

Feminist critiques of cosmetic surgery follow similar lines as those of the beauty industry in general. There are those who see cosmetic surgery as an oppressive way to discipline or normalise bodies. They see the participation of women in such practices as an example of false consciousness. Some read cosmetic surgery from within the liberal discourse of choice; they view cosmetic surgery in an almost celebratory fashion, arguing that these women are not victims, but rather are taking control of their own bodies and exploiting medical technologies for their own ends. Others analyse cosmetic surgery and the role it plays in the discourse of femininity. In other words, the approaches that feminist analysis has taken to cosmetic surgery have mirrored the major critiques of the beauty system we outlined above.

One recent discussion of cosmetic surgery is particularly interesting for us, for it incorporates the major lines of past critiques of body surgery, but takes them in a new direction. It focuses on the question of feminine embodiment. Kathy Davis's book, *Reshaping the Female Body: The Dilemma of Cosmetic Surgery* (1995), was motivated, as she writes, by an 'equally feminist desire to treat women as agents who negotiate their bodies and their lives within the cultural and structural constraints of a gendered social order' (p. 5). Davis wanted to move beyond the traditional explanations of the success of beauty culture as being in the female propensity to narcissism, lack of self-esteem or susceptibility to the lure of consumer capitalism. She argues against the notion that women are blindly complying with cultural definitions of feminine beauty, and, like discourse analysts, she too is suspicious of the possibility of discovering an authentic feminine self who is able to free herself from the constraints of the beauty system. She finds discursive analysis of beauty culture to be 'a sophisticated framework for linking individual beauty practices to a broader context of power and gender hierarchies' (p. 56). But she also is not completely convinced by the lack of strategic direction which reading the discourse of beauty and femininity offers. All that seems to be available, she sighs, is 'waiting until some miraculous shifting in the discursive constellations enables this particularly nasty cultural phenomenon to make way for other – less oppressive, it is hoped – cultural practices' (p. 58).

Davis's work attempts to situate cosmetic surgery in a feminist analysis of the cultural constraints of femininity – an analysis of the corset of cosmetic surgery beauty practices. At the same time, she also sees women as agents who participate in a gendered social order where they also experience their bodies as vehicles for enacting their desires or reaching out in the world. She relies on Iris Young's (1990a) articulation of the tension between the female body as object and the embodied feminine subject as a theoretical starting point for understanding women's everyday struggles with their bodies. For Davis, cosmetic surgery becomes an expression of both the objectification of the female body and women's struggles to become embodied subjects rather than mere bodies. She shows how Dorothy Smith's work on how women 'do' beauty as an opportunity for action, and view their bodies as objects – not as sex objects for others – but rather as objects of work, as something to be improved, fixed or transformed leads to a different way of thinking about women's participation in beauty culture (1995, p. 62). This new turn draws on discursive analysis, but also relies on women's own narratives, the stories of those who participate in such processes to analyse the meanings of that participation. To think of our bodies as a kind of plastic, and to do research which encourages this kind of self-conscious and analytical exploration of the experience of embodiment, the production of one's own body in a social context, may be one way out of the dilemma of power dupe versus discursive description.

Of course, there are other possible responses to the dilemma of cosmetic surgery. Kathryn Morgan (1991) suggests a few amusing ones in her article 'Women and the Knife: Cosmetic Surgery and the Colonization of Women's Bodies'. Aside from the feminist response of refusal to the coercive practices of cosmetic surgery, which Morgan argues is utopian, because it hopes for a place outside patriarchy, parody could be invoked, in a feminist response of appropriation. Feminists informed by the idea of gender performance (with or without poststructuralism) could erect booths at medical conferences with before and after pictures of 'The penis you were meant to have' or have themselves surgically altered to participate in Ms Ugly contests.

This section on fashioning the body reveals some of the ways in which men and women perform different ideas of masculinity and femininity through their bodies, and the breaking down of the dichotomy between nature and culture which seems to be the result of the new plastic body. While looking at the fashioning of bodies showed us how the question of the agency of individuals had a role to play in imagining change, this next section looks at some of the laws which attempt to codify or restrict such play.

The Body of the Law

Here we look at some of the ways in which 'laws' make bodies. 'Laws' is in quotation marks here, because we will be looking not only at legislation – which enforces the construction of certain kinds of bodies – but also common practices, everyday etiquette and social taboos, which also enact certain kinds of bodies. As the French sociologist Michel de Certeau (1984) noted: 'There is no law that is not inscribed on bodies.' Those who write on gender and the law, or on gender identity in general, show clearly that legal discourse is an important site for the constitution, consolidation and regulation of sexuality. In particular, the law produces and consolidates the dichotomy between heterosexuality and homosexuality (Stychin 1995, p. 7). The law can produce and legitimise identity categories (for example black, Aboriginal, or woman) and it can fail or refuse to produce them (for example 'half-breed', lesbian, transsexual) (Butler 1993, p. 8). In Canada, for example, until the repeal of section 21(1)(b) of The Indian Act, children born to indigenous women of white fathers were not accorded status as native children (see Silman 1987 for an account of some Aboriginal women's fight against this section of the Act). This kind of procedural or legislative genocide is common in many of the settler countries such as Canada, Australia and the United States.

To illustrate this question of the production of bodily identities by the law, we will look closely at one particular example of how legislation enforces the

construction of certain kinds of bodies. In the last three decades, gender reassignment surgery – surgery which enables men to chose to become women,
and women men (that is, to adopt the normative physical attributes of men
and women) – has become increasingly sophisticated. As it grows more
successful, and is more frequently turned to, legal questions have begun to
cluster around transsexuality and the transgendered body (see also Chapter
4). While these cases may seem to apply only to a small minority of people
and are removed from the everyday lives of many, they show us quite clearly
the principles by which the law operates in the great majority of people's lives.
The cases we refer to in the next page or two are drawn from Australia, but
similar cases could be found in Canada, the United States, England and so on.

Your legal sex is what is used to determine your legal eligibility for various
kinds of social welfare provisions, such as pensions for example, and your
legal status in the community. It can be used in deciding who you can marry,
or whether you can be charged with criminal acts such as sexual assault on
another person. For example, a ruling in an Australian court on social security legislation determined that a male-to-female transsexual had the right to
receive the retirement pension at age 60 rather than the male age of 65 (see
Sharpe 1997 for this and other examples).

The determination of a person's legal sex is tightly linked to sexuality.
Depending on the particular subject for litigation, the law puts a great deal of
emphasis on the capacity and desire for heterosexual intercourse. It relies on
penetrative, vaginal sex as defining female heterosexuality. So, for example, to
take a case from Australia again, it was ruled that a pre-operative male-
to-female transsexual could not have been raped by a man because she did
not yet possess the vagina that would make her a legal woman (Sharpe 1994).
Moreover, medical discourse and legal discourse operate together here. For
male-to-female transsexuals attempting to secure gender reassignment
surgery, evidence of homosexual activity prior to operations has worked
against them, making their claims of heterosexual desire inauthentic and
turning the legal and medical machinery, which sanctions the surgical procedures and their outcomes, against them. In short, the male-to-female transsexual has the right to change bodies, but is legally compelled to be
heterosexual. In the formation of a new kind of legal subject, a new identity
category – the trans-sexual – the category of homosexuality is rendered
unavailable. This presents us with a conundrum: while on the one hand,
gender reassignment surgery seems to herald a new fluidity in gender, on the
other hand, the rigid binary system of gender is reinscribed through enforcing
heterosexuality. The transsexual's psychological sex comes to take the place of
their biological sex, but only on the proviso that this cultural sex be as rigidly
patriarchal as the natural sex was. And for those of us reading gender at the
start of the twentieth-first century, these porous boundaries between
gay/straight; nature/culture; male/female provide us with a good oppor-

tunity to see gender in movement. To summarise then, what we might think of as our legal body provides us with the physical limits of sanctioned and punishable behaviour. But legislation is not the only kind of law governing our bodies. Some gay and lesbian communities initially refused to acknowledge transsexuals' demands for recognition of their desire and right to take part in homosexual communities. But this refusal took place in the realm of social regulation, not in the courts.

While it is clear that what we think of as the law governs the possibilities for embodiment available to us, so too do other informal laws. Our daily ways of acting and interacting are governed by laws of ritual. In his book *The Practice of Everyday Life* (1984), Michel de Certeau attributes to the law a voice that says: 'Give me your body and I will give you meaning, I will make you a name and a word in my discourse' (p. 149). The rules of ritual place us, make us comfortable and comprehensible. By adhering to these rules, a subject is comprehended by culture, marked and owned by it. To take a familiar example from the Western world, among white able-bodied male professionals, a firm handshake (whether offered in a bar, an office or a factory) marks him as competent, masculine and authoritative. A man with arthritis who avoids such contact or a woman with a gentle grip is not obeying the rules of this everyday ritual and hence fails to embody authority.

This is a simple example of the ways in which power is embodied. The sociologist Pierre Bourdieu has developed some concepts which encapsulate these principles and many gender theorists and feminists have found his work useful. Bourdieu (1977) links power to the nature of the dominant modern economic system – capitalism. He argues that along with economic capital, which its holders can use to acquire material resources and political power for themselves, there is also cultural capital: forms of language, dress, social manners, and certain kinds of knowledge provided by institutions such as museums and schools.

This idea of cultural capital is worth considering at greater length, for this is one theory where we can see the idea of the embodiment of power clearly developed. Cultural capital can be: embodied in its owner (for example language skills or personal familiarity with works or art); objectified (in books, paintings, machines and so on); and certified, as with diplomas and formal credentials. Linked to this idea of cultural capital is the idea of the 'habitus', a word Bourdieu used to refer to a set or system of dispositions, a way of organising action, a way of being, habits (particularly of the body) and predispositions or inclinations. These are repeated behaviours, actions, tastes, which produce the everyday world. Bourdieu derived this concept from the work of Marcel Mauss (1992) whose work was discussed briefly in Chapter 2. Our habitus makes our own repeated actions make sense in relation to similar or identical experiences of other people, whether these are individual, collective (festivals or ritual), improvised or programmed (commonplaces or sayings). Moreover, these various practices of living among a certain class or group are harmonised with its specific living conditions. This sameness, this homogeneity, integrates different aspects of lifestyle – taste in diet, housing, style of dressing, domestic division of labour, aesthetic codes and so on – into a consistent whole. Thus the same principles (or meaning structures) that appear in working-class clothing should be found in its dietary patterns and artistic taste. Our habitus is what allows us to deal with change, to cope with new situations; it isn't just a set of norms, rather it generates strategies for living. Nor is it matched directly to our living conditions; pre-colonial, peasant ways of life can exist side by side with modern ways of life within the same person, for example.

Habitus describes the unconscious habits of embodiment, meaning-making and relationships which characterise our behaviour and our being in the world. For Bourdieu, habitus is not idiosyncratic but is derived primarily from an individual's social class and educational background.

So for those of us who would like to read gender and its effects in our everyday lives, and on the elaboration of our very bodies, this theory makes it clear that it is not enough to note someone's biological sex to make general observations about what their domestic arrangements are, or how they drive their car. We must take into account class and race, of course, but also provenance (where someone comes from and where their family comes from), current living conditions, education and so on. We must identify the habitus.

Another form of capital, however, is not economic or cultural capital, but symbolic capital. Bourdieu would define this as the means to convert or transform economic or cultural capital into real, material resources and social authority. If you are a Rockefeller, and you donate the funding necessary for the establishment of the Rockefeller professorial chair in business management at a university, the prestige and social credit you acquire would be symbolic capital; you have used your economic capital to acquire symbolic capital. If you have cultural capital without symbolic capital, then you may still find yourself excluded from the vital resources of society (Bourdieu 1984). This model of power would explain, for example, why women in management, or black men in politics, may be invested with a highly paid or politically powerful position, but because of a deficit in cultural capital (they don't wear the right clothes, shake hands the right way, haven't gone to the right schools) are unable to translate their economic capital into symbolic capital – into real material resources and social authority. In short, they don't embody power correctly.

The Hysterical Body

The last kind of law we would like to consider in this section on the body of the law is taboo, and its impact on sexual difference. In Chapters 2 and 4, where psychoanalytic discourse was discussed extensively, we dwelt on the Oedipus complex at some length. In these next few pages, we will consider the effects of the incest taboo on the body, particularly the woman's body.

In psychoanalytic theory, the development of subjectivity involves success-fully traversing the Oedipal complex and incorporating the incest taboo. In the nineteenth century, there were considerable numbers of women whose hyster-ical behaviour was interpreted by nascent Freudian psychoanalysis as due to a failure to traverse this Oedipal territory. In the nineteenth century, socially as well as medically, female hysterics were treated as deviant and abnormal. They were subjected to theories of hereditary degeneration and therapies in the form of physical and mental punishment. These therapies included enforced clitoridectomy (Charcot 1987; Jahoda 1995), the surgical removal of the clitoris. Although Freud may come across to the present-day reader as paternalistic, he displayed deep respect and sympathy for the suffering of his female patients; in his time his practice was revolutionary. Importantly, he did not think that the cause of hysteria was biological. He analysed hysteria as a neurosis arising from unconscious sexual desires and he hoped to cure his patients of hyster-ical symptoms by making these desires conscious. Freud argues that the hysterical woman is suffering from her memories. A trauma keeps her tied to her past, which is then expressed in dreams and hallucinations. The cure consists of releasing these memories by working backwards. In psychoanalytic practice, this illness and its symptoms become signs which need interpretation: they are caused by and connected to unconscious, sexual desires. The Freudian unconscious has its own logic far removed from conscious thought; unrecog-nised wishes and desires constitute the unconscious, but because they have been repressed, their content is inaccessible to consciousness. This repression can surface, however, in the form of a symptom or somatic (physical) distur-bance: gestures, dreams, slips of the tongue, nervous tics, delusions, halluci-nations and so on. This forms the material which psychoanalysis attempts to decipher (we introduced several of these ideas in Chapter 2).

In the talking cure, the hysterical body, with all its symptoms, becomes a text, that is to say, a collection of signs that demand interpretation. The hyster-ical woman speaks in a language that not even she herself fully understands: there is a language there, but no one yet speaks it. The cure consists of finding adequate expression for the symptoms in everyday language. Freud explains, however, that the symptom, as an unconscious sign, cannot be translated immediately into a conscious meaning because access to it is blocked by the structure of unconscious desires. The neurotic symptom is, as it were, a text which is written without the will of the patient; thus interpreting the symptoms implies making manifest the latent meaning of the patient's behaviour.

Some feminists have interpreted these nineteenth-century cases of hysteria as a rebellious outlet for the domesticated woman, 'an alternative role option of middle-class women faced with conflicting expectations about their behaviour' (Smith-Rosenberg 1972, p. 665). Susan Bordo (1988) suggests that in the twentieth century, eating disorders such as anorexia nervosa, or bulimia, and the bodies they produce could be regarded as a parallel form of feminist protest, in that women attempt to exercise agency by controlling their own bodies. These bodies are marked not just by a childhood trauma, but by an early social trauma. Patriarchal pressure constitutes a trauma for some young women, the argument goes, and so their bodies incorporate this trauma and become ill. Anorexia and bulimia can be the result. For the French feminist Catherine Clément (1980, 1989), the hysterics' deviance is carefully programmed by the social order. For Clément, female hysteria constitutes a kind of safety valve which permits, even encourages, discontented women to express their wrongs through illness (rather than demanding economic and legal rights). Similarly, Bordo comes to the conclusion that in the question of anorexia, 'potential resistance is not merely undercut but utilised in the maintenance and reproduction of existing power relations' (Bordo 1989, p. 15). For Bordo, what might start out as a rebellious act eventually becomes constituted and incorporated by the dominant order, the order with the power to produce certain bodies. She follows a more Foucauldian, rather than psychoanalytic, approach here, when she locates in the body itself, in a self-surveillant, self-correcting body, a 'direct locus of social control' (Bordo 1993b, p. 191). And finally, Elizabeth Grosz (1994) suggests that the hystericisation of women's bodies is a procedure that 'depending on its particular context, location and subjects' (p. 158) may function as complicit or resistant to patriarchal inscription.

The flip side of reading the body as a kind of hysterical text would be writing the hysterical body into the text as a kind of rebellion. The work of Luce Irigaray (1985a, 1985b), a psychoanalyst from Lacan's school who was dismissed by him after writing a critical dissertation about his work, is a prominent theoretical underpinning to this idea that a female feminist might produce a different kind of text. Briefly, Irigaray argues that Lacan, following in Freud's footsteps, does not recognise any individual specificity for the female subject. He again essentialises the feminine as a lack or excess; whether the feminine is signified as too little or too much, in both cases it refers to a symbolic absence: femininity is not represented within the symbolic order. According to Irigaray, the feminine is fundamentally unrepresentable because woman defies the phallocentric system of representation. (This does not mean that woman is not represented in culture; on the contrary, she is overrepresented as the eternal feminine.) Irigaray believes in the idea of a female symbolic order as a totally different system. The concept of 'difference' is understood here not as a sign of inferiority, but rather as a positive source of alternative values. Irigaray's work has inspired some feminist cultural critics to look for a female aesthetic in art and literature by women. Other writers associate her work with what is known as *écriture féminine*. French writers such as Hélène Cixous or Chantal Chawaf, as well as many writers in Canada, Australia, the USA and the UK, foreground the physical self, that is, sexuality and *jouissance* (a word taken from French for sexual pleasure, but also meaning pleasure more generally, and enjoying the use of something). They write from the body – the female body – and reject a phallic position within language. Where psychoanalysis speaks of loss and castration, *écriture féminine* tries to find positive terms: women's unconscious dreams, wishes and traumas form the source of their fictional work.

Laws of all kinds govern our embodiment. Legal sex and gender formulate for us what we are permitted; habit moulds our daily lives, and unconscious laws can affect our bodies' desires. But whether it is conscious or unconscious laws which form our bodies and which our bodies in turn formulate, these differ from site to site. In the next section, we will look at how bodies differ in space. We will examine how the idea of place is gendered, and look at the gendering of some specific sites as well.

Gendered Bodies in Space

To consider the gendering of bodies in relation to place and space, it seems sensible to start with the question of public and private space. We began this chapter by considering how bodies have minds; in this section we'll begin by looking at how certain ideas seem to call for particular kinds of bodies.

One of the classic texts of second-wave feminism outlines a hierarchical difference between the public and private that maps onto male dominance and female oppression. In her 1974 essay, 'Women, Culture and Society: A Theoretical Overview', Michelle Rosaldo draws analogies between the binary of gender – male versus female – and the binaries of nature and culture and public and private. She argued that the association of women with domestic space and the hierarchy between the gendered public and private was fundamental to the universal oppression of women. This dichotomy is still used very powerfully by feminist analysts. For example, Carole Pateman's work (1988, 1989) argues that the public/private split is the key to the feminist struggle of the nineteenth and twentieth centuries.

Yet the easy mapping of public versus private onto male versus female has been contested from the point of view of race, class and sexuality. Working-class women have sometimes had difficulty in joining in with the enthusiasm for getting women out of the domestic space. For many working-class women, their mothers were in fact very much in the public realm, and worked long hours. The idea of retreating to the home was a good thing, it was a place to put your feet up, and a fancy suburban home offered out-of-reach comforts. How to define public and private space is complicated, then, and the assumption that all women have been excluded from the public workforce is not always helpful. The history of the elaboration of the public/private dichotomy along the lines of male/female served to distinguish the middle class, the bourgeoisie, from the working class; 'Their women' don't work (Davidoff and Hall 1987). Black women too have pointed out that their participation in the elaboration of a realm of ladies was tenuous at best and, in general practice, unrealisable. For black women in the USA, overshadowed by a history of slavery in which 'the house' was 'massa's' and, although an improvement on working in the fields, hardly a safe haven, the automatic linking of femininity and domesticity is skewed. Moreover, for black communities in general, both past and present, whose neighbourhoods are over-policed and whose houses are often not havens, this doubled dichotomy doesn't map true.

It is important to take from these critiques not the impossibility of analysing space and gender, but rather the importance of developing what might be called, following Adrienne Rich (1986), a 'politics of location'.

> The politics of location investigates how place is gendered (masculinised or feminised) and how this delineates what kinds of bodies are permitted and welcomed in certain kinds of spaces, and what kinds are not.

We might take as a brief example here Bob Connell's (1987) work which analyses how the street is experienced in significantly different ways depending on one's gender and sexuality. A mother with a baby in a pram, a lesbian on a gay-pride march, a businessman, or a gay man with his lover all experience the street differently – as safe or not safe, reassuring or threatening, welcome respite or obstacle to be traversed, or a site of public statement or silencing.

Having said that, we can certainly trace in nineteenth- and twentieth-century Europe and North America how private space was increasingly defined as a haven of domesticity and femininity, while out in the rat race of public space, aggressive competition and masculinity held sway. We still need, then, to return to this question of the public and private, while keeping in mind the limited usefulness of grand, essentialist pronouncements about all men and all women. We'd like to concentrate on the 'body politic', a phrase which seems, at first glance, to stitch together the public and private. It is one of those phrases which conjures up ideas of enfranchisement, civil society and democracy – ideas which seem to be universal. On closer examination, the construction of the body politic in political and legal discourse privileges masculine bodies (Gatens 1991; Jones 1993; Corrigan and Meredyth 1997). Why is this?

In her article 'Are Small Penises Necessary for Civilisation? The Male Body and the Body Politic', Mary Spongberg (1997) argues that ideas of civilisation and good government which developed during the eighteenth century relied on the disappearance of not just the sexed bodies of women (their confinement in the domestic realm), but also certain kinds of male bodies as well. She traces imperial representations of black male bodies, and shows how colonialist anxieties about the size of 'African penises' (at the same time coupled with a belief in their impotence) indicates that the body politic and the political body itself must be unsexed. Furthermore, she argues, those who were evacuated from the political realm in the theories of eighteenth-century liberal political philosophers (women, the working classes, people of colour) had too much body.

We've already come across this idea that the bodies of categories of people – women, blacks, workers – rendered them ineligible for participation in certain aspects of life. Early in this chapter we discussed how having too much body meant that you would be incapable of rational thought (or, to put it another way, it was decided in advance that certain kinds of bodies would not be capable of rational thought). Here we have a twist on this kind of thinking. Certain kinds of bodies are not only not rational, but also are not legitimate candidates for the public realm. To disqualify entire categories of people from the public realm, it was merely necessary to develop representations of those people which characterised them as too close to sexuality. For women, as a category, their hysterical wombs disqualified them. For black and working-class men, overactive sexual appetites (represented particularly in black men by the myth of the large penis) disqualified them from the reasoned, civilised and unsexed realm of political life. For black working-class women, their hysterical wombs were coupled with this representation of wanton and overwhelming sexuality. It is important, then, to examine the history and present reproduction of the gendering of spaces. Not only to ask, along with popular songwriter Tracy Chapman, 'Across the lines, who would dare to go, over the bridge and under the tracks, that separate whites from blacks?', but also, what is the history of those lines and how do they function?

The gendering of categories of bodies is matched by a gendering of the spaces they are allowed or forbidden to enter and occupy. Various private spaces are perceived in Western societies as metaphorically and idealistically feminine: the domestic, the space of the body itself, the natural world, the family, property and the household. This explains in part the attractiveness of the stereotype of gay men as interior decorators – their feminine sexuality attaches them to feminine space. Various public places are likewise perceived as masculine: the marketplace, the economy, the polis and the state. This might explain the popularity of characterisations such as the 'Iron Lady' (past prime minister of England, Margaret Thatcher) of women politicians. The point here is not whether Thatcher is in fact tough as nails, but that the media and the public feel a certain anxiety about a 'lady' being prime minister of the nation, which is caught up in the play of images and descriptions of her which speculate on how hard (read masculine) she is.

Moreover, to constrain the space someone can easily occupy feminises them: enclaves such as the harem, suburbia, the ghetto, the dark continent and the closet are associated with weakness, passivity, mystery, ignorance and femininity. Similarly, open places, frontiers and places of exploration become associated with conquest, activity, the pursuit of knowledge and even aggression: think of the taming of the Wild West, the glorious metaphors associated with space travel and the heroic dedication of the scientist. Analysts examining the texts and contexts of nineteenth-century British imperialism often describe how, in a country such as India, the ruling British policed rigid gender boundaries between the militarised realms of the male governors and the domestic realm of the memsahibs. While nineteenth-century Britain was already a place where the construction of a rigid distinction between masculine and feminine space was in train, these divisions seemed particularly acute in the colonising exploits of the British Empire. Out in the Empire, extreme forms of masculinity seemed de rigueur: in Australia, for example, it was exemplified in the nationalist myth of the bush (Schaffer 1988, 1995). In India, hypermasculinist military virtues were the vogue (Mills 1991).

Of course, the hypermasculinist rhetoric of colonialist ventures and the Empire did not die out with the nineteenth century. To take an example closer to home, the first series of the popular television show *Star Trek* opened with a voice-over announcing: 'These are the voyages of the starship *Enterprise*. Her five-year mission: To seek out new worlds ... To boldly go where no man has gone before.' With this triumphant affirmation, each episode saw Captain James T. Kirk set off in search of new spaces, new galaxies, new knowledge. The voyages of the *Enterprise* conquered in hypermasculinist mode a feminised space (the space of space – chaotic, unruly, irrational). In the new series, *Star Trek: The Next Generation*, the opening voice repeats the earlier series' mission statement, with one important change: the starship *Enterprise* will 'boldly go where no *one* has gone before'. But despite the actively affirmative inclusiveness of this phrase, the mission statement still rings with a masculinised, conquering fervour. However, imagining space travel and exploration as masculine is tempered in this later series by the increased importance of 'the prime directive'. The prime directive is an injunction on space travellers in the federation not to interfere with the cultural and political life of populations with which the starships come into contact. This directive (and adhering to it provides the dramatic impetus for many of the episodes in the new *Star Trek* series) somehow makes less bold the exploration that seeking out strange new worlds entails. It seems a more cautious, more tentative, dare we say it, more feminine kind of exploration.

But it might be worthwhile to make a comment on this improved kind of exploration. In just one more example of the intricate weave of space with gender, class and race, we might look at nineteenth-century and early twentieth-century travel writing. Part of second-wave feminism involved the rediscovery of several women explorers and their writings; Virago Press reprinted the out-of-print works of women such as Mary Kingsley (1982), Alexandra David-Neel (1983), and Flora Tristan (1982, 1986). The critical response to the rediscovery of nineteenth-century women's travel writing during second-wave feminism tended to celebrate the brave and adventurous exploits of these white women who refused to be constrained by Victorian strictures on the proper behaviour of ladies. At the same time, their travel writings were also seen as more individual, personal and domestic. While the accounts of men conquering new worlds tended to produce scientific know-ledge (which involved a kind of messing around with the native populations which would have certainly violated the *Star Trek* prime directive, had such a thing existed), women travel writers' observations seemed more innocuous. Recipes, descriptions of the habits of local women, drawings of local flowers were not, it was argued, part of the knowledge-gathering expeditions targeted at native populations; they lacked the heroic exploits of men's travel writing. Bearing witness to the treatment of women and adopting the high moral ground (while not, of course, interfering with the local customs) had the effect of justifying the presence of colonial forces. Analysts have argued that the production of personalised texts on the colonies also had their place in consolidating the Empire, by consolidating different modes of knowledge (Mills 1991; Pratt 1992; Blunt 1994). Untangling the intersections of powerful systems of social life such as race, gender and class can be quite complex, and an easy division of public man/private woman seems bound to be less than effective, both analytically and politically.

Finally, it might be interesting to look at a space which isn't a space, and bodies which have no blood. Where might this be? The internet, of course. The experience of some surfers of the World Wide Web may highlight some of these questions about the ways in which embodiment is woven through subjectivity. The question of whether the net is a masculine space or not can be approached in many ways. Sherry Turkle (1984, 1995) has done some very interesting studies on the inscriptions of masculinity and femininity consis-tent with different kinds of developing computer technologies. Going against the grain, Sadie Plant (1997) suggests that there is more that is feminine than masculine about cyberspace, both in terms of the history of the women who were involved in the development of digital technologies, and in terms of the feminine nature of the space. Some writers look more closely and specifically at the gendering of any of the several technologies which are bundled together, rather amorphously, to make it up. Whether it's email, World Wide Web pages, online fan groups, listservers, Usenet and newsgroups, or MUDs and MOOs, the question of the gendering of communication and comm-unities in cyberspace is a vexed one. Are there more women than men on the web? And how would we know? Is cyberspace an unredeemable and irrem-ediable bastion of misogyny? Or is it so large and amorphous as to permit a breaching of this macho facade?

To draw out some of the implications of these questions, we're going to pause over the question of MUDs, or MOOs (object-oriented MUDs). These are sites on the net which originally were known as 'multi-user dungeons', online interactive role-playing sites for games such as Dungeons and Dragons. This soon transformed to multi-user 'dimensions' or 'domains' and their uses range from role-playing games to the elaboration of virtual univer-sities. By using some reasonably simple software commands onscreen and online, a participant in a MUD can build classrooms, develop a persona or character, talk with other characters or participants in the MUD in real time, and so on.

One writer on MUDs has argued that, even in those MUDs which encourage female characters, the sometimes violent or hostile reactions to women, and the gender stereotypes in operation there would discourage women from participating in many MUDs (Kendall 1996). It may depend though, on the uses for which the MUD has been designed. Tari Lin Fander-clai (1996), a college composition teacher, uses MUDs to link writing classes from different universities for collaborative learning and peer review. She has found that the bodily anonymity of the MUD encouraged some of her quieter students to participate in discussions.

In most MUDs, the participant has the option on entering of choosing their gender: there are several to choose from – he, she, it, the royal we, 'spivak' (an invented gender – a fluid concatenation of he and she with its own pronouns: e, em, eirs, eirself) (see McRae 1996, p. 257; Kendall 1996, pp. 217–19). There is no requirement to choose any particular gender, a man can be a woman, a woman a man, a transgender woman can be the royal we, whatever. He and she are the genders most frequently chosen, but there is a good deal of evidence to suggest that many people use MUDs as a place to experiment with gender, and choose a virtual gender which is at odds with their real-life gender. Shannon McRae (1996) suggests that, despite the preva-lence of gender stereotypes, MUD participants' experimentation with gender/sex roles and erotic pleasure 'may well afford some measure of resistance against social and technological forces that would divide us from each other and prevent us from naming and shaping our own experience' (p. 262). And because the web is represented as a colonial space at the moment, a frontier, some of the hypermasculinist rhetoric of bold conquering, which we discussed above, may pervade it, while at the same time, through its technologies of virtual reality, it permits an unprecedented exploration of gender roles.

We blunder into a hypermasculinist chat room, or climb the forbidding stairs of the university library with trepidation; we sit uncomfortably in the bank manager's office, or slouch with forced nonchalance down a tough street in a strange town. Bars, university libraries, dark streets, parking lots, shopping malls can all impart a sense of belonging or dislocation. Being in some spaces may even make us anxious to the point of illness. We carry the boundaries of these spaces within ourselves, we embody the cultural land-scape. Iris Young (1990b) took this idea into the political realm in her book, *Justice and the Politics of Difference*. In a chapter called 'The Scaling of Bodies and the Politics of Identity', Young suggests that bodily characteristics in Euro-American society are ranked, or scaled. Race, sex, sexuality, age and ability are categories that are used to rank bodies and assign them to a hier-archical place. She uses Julia Kristeva's idea of the abject (which we discussed briefly in Chapter 2 and again in Chapter 4) to argue that the bodies of those groups who are denigrated produce physical or corporeal reactions in those who denigrate them. The reaction of aversion or disgust that some people have to others is, for Young, like the process of abjection that Kristeva describes, part of the way subjects are produced. In the process of learning to draw the boundaries between what is proper to 'me' and what is 'not-me', the subject develops a disgusted fascination with the abject products of the body (blood, sweat, urine, mucus, faeces and so on). This fascination is one with boundaries, the borderlines of the self, and the reaction of disgust is due in part to how tenuous, how porous this boundary between outside and inside, between Self and Other, can be. (Kristeva 1982) This repressed and uncon-scious visceral response of aversion is something that Young argues is part of the way in which bodies which do not conform to the generic human ideal (that is, old people, black people, women, disabled people and so on) come to be shunned. The threat to corporeal integrity that the abject represents, the tenuousness of the self's borders, is projected onto entire categories of people: these bodies represent a threat to the perfect borders of the generic human body, and so we shun them. This reaction of aversion is part of the complex production of categories of Self and Other. And although such a construction is cultural, we experience it as natural, where the very marked bodies of these non-generic humans affront our imagination of ourselves who inhabit unmarked bodies.

If we are young, we might turn away from the inevitable onset of age embodied in the wrinkled woman; if we are mobile, the fragility embodied by the man in the wheelchair might frighten us. If we are white, we might swallow painfully while we cross the street to avoid the group of black kids on the corner. Despite even the best intentions of those of us who adopt liberal attitudes, or who may in fact be members of these abject categories, we harbour the learned, unconscious and visceral response of aversion and these reactions are an attempt to maintain and police the limits of the body. A similar kind of point about the cultural and socially inscribed limits of the body was made quite early by the anthropologist Mary Douglas (1966). For Douglas, the body is 'bounded' as both symbol and matter of culture. As she affirmed in her book *Purity and Danger: An Analysis of Concepts of Pollution and Taboo*, 'all margins are dangerous' (p. 120) because the margin represents the limits and boundaries of social identity.

Marked Bodies

In 'Encounters: The Body Silent in America', Robert Murphy (1995) explains how his sense of self and his relations with others changed radically when he began to rely on a wheelchair for his mobility. Life in the wheelchair meant that a black campus policeman who never before had greeted him, now began to say hello. Women would speak to him, and more personally than before. Graduate students began to call him by first name, and undergraduates lightly touch his arm or shoulder when taking leave of him. For Murphy, it seemed as if he had arrived in a different territory. What this territory is might become clear if we consider his experience in the light of some of the critiques of Merleau-Ponty which writers such as Diprose (1994) and Young (1990b) have elaborated.

We discussed Merleau-Ponty's ideas on the phenomenology of perception, the body thinking itself, early in this chapter. Some of the feminist philosophers who have welcomed Merleau-Ponty's insights have also taken him to task for imagining a certain mastery of movement as being universal; they have argued that this may more accurately portray the self-assured carriage through the world of the normal male. In *Throwing Like a Girl*, Young (1990a) argues that women are less likely to take up and move through the full range of body movements and spaces available to them. Couple this with the idea that women often imagine themselves as objects, or approach their presence in the world self-consciously, and you have the explanation for the three 'contradictory modalities of feminine bodily existence' which Young (1990a, p. 147) posits (ambiguous transcendence, inhibited intentionality and discontinuous unity with its surroundings). 'Feminine bodily existence', she writes, 'is frequently not a pure presence to the world because it is referred onto itself as well as onto possibilities in the world' (1990a, p. 150). But surely these restrictions are not solely the property of women? While girls may not throw like boys, and hence 'fail to make full use of the body's spatial and lateral potentialities' (p. 145), we might say the same of any body which has been habitually and socially restricted to a constricted space: the closet, the ghetto, the wrong side of the tracks. In other words, part of Merleau-Ponty's development of the thinking body relies on that idea of the generic human body.

Perhaps our example of Robert Murphy, the man who took up a new life with others when he began to live in a wheelchair, will be helpful here. Murphy attributed this new and welcome change in his human relations to a sense on the part of these 'other' groups that he was no longer a threat, or that he now 'occupied the same devalued status as ex-convicts, certain ethnic and racial minorities, and the mentally ill, among others' (1995, p. 140). And it does seem obvious that admission to the status of the devalued would in fact be part of the disabled experience. But is there not some way to imagine this bodily situation as other than entirely negative, as only in the realm of devalued status? Perhaps what is also at issue here is the ways in which the disabled Murphy no longer seemed a candidate for the unmarked generic human body, and with his new marked body, he entered a space peopled with other marked bodies. He entered the space where no one is pure, in the sense that Mary Douglas uses it, where all the bodies are marginal. Yet if our bodies are all marked and traverse gendered spaces which realise themselves in different ways on them and in them, then we must negotiate our relations with one another without having recourse to an unmarked generic human. We become hybrid bodies, negotiating our everyday contacts with one another.

Hybrid Bodies

This is the last space we will discuss, this space of hybrid bodies. Perhaps one of the easiest ways of imagining this space is to invoke the experience of people who are bilingual. People who speak more than one language often describe how they switch not just from one set of words to another, or even from one cultural context to another, but how they *feel* different. They move their shoulders differently, enter the room differently, drive differently, eat dinner with different manners and so on. Anyone who has spent a lengthy period of time in another culture, whether working or travelling, has had a taste of this process of embodiment – it's called culture shock. Gloria Anzaldúa (1991) tries to capture this doubled-body experience in her collection of essays, *Borderlands/La Frontera: The New Mestiza*. Particularly in 'La conciencia de la mestiza/Towards a New Consciousness' she creates a different experience of reading by writing portions of her text in Chicana Spanish and portions in American English. Two languages which are already hybrids come together to make the experience of reading vastly different depending on who the reader is.

Jennifer Biddle (1993), an Australian anthropologist, describes a similar process. After breaking her neck in a car accident while doing fieldwork among the Walpiri in northern Australia, Biddle wrote an article which explained that, although anthropologists-in-training should certainly be warned of the dangers of fieldwork (and buy extra medical insurance), the process of doing fieldwork, coming into contact with another culture, living in that culture and embodying that culture personally entails a risk, not just intellectual, not just ethical, but bodily. It involved a double embodiment, of the kind which Chicana writers such as Anzaldúa and Moraga (1983) in the USA are invoking in their double-voiced texts. It seemed impossible to Biddle to imagine a prophylactic for the anthropological endeavour. 'To do fieldwork is to live difference. It is both to confront and, to a greater or lesser degree, transgress the safety, the certainty, the habits, the contours and definitions of a single corporeal schema' (p. 193).

Texts such as Biddle's, Murphy's, Young's and Anzaldúa's point out for us the fuzziness of the boundaries of the bodily self, and its intersection with the social body. They remind us not only that there is no generic human, but that embodied people, people with marked bodies, are constantly risking themselves in contact. Culture shock, breaking your neck in the field and the abject response of racism – these remind us that we think with our bodies.

Summary

What we have tried to do in this chapter is introduce you to some of the more important writers and ideas in relation to gender and bodies: from Merleau-Ponty to Foucault, Bourdieu, Diprose, Walkerdine, Young and Douglas. Their writings on the operations of power, in particular Foucault's notion of bio-power, have been particularly influential, and offer gender analysts ways of approaching issues such as regimes of beauty and cosmetic surgery, the management of reproduction and the cultural constructions of mothering. We also considered some of the critiques of the major (mostly male) theorists who tend to work with the notion of a generic (that is, masculine) body.

We also canvassed some of the more prevalent dualisms that come up in relation to bodies and gender: mind/body; public/private; and nature/culture. In critiquing notions such as the generic human body and abstract thinking (with its assumptions about the disembodied, neutral observer/learner/knowledge producer) we show both how these concepts serve to rob everyone of the joyful particularities of being and how they exclude specific bodies from particular sites and activities. Theories about gendered bodies and the process of embodiment enable us to look closely at the practices that regulate our gendering, but also permit us to engage in debates and playfulness at the sites where gender is ambiguous. The analysis of bodies in space enables us to consider the many specificities involved in our occupation of spaces and places – public and private, institutional and domestic. The material in this chapter should provide you with opportunities to enter into critical debates and playful questionings. Our final chapter deals with the workplace and its genderings.

Recommended Reading

Anzaldúa, Gloria (1991) 'La conciencia de la mestiza/Towards a New Consciousness' in *Borderlands/La Frontera: The New Mestiza*, Aunt Lute Books, San Francisco, pp. 77–91.

Biddle, Jennifer (1993) 'The Anthropologist's Body or What it Means to Break Your Neck in the Field', *Australian Journal of Anthropology*, 4(3):184–97.

Braidotti, Rosi (1991) 'Radical Philosophies of Sexual Difference', *Patterns of Dissonance*, Polity, Oxford.

Cartwright, Lisa (1995) *Screening the Body: Tracing Medicine's Visual Culture*, University of Minnesota Press, Minneapolis.

Connell, R.W. (1987) *Gender and Power*, Polity, Cambridge.

Connell, R.W. (1996) *Masculinities*, Allen & Unwin, Sydney.

Cranny-Francis, Anne (1995) *The Body in the Text*, Melbourne University Press, Melbourne.

Mascia-Lees, Frances E. and Paytricia Sharpe (eds) (1992) *Tattoo, Torture, Mutilation, and Adornment: The Denaturalization of the Body in Culture and Text*, State University of New York Press, Albany.

Haraway, Donna (2001) 'Modest_Witness@Second_Millenium' *Modest_Witness@ Second_Millenium.FemaleMan©_Meets_OncoMouse™: Feminism and Technoscience*, Routledge, New York.

Irigaray, Luce (1985) *This Sex Which Is Not One*, (trans. Catherine Porter and Carolyn Burke), Cornell University Press, Ithaca, NY.

Jenkins, Richard 1992) *Pierre Bourdieu*, Routledge, London.

Murphy, Robert (1995) 'Encounters: The Body Silent in America' in B. Ingstad and S. White (eds) *Disability and Culture*, University of California Press, Berkeley, pp. 140–58.

Orlan Panel (1998) http://filament.illumin.co.uk/ica/Bookshop/video/performance.html.

Pateman, Carole (1988) *The Sexual Contract*, Polity, Cambridge.

Plant, Sadie (1997) *zeros + ones: Digital Women + the New Technoculture*, Fourth Estate, London.

Sparke, Penny (1995) *As Long As It's Pink: The Sexual Politics of Taste*, Pandora, London.

Walkerdine, Valerie (1990) *Schoolgirl Fictions*, Verso, London.

Exercises

1. How are bodies gendered in your disciplinary background?

2. Discuss the functioning of gender on bodies at a level of education with which you are familiar.

3. What ways of thinking have you acquired that allow you to connect everyday life with the analysis of the social institutions that shape that life? Map out the theorists whose work seems most useful to you for analysing embodied existence.

4. Are you part of a community that knows? Describe it and some of the contradictions that this sometimes involves. Pay particular attention to the kinds of knowledges that your knowing community marginalises and/or excludes.

5. Discuss the discourse of masculinity with reference to beauty culture. How do you think men are currently influenced by contemporary notions of masculinity? You might consider looking at some of the magazines targeted at a male audience, for example sports magazines of various kinds (football, cricket, surfing, racing and so on), men's fashion and lifestyle magazines, as well as those with a more ambiguous audience, such as business and popular science magazines.

6. What are the political or social implications of thinking of the body as a kind of plastic?

7. What kind of agency (limits/possibilities) does cosmetic surgery offer (a) men, (b) women, and (c) people of colour? What do you think the new cosmetic surgery for men means? How does gender reassignment surgery fit into these debates?

8. What are the laws governing transsexual bodies in your state or country? Do your laws make it possible to imagine a lesbian transsexual?

9. Where do you stand in the debate on anorexia and agency? Can extreme dieting be personally empowering? Does pathological protest have the power to effect cultural change?

10. Consider various kinds of body modification such as tattooing, piercing and scarring. What do you think are the meanings of such practices? How do they differ from culture to culture? Focus on a popular practice among your own friends: what meanings do you think this practice makes? And how does the meaning change in different contexts?

11. Describe the gendered functioning of a ritual in your own habitus. How does it mirror other aspects of your habitus?

12. What are the implications for thinking about gendered and colonised space of the leadership styles of Jean-Luc Picard (of *Star Trek: The Next Generation*) versus Catherine Janeway (of *Star Trek: Voyager*)?

13. What have your experiences on the net taught you about the boundaries of the gendered body?

6

Ways of Living

In previous chapters we have discussed ways in which gender operates as a social practice rather than a natural attribute. In considering contrasting areas such as the construction of subjectivity, the mediating role of language and the capacity of literary and media representations to both reflect and shape our identities, we have demonstrated how gender is political rather than natural in the ways it operates. Our discussion has also shown that the category of the social relates as much to internal, private domains as to external, public ones. This chapter considers how we live and 'do' gender in light of these connections. It does so in the immediate context of everyday life, in particular with reference to the workplace, home life, the use of space and the negotiation of gender roles by young children.

Where the Structural and the Psychic Meet: Gendered Labour and the Politics of Work

The workplace is profoundly gendered in ways that are both more and less obvious. Therefore it is important to be attuned to the different levels at which gender operates in the world of paid work, and in our very definitions of what work is. Take the term 'workplace', for example. While conjuring up a range of different jobs, professions and practices, there is still a popular perception that the term 'work' refers to waged labour alone. New technologies, changing economic and social conditions and demands for increased flexibility have challenged the view that home and workplace (private and public) can be neatly separated. But the idea that real work is financially remunerated remains widespread. Early feminist work on the unpaid labour of housekeeping showed that our very conceptions of what work is relate to what we are prepared to recognise as work.

> Discussions of work almost always exclude unpaid labour, such as work performed in the home. Work is conventionally equated with waged or salaried labour.

Changes in the nature of paid work, and women's contemporary visibility in the paid labour force, can mask underlying continuities in the inequitable organisation of labour. As early as the 1950s, sociologist Talcott Parsons predicted that women would increasingly remain in the workforce after marriage and children, but that their work in the home would remain primary (see Wearing 1996, pp. 103, 143). This, he argued, would reflect the caring and expressive dimensions of female socialisation (women are commonly represented, or constructed, as being more caring and emotionally expressive, and so more suited to maintain home and family life). The result would be that the pay and status of women in the workforce would be lower than that of their partners (reflecting women's lower interest in career development) and complementarity of gender roles would be assured. Fifty years later, after the turn of the millennium, this reading clearly needs to be challenged in some respects, but there are also some senses in which it accurately describes contemporary gendered reality.

Note, for example, the frequent disparity between the expectations that young girls often have about their futures (for example an envisaged seamlessness of their working and home lives) and the structural inequities on which such expectations are likely to founder. In Western societies, as feminist critics point out, such expectations are shaped more by media representations of superwomen having it all than by any clear understanding of economic inequity. For example, the female leads of popular soaps and sitcoms often maintain a demanding job and a complex emotional life without any apparent conflict between the two. Vastly increased female participation in the paid workforce over the last decade has not seen any parallel diminution in family and household responsibilities. The expansion of socially acceptable roles for women has come 'largely through adding on new responsibilities and possibilities to those already assigned to them rather than through structural changes in social institutions or interpersonal relationships' (Jaggar and Rothenberg 1993, p. 3).

Both the paid workplace per se, and the myriad practices which sustain it, are deeply gendered. There exists a crucial nexus between what we call work and conceptions of femininity and masculinity, which suggests that the work that is available to and appropriate for particular individuals is influenced by conceptions of gender. Betsy Wearing (1996, p. 167) gives a summary of the factors that combine to maintain the gendered character of labour:

- women's responsibility for childcare and domestic tasks;

- the vertical and horizontal gendered segregation of the workforce;

- differential definitions of male and female skills;

- lack of recognition for skills acquired outside the workplace;

- lack of recognition of responsibilities outside the workplace;

- the low status of part-time work;

- the positive recognition of masculine bureaucratic rationality;

- the devaluation of traditionally feminine interpersonal skills.

Some of these factors are changing, with greater recognition of domestic responsibility included in some workplace agreements, and the growth in other modes of work, such as working from home and consultancy work. However, in the main, Wearing's analysis remains accurate, and the factors which devalue women's participation in the paid workforce continue to operate – whether as blatantly differential valuations of work (for example in Australia it has been noted that full-time childcare workers are paid less than apprentice nurserymen, although the level of responsibility expected of the former is immeasurably greater), or as more subtle reflections on women's ability to perform (for example the refusal to accommodate the time constraints of women who have young children).

We have noted that neither women nor men are a homogeneous group. Do the differentials of ethnicity and class – as well as others such as age and sexual preference – qualify the extent to which women at work can be depicted as generally discriminated against? After all, the status and salaried remuneration of, for example, a white female professional and a black male labourer are very different. How central is the axis of gender to workplace discrimination? There are many forms of oppression which are not reducible to any one type.

Gender politics is frequently subtle rather than obvious. For example, in relation to the case above (white female professional/black labourer) we need to take into account a number of gendered elements. First, subordination at work tends to be feminised (equated with women's work) no matter who (male or female) is in the subordinate role. Second, manual labour is defined in opposition to intellect, in a version of the classic gendered dichotomy (male/female; mind/body) we have discussed throughout the book and described in Chapter 1. Taking these elements into account, it is not surprising that a white *female* professional is more highly paid and has higher status than a *black* labourer, since his work is systematically feminised (and hers, contrastingly, masculinised). Note that we haven't even taken into account the effect of race issues in this comparison.

Some gender theorists (for example Naffine 1990) contend that feminism is most powerful and provocative when used as a site to critique *multiple* exclusions. To the extent that the implicit norm of major societal institutions is that of the *white, middle-class* male, it is not only women who are discriminated against. In the context of the labour market – where expanding globalisation entails massively increased casualisation of labour and increasingly restrictive work practices – Jan Pettman (1996) points out that an examination of the term 'women' actually shows it to include large numbers of children of both sexes, many of whom are non-white (that is, the term 'women' is not a biological category, but a sign with a number of specific meanings which include subordinate, non-autonomous, manual and low status). Once again, gender suggests a tool of analysis which can expose a range of inequities.

Gender analysis suggests that an examination of the workplace requires a more sustained exploration than a superficial reference to gender bias might allow. An acknowledgment of gender bias can even deflect attention from the more complex structural relationships that sustain gendered labour practices. Consider again Parsons' 1950 contention that women would remain in the (paid) workforce after marriage and children, that their work in the home – reflecting the caring and expressive aspects of their socialisation – would remain primary, and that their pay and status would stay lower than that of their partners in ways which would guarantee complementarity of gender roles. As we have noted, there are some senses in which this contention would seem to be borne out (as well as some in which contemporary feminist critics can agree with his prediction, if not his values). But does this reading comprise gender *analysis*, particularly in light of Parsons' acceptance that family stability and that of the wider society benefit from such complementarity, as well as benefiting from the ensuing absence of competition between the sexes? Notions of gender complementarity, and the social benefits derived from it, are hardly feminist friendly. Parsons' contention that employment in the paid workforce comprises an extension of family roles has also been challenged by contemporary gender theorists. Game and Pringle (1983), for example, argue that gender is not so much taken to work after being formed within the family as it is actively constructed within the workplace itself; that is, the workplace is a major site for the generation of gender ideas and norms, which are then referred back to family life.

How, then, is gender actively constructed through the workplace, rather than as the product of socialisation as was for so long believed (and to a significant extent still is)? Here we might be seeing the limitations imposed by dichotomous (either/or) thinking. It may not be a case of socialisation counterposed against other factors. An alternative reading is to see these contrasting dimensions as *reinforced* by gendered socialisation practices. For example, with reference to the work of Game and Pringle (1983), Betsy Wearing (1996) notes the extent to which the division of labour in the white-goods industry is structured around dichotomies. These include heavy/light, skilled/unskilled, dangerous/safe and dirty/clean, in which the first of these pairs is seen as appropriate for men, and the second for women:

There is nothing inherently different in the quality of the work, it is the meaning given to it by the men and women themselves, and men's work is perceived as superior. (pp. 103–4)

Once again, class and race differences are crucial and complicating; however, gendered categories continue to shape and even structure inequities related to work. White middle-class masculinity is predicated on a confidence and dominance to which working-class and non-white men have less access vis-à-vis their (white middle-class) employers. But for men who do not fit the privileged positioning (because of class, ethnicity and/or ability) compensation can be sought via aspirations for higher education for sons, and a sense of pride in physical strength. (It is interesting to note the flexibility of constructions of male physicality in ways that perpetuate gender inequity – from brute strength detached from intellect, to the equally tenacious notion of the real man who scorns effete presentation.) In these scenarios, as Wearing (1996, p. 104) highlights:

the term socialization takes on a different meaning. No longer can it be claimed to be fitting men and women for their different adult roles in society. Rather it is a means of reinforcing women's inferiority and subordination, and for some men a struggle to maintain a dominant form of masculinity.

The proposition that gender (subordination) is actively constructed by and within the workplace, and is not necessarily the product or outcome of prior socialisation within the family, raises a range of questions about which gender theorists themselves disagree (see, for example, Adkins' (1995) critique of Game and Pringle's account). But it is helpful to note something of a shift away from the emphasis on socialisation practices as an explanation of gender discrimination in the workplace. Wearing (1996, p. 104) sees this shift as mirrored in the contemporary feminist preference for the term 'construction of gender' rather than gender socialisation – gender as constantly produced and renegotiated, rather than a fixed category and set of qualities. It is also helpful to note a corresponding reappraisal of terms such as 'exploitation' and 'alienation', to more accurately reflect the kinds of gender subordination which occur.

It is particularly important to address the ways in which exploitation operates in the contemporary gendered workplace. This is because the concept of exploitation speaks directly to issues of discrimination, marginalisation and harassment which relate to the everyday experience of working life. There is also agreement among gender theorists that the more familiar Marxist/socialist conceptions of the term need refining in light of more recent developments. It is in this context that the concept of emotional labour (which, for reasons which will become clear, has been particularly elaborated by feminists) is suggestive. The concept of emotional labour is also helpful in highlighting some of the gendered links between work and intimacy which we will go on to develop.

So what is emotional labour? In her 1983 text *The Managed Heart*, Arlie Russell Hochschild powerfully dissects the dynamics of emotional labour. Hochschild wants to contrast traditional, Marxist-inspired conceptions of labour and exploitation (according to which workers give their time and energy, but not necessarily their feelings) with the contemporary, less obvious, requirement of workers that they manage their feelings in the interests of the workplace which employs them. The management of feelings requires stringent self-surveillance (at least initially, or until that management becomes habitual). It thus comprises work, and can involve insidious exploitative elements. To the extent that women are overrepresented in the aptly named 'service' industries, there is a gendered aspect to such exploitation to which women are disproportionately subject.

Emotional labour is the work of controlling and managing feelings in the workplace. It may mean enhancing emotional expression or suppressing that expression, but in both cases is aimed at constructing a positive image of the company and maximising company profit.

Hochschild's account is a fine-grained analysis of the work and training practices of Delta Airlines, which substantiates her more general claims about 'the commercialization of human feeling', particularly as this affects women. She speaks of a businessman's casual but calculated request for 'a smile' from the female flight attendant:

> In some versions of this smile war the flight attendant works for United; in others, TWA or World Airways. In some versions the businessman says, 'What's the matter, not smiling today?' or 'Baby, where's my smile?' In some versions the man is old, in others young. But in all the times I've heard this story, one detail goes unchanged. It is always a man who claims the smile and always a woman's smile that he claims. (Hochschild 1983 in Jaggar and Rothenberg 1993, p. 328)

The association of women with caring and nurturance (as of the male with intellect and productivity) is persistent (we will see the subtle forms this assumes in intimate relationships later on). Hochschild's contention is that this association becomes an expectation and an implicit requirement in the world of paid work. Women's very employability comes to depend on adherence to the stereotype. While race and class politics are also operative, it is the gendered politics of emotional labour that she particularly wants to expose.

In the course of so doing, Hochschild considers a range of subtle ways in which power is exercised, and structural gendered inequalities both produced and reproduced in the workplace. For example, in the context she studies, and in a striking illustration of the relationship between language and power (see Chapter 3), there is no such thing as an obnoxious passenger. Despite mounting evidence to the contrary, there are only mishandled passengers: 'By linguistically avoiding any attribution of blame, the companies smuggle out of discourse the very idea of a right to be angry at a passenger' (Hochschild 1983 in Jaggar and Rothenberg 1993, p. 334). The onus of responsibility for bad passenger (customer, consumer, client) behaviour is placed squarely with the (female) employee. This is a situation which requires considerable emotional labour on the part of these employees, which at the same time reproduces and reinforces the stereotype of the female carer.

Emotional labour, then, is a form of exploitation, for the very reason that it is unacknowledged, unrewarded and its specific gendering is not acknowledged by employers. It is also on the increase. In an accelerating, globalised economy, service providers are 'like workers on an assembly line that have been speeded up ... asked to hand out commercial love at an ever faster rate, to more people in the same amount of time' (Hochschild 1983 in Jaggar and Rothenberg 1993, p. 328). Thus, the commodification of feeling goes far beyond the interests or idiosyncrasies of particular individuals (significantly, Hochschild notes that the 'trainers' in this emotional commercialisation seemed 'deeply decent people'). Rather, it is necessitated by the commercial logic of the system itself. Hochschild's achievement is to show the often unrecognised relationship between economic and emotional organisation, and the pivotal role of gender in their constant interplay. In the course of so doing, she shows that the concept of exploitation needs refining to address the emotional and psychic dimensions traditionally counterposed against the hard material domain of labour practices and economic structure.

The idea of emotional labour (in contrast to more traditional Marxist conceptions of exploitation) can also shed light on ways in which gender, class and race exploitation collide. Menial work in Western liberal democracies is often performed by non-white people of low socioeconomic background. In an area of employment such as domestic service (which is heavily racialised and classed as well as feminised), traditional conceptions of exploitation fail to capture the emotional oppression which is part of the job. In her study of the politics of domestic service, Judith Rollins argues that the power dynamics at issue 'go ... far beyond the exploitation in the economic sense in which the term is usually used' (Rollins in Jaggar and Rothenberg 1993, p. 335). The gendered concept of emotional labour can access these less visible forms of discrimination in ways that gender-blind accounts are unable to do.

In a fascinating discussion of the nuances involved, Rollins reveals the extent to which employers of domestics extract far more than labour in the commonly understood sense:

> This fact was suggested by the employers' preference for an individual woman over a cleaning service and the numerous statements in which employers made clear that work performance was not their highest priority in evaluating their domestics. (p. 335)

What, then, was valued more highly? Interestingly, it was the validation and psychological reinforcement the employers' lifestyles. This came in the form of *deference* – often subtle displays of appreciation – from those constructed as social subordinates. And who, in this context, were subordinates? Frequently working-class, non-white women, revealingly referred to as 'girls'.

With reference to the work of sociologist Erving Goffman (1963, 1971), Rollins dissects the politics and rituals of deference, 'which function as a symbolic means by which appreciation is regularly conveyed to a recipient' (Rollins in Jaggar and Rothenberg 1993, p. 336). Employers of domestics accord themselves the 'privilege of familiarity' with their girls, along with a range of liberties (for example intrusive questions about their private lives and the use of their given names) which, it scarcely needs to be noted, are not reciprocated. In this context, it is yet again pertinent to note the role of language (for example the use of the term 'girl' rather than 'woman' for an adult and the very label 'domestic' itself) in the maintenance and reinforcement of gendered power relations. Also apparent from this particular illustration is how readily these can converge with discrimination on the basis of race and class (in that domestics are frequently women of colour and low socioeconomic status).

In Chapter 4, the gendered politics of performativity, and its relationship to subjectivity, was discussed. Rollins' study of domestic service – and the importance that employers accord to particular rituals of behaviour in their domestics – well illustrates this point. For example, Rollins relates how a prospective employer expressed doubts about her suitability for the work in the absence of the 'deliberately subservient' presentation she had assumed during earlier interviews. To allay the woman's suspicions, Rollins assumed the full dress and demeanour of subservience, complete with docile body language and expression. She was, she says:

> rather shocked at her [that is, the prospective employer's] obvious pleasure over and total lack of suspicion about this performance, especially since she had encountered me without it the previous week ... She did not question the change; my behavior now expressed my belief in my inferiority in relation to her and thus my acceptance of her superiority in relation to me. (Rollins in Jaggar and Rothenberg 1993, p. 337)

Having adopted the protective disguise of deference, Rollins had constructed her own subjectivity (and thus suitability) for the gendered, classed and racialised requirements of domestic labour.

A number of studies have been undertaken on the gendered politics of labour, and on the crucial if often covert role of the corresponding construction of subjectivity. (See, for example, Lisa Adkins' analysis of the tourist industry (1995) and Cynthia Enloe (1989) and Jan Pettman (1996) on the centrality of gender, racial and class hierarchies in the globalised economy.) Such studies illustrate the wide potential of gender as a lens through which to examine a vast array of work practices. They also suggest that the gendered politics of labour will remain an important exploratory site in any consideration of the politics of inequity.

> The study of the gendering of labour, and of the markers of that gendering, reveal not only how work is differentially gendered, but also how it is classed, ethnically specific, able-bodied and sexed.

Home is Where the Heart Is?: The Gendered Politics of Intimacy

To shift our focus to the domain of home, family and intimate life is to address sites quite different from those of the (paid) workplace. Yet here, too, the politics of gender is operative in ways that can mask the continuities between our public and private lives. Our intimate relationships do not operate in a vacuum, untouched by the structural political and economic inequities we have noted. The very questioning of the public/private dichotomy suggests that the gendered relations of the workplace do not cease to operate in the home, or even in the bedroom.

Gender theorists chart important connections in this context. For example, Adkins (1995) and others highlight the significance of family labour to the economy. In her pioneering study *The Sexual Contract* (1988), Carole Pateman traces links between the marriage contract and the wider exploitation of women. Even outside the traditional institutions of marriage and family, gender theorists have found a politics of intimacy to operate along decidedly (if often subtly) gendered lines. Thus Stevi Jackson (1995, p. 50) shows how the notion of romance is 'implicated in maintaining a cultural definition of love which is detrimental to women'. Similarly, Sandra Lee Bartky (1990, p. 100) elaborates a 'gendered imbalance in the provision of emotional support' which sees women give more and receive less than do men ('men get the benefits; women run the risks'; p. 113). Such accounts suggest that the concept of 'emotional labour' is no less applicable to the realm of intimate relation-ships than it is to commercial relationships.

Exactly *how* it is applicable needs to be considered, however, since there are significant differences between the gendered emotional labour of the workplace, and that expended on those we love. The gendered politics of the workplace and public sphere cannot simply be extrapolated across to the private realm of intimacy. How, then, to conceptualise the emotional labour involved in the norm of heterosexual love; the challenging inter-relationship of structural and psychic in this undertheorised (but now increasingly interrogated) domain? How to theorise the politics of intimacy when part of us is likely to reject the very suggestion that theory and politics apply to the realm of emotion?

These questions are confronting and difficult to answer. But they also evoke our previous theme that we are not unitary subjects. The way we think and the way we feel do not fit seamlessly together, and it would be simplistic to deny this. So the notion of *disjuncture* can be helpful here – a recognition that intimacy and the deep feelings associated with it do not necessarily coincide with our conscious politics. Previous attempts to deny this led to some painful splits among an earlier generation of feminists (Segal 1994, for example, argues that it was not until the 1970s that the limits of consciousness were confronted within feminism). The terrain of romance, love and desire is necessarily contradictory. It also forces confrontation with one of the most powerful claims to which our subjectivities are vulnerable, the seemingly transcendental allure of romantic love (and note the gendered character of this construct – that the myth of romantic love applies to women alone). No wonder there is widespread resistance to the very suggestion that love relates to social, much less political, factors.

To say that the realm of love, care and intimacy cannot be detached from gendered power relationships (and the public dimensions of these) is not to say that this is all love comprises. Nor is it to dispute that great pleasure and gratification can be derived from intimate relationships. Women are not simply victims of their close relationships. Recent work on the gendered politics of intimacy does not contest the myriad pleasures associated with the ideal of romantic love. This is in contrast to earlier feminist writing (for example Kollantai (1977[1919]), de Beauvoir (1972[1949]) and Firestone (1970) which tended to be extremely critical of the very notion of romance. For contemporary gender theorists such as Jackson (1995, p. 50) it is unnecessary to deny 'the pleasures of romance or the euphoria of falling in love' while being 'sceptical about romantic ideals and many of their consequences' (such as loss of autonomy, merged identity and reduced career prospects when the needs of male partners are accorded higher priority). Few today would underestimate the complexity of theorising desire in a way which can address both its social and subjective dimensions.

So how can these connections – the social and political aspects of love and intimacy – be explored? Gender theorists contest the ideal that there could be something called love, romance or even emotion outside particular social and historical contexts. Just as gender is shown to be a social practice rather than a natural attribute, so the apparent naturalness and universality of love are questioned. Another way of putting this would be to say that while the need for affection and affective ties may be natural and universal, there is nothing natural about the form, and particularly the institutional expression, this need takes. With reference to the apparent universal appeal of Mills and Boon novels, Stevi Jackson (1995, p. 51, citing Taylor 1989) suggests that an alternative interpretation is possible:

> these romances derive from a specifically Western culture tradition – if they are being consumed worldwide we need to know why they are being read. It cannot simply be assumed that all women everywhere make sense of them in exactly the same way.

For Jackson, we need to analyse love as a culturally constructed emotion, and chart its connections to specific social contexts of intimate relationships.

Such analyses are now being undertaken. In her 1998 text *Intimacy* (and with reference to a range of theorists), Lynn Jamieson proposes that what she calls 'disclosing intimacy' may be specific to the social conditions of the late twentieth century. Unlike previous eras, in which more rigidly hierarchical social relationships were the norm, disclosing intimacy (involving the constant mutual revelation of inner thoughts and feelings) can only exist if the social and structural barriers between the participants are removed. This particular form of intimacy is thus correlated with 'significant changes in both social divisions and social cohesion, particularly in inequalities and differences between men and women' (Jamieson 1998, p. 14).

Romantic love, as it is constituted in contemporary Western society, can be seen as the construct of a particular time and place, when hierarchical relationships are less common than in the past. Now, disclosure between partners is a feature of intimacy; in earlier times this may not have been the case.

Once again, to contend that love, desire and emotion are shaped by social factors is not to say that they are necessarily reducible to them (for a helpful account which critiques both naturalist and constructivist readings of emotion, see Armon-Jones 1986, pp. 32–56). The key point to note is that emotions cannot be detached from the specific sociocultural contexts in which they are embedded. When it is considered that personal relationships are both 'a key form of social cohesion' and 'also crucial in maintaining social divisions' (Jamieson 1998, p. 3), the limits of a purely personal focus become clear. Personal intimacy and social life are irrevocably intertwined.

Where, though, does gender figure in the dynamics of intimacy, particularly if more equal relationships between the sexes are now apparent? For many gender theorists (for example Jackson 1995, p. 52) the connections between Western concepts of self, subjectivity and romantic love mean that gender must correspondingly be central. The gendered subject/object division continues to have effects, even as it is increasingly criticised. Here it is also significant that emotion tends to be coded as feminine. According to the binary opposition which is symbolically reproduced throughout our culture, emotion is counterposed against a masculine rationality in ways which imply that matters to do with feeling are still largely the preserve of women. Intimacy is gendered because emotion is gendered. As Alison Jaggar (1992, p. 157) points out, the implications of this in societies which are also hierarchised along class, age and race lines are considerable:

> the western tradition has not seen everyone as equally emotional. Instead, reason has been associated with members of dominant political, social and cultural groups and emotion with members of subordinate groups.

Yet again, the lens of gender provides an insight into wide-ranging forms of discrimination and marginalisation.

To the extent that we live in a society that is structured according to the norms of heteronormativity, the gendered politics of heterosexual love provides a fertile site for exploration. What we find when we analyse heterosexual love are the twin dimensions and disjunctures we have noted – both the structural and gendered inequities of social power, and the frequently contrasting subjective feeling that love relationships are immune from these. Recognising the political dimensions of intimacy is often difficult because in some ways there is increased equality between the sexes. In the past, it was relatively easy for feminists to show that the institutional expression of heterosexual love – in the form of the marriage contract – subordinated women economically while denying them social power and freedoms comparable to those of men. But in the contemporary period, it is sometimes harder to appreciate that a gendered politics of intimacy operates. Consider, for example, the greater participation of women in the public sphere, the increased legitimacy and popularity of de facto liaisons, and the many shifts in the economy that see increasing numbers of male casualties. How, in light of these contemporary shifts, can it be claimed that a gendered politics of intimacy continues to operate?

It is here that the more recent work of gender theorists – particularly in relation to the dual notions of romance and caring – is illuminating. Such analysis suggests that, irrespective of the institutional form that heterosexual relationships take (that is, whether the partners are married, cohabit or live separately), notions such as the 'nurturing female' continue to influence intimate (and, as we have seen, commercial) relationships. Moreover, they do so in ways which threaten otherwise significant shifts towards egalitarianism. For example, even when there is formal recognition of equal pay for equal work, the gendered double shift of disproportionate household duties continues to be borne by women and this is not formally recognised.

The gendered politics of caring in intimate relationships is different from that of the commercial caring we have discussed. So different, in fact, that the parallels between them risk being denied or even overlooked altogether. Here it is helpful to recall the lack of expressiveness and tenderness according to which conventional masculinity has been constructed. Since we have already noted that exploitation can be far more subtle than brute dominance – and that it is likely to be particularly insidious when it is not recognised as such – the outlines of a gender critique of intimacy can start to be drawn. That heterosexual relationships may in some ways be reciprocal does not invalidate such a critique. After all, we have already had ample grounds to be wary of readings which depict complementarity between the sexes in positive terms. In any case, as Sandra Lee Bartky (1990) notes, it is precisely the *un*reciprocated dimensions of caring in heterosexual relationships of which women routinely complain.

For Bartky, the risks to women of unreciprocated caring in intimate relationships are profound. Chief among these is the disempowerment that stems from the temptation, and even the subtle imperative – it 'goes with the territory'– for a woman to adopt her partner's perspective on the world (1990, p. 111). Desiring so ardently to share his troubles and lighten his burden (aims which, so familiar in the discourse of intimacy, can be seen to operate in gendered rather than neutral ways), women risk accepting their partner's orientation towards the world rather than exploring and respecting their own. Thus, in addition to disproportionate emotional giving, women risk a subtle subsuming of identity which can inhibit their own development in a range of ways.

It might be said that this risk is not political, since assimilation of the perspectives of the loved one is not confined to women, and since the particularities of these will in any case vary from couple to couple and from case to case. But it is here that the wider structural context becomes relevant. This is because the continuing conservatism of major social institutions, and the recentness of women's legitimacy as actors in the public world, ensures that it is the views of men (whatever their internal diversity) which are still accorded more sanction and status. Disempowerment is imbibed in 'the

world according to him', since 'there is no corresponding affirmation, in intimacy, of the world according to *her*' (Bartky 1990, p. 112).

Thus, the structuring effects of social and economic inequity on intimate
relationships are potentially profound. They are also less overt than a focus
on gendered pay differentials and numerical representation in the workforce
can convey (revealing as these continue to be). At issue here is the weight and
respect accorded to so-called women's views, that is, those which have traditionally been depreciated, in the public world. For Jackson (1995, p. 55) the
question is not simply 'an imbalance of values', but 'a material, structural
imbalance' in which female nurturing capacities 'are closely interwoven with
[women's] location within patriarchal relations'. It is here that conventional
(apolitical) constructions of caring and intimacy – as well as romance and
passion – work as disincentives to examine the inequities which may actually
be operating.

It is also in this context that the perceptual, experiential dimensions of
heterosexual love need to be considered. As noted previously, thinking and
feeling do not necessarily coincide. Nor can we address the reality of female
complicity in inequitable relationships if we use an approach that equates
emotion and intellect. As Bartky (1990, p. 114) notes, women may well
concede that 'men in general have more power than women in general'. But
this abstract fact is likely to recede in comparison with the physical imme-
diacy of the loved one. To be compelling, and even adequate, theories of intimacy must be attuned to this disjuncture. They must account for both the
social context in which private relationships take place, and the strength of
feeling which, particularly in contexts of intimate relationships, wants to deny
that power is operative.

Reference to female complicity in the disproportionate caring of heterosexual relationships suggests the potential of psychoanalytic theory to address
the subjective dynamics involved. There is a vast literature in this broad area
(see the recent work of Benjamin (1988, 1995) and Flax (1990, 1993) as well as
the pioneering texts of Dinnerstein (1976, 1978) and Chodorow (1978b, 1989)).
But consistent with our theme of the need to interrogate both social *and*
subjective terrain – as well as the problematic areas of their intersection – it is
crucial that both axes are kept firmly in focus. Despite the untenability of
either/or approaches, it is still hard to simultaneously address contrasting
emphases. It is significant, for example, that while Jackson and Bartky
welcome psychoanalytic contributions to the study of the politics of intimacy,
both also worry about the analytical skewing which can result; that is, the risk
that subjectivity will be privileged over the social – or vice versa – rather than
their interconnections explored. Such skewing can be extremely subtle. For
example, Lacanian conceptions of desire (whereby terms of entry into
language and culture are crucial; see Chapter 2) clearly address both social
and subjective registers. But they arguably say insufficient about the specifics

of *particular* cultures and social arrangements (Jackson 1995, p. 57). Even when the intersections (between social and psychic, private and public, inner and outer) are focused on, disciplinary boundaries and specialties often mean that particular domains become privileged over others in theoretical analysis.

In analysing interpersonal relationships, we are constantly tracing the interplay of social and psychic in their practice. While attempts to restructure patterns of psychological response may well be valuable in advancing gender equity, the restructuring of labour practices and the status accorded to them must remain at least as significant (Bartky 1990, p. 118; also see Segal 1987). Of course the two impact on one another: for example, tangible changes to the workplace and childcare practices presuppose changed attitudes and psychological responses. But the long legacy of dichotomies means that the material, public world still risks being counterposed to the internal, subjective one, even as the limits of doing so are consciously recognised (here again, disciplinary boundaries have not assisted the study of interconnections between contrasting domains).

Within the diffusely defined realm of heterosexual love, myriad expressions of the gendered politics of emotional labour are played out. These range from the covert depletions of caring, to the overt manifestations of physical violence and abuse. (Interestingly, to the extent that love is not necessarily a gentle feeling, Jackson (1995, p. 54) and, in a different way, Benjamin (1988, 1995) postulate links between aggression, violence and love.) Gender theory does not conflate such diverse practices, nor the varied pay-offs which may be associated with them. Neither does it dispute the intense pleasure which being in love can afford. But it invites us to locate the realm of intimacy within specific social and cultural practices that are themselves gendered and cannot be willed away. As Jackson (1995, p. 52) points out, a range of diverse material now suggests 'that "love" is not a fixed, unchanging emotion, and that its shifting meanings are the outcome of gendered struggles'.

Sexual Space, Citizenship and Democracy

Both the public workplace and the more intimate realm of private relationships comprise key sites at which gender is operative. Consideration of these contrasting spaces suggests that our focus might be expanded even further – to the possibility that *space itself* may be gendered in ways which differentially affect the various groups which occupy it. Recent work on the body (which stresses the social, rather than natural dimensions of corporeality) is now being extended to the realm of geography (traditionally a particularly masculine domain, as Bell and Valentine, 1995 argue). While drawing on and elaborating some of this material, our aim here is to explore the relationship between gender and space – sexual geography – and the implications of this relationship for democratic and citizenship rights within liberal democracies. How we live and 'do' gender is crucially shaped by the politics of space, and the corollary of this – that space itself may be gendered – has widespread implications (and remember that we began the study of the gendering of space in Chapter 5).

Before such links can begin to be explicated, however, some preliminary questions need to be addressed. It is probably clear at this point (even before engagement with the more specific literature on sexualised geography) that concrete social practices are spatially contingent. What we do is performed in particular spatial contexts. But this may seem a long way from the contention that space per se is gendered and sexualised. Acknowledgement of the traditionally masculinist parameters of geographical (as other) discourse need not entail the more far-reaching recognition that space itself cannot be neutral. Yet it is precisely this latter recognition that illustrates the strength of the power relations at issue, and forms the context in which democratic rights are articulated.

In his account of the relationship between space, HIV and identity construction, David Woodhead (1995, p. 235) contests the 'standard' geographical conception 'that there exist imagined spaces that are somehow less significant, less *real*, than material, physically bounded spaces'. Directly confronting the familiar counterposing of the material and the imaginary, Woodhead (1995, p. 236) argues 'that space does not stand awaiting us to give meanings to it, but that space *becomes*, that space is *constituted*, through meaning'. Thus he wants to consider the materialisation of imagined spaces. Such a (re)conceptualisation of space is powerfully indicative of the radical politics that such work entails, and the illegitimacy of exempting *any* domain from political analysis. Even as the notions of objectivity and neutrality are increasingly questioned, there are some contexts in which they are still assumed to be apparent, and space and geography are striking illustrations. To this extent, the gendered nature of space (recognition of which is a prelude to the implications of such gendering for the attribution of rights within liberal democracies) may be harder to apprehend than, say, the gendered politics of the workplace and even the family. A common initial reaction might be 'if space and geography aren't neutral and objective, then what is?'.

> Space is not an empty material reality waiting for people to give it meaning; rather meaning creates space. And as meaning is a sociocultural and political construct, and so is gendered, then the space it creates is gendered.

How, then, are space and geography gendered, rather than objective and neutral? And what are the links between such gendering of geography and citizenship rights in liberal democracies? In relation to the first question, one way of addressing it is to note implications of the heteronormativity according to which dominant institutions are structured. The gendered equation between masculinity and the public realm has its correlate not only in the masculinised design and constructions of public space, but in the extent to which, irrespective of its particular design, public space is the space of men. Both feminist critique and untheorised everyday experience testify to the continuing anomaly of women's bodies in the public sphere, in ways in which it is beyond liberal affimative action-style programmes to rectify. The increased visibility, and in many ways legitimacy, of women as public actors need not in itself alter the masculinised operation of public space (consider the ambivalence still evoked by the woman who breastfeeds in public). Public space is also structured according to norms which are heterosexist. This is testified to by gay and lesbian critics, whose (complex and contrasting) marginalisation is reinforced in ways the unreflective heterosexual actor is not only discouraged from seeing, but may be quite unable to recognise.

Another approach to the topic of the gendered nature of (public) space has to do with the more specific equation of geographical domains with particular groups and processes. Thus the city (itself an amorphous entity) is implicitly and explicitly associated with production, vitality and middle-class masculinity. This is in contrast to a feminised rural realm in which traditional practices and values prevail (the crudity and untenability of this dichotomy is a dramatic illustration of its continued reproduction and symbolic power). As Knopp (in Bell and Valntine (eds) 1995, p. 154) notes, in Western cities, 'power is still quite closely associated with the production and consumption of commodities, and with white, non-working-class, heterosexually identified men'. But power is appropriated and exercised via mechanisms in which people who are oppressed in one way (for example as working class or non-white) may benefit in others (for example as men). Once again – as in our previous illustration of the black male labourer and the white female professional – the gender politics which operates is not simple or transparent. But the contrasts and contradictions at issue do not diminish the significance of the gendered politics of space. Contrasting experiences and contradictions are themselves dependent in part on the spatial and social locations in which different people are situated.

> The masculinised nature of public space means that it is more accessible to some people – particularly white, middle-class men – than to others.

How, though, does the reality of gendered (classed and racialised) space relate to the seemingly different domain of citizenship rights? From its very inception, the neutrality of the term 'citizen' was belied by its gendered (and in other ways discriminatory) practice. In ancient Greece, it was *arms-bearing men* who were citizens; a qualification which precluded not only women, but slaves and resident aliens as well. It is significant that conceptions of space – and of which people were appropriate to occupy particular spaces – figured prominently in such exclusions. Masculinised, militarised space was the realm from which citizenship rights issued; those who did not inhabit this space were, quite simply, not citizens.

The implication of citizenship in militarism, as well as masculinity, is interesting, if problematic, in the contemporary context, where citizenship rights are more broadly conferred. At one level, the nexus between the two, as the determining significance of either, would seem to be broken (women now possess formal citizenship rights and the criterion of participation in militarism would seem to be redundant). Yet, as feminist critics have argued, the mother/soldier dichotomy remains resilient, even (and perhaps especially) now that in Western societies (some) women *are* soldiers. To what extent, if women are to enjoy citizenship rights, must they prove themselves capable of defending their country in ways analogous to men? To what extent must women occupy particularised, masculinised spaces (in addition to more generalised public space) in order to access rights formerly reserved for (particular) men?

While the military context may seem to be extreme and atypical – in that women's citizenship rights today are hardly dependent on active military participation – the question it raises cannot be dismissed so easily. To what degree is female access to rights traditionally denied them dependent on their becoming more like (traditional conceptions of) men? Long-term construction of the private realm as non-political has clearly disqualified women from many of the citizenship rights accorded to men. It is here that male domination of public space (literal in an earlier period, symbolic but no less real in its material effects today) remains significant.

To contend that women (now as in the past) do not enjoy the same citizenship rights as men raises a range of issues, and the need to engage with a wide and varied literature. Feminist critics have considerably expanded conceptions of what citizenship entails (see, for example, Jones 1990, pp. 781–812; Yuval-Davis 1991, pp. 58–68; Phillips 1993, pp. 75–89). A key theme of such work is that it is not enough to focus on formal rights alone. In theory, and even in legislation, we may all be equal, but when it comes to *accessing* the rights to which we are all supposedly entitled, covert forms of discrimination operate and many of these are gendered. So it is not necessarily at the formal political level that disenfranchisement takes place.

Gender theorists are not alone in showing the inadequacy of standard (that is, narrow) conceptions of citizenship. Broader definitions than those that pertain to formal rights date to the 1950s (that is, before the explosion of the second wave of feminism). For T.H. Marshall (1950) – whose definition forms the point of departure for contemporary readings – citizenship pertains to a wide range of civil, political and social rights, and relates to 'full membership in a community'. But seemingly gender-neutral definitions such as this only underline the importance of gender. At one level, Marshall's expanded conception of citizenship seemed promising for those who suffered under technical inclusion criteria alone. Once more wide-ranging contributions to the nation other than those of active military service and wage-earning were recognised, this widened the range of people who could lay claim to citizenship status. But in paving the way for a more active conception of civic participation – in terms of responsibilities as well as rights – it entailed the risk that some forms of participation would be valued over others.

Since gender is one of the primary axes according to which social organisation is structured, and to the extent that the feminine is equated with subordination, how could this not elevate masculine modes of participation? One outcome of expanded conceptions of citizenship, as feminist critics (for example Phillips 1993, p. 78) were quick to point out, could be a corresponding expansion of the characteristics of those who are already dominant. Nor do long-standing socialist concerns about economic inequity lose their pertinence in expanded conceptions of citizenship. Accessing one's rights is more difficult in the absence of financial resources, such that the feminisation of poverty has wider implications than the obvious material ones.

Ironically, then, broader Marshallian-inspired conceptions of citizenship can multiply the areas of exclusion, rather than extend the grounds on which *in*clusion can occur. This is because criteria for citizenship remain largely male-defined, even as more modes of activity may be recognised. Citizenship is gendered, and 'the citizen is less universal in scope than he likes to pretend' (Phillips 1993, p. 78). In an example that dramatises the gendered politics of culture, the double-edged nature of female citizenship rights was underlined even at the time Marshall was writing. Of what use to women was the right to employment in the 1950s, when social pressure virtually dictated that the breadwinner be male? As feminist writers have shown, the more broadly citizenship is conceptualised, the more clearly its gendered character can be appreciated. And sexualised geography, the gendered politics of space – which bodies are appropriate presences in which spaces – becomes a crucial component of marginalisation in this context.

> The ability to occupy the public space without fear of violence or threat is an aspect of citizenship to which men and women do not have equal access; to this extent citizenship, constituted as the ability to be publicly part of a community, is differentially gendered.

Some further examples are useful here, particularly since the challenges to the view that space is neutral are so far-reaching. Correspondingly, it is helpful to consider necessary preconditions for the exercise of citizenship rights in any meaningful sense. Conventional criteria are physical freedom – the need to be free from the threat of bodily violation – and the need to be free from the risk of material destitution. Once again, while seemingly gender-neutral, such criteria do not operate that way. Women's bodies are manifestly *not* free from physical threat in the same way as are men's (which is not to deny the reality of male violence directed at men). Nor are the risks of material deprivation comparable. Susan James (1992, p. 50) also adds 'a third kind of independence' to the criteria for citizenship – a degree of *emotional* freedom. For James there are important connections 'between self-esteem and the emotional independence that full citizens need' (p. 61). When viewed in this light, the corresponding connections between the masculinised ethos of public space and the capacity to exercise citizenship rights become clearer.

We have noted consistently that values and activities associated with the feminine are still routinely disparaged in public life. And women's bodies are not only anomalous in key areas of public space, but also more vulnerable to physical threat than those of men in public space. How, then, can the criteria for 'full [civic] membership in [the] community' be said to apply? The case of the woman who breastfeeds in public is again illustrative, and provides a test case in itself of the (un)ease with which the polity regards practices and processes heavily coded as private. To the extent that women in Western societies are frequently reminded of their late and tenuous entry to public space, the discomfort experienced is a constant check on the confident exercise of full citizenship rights.

Queer theory can also cast new light on the spatial politics of citizenship. If the public/private dichotomy has been coercive in its restrictive construction of the feminine, it has been coercive in a different way for those who are not heterosexual. As Bell (Bell and Valentine 1995, p. 312) points out, there is a sense in which those constructed as perverted are 'irreducible to either domain', and as gay and lesbian critics routinely highlight, construction of a space as private does not necessarily translate to the experience of privacy *in* the space so described. Many who are not heterosexual are subject to the periodic intrusion of homophobic relatives and acquaintances within their own homes. To this extent, they are forced to seek privacy within designated realms of the public sphere, and thereby force redefinition of what the very concepts of private and public signify (see Bell and Valentine 1995, pp. 306–13). Consideration of the many exclusions on which the white heterosexual male norm is predicated reveals the limits of claims about the full exercise of citizenship rights within liberal democracies. It also suggests the crucial role of the politics of space in normalising such exclusions.

Mirror, Mirror on the Wall: Negotiation of Gender Duality in Young Children

All the material we have considered to date suggests the deep-rootedness, as well as variety, of the processes which shape who we come to be. They are processes over which we exert little control at one level, but which themselves are shaped by innumerable acts of agency at another. The depth of such processes means that study of the realm labelled 'childhood' might provide crucial insight into the ways in which subjectivities are constituted in relation to the social. It is in the very early (and thus extremely difficult to access) years that crucial input into identity construction occurs.

> Childhood is another concept (temporal rather than spatial) that is open to multiple definitions and explorations, and where the work of gendering can be observed in many different ways.

Simultaneously, modes of mediating such input also develop. This being the case, recognition of the importance of these early years is as central to the project of better understanding who we are *now* as it is to enhanced appreciation of possibilities for what we might become. And since the taking up of gendered identities is part of – constitutive of – what childhood entails, gender analysis again has enormous potential to revise existing ways of living and being.

Once again, too, the predisposing function of language becomes apparent. This is because childhood is not a discrete domain from which we move in a predictable linear fashion (even as certain physiological and socially designated benchmarks signify senses in which it is left behind). The existence of an inner child is a truism of popular culture as much as of psychoanalytic discourse. We are not unitary beings, so that the many aspects of ourselves – including the experiences which shape who we are – cannot be demarcated neatly. The familiar terms 'immature adult' and 'mature child' are illustrative here; the labels we use belie the complexity which operates. When coupled with the relative inaccessibility of the early years to conscious adult reflection, the continued existence of childhood within the mature adult raises challenging theoretical (as real-life) problems.

There is, of course, a huge and challenging literature in relation to these issues, however, since the aim of this section, as of the previous ones, is to highlight the need for recognition of the significance of key sites and contexts, broad themes, rather than exhaustive analysis, will be presented. One of the most obvious preliminary points in relation to this area concerns the powerful investments that still surround attempts to conceptualise childhood at all. To the extent that infancy is perceived as a period of innocence (see Elder 1993), there can be a reluctance to introduce, much less impose, what is regarded as misplaced political and social analysis. Such reluctance is discernible even on the part of those who are otherwise socially committed. For example, many who contest sexist, classist and racist stereotypes stop short of applying such criteria to the stories they read their children.

Yet such reluctance shows a reinscription of the very dichotomies (child/society; innocence/experience) that we are attempting to get beyond. Attempts to construct childhood as a pristine realm uncontaminated by ideology and power relations are highly unrealistic. This is because, in contrast to what we may want to believe, the politics is already there. Efforts to deny this, therefore, work to sanction the status quo, and to this extent buttress conservative politics (even and especially when they come in a liberal guise). Attempts to introduce gender awareness into school curricula make this point strongly. Child-centred philosophies that stress minimal adult intervention on the grounds that the values of the child should be respected may sound good at one level, but they leave untouched and unrecognised the politics which is already operating:

> If teachers resist the temptation to intervene and they make every effort to respect the integrity of children's current understandings, issues of social justice can take on secondary importance. (Alloway 1995, p. 57)

Even a cursory consideration of familiar childhood activities suggests the naturalising dimensions of socialising processes. We expect little girls to like dolls and little boys to like fire engines. The power of such processes lies in the fact that by the time they come to be recognised (if indeed they are focused on at all), they have already been imbibed in ways which render their deconstruction problematic. For example, in two important texts on acquisition of gender identity in young children, Bronwyn Davies (1989, 1993) shows, as she puts it, 'the impressive power of traditional storylines to assert oppressive gender relations as natural and correct' (1993, p. 30). From dragon-slaying heroes and domesticated heroines to happy (heterosexual) ever after, the gendered hierarchies acquire legitimacy for seeming normal and inevitable.

Much has now been written on the extremely gendered character of fairy tales long regarded as beyond the reach of the political. It is now widely recognised that such tales consistently rest on gendered stereotypes of passive women and active men. It is the kiss of the male – as in Snow White – which literally brings the female to life. The implications of such early associations for patterns of adult intimacy, as previously discussed, are striking. The dichotomies and associated connotations of (active) masculinity and (passive) femininity, (good) beauty and (evil) ugliness, and (pure) whiteness and (corrupt, contaminated) blackness recur as potent archetypes within a range of favourite children's stories. As such, they become inscribed on developing psyches as heavily encoded and covert signifiers of societal values, and from the point of view of gender, race and class analysis, they are far from egalitarian. To this extent, and as Chilean writer Ariel Dorfman elaborated in a text famously titled *How to Read Donald Duck* (1984), the phrase 'suitable for children' can be seen as alarming rather than reassuring.

To consciously acknowledge the political power of narrative and filmic representations in constructing young subjectivities is thus a partial achievement when it is at the sub- and *un*conscious levels that they most powerfully resonate. But it is also important to note that such representations are not simply and passively incorporated. Psychic dynamics are neither so compliant nor reducible to the social. Ways in which they are mediated can open up the space of possibility as well as suggest the limits of constraint. It is here that earlier discussion of the active dimensions of textual practice (Chapter 3) again becomes relevant. Davies's work shows how encouragement of even very young children to take issue with expected readings of texts can disrupt some of the powerful binaries on which traditional narratives rest. Children also read differently according to the gender, class and race dynamics of their own lives. This is itself a potential challenge to the homogenising (and politically paralysing) perception that even very familiar stories are necessarily consumed in the same way.

The resilience of the powerfully gendered construction of subjectivity in childhood is thus potentially undercut by the capacity that still exists to valorise alternative perspectives. At one level, Davies's work clearly establishes how early it is that children assume and (partially) identify with profoundly gendered subject positions. But the challenge of her work lies in its equally clear illustration of the capacity of children to mediate at a quite sophisticated level *between* and *within* the gendered positionings that constrain as well as define them. The respective cases of Joanne (who, knowing she had to be identifiable as a girl, was nevertheless determined to access masculine activity) and George (who while embracing, as he had to, male identity, was regularly drawn to feminine play) are particularly interesting here. Both children showed great skill and sophistication in transgressing some of the gendered expectations of their play, while taking care to remain identifiably feminine and masculine respectively. A too-ready (adult) belief in the formative power of socialisation (see previous discussion) can blind us to the many opportunities which do exist to unsettle familiar assumptions. This applies particularly to young children who, while powerfully moulded in some ways, retain great receptivity to diverse influences in others.

The injunction to think beyond gender dualisms may sound utopian in light of their insistent reproduction at every level of the construction of childhood subjectivity. But even so, the micropolitics of everyday life affords considerable room for their unsettling. Consistent with our previous points about the need for disciplinary and methodological eclecticism, gender analysis can draw on a range of approaches to challenge the taken for grantedness of the acquisition of gender identity. Davies (1993) is explicit about the potential of poststructuralist analysis in this context, insights of which 'allow a different relationship to structure, a recognition of it as something which is not absolute, which can be acted upon by individuals and by collectivities' (p. 198). A focus on childhood provides a rich site for the exploration of the possibilities and limits of conceptual combination(s). It also increases the likelihood of further insights into the simultaneous tenaciousness and fragility of the gendered identities which inform our adult lives.

Summary

It is problematic to attempt a summary at this point, much less to construct a concluding comment that could draw together such contrasting material. Nevertheless, the very diversity of this material is itself suggestive of some key points that emerge from the preceding discussion. The first relates not only to the applicability of gender analysis to contrasting topics and sites, but to the radical potential of a focus on gender at both practical and theoretical levels. That new theoretical light can be shed on contexts as diverse as the workplace, personal relationships, the politics of spatiality and the constitution of childhood subjectivity is itself a powerful testament to the capacity of gender analysis to envisage alternative ways of doing and being. The applicability of gender analysis to such diverse contexts entails a corresponding recognition of the untenability of many of the dichotomies (social/psychic; material/symbolic; concrete/abstract) with which we still have to contend.

It is simply not possible to confine the application of gender to specifically demarcated fields and approaches. This is because gender is necessarily a transdisciplinary concept, and is as intimately related to social practice as to the workings of subjectivity. The processes and issues that gender analysis calls into question do not correlate neatly, and we have seen that the notion of disjuncture is a helpful one. But the difficulty of charting links between contrasting domains does not undermine the legitimacy of the attempt. Since gender permeates so many aspects of life, it is not only necessary but urgent that its myriad workings are explored in as much detail as possible.

Recommended Reading

Bell, David and Valentine, Gill (eds) (1995) *Mapping Desire: Geographies of Sexualities*, Routledge, London.

Davies, Bronwyn (1989) *Frogs and Snails and Feminist Tales: Preschool Children and Gender*, Allen & Unwin, Sydney.

Davies, Bronwyn (1993) *Shards of Glass: Children Reading and Writing Beyond Gendered Identities*, Allen & Unwin, Sydney.

Game, Ann (1983) *Gender at Work*, Allen & Unwin, Sydney.

Jackson, Stevi (1995) 'Women and Heterosexual Love: Complicity, Resistance and Change', in Lynne Pearce and Jackie Stacey (eds) *Romance Revisited*, Lawrence & Wishart, London, pp. 49–62.

Jaggar, Alison and Rothenburg, Paula (eds) (1993) *Feminist Frameworks: Alternative Theoretical Accounts of the Relations Between Women and Men*, McGraw-Hill, New York.

James, Susan and Gisela Bock (eds) (1992) *Beyond Equality and Difference: Citizenship, Feminist Politics and Female Subjectivity*, Routledge, London.

Naffine, Ngaire (1990) *Law and the Sexes: Explorations in Feminist Jurisprudence*, Allen & Unwin, Sydney.

Pateman, Carole (1989) *The Disorder of Women: Democracy, Feminism and Political Theory*, Polity Press, Cambridge.

Pettman, Jan (1996) *Worlding Women: A Feminist International Politics*, Allen & Unwin, Sydney.

Phillips, Anne (1993) *Democracy and Difference*, Polity, Cambridge.

Pringle, Rosemary (1989) *Secretaries Talk: Sexuality, Power and Work*, Allen & Unwin, Sydney.

Wearing, Betsy (1996) *Gender: The Pain and Pleasure of Difference*, Longman, Melbourne.

Exercises

1. Think of the many kinds of labour performed outside the paid workplace (by men as well as women). Who performs this labour and why do you think it is valued as it is? What alternative ways are there for valuing this non-waged labour? What kinds of social changes would be needed for your valuations to be accepted?

2. Read through a newspaper or magazine, or watch a television news programme or a sit com, and record the ways in which work is characterised. What does this reveal about the ways in which our society evaluates work?

3. Apply Betsy Wearing's list of factors ensuring the gendering of work to a workplace situation in which you have participated. How effectively does it describe your workplace?

4. Describe your experience of emotional labour, either as an initiator or a receiver. How did that emotional labour operate to ensure the workplace interaction went smoothly? How do you think that kind of labour could be effectively acknowledged?

5. How do you react to the idea that love is a cultural construct? Can you map the characteristics of romantic love as it functions in contemporary Western society?

Can you imagine a different kind of intimate relationship – for example one that doesn't involve disclosure? How would a different conception of love and romance change the way we live our everyday lives? Think this through in relation to inter-personal relationships, friendships, ways of reading and seeing, and ways of thinking and feeling.

6. Consider David Woodhead's interesting idea that space is created through, rather than pre-exists, meaning. How can you see this operating at a particular site? You might, for example, consider the ways that different value systems create a partic-ular location: do they construct the same space? (An example might be drawn from the Western construction of latitude and longitude and the use of the mercator grids to define geographical location, compared with the non-Western constructions of the same space.)

7. How do you see the relationship between citizenship and the ability to occupy the public sphere? Does this explain certain apparent conundrums in Western democ-racies, such as the comparatively small number of women in public office?

8. Explore the images of masculinity and femininity presented in a number of fairy tales. How would you describe the attributes of these gendered images? Read Bronwyn Davies' accounts of the ways that children gender these stories differently and map the attributes of their alternative readings and rewritings.

7

Conclusion

We prefaced this study by reference to Ursula Le Guin's novel *The Left Hand of Darkness* (1981), a science fiction novel set on a world called Gethen. The indigenous inhabitants of Gethen spend most of their time in a state described by one observer as 'manwoman' – without a specific gendering – and once a month enter a sexual phase (*kemmer*) in which they adopt the primary sexual characteristics of one gender only. While this novel has since been criticised in many ways (for example its failure to include same-sex couplings in the *kemmer* period), it nevertheless remains a powerful interrogation of contemporary gendering. The field notes of Investigator Ong Tot Oppong note that:

> When you meet a Gethenian you cannot and must not do what a bisexual naturally does, which is to cast him in the role of Man or Woman, while adopting towards him a corresponding role dependent on your expectations of the patterned or possible interactions between persons of the same or the opposite sex. Our entire pattern of socio-sexual interaction is nonexistent here. (Le Guin 1981, p. 85)

When a human envoy, Genly Ai first visits Gethen, this different gendering proves a major problem for him. He constantly attempts to see his hosts as either male or female, finding their aberrations from his imposed gendering threatening or sickening. And, as Oppong had warned, he finds their disregard of binaristic sexuality (which Oppong terms 'bisexuality') very disturbing. In fact, it comes as a great shock to Genly to realise, as he does in one shared-mind experience, that the Gethenians regard him as a pervert, some kind of gendered monstrosity, stuck forever with the primary (and prominently displayed) sexual characteristics of one gender only and unable, unlike them, to enjoy the pleasures of male and female, including the bearing of children.

The Left Hand of Darkness, despite its flaws, can still serve as an imaginative catalyst for us now, as we rethink the ways in which our society has imagined and categorised gender. The monstrosity which Genly projects onto the Gethenians, and which he experiences as their projection of him, is the limit case of our social(ised) thinking about and acting out of gendering. As Liz Grosz (1995) notes:

> Freaks cross the borders which divide the subject off from all ambiguities, inter-connections and reciprocal classifications. They imperil the very definitions we rely on to classify humans, identities, sexes – our most fundamental categories of self-definition. (p. 25)

This study has moved between the two areas of definition and ambiguity. We began with a survey of many of the terms and theories used to define and describe gender in our society. The history of these gendering terms traces not only their social function but also the way in which they operate as social regulation. Like Genly's assumptions, they can construct others as monsters – not for any essentialist reason, but because they do not fit in with the defin-itions we bring to them. The theories that have been developed to account for gendering and sexual behaviours and interrelations may be either and both part of the problem and part of the solution. On the one hand, they can and have been used to regulate acceptable gendering and judge whether individ-uals are viable individual subjects. On the other hand, they have also located and identified the grounds on which our gendering is performed – its struc-turing fantasies and behavioural consequences. Our theories of gendering locate both the genders with which we operate and the ambiguities and inconsistencies of that gendering.

We then moved to the cultural productions and practices of gendering, including practices of reading and viewing. On Gethen, Genly Ai spent part of his time exploring the cultural products of this new world – the myths and stories which the Gethenians use to explain themselves to themselves. Our study made a parallel move, tracing in the practices of reading and viewing some of the means by which our society engenders us – and also tracing some of the tactics used by individual subjects to resist this engendering practice. In general terms, we discussed theories of reading and viewing, which can be used to understand the kinds of meanings readers/viewers make from texts. We also related these theories specifically to the ways in which the reading and viewing of texts works as a gendering practice, creating and reinforcing notions about gender and gendered behaviours which ultimately influence the ways in which we, as individual subjects, are both gendered and gender ourselves.

Like Genly Ai, we also confronted the ways in which gendering is embodied. For Genly this confrontation with embodiment takes place when he is caught in a blizzard with a Gethenian and must confront his own preju-dices. Genly reveals to his companion during the blizzard that:

I can't tell you what women are like. I never thought about it much in the abstract, you know, and – God! – by now I've practically forgotten. I've been here two years. … You don't know. In a sense, women are more alien to me than you are. (p. 200)

By contrast, the gendering of the Gethenians is figured as 'Both and one. A shadow on snow' (p. 225).

In our everyday embodied existence we too must confront social prejudices about gendering in all our interpersonal and institutional encounters. The ways in which bodies are processed by institutions such as education, medicine, the law and the fashion industry gender us in specific ways – mostly in terms of a normative heterosexuality with which we may or may not agree and in the process our experience of gender is delimited in specific ways.

Finally, we addressed some aspects of everyday living – as Genly Ai constantly explored the practices of everyday life on his adopted world, Gethen. Like him we explored a range of public and private experiences, and looked for ways to theorise their gendering. Oppong's field notes warn Genly about the critical differences between work practices on Gethen and elsewhere:

Consider: Anyone can turn his hand to anything. This sounds very simple, but its psychological effects are incalculable. The fact that everyone between seventeen and thirty-five or so is liable to be (as Nim put it) 'tied down to childbearing', implies that that no one is quite so thoroughly 'tied down' here as women, elsewhere, are likely to be – psychologically or physically. (pp. 84–5)

Through the field notes and then through his own observations and experiences, Genly learns by contrast just how gendered is the experience of the workplace on his home planet, Earth. In this extract, Oppong comments on the way attitudes to childbearing gender the workplace – how the fact that women have, or potentially might have, children leads to practices, both material and psychological, that disadvantage them. Further, Oppong's statement recalls another of the elements of our discussion of everyday life, which was the gendered nature of citizenship. The ways that women are treated in the public sphere do more than disadvantage them financially; they limit their liberty ('tie them down'). And Oppong goes on to note that even childhood is different on Gethen:

Consider: A child has no psycho-sexual relationship to his mother and father. There is no myth of Oedipus on Winter. (p. 85)

Gethenian children live their lives being treated only as human beings, not as men or women. As noted in the Preface, Oppong goes on to warn later ambassadors to Gethen:

A man wants his virility regarded, a woman wants her femininity appreciated, however indirect and subtle the indications of regard and appreciation. On Winter they will not exist. One is respected and judged only as a human being. It is an appalling experience. (p. 86)

Oppong's wry horror is a measure of the extent to which we rely on gendered responses to affirm our sense of self – and why childhood is such a locus for training in gendered behaviour and (self-)representation. And we also explore briefly some of the ways in which children resist that gendering.

The purpose of this study has been to open up the ways in which we experience, talk about, think about, read, see and embody gender and to provide readers with a framework to move forward. In a sense this has been the tracing of a terrain, in the same way that Genly Ai's journey took him over the planet Gethen. As Genly's journey revealed to him the assumptions which structure his own gendering and the cultural practices which generated and reinforced those assumptions, so we have attempted to trace the gendering practices of our society and the kinds of assumption they inscribe. Genly ends his journey with changed perceptions – about Gethen, himself and the gendering practices of his world. When Genly encounters humans again, the experience is shocking:

But they all looked strange to me, men and women, well as I knew them. Their voices sounded strange: too deep, too shrill. They were like a troupe of great, strange animals, of two different species. (p. 249)

We hope that we, like Genly, have opened up some questions about gendering which will change (or perhaps simply support) your own perceptions of contemporary gendering, and will provide a catalyst for an ongoing engagement with its delimiting and regulatory practices.

Bibliography

Abelove, Henry, Barale, Michèle Aina and Halperin, David (1993) *The Lesbian and Gay Studies Reader*, Routledge, New York.

Adam, Barry D. (1995) *The Rise of a Gay and Lesbian Movement* (rev. edn) Twayne, New York.

Adkins, Lisa (1995) *Gendered Work: Sexuality, Family and the Labour Market*, Open University Press, Buckingham.

Alloway, Nola (1995) *Foundation Stones: The Construction of Gender in Early Childhood*, Curriculum Corporation, Victoria.

Althusser, Louis (1971) 'Ideology and Ideological State Apparatuses' (trans. Ben Brewster) in *Lenin and Philosophy and Other Essays*, Monthly Review Press, New York, pp. 131–87.

Ang, Ien (1985) *Watching Dallas: Soap Opera and the Melodramatic Imagination*, (trans. Della Couling) Methuen, London.

Anzaldúa, Gloria (1991) 'La conciencia de la mestiza/Towards a New Consciousness' in *Borderlands/La Frontera: The New Mestiza*, Aunt Lute Books, San Francisco, pp. 77–91.

Anzaldúa, Gloria and Moraga, Cherrie (eds) (1983) *This Bridge Called My Back: Writings by Radical Women of Color*, Kitchen Table: Women of Color Press, New York.

Aristotle (1968–69) *The Metaphysics* (trans. Hugh Tredennick); *Oeconomia and Magna Moralis* (trans. G. Cyril Armstrong) W. Heinemann, London.

Armon-Jones, Claire (1986) 'The Thesis of Constructionism' in Rom Harre (ed.) *The Social Construction of Emotion*, Blackwell, Oxford, pp. 32–56.

Balsamo, Anne Marie (1996) *Technologies of the Gendered Body: Reading Cyborg Bodies*, Duke University Press, Durham.

Banner, L. (1983) *American Beauty*, University of Chicago Press, Chicago.

Barr, Marleen (1993) *Lost in Space: Probing Feminist Science Fiction and Beyond*, University of North Carolina Press, Chapel Hill & London.

Barthel, Diane (1988) *Putting on Appearances: Gender and Advertising*, Temple University Press, Philadelphia.

Barthes, Roland (1977) *Image/Music/Text* (trans. Stephen Heath) Fontana, London.

Bartky, Sandra Lee (1990) *Femininity and Domination: Essays in the Phenomenology of Oppression*, Routledge, New York.

Bell, David and Valentine, Gill (eds) (1995) *Mapping Desire: Geographies of Sexualities*, Routledge, London.

Belsey, Catherine (1980) *Critical Practice*, Methuen, London.

Belsey, Catherine (1985) 'Constructing the Subject: Deconstructing the Text' in Judith Newton and Deborah Rosenfelt (eds) *Feminist Criticism and Social Change: Sex, Class and Race in Literature and Culture*, Methuen, New York.

Benveniste, Emile (1971) *Problems in General Linguistics* (trans. M.E. Meek) University of Miami Press, Coral Gables, FL.

Benjamin, Jessica (1988) *The Bonds of Love: Feminism, Psychoanalysis, and the Problem of Domination*, Virago, London.

Benjamin, Jessica (1995) *Like Subjects, Love Objects: Essays on Recognition and Sexual Difference*, Yale University Press, New Haven.

Berger, John (1972) *Ways of Seeing*, BBC and Penguin, London.

Bernheimer, Charles and Kahane, Claire (eds) (1985) *In Dora's Case: Freud, Hysteria, Feminism*, Virago, London.

Best, Sue (1994) 'This Style Which is Not One' in Catriona Moore (ed.) *Dissonance: Feminism and the Arts 1970–90*, Allen & Unwin, Sydney.

Biddle, Jennifer (1993) 'The Anthropologist's Body or What it Means to Break Your Neck in the Field', *Australian Journal of Anthropology*, 4(3): 184–97.

Blunt, Alison (1994) *Travel, Gender, and Imperialism : Mary Kingsley and West Africa*, Guilford Press, New York.

Bordo, Susan (1988) 'Anorexia Nervosa: Psychopathology as the Crystallization of Nature' in Irene Diamond and Lee Quimby (eds) *Feminism and Foucault: Reflections on Resistance*, Northeastern University Press, Boston, pp. 87–118.

Bordo Susan (1989) 'The Body and the Reproduction of Femininity: A Feminist Reappropriation of Foucault', in Alison M. Jaggar and Susan R. Bordo (eds) *Gender/Body/Knowledge: Feminist Reconstructions of Being and Knowing*, Rutgers University Press, New Brunswick, NJ, pp. 13–33.

Bordo, Susan (1992) 'Eating Disorders: The Feminist Challenge to the Concept of Pathology', in Drew Leder (ed.) *The Body in Medical Thought and Practice*, Kluwer Academic Publishers, Dordrecht.

Bordo, Susan (1993a) *Unbearable Weight: Feminism, Western Culture & the Body*, University of California Press, Berkeley.

Bordo, Susan (1993b) 'Feminism, Foucault and the Politics of the Body' in Caroline Ramazanoglu (ed.) *Up Against Foucault: Explorations of Some Tensions between Foucault and Feminism*, Routledge, New York.

Bourdieu, Pierre (1977) *Outline of a Theory of Practice* (trans. Richard Nice) Cambridge University Press, Cambridge.

Bourdieu, Pierre (1984) *Distinction: A Social Critique of the Judgement of Taste* (trans. Richard Nice) Routledge & Kegan Paul, London.

Braidotti, Rosi (1991) 'Radical Philosophies of Sexual Difference', *Patterns of Dissonance*, Polity, Oxford, pp. 209–73.

Braidotti, Rosi (1994) *Nomadic Subjects: Embodiment and Sexual Difference in Contemporary Feminist Theory*, Columbia University Press, New York.

Braidotti, Rosi (1995) 'In the Footsteps of Anna and Dora: Feminism and Psychoanalysis' in Rosemarie Buikema and Anneke Smelik (eds) *Women's Studies and Culture: A Feminist Introduction*, Zed Books, London.

Bray, Abigail (1994) 'The Edible Woman: Reading/Eating Disorders and Femininity', *Media Information Australia*, **72**: 3–10.

Brod, Harry and Michael Kaufman (eds) (c. 1994) *Theorizing Masculinities*, Sage, Thousand Oaks, CA.

Brown, Mary Ellen (ed.) (1990) *Television and Women's Culture: The Politics of the Popular*, Currency Press, Sydney.

Brown, Wendy (1987) 'Where is the Sex in Political Theory?', *Women and Politics*, **7**(1): 3–23.

Buchbinder, David (1994) *Masculinities and Identities*, Melbourne University Press, Melbourne.

Buchbinder, David (1998) *Performance Anxieties: Re-producing Masculinity*, Allen & Unwin, Sydney.

Bullough, Vern L. and Bonnie Bullough (c.1993) *Cross Dressing, Sex, and Gender*, University of Pennsylvania Press, Philadelphia.

Butler, Judith (1990) *Gender Trouble: Feminism and the Subversion of Identity*, Routledge, New York.

Butler, Judith (1993) *Bodies that Matter: On the Discursive Limits of 'Sex'*, Routledge, New York.

Cameron, Deborah (1985) *Feminism and Linguistic Theory*, Macmillan – now Palgrave Macmillan, Basingstoke.

Cameron, Deborah (ed.) (1990) *The Feminist Critique of Language: A Reader*, Routledge, London.

Cameron, Deborah (1995) *Verbal Hygiene*, Routledge, London.

Camri, Leslie (1993) 'Stealing Femininity: Department Store Kleptomania as Sexual Disorder', *Difference* **5**(1): 26–50.

Cartwright, Lisa (1995) *Screening the Body: Tracing Medicine's Visual Culture*, University of Minnesota Press, Minneapolis.

Case, Sue-Ellen, Philip Brett, and Susan Leigh Foster (eds) (1995) *Cruising the Performative: Interventions into the Representation of Ethnicity, Nationality, and Sexuality*, Indiana University Press, Bloomington.

Cawelti, John G. (1976) *Adventure, Mystery, and Romance: Formula Stories as Art and Popular Culture*, University of Chicago Press, Chicago.

Charcot, Jean-Martin (1987) *Charcot, The Clinician: The Tuesday Lessons: Excerpts from Nine Case Presentations On General Neurology Delivered at the Salpêtrière Hospital in 1887–88 by Jean-Martin Charcot* (trans. Christopher G. Goetz) Raven Press, New York.

Chodorow, Nancy (1978a) *Feminism and Psychoanalytic Theory*, Yale University Press, New Haven.

Chodorow, Nancy (1978b) *The Reproduction of Mothering: Psychoanalysis and the Sociology of Gender*, University of California Press, Berkeley.

Citron, Marcia J. (1993) *Gender and the Musical Canon*, Cambridge University Press, Cambridge.

Cixous, Hélène (1980) 'Sorties', in Elaine Marks and Isabelle de Courtivron (eds) *New French Feminisms*, Harvester, Brighton, pp. 90–8.

Clément, Catherine (1980) 'Enslaved Enclave' in Elaine Marks and Isabelle de Courtivron (eds) *New French Feminisms*, New York, Schocken Books.

Clément, Catherine (1989) *Opera, or, The Undoing of Women* (trans. Betsy Wing) Virago, London.

Coates, Jennifer (1996) *Women's Talk*, Blackwell, Oxford.

Coates, Jennifer and Cameron, Deborah (eds) (1989) *Women in their Speech Communities: New Perspectives on Language and Sex*, Longman, London.

Code, Lorraine (1995) *Rhetorical Spaces: Essays on Gendered Locations*, Routledge, New York.

Connell, Robert W. (1987) *Gender and Power*, Polity, Cambridge.

Connell, Robert W. (1996) *Masculinities*, Allen & Unwin, Sydney.

Corea, Gena (1985) *The Mother Machine: Reproductive Technologies from Artificial Insemination to Artificial Wombs*, Women's Press, London.

Corrigan, Annette and Meredyth, Denise (1997) 'The Body Politic' in Kate Pritchard Hughes (ed.) *Contemporary Australian Feminism*, Longman, Melbourne, pp. 52–75.

Coward, Rosalind (1985) 'Are Women's Novels Feminist Novels?' in Elaine Showalter, (ed.) *The New Feminist Criticism: Essays on Women, Literature and Theory*, Virago, London, pp. 225–39.

Cranny-Francis, Anne (1988) 'Gender and Genre: Feminist Rewritings of Detective Fiction', *Women's Studies International Forum*, **11**(1): 69–84.

Cranny-Francis, Anne (1990) *Feminist Fiction: Feminist Revisions of Generic Fiction*, Polity, Cambridge.

Cranny-Francis, Anne (1992) *Engendered Fiction: Analysing Gender in the Production and Reception of Texts*, New South Wales University Press, Sydney.

Cranny-Francis, Anne (1995) *The Body in the Text*, Melbourne University Press, Melbourne.

Cranny-Francis, Anne (1997) 'Different Identities, Different Voices: Possibilities and Pleasures in Some Trek Novels by Jean Lorrah', *Science-Fiction Studies*, **24**(2): 245–55.

Creed, Barbara (1990) 'Alien and the Monstrous-Feminine' in Annette Kuhn (ed.), *Alien Zone: Cultural Theory and Contemporary Science Fiction Cinema*, Verso, London.

Creed, Barbara (1993) *The Monstrous-Feminine: Film, Feminism, Psychoanalysis*, Routledge, London.

Culler, Jonathan (1991) 'Reading as a Woman' in Robyn R. Warhol and Diane Price Herndl (eds) *Feminisms: An Anthology of Literary Theory and Criticism*, Rutgers University Press, New Brunswick, N.J.

Daly, Mary (1978) *Gyn/Ecology: The Metaethics of Radical Feminism*, Women's Press, London.

David-Neel, Alexandra (1983) *My Journey to Lhasa*, Virago, London.

Davidoff, Leonore and Hall, Catherine (1987) *Family Fortunes: Men and Women of the English Middle Class 1780–1850*, Hutchinson, London.

Davies, Bronwyn (1989) *Frogs and Snails and Feminist Tales: Preschool Children and Gender*, Allen & Unwin, Sydney.

Davies, Bronwyn (1993) *Shards of Glass: Children Reading and Writing Beyond Gendered Identities*, Allen & Unwin, Sydney.

Davis, Kathy (1995) *Reshaping the Female Body: The Dilemma of Cosmetic Surgery*, Routledge, New York.

Day, Marele (1988) *The Life and Crimes of Harry Lavender*, Allen & Unwin, Sydney.

de Beauvoir, Simone (1972) *The Second Sex* (trans. H.M. Pashley) Penguin, Harmondsworth.

de Certeau, Michel (1984) *The Practice of Everyday Life* (trans. Steven Rendall) University of California Press, Berkeley.

de Lauretis, Teresa (1984) *Alice Doesn't: Feminism, Semiotics, Cinema*, Indiana University Press, Bloomington.

de Lauretis, Teresa (1987) *Technologies of Gender: Essays on Theory, Film and Fiction*, Indiana University Press, Bloomington.

de Lauretis, Teresa (1991) 'Queer Theory: Lesbian and Gay Sexualities', *Differences: A Journal of Feminist Cultural Studies*, **3**(2): iii–xviii.

Deleuze, Gilles and Guattari, Felix (1983) *Anti-Oedipus: Capitalism and Schizophrenia* (trans. Robert Hurley, Mark Seem and Helen R. Lane) University of Minnesota Press, Minneapolis.

Deleuze, Gilles and Guattari, Felix (1987) *A Thousand Plateaus: Capitalism and Schizophrenia* (trans. Brian Massumi) University of Minnesota Press, Minneapolis.

Delphy, Christine (1984) *Close to Home: A Materialist Analysis of Women's Oppression* (trans. and ed. Diana Leonard) University of Massachusetts Press, Amherst.

Derrida, Jacques (1978) *Writing and Difference* (trans. Alan Bass) University of Chicago Press, Chicago.

Derrida, Jacques (1980) 'La loi du genre/The Law of Genre', *Glyph*, **7**: 176—232.

Descartes, René (1979) *Discourse on Method and the Meditations* (trans. F.E. Sutcliffe) Penguin, Harmondsworth.

Deutsch, Helene (1944) *The Psychology of Women: A Psychoanalytic Interpretation*. Grune & Stratten, New York.

Dinnerstein, Dorothy (1976) *The Mermaid and the Minotaur: Sexual Arrangements and Human Malaise*, Harper Colophon Books, New York.

Diprose, Rosalyn (1994) *The Bodies of Women: Ethics, Embodiment and Sexual Difference*, Routledge, New York.

Doane, Mary Ann (1991) *Femmes Fatales: Feminism, Film Theory, Psychoanalysis*, Routledge, New York.

Dorfman, Ariel (1984) *How to Read Donald Duck: Imperialist Ideology in the Disney Comic* (trans. David Kunzle) International General, New York.

Dorman, Sonya (1978) 'When I Was Miss Dow' in Pamela Sargent (ed.) *Women of Wonder: Science-fiction Stories by Women about Women*, Penguin, Harmondsworth, pp. 141–54.

Douglas, Mary (1966) *Purity and Danger: An Analysis of Concepts of Pollution and Taboo*, Routledge & Kegan Paul, London.

Edley, Nigel and Wetherell, Margaret (1995) *Men In Perspective: Practice, Power and Identity*, Prentice Hall, London.

Ehrenreich, Barbara and English, Dierdre (1978) *For Her Own Good*, Doubleday, Garden City, NY.

Elder, Glen H. Jr, Modell, John and Parke, Ross D. (eds) (1993) *Children in Time and Place: Developmental and Historical Insights*, Cambridge University Press, Cambridge.

Enloe, Cynthia (1989) *Bananas, Beaches and Bases: Making Feminist Sense of International Politics*, Pandora, London.

Ervin-Tripp, Susan M. (1971) 'Sociolinguistics' in Joshua A. Fishman (ed.) *Advances in the Sociology of Language*, Vol. 1, Mouton, The Hague.

Fanon, Frantz (1967) *Black Skin, White Masks* (trans. Charles Lam Markmann) Grove Press, New York.

Faraday, Annabel (1981) 'Liberating lesbian research' in Kenneth Plummer (ed.) *The Making of the Modern Homosexual*, Hutchinson, London.

Farley Tucker, Pamela (1985) 'Lesbianism and the Social Function of Taboo' in Hester Eisenstein and Alice Jardine (eds) *The Future of Difference*, Rutgers University Press, New Brunswick, pp. 267–73.

Ferrell, Robyn (1996) *Passion in Theory: Conceptions of Freud and Lacan*, Routledge, London.

Fetterley, Judith (1978) *The Resisting Reader: A Feminist Approach to American Fiction*, Indiana University Press, Bloomington.

Finkelstein, Joanne (1991) *The Fashioned Self*, Polity, Cambridge.

Firestone, Shulamith (1970) *The Dialectic of Sex*, Bantam Books, New York.

Fiske, John (1989) *Understanding Popular Culture*, Hyman Unwin, Boston.

Flax, Jane (1990) *Thinking Fragments: Psychoanalysis, Feminism and Postmodernism in the Contemporary West*, University of California Press, Berkeley.

Flax, Jane (1993) *Disputed Subjects: Essays on Psychoanalysis, Politics and Philosophy*, Routledge, New York.

Flood, Michael (1996) 'State of the Movement', *XY: men, sex, politics*, 6(3).

Foucault, Michel (1977) *Language, Counter-Memory, Practice: Selected Essays and Interviews* (trans. Donald F. Bouchard and Sherry Simon; ed. Donald F. Bouchard) Basil Blackwell, Oxford.

Foucault, Michel (1979) *Discipline and Punish: The Birth of the Prison*, Vintage, New York.

Foucault, Michel (1980) 'Lecture Two: 14 January 1976' in Colin Gordon (ed.) *Power/Knowledge*, Pantheon, New York.

Foucault, Michel (1981) *The History of Sexuality*, Vol. I (trans. Robert Hurley) Pelican, Harmondsworth.

Foucault, Michel (1986) *The Use of Pleasure: The History of Sexuality*, Vol. II, Viking, London.

Foucault, Michel (1988) *The Care of the Self: The History of Sexuality*, Vol. III, Allen Lane, London.

French, Marilyn (1977) *The Women's Room*, Summit Books, New York.

Freud, Anna (1967) *The Writings of Anna Freud*, International Universities Press, New York.

Freud, Sigmund (ed.) (1905) 'Three Essays on the Theory of Sexuality' *Standard Edition of the Complete Psychological Works* (trans. James Strachey) Vol. 7, pp. 125–248.

Freud, Sigmund (ed.) (1925) 'Some Psychical Consequences of the Anatomical Distinction between the Sexes' *Standard Edition of the Complete Psychological Works* (trans. James Strachey) Vol. 19, pp. 243–58.

Freud, Sigmund (ed.) (1931) 'Female Sexuality', *Standard Edition of the Complete Psychological Works* (trans. James Strachey) Vol. 21, pp. 223–43.

Freud, Sigmund (ed.) (1933) 'Femininity', *Standard Edition of the Complete Psychological Works* (trans. James Strachey) Vol. 22 .

Friedan, Betty (1974) *The Feminine Mystique*, Dell, New York.

Fuss, Diane (1992) 'Fashion and the Homospectatorial Look', *Critical Inquiry* **18** (Summer): 713–37.

Fuss, Diane (1995) *Identification Papers*, Routledge, New York.

Gaines, Jane (1988) 'White Privilege and Looking Relations: Race and Gender in Feminist Film Theory', *Screen*, **29**(4): 12–27.

Gallop, Jane (1982) *Feminism and Psychoanalysis: The Daughter's Seduction*, Macmillan – now Palgrave Macmillan, Basingstoke.

Game, Ann and Rosemary Pringle (1983) *Gender at Work*, Allen & Unwin, Sydney.

Gamman, Lorraine and Marshment, Margaret (eds) (1988) *The Female Gaze: Women as Viewers of Popular Culture*, Women's Press, London.

Garber, Marjorie (1992) *Vested Interests: Cross-dressing and Cultural Anxiety*, Penguin, London.

Garber, Marjorie (1995) *Vice Versa: Bisexuality and the Eroticism of Everyday Life*, Simon & Schuster, New York.

Gatens, Moira (1991) 'Corporeal Representations In/and The Body Politic' in Ros Diprose and Robyn Ferrell (eds) *Cartographies: Poststructuralism and the Mapping of Bodies and Spaces*, Allen & Unwin, Sydney.

Gever, Martha, Pratibha Parmar and John Greyson (eds) (1993) *Queer Looks: Perspectives on Lesbian and Gay Film and Video*, Routledge, New York.

Gilbert, Pam (1989) 'Stoning the Romance: Girls as Resistant Readers and Writers' in Frances Christie (ed.) *Writing in Schools*, Deakin University Press, Geelong, Victoria, pp. 73–80.

Gledhill, Christine (ed.) (1987) *Home is Where the Heart Is: Studies in Melodrama and the Woman's Film*, British Film Institute, London.

Goffman, Erving (1963) *Behaviour in Public Places: Notes on the Social Organization of Gatherings*, Free Press of Glencoe, New York.

Goffman, Erving (1971) *Relations in Public: Micropolitics of the Public Order*, Basic Books, New York.

Greer, Germaine (1970) *The Female Eunuch*, Paladin, London.

Grosz, Elizabeth A. (1989) *Sexual Subversions: Three French Feminists*, Allen & Unwin, Sydney.

Grosz, Elizabeth A. (1994) *Volatile Bodies: Toward a Corporeal Feminism*, Allen & Unwin, Sydney.

Grosz, Elizabeth A. (1995) *Space, Time, and Perversion: Essays on the Politics of Bodies*, Allen & Unwin, Sydney.

Guntrip, Harry (1968) *Schizoid Phenomena, Object-relations and the Self*, Hogarth Press and the Institute of Psycho-analysis, London.

Guntrip, Harry (1971) *Psychoanalytic Theory, Therapy, and the Self: A Basic Guide to the Human Personality in Freud, Erikson, Klein, Sullivan, Fairbairn, Hartmann, Jacobson, and Winnicott*, Basic Books, New York.

Hall, Radclyffe (1982)[1928] *The Well of Loneliness*, Virago, London.

Hall, Stuart (1992) 'The Question of Cultural Identity' in Stuart Hall, Daniel Held and Tony McGrew (eds) *Modernity and its Futures*, Polity Press, Cambridge, pp. 273–325.

Hall, Stuart (ed.) (1996a) *Representation: Cultural Prepresentations and Signifying Practices*, Sage, London.

Hall, Stuart (1996b) 'Introduction: Who Needs "Identity"?' in Stuart Hall and Paul du Gay (eds), *Questions of Cultural Identity*, Sage, London, pp. 1–17.

Halperin, David (1996) 'A Response from David Halperin to Dennis Altman', www.lib.latrobe.edu.au/AHR/emuse/Globalqueering/halperin.html.

Haraway, Donna (1991) 'A Cyborg Manifesto: Science, Technology, and Socialist-Feminism in the Late Twentieth Century' in *Simians, Cyborgs and Women: The Reinvention of Nature*, Routledge, New York, pp. 149–81.

Haraway, Donna (2001) 'Modest_Witness@Second_Millenium' in *Modest_Witness @Second_Millenium.FemaleMan©_Meets_OncoMouse™: Feminism and Technoscience*, Routledge, New York, pp. 23–45.

Hartsock, Nancy (1983) *Money, Sex, and Power: Toward a Feminist Historical Materialism*, Longman, New York.

Heath, Stephen (1986) 'Joan Rivière and the Masquerade', in V. Burgin, J. Donald and C. Kaplan (eds), *Formations of Fantasy*, Routledge, London, pp. 45–61.

Hill Collins, Patricia (1990) *Black Feminist Thought: Knowledge Consciousness and the Politics of Empowerment*, Unwin Hyman, Boston.

Hochschild, Arlie Russell (1983) *The Managed Heart: Commercialization of Human Feeling*, University of California Press, Berkeley.

Hodge, Robert and Tripp, David (1986) *Children and Television*, Polity, Cambridge.

hooks, bell (1990) *Yearning: Race, Gender and Cultural Politics*, South End Press, Boston.

Horney, Karen (1973) *Feminine Psychology*, W.W. Norton, New York.

Horrocks, Roger (1994) *Masculinity in Crisis: Myths, Fantasies and Realities*, St Martin's Press, New York.

Hunter, Dianne (ed.) (1989) *Seduction and Theory: Readings of Gender, Representation, and Rhetoric*, University of Illinois Press, Urbana.

Irigaray, Luce (1985a) *Speculum of the Other Woman* (trans. Gillian C. Gill) Cornell University Press, Ithaca, NY.

Irigaray, Luce (1985b) *This Sex Which Is Not One* (trans. Catherine Porter and Carolyn Burke) Cornell University Press, Ithaca, NY.

Jackson, Stevi (1995) 'Women and Heterosexual Love: Complicity, Resistance and Change', in Lynne Pearce and Jackie Stacey (eds) *Romance Revisited*, Lawrence & Wishart, London, pp. 49–62.

Jaggar, Alison M. (1992) 'Love and Knowledge: Emotion in Feminist Epistemology' in Alison Jaggar and Susan Bordo (eds) *Gender/Body/Knowledge: Feminist Reconstructions of Being and Knowing*, Rutgers University Press, New Brunswick, NJ, pp. 145–71.

Jaggar, Alison M. and Bordo, Susan (eds) (1989) *Gender/Body/Knowledge: Feminist Reconstructions of Being and Knowing*, Rutgers University Press, New Brunswick, NJ.

Jaggar, Alison and Rothenburg, Paula (eds) (1993) *Feminist Frameworks: Alternative Theoretical Accounts of the Relations between Women and Men*, McGraw-Hill, New York.

Jagose, Annamarie (1996) *Queer Theory*, Melbourne University Press, Melbourne.

Jahoda, Susan (1995) 'Theatres of Madness', in Jennifer Terry and Jacqueline Urla (eds) *Deviant Bodies: Critical Perspectives on Difference in Science and Popular Culture*, Indiana University Press, Bloomington, pp. 251–76.

James, Susan (1992) 'The Good-Enough Citizen: Female Citizenship and Independence', in Susan James and Gisela Bock (eds) *Beyond Equality and Difference: Citizenship, Feminist Politics and Female Subjectivity*, Routledge, London, pp. 48–65.

Jameson, Fredric (1981) *The Political Unconscious: Narrative as a Socially Symbolic Act*, Methuen, London.

Jamieson, Lynn (1998) *Intimacy: Personal Relationships in Modern Societies*, Polity, Cambridge.

Jenkins, Henry (1991) 'Star Trek Rerun, Reread, Rewritten: Fan Writing as Textual Poaching' in Constance Penley, Elisabeth Lyon, Lynn Spigel, and Janet Bergstrom (eds) *Close Encounters: Film, Feminism, and Science Fiction*, University of Minnesota Press, Minneapolis, pp. 170–203.

Jenkins, Henry (1992) *Textual Poachers: Television Fans and Participatory Culture*, Routledge, New York.

Jenkins, Henry (1995) '"Out of the Closet and into the Universe": Queers and Star Trek' in John Tulloch and Henry Jenkins (eds) *Science Fiction Audiences*, Routledge, London, pp. 237–65.

Jenkins, Richard (1992) *Pierre Bourdieu*, Routledge, London.

Jones, Kathleen (1990) 'Citizenship in a Woman-Friendly Polity', *Signs* **15**(4): 781–812.

Jones, Kathleen (1993) 'What Sort of Body is the Body Politic', *Compassionate Authority: Democracy and the Representation of Women*, Routledge, London.

Kaplan, E.A. (1984) 'Is the Gaze Male' in Ann Snitow, Christine Stansell and Sharon Thompson (eds) *Desire: The Politics of Sexuality*, Virago, London, pp. 321–38.

Kaplan, Louise J. (1997) *Female Perversions: The Temptations of Emma Bovary*, Jason Aronson, Northvale, NJ.

Kaw, Eugenia (1993) 'Medicalization of Racial Features: Asian-American Women and Cosmetic Surgery, *Medical Anthropology Quarterly*, **7**(1): 74–89.

Kaw, Eugenia (1994) 'Opening Faces: The Politics of Cosmetic Surgey and Asian-American Women' in Nicole Landry Sault (ed.) *Many Mirrors: Body Image and Social Relations*, Rutgers University Press, New Brunswick, NJ, pp 241–65.

Kendall, Lori (1996) 'MUDder? I Hardly Know 'Er! Adventures of a Feminist MUDder' in Lynn Cherny and Elizabeth Reba Weise (eds) *Wired Women: Gender and New Realities in Cyberspace*, Seal Press, Boston, pp. 207–23.

Kingsley, Mary Henrietta (1982[1897]) *Travels in West Africa: Congo Français, Corsico, and Cameroons*, 5th edn, Virago, London (originally published by Macmillan, London).

Kitzinger, Sheila (1988) *Freedom and Choice in Childbirth: Making Pregnancy Decisions and Birth Plans*, Penguin, Harmondsworth, p. 145.

Klein, Melanie (1963)[1949] *The Psycho-analysis of Children* (trans. Alix Strachey) Hogarth Press, London.

Klein, Melanie (1975a) *The Writings of Melanie Klein*, Hogarth Press, London.

Klein, Melanie (1975b) *The Psychoanalysis of Children*, Delacourt Press, New York.

Klein, Melanie (1975c) *Love, Guilt and Reparation, and Other Works, 1921–1945*, Hogarth Press, London.

Kollantai, Alexandra (1977)[1919] *Selected Writings of Alexandra Kollantai* (trans. Alix Holt) Allison & Busby, London.

Kolodny, Annette (1980) 'Reply to Commentaries: Women Writers, Literary Historians, and Martian Readers', *New Literary History*, **11**: 587–92.

Kramarae, Cheris (ed.) (1980) *The Voices and Words of Women and Men*, Pergamon, Oxford.

Kramarae, Cheris (1981) *Women and Men Speaking: Frameworks for Analysis*, Newbury House, Rowley, MA.

Kramarae, Cheris (ed.) (1988) *Technology and Women's Voices: Keeping in Touch*, Routledge & Kegan Paul, London.

Kramarae, Cheris, B. Thorne and N. Henley (eds) (1983) *Language, Gender and Society*, Newbury House, Rowley, MA.

Kramarae, Cheris and Treichler, Paula A. with Russo, Ann (eds) (1985) *A Feminist Dictionary*, Pandora, London.

Kress, Gunther (1985) *Linguistic Processes in Sociocultural Practice*, Deakin University Press, Geelong, Victoria.

Kristeva, Julia (1982) *The Powers of Horror: An Essay on Abjection* (trans. Leon Roudiez) Columbia University Press, New York.

Kunzle, David (1982) *Fashion and Fetishism: A Social History of the Corset, Tight-lacing, and Other Forms of Body-sculpture in the West*, Rowman & Littlefield, Totowa, NJ.

Lacan, Jacques (1977a) *Ecrits: A Selection* (trans. Alan Sheridan) Norton, New York.

Laqueur, Thomas (1990) *Making Sex: Body and Gender from the Greeks to Freud*, Harvard University Press, Cambridge, MA.

Le Guin, Ursula K. (1981) *The Left Hand of Darkness*, Futura, London.

Lewis, Lisa A. (1990) *Gender Politics and MTV: Making the Difference*, Temple University Press, Philadelphia.

Lieberman, Rhonda (1993) 'Shopping Disorders' in Massumi, Brian (ed.) *The Politics of Everyday Fear*, University of Minnesota Press, Minneapolis.

Lorde, Audre (1984) *Sister Outsider: Essays and Speeches*, Crossing Press, Freedom, CA.

Lorrah, Jean (1984) *The Vulcan Academy Murders*, Pocket Books, New York.

Lubiano, Wahneena (1993) 'Black Ladies, Welfare Queens and State Minstrels: Ideological War by Narrative Means' in Toni Morrison (ed.) *Race-ing Justice, En-gendering Power: Essays on Anita Hill, Clarence Thomas, and the Construction of Social Reality*, Chatto & Windus, London, pp. 323–63.

Lumby, Catharine (1997) *Bad Girls: The Media, Sex and Feminism in the 90s*, Allen & Unwin, St Leonards, NSW.

Mac An Ghail, Martin (ed.) (1996) *Understanding Masculinities*, Open University Press, Buckingham.

McClary, Susan (1991) *Feminine Endings: Music, Gender, and Sexuality*, University of Minnesota Press, Minnesota.

McRae, Shannon (1996) 'Coming Apart at the Seams: Sex, Text and the Virtual Body' in Lynn Cherny and Elizabeth Reba Weise (eds) *Wired Women: Gender and New Realities in Cyberspace*, Seal Press, Boston, pp. 242–63.

Mackenzie, Catriona (1992) 'Abortion and Embodiment', *Australian Journal of Philosophy*, **70**(2): 136–55.

Mansfield, Nick (2000) *Subjectivity: Theories of the Self from Freud to Haraway*, Allen & Unwin, St Leonards, NSW.

Marshall, Donald G. (1993) *Contemporary Critical Theory: A Selective Bibliography*, Modern Language Association of America, New York.

Marshall, T.H. (1950) *Citizenship and Social Class and Other Essays*, Cambridge University Press, Cambridge.

Mascia-Lees, Frances E. and Paytricia Sharpe (eds) (1992) *Tattoo, Torture, Mutilation, and Adornment: The Denaturalization of the Body in Culture and Text*, State University of New York Press, Albany.

Mauss, Marcel (1992) 'Techniques of the Body' in Jonathan Crary and Stanford Kwinter (eds) *Incorporations*, Zone Books, New York, pp. 455–77.

Mead, Jenna (ed.) (1997) *Bodyjamming: Sexual Harassment, Feminism and Public Life*, Vintage, Sydney.

Mead, Margaret (1949) *Male and Female*. Morrow Quill, New York.

Merleau-Ponty, Maurice (1962) *Phenomenology of Perception* (trans. Colin Smith) Routledge & Kegan Paul, London.

Merleau-Ponty, Maurice (1964) *Signs* (trans. Richard C. McCleary) Northwestern University Press, Evanston, IL.

Michie, Elsie (1992) 'From Simianized Irish to Oriental Despots: Heathcliff, Rochester and Racial Difference', *Novel: A Forum on Fiction* **25**(2): 125–40.

Millett, Kate (1970) *Sexual Politics*, Doubleday, New York.

Mills, Sara (1991) *Discourses of Difference: An Analysis of Women's Travel Writing and Colonialism*, Routledge, London.

Modleski, Tania (1984) *Loving with a Vengeance: Mass-Produced Fantasies for Women*, Methuen, New York.

Modleski, Tania (ed.) (1986) *Studies in Entertainment: Critical Approaches to Mass Culture*, Indiana University Press, Bloomington.

Morgan, Kathryn (1991) 'Women and the Knife: Cosmetic Surgery and the Colonization of Women's Bodies', *Hypatia*, **6**(3): 111–24.

Morris, Meaghan (1997) 'Sticks and stones and stereotypes' in Phillip Adams (ed.) *The Retreat from Tolerance*, ABC Books, Sydney.

Morrison, Toni (ed.) (1993a) *Race-ing Justice, En-gendering Power: Essays on Anita Hill, Clarence Thomas, and the Construction of Social Reality*, Chatto & Windus, London.

Morson, Gary Saul (1981) *The Boundaries of Genre: Dostoyevsky's Diary of a Writer and the Traditions of Literary Utopia*, University of Texas Press, Austin, TX.

Mulvey, Laura (1975) 'Visual Pleasure and Narrative Cinema', *Screen*, **16** (reprinted in Mulvey, Laura (ed.) (1989) *Visual and Other Pleasures*, Indiana University Press, Bloomington, pp. 14–28).

Mulvey, Laura (1989) *Visual and Other Pleasures*, Indiana University Press, Bloomington.

Murphy, Robert (1995) 'Encounters: The Body Silent in America' in B. Ingstad and S. White (eds) *Disability and Culture*, University of California Press, Berkeley, pp. 140–58.

Naffine, Ngaire (1990) *Law and the Sexes: Explorations in Feminist Jurisprudence*, Allen & Unwin, Sydney.

Nava, Mica (1992) *Changing Cultures: Feminism, Youth and Consumerism*, Sage, London.

Omolade, Barbara (1985) 'Black Women and Feminism' in Hester Eisenstein and Alice Jardine (eds) *The Future of Difference*, Rutgers University Press, New Brunswick, pp. 247–57.

Orlan Panel (1998) http://filament.illumin.co.uk/ica/Bookshop/video/performance.html.

Painter, Nell Irvin (1993) 'Hill, Thomas, and the Use of Racial Stereotype', in Toni Morrison (ed.) *Race-ing Justice, En-gendering Power: Essays on Anita Hill, Clarence Thomas, and the Construction of Social Reality*, Chatto & Windus, London, pp. 200–14.

Pateman, Carole (1988) *The Sexual Contract*, Polity, Cambridge.

Pateman, Carole (1989) *The Disorder of Women: Democracy, Feminism and Political Theory*, Polity, Cambridge.

Peiss, Kathy (1990) 'Making Faces: The Cosmetics Industry and the Cultural Construction of Gender, 1890–1930', *Genders* **7**: 143–70.

Penley, Constance (1991) 'Brownian Motion: Women, tactics, and Technology' in Constance Penley and Andrew Ross (eds) *Technoculture*, University of Minnesota Press, Minneapolis, pp. 135–61.

Penley, Constance (1992) 'Feminism, Psychoanalysis and the Study of Popular Culture' in Lawrence Grossberg, Cary Nelson and Paula A. Treichler (eds) *Cultural Studies*, Routledge, New York, pp. 479–500.

Penley, Constance (1997) *NASA/TREK: Popular Science and Sex in America*, Verso, London.

Perkins, T.E. (1979) 'Rethinking Stereotypes', *Ideology and Cultural Production*, St Martin's Press, New York.

Petchesky, Rosalind Pollack (1987) 'Fetal Images: The Power of Visual Culture in the Politics of Reproduction', *Feminist Studies*, **13**(2): 263–92.

Pettman, Jan (1996) *Worlding Women: A Feminist International Politics*, Allen & Unwin, Sydney.

Pfeil, Fred (1995) *White Guys: Studies in Postmodern Domination and Difference*, Verso, London.

Phelan, Shane (1994) *Getting Specific: Postmodern Lesbian Politics*, University of Minnesota Press, Minneapolis.

Phillips, Anne (1993) *Democracy and Difference*, Polity, Cambridge.

Plant, Sadie (1997) *zeros + ones: Digital Women + the New Technoculture*, Fourth Estate, London.

Plummer, Ken (ed.) (1981) *The Making of the Modern Homosexual*, Hutchinson, London.

Poynton, Cate (1985) *Language and Gender: Making the Difference*, Deakin University Press, Geelong, Victoria.

Pratt, Mary Louise (1992) *Imperial Eyes: Travel Writing and Transculturation*, Routledge, London.

Pringle, Rosemary (1989) *Secretaries Talk: Sexuality, Power and Work*, Allen & Unwin, Sydney.

Rabinowitz, Peter (1987) *Before Reading: Narrative Conventions and the Politics of Inter-pretation*, Cornell University Press, Ithaca, NY.

Radicalesbians (1973) 'The Women-identified Woman' in Anne Koedt, Ellen Levine and Anita Rapone (eds) *Radical Feminism*, Quadrangle Books, New York, pp. 240–5.

Radway, Janice A. (1984) *Reading the Romance: Women, Patriarchy, and Popular Culture*, University of North Carolina Press, Chapel Hill, NC.

Radway, Janice A. (ed.) (1986) *The Progress of Romance: The Politics of Popular Fiction*, Routledge & Kegan Paul, London.

Reekie, Gail (1993) *Temptations: Sex, Selling and the Department Store*, Allen & Unwin, Sydney.

Reinharz, Shulamit (1992) *Feminist Methods in Social Research*, Oxford University Press, New York.

Reiser, Stanley Joel (1978) *Medicine and the Reign of Technology*, Cambridge University Press, Cambridge.

Rich, Adrienne (1986) *Blood, Bread, and Poetry: Selected Prose, 1979–1985*, Norton, New York.

Rich, Adrienne (1993a) 'Compulsory Heterosexuality and Lesbian Existence' in Barbara Charlesworth Gelpi and Albert Gelpi (eds) *Adrienne Rich's Poetry and Prose*, W.W. Norton, New York, pp. 203–23.

Rich, Adrienne (1993b) 'Planetarium' in Barbara Charlesworth Gelpi and Albert Gelpi (eds), *Adrienne Rich's Poetry and Prose*, W.W. Norton, New York, pp. 38–9.

Rich, Adrienne (1993c) 'Blood, Bread and Poetry: The Location of the Poet (1984)' in Barbara Charlesworth Gelpi and Albert Gelpi (eds) *Adrienne Rich's Poetry and Prose*, W.W. Norton, New York, pp. 239–52.

Rivière, Joan (1986)[1929] 'Womanliness as Masquerade' in V. Burgin, J. Donald and C. Kaplan (eds) *Formations of Fantasy*, Routledge, London, pp. 35–44.

Rosaldo, Michelle Zimbalist (1974) 'Woman, Culture and Society: A Theoretical Overview' in Michelle Zimbalist Rosaldo and Louise Lamphere (eds) *Women, Culture and Society*, Stanford University Press, Stanford, CA, pp. 17–42.

Rubin, Gayle (1974) 'The Traffic in Women: Notes on the "Political Economy" of Sex' in Rayne R. Reiter (ed.) *Toward an Anthropology of Women*, Monthly Review Press, New York, pp. 157–210.

Rubin, Gayle S. (1992) 'Thinking Sex: Notes for a Radical Theory of the Politics of Sexuality' in Henry Abelove, Michèle Aina Barale and David Halperin (eds) *The Lesbian and Gay Studies Reader*, Routledge, New York, pp. 3–44.

Sandoval, Chela (1991) 'U.S. Third World Feminism: The Theory and Method of Oppositional Consciousness in the Postmodern World', *Genders*, **10**: 1–24.

Sandoval, Chela (1995) 'New Sciences: Cyborg Feminism and the Methodology of the Oppressed' in Charles Hables Gray (ed.) *The Cyborg Handbook*, Routledge, New York, pp. 407–22.

Sargent, Pamela (ed.) (1978) *Women of Wonder: Science-fiction Stories by Women about Women*, Penguin, Harmondsworth.

Sargent, Pamela (ed.) (1979) *More Women of Wonder: Science-fiction Novelettes by Women about Women*, Penguin, Harmondsworth.

Sawicki, Jana (1991) 'Disciplining Mothers: Feminism and the New Reproductive Technologies', *Disciplining Foucault: Feminism, Power and the Body*, Routledge, New York.

Schaffer, Kay (1988) *Women and the Bush: Forces of Desire in the Australian Cultural Tradition*, Cambridge University Press, Melbourne.

Schaffer, Kay (1995) *In the Wake of First Contact: the Eliza Fraser Stories*, Cambridge University Press, Melbourne.

Scott, Joan W. (1992) 'Experience' in Judith Butler and Joan W. Scott (eds), *Feminists Theorize the Political*, Routledge, New York, pp. 22–40.

Segal, Lynne (1987) *Is the Future Female? Troubled Thoughts on Contemporary Feminism*, Virago, London.

Segal, Lynne (1994) *Straight Sex: The Politics of Pleasure*, Virago, London.

Sharpe, Andrew (1994) 'The Precarious Position of the Transsexual Rape Victim' *Current Issues in Criminal Justice*, **6**(2): 303–7.

Sharpe, Andrew (1997) 'Anglo-Australian Judicial Approaches to Transsexuality: Discontinuities, Continuities and the Wider Issues at Stake', *Social and Legal Studies*, **6**: 51–78.

Showalter, Elaine (1971) 'Women and the Literary Curriculum', *College English*, **32**: 855–62.

Showalter, Elaine (1985a) 'Towards a Feminist Poetics' in Elaine Showalter (ed.), *The New Feminist Criticism: Essays on Women, Literature and Theory*, Virago, London, pp. 125–43.

Showalter, Elaine (1985b) *The Female Malady: Women, Madness and English Culture, 1830–1980*, Virago, London.

Silman, Janet (ed.) (1987) *Enough is Enough: Aboriginal Women Speak Out*, The Women's Press, Toronto.

Silverberg, Robert (1975) 'Who Is Tiptree, What Is He?' in Robert Silverberg (ed.) *Warm Worlds and Otherwise by James Tiptree Jr*, Ballantine, New York, pp. ix–xviii.

Silverman, Kaja (1983) *The Subject of Semiotics*, Oxford University Press, New York.

Silverman, Kaja (1988) *The Acoustic Mirror: The Female Voice in Psychoanalysis and Cinema*, Indiana University Press, Bloomington.

Silverman, Kaja (1992) *Male Subjectivity at the Margins*, Routledge, New York.

Sinfield, Alan (1994) *Cultural Politics – Queer Reading*, Pennsylvania University Press, Philadelphia.

Smith, Dorothy (1990) 'Women's Perspective as a Radical Critique of Sociology', *The Conceptual Practices of Power: A Feminist Sociology of Knowledge*, Northeastern University Press, Boston.

Smith-Rosenberg, Carroll (1972) 'The Hysterical Woman: Sex Roles in 19th century America', *Social Research*, (39): 652–78.

SOED (Shorter Oxford English Dictionary), 3rd edn, Clarendon, Oxford.

Sparke, Penny (1995) *As Long As It's Pink: The Sexual Politics of Taste*, Pandora Press, London.

Spender, Dale (1989) *The Writing or the Sex? Or Why You Don't Have to Read Women's Writing to Know it's No Good*, Pergamon, New York.

Spongberg, Mary (1997) 'Are Small Penises Necessary for Civilisation? The Male Body and the Body Politic', *Australian Feminist Studies*, **12**(25): 19–28.

Stabile, Carole (1992) 'Shooting the Mother: Fetal Photography and the Politics of Disappearance', *Camera Obscura*, **28**: 179–205.

Stanworth, Michelle (1990) 'Conceptive Technologies and the Threat to Motherhood' in Marianne Hirsch and Evelyn Fox Keller (eds) *Conflicts in Feminism*, Routledge, London.

Steedman, Carolyn (1986) *Landscape for a Good Woman: A Story of Two Lives*, Virago, London.

Stephan, Nancy Leys (1986) 'Race and Gender: The Role of Analogy in Science,' *Isis*, **77**: 261–77.

Stoller, Robert J. (1968–75) *Sex and Gender*, Hogarth Press and the Institute of Psychoanalysis, London.

Stone, Sandy (1991) 'The "Empire" Strikes Back: A Posttranssexual Manifesto', http://www.sandystone.com/empire-strikes-back.

Sturken, Marita and Lisa Cartwright (2001) *Practices of Looking: An Introduction to Visual Culture*, Oxford University Press, Oxford.

Stychin, Carl, (1995) 'Equality Rights, Identity Politics and the Canadian National Imagination' *Law's Desire*, Routledge, New York, pp. 102–15.

Synnott, Anthony (1993) 'Dualism and the Opposite Sex', *The Body Social: Symbolism, Self, and Society*, Routledge, London, pp. 38–72.

Tannen, Deborah (1990) *You Just Don't Understand: Men and Women in Conversation*, Ballantine, New York.

Tannen, Deborah (1993) *Gender and Conversational Interaction*, Oxford University Press, New York.

Tannen, Deborah (1994) *Gender and Discourse*, Oxford University Press, New York.

Teitelman, Robert Gene (1989) *Dreams: Wall Street, Academica and the Rise of Biotechnology*, Basic, New York.

Throop, David (1996) 'What Are Men's Issues', http://www.vix.com/pub/men/history/accounts/throop5.html

Thurber, James (1983) 'The Little Girl and the Wolf' in Jack Zipes (ed.) *The Trials and Tribulations of Little Red Riding Hood*, Heinemann, London, p. 210.

Thurston, Carol (1987) *The Romance Revolution: Erotic Novels for Women and the Quest for a New Sexual Identity*, University of Illinois Press, Urbana.

Thwaites, Tony, Lloyd, Davis and Mules, Warwick (1994) *Tools for Cultural Studies: An Introduction*, Macmillan Education Australia, South Melbourne.

Tiptree Jr, James (1981) 'The Screwfly Solution' in *Out of the Everywhere, And Other Extraordinary Visions*, Ballantine, New York, pp. 53–75.

Todorov, Tzevetan (1984) *Mikhail Bakhtin: The Dialogical Principle* (trans. Wlad Godzich) Manchester University Press, Manchester.

Tompkins, Jane P. (1985) 'Sentimental Power: Uncle Tom's Cabin and the Politics of Literary History' in Elaine Showalter (ed.), *The New Feminist Criticism*, Virago, London, pp. 81–104.

Treichler, Paula (1990) 'Feminism, Medicine and the Meaning of Childbirth' in Mary Jacobus, Evelyn Fox Keller and Sally Shuttleworth (eds) *Body/Politics: Women and the Discourses of Science*, Routledge, New York, pp. 113–38.

Trinh, T. Minh-Ha (1991) *When the Moon Waxes Red*, Routledge, New York.

Tristan, Flora (1982) *The London Journal of Flora Tristan, 1842 or, The Aristocracy and the Working Class of England/A Translation of Promenades dans Londres by Jean Hawkes*, Virago, London.

Tristan, Flora (1986) *Peregrinations of a Pariah: 1833–1834* (Jean Hawkes trans. and ed.) Virago, London.

Turkle, Sherry (1984) *The Second Self: Computers and the Human Spirit*, Granada, London.

Turkle, Sherry (1992) *Psychoanalytic Politics: Jacques Lacan and Freud's French Revolution*, Free Association Books/Guilford Press, London/New York.

Turkle, Sherry (1995) *Life on the Screen: Identity in the Age of the Computer*, Simon & Schuster, New York.

Volpe, E. Peter (1987) *Test-tube Conception: A Blend of Love and Science*, Mercer, Macon, GA.

Wajcman, Judy (1991) 'Reproductive Technology: Delivered into Men's Hands' in *Feminism Confronts Technology*, Allen & Unwin, Sydney.

Walkerdine, Valerie (1990) *Schoolgirl Fictions*, Verso, London.

Wearing, Betsy (1996) *Gender: The Pain and Pleasure of Difference*, Longman, Melbourne.

Webber, David (ed.) (1990) *Biotechnology: Assessing Social Impacts and Policy Implications*, Greenwood, New York.

Weeks, Jeffrey (1977) *Coming Out: Homosexual Politics in Britain, from the Nineteenth Century to the Present*, Quartet, London.

Weeks, Kathi (1996) 'Subject for a Feminist Standpoint' in Saree Makdisis, Cesare Casarino, and Rebecca E. Karl (eds) *Marxism Beyond Marxism*, Routledge, New York, pp. 89–118.

Winnicott, Donald Woods (1975) *Through Paediatrics to Psycho-analysis*, Hogarth Press and the Institute of Psycho-analysis, London.

Wittig, Monique (1992) *The Straight Mind and Other Essays*, Harvester Wheatsheaf, New York.

Wolf, Naomi (1991) *The Beauty Myth: How Images of Beauty Are Used Against Women*, William Morrow, New York.

Wollstonecraft, Mary (1975)[1792] *A Vindication of the Rights of Woman*, Penguin, Harmondsworth.

Woodhead, David (1995) '"Surveillant Gays": HIV, Space and the Constitution of Identities' in David Bell and Gill Valentine (eds) *Mapping Desire: Geographies of Sexualities*, Routledge, London.

Woodhouse, Annie (1989) *Fantastic Women: Sex, Gender and Transvestism*, Macmillan – now Palgrave Macmillan, Basingstoke.

Woolf, Virginia (1977) *A Room of One's Own*, Panther, London.

Young, Iris Marion (1990a) *Throwing Like A Girl and Other Essays in Feminist Philosophy and Social Theory*, Indiana University Press, Bloomington.

Young, Iris Marion (1990b) 'The Scaling of Bodies and the Politics of Identity', *Justice and the Politics of Difference*, Princeton University Press, Princeton, NJ, pp. 122–55.

Yoxen, Edward (1983) *The Gene Business: Who Should Control Biotechnology?* Oxford University Press, New York.

Yuval-Davis, Nira (1991) 'The Citizenship Debate: Women, Ethnic Processes and the State', *Feminist Review*, **39**: 58–68.

Zipes, Jack (1983) *The Trials and Tribulations of Little Red Riding Hood: Versions of the Tale in Sociocultural Context*, Heinemann, London.

Index